"*More* takes a vast 10,000-year sweep of economic history and melds it into a compelling story of countries and conflicts, civilisations and civic institutions, stagnations and transformations. All in little more than 300 pages of lucid prose. It is a majestic must-read."

Andy Haldane, Chief Economist at the Bank of England

"*More* is an extraordinary achievement. How can it be possible to turn 10,000 years of human endeavour into a tale which is at once exciting, coherent and surprisingly optimistic? *The Economist*'s Philip Coggan has a very rare gift. Economics books usually overwhelm the reader with heavy analysis and too many statistics, or frustrate with oversimplification. Coggan distils a vast expanse of human history – the history of trade and economic advance – into a beautifully light and elegantly written tale, full of surprises, and free of ideology. If you have never read any economics, I can think of no better place to start. If you are a seasoned economist, you will discover there is much to learn. I cannot recommend this book highly enough."

Eric Lonergan, author of *Money: The Art of Living*

"Philip Coggan tells his epic story of humankind's economic development with both wisdom and wit. Brilliantly weaving together a sweeping historical narrative with a focus on the 'drivers' of development – energy, transportation, government and so on – Coggan has written a book that should be essential reading for anyone seeking to understand how our modern day economy came into being."

Stephen D. King, author of *Grave New World: The End of Globalization, the Return of History*

"An engaging and highly accessible narrative about the long historical development of global trade, commerce, and innovation. Philip Coggan writes clearly about how and why it all happened, and gives us cause for optimism in difficult times."

George Magnus, author of *Red Flags: Why Xi's China Is in Jeopardy*

"Philip Coggan's *More* is a monumental work of scholarship that never feels like one while you are reading it. All of human economic history is here, with something you didn't know on every page, and today's apparently terrible economic problems put into a clear context. It should be recommended reading for students, economists, anyone who works in business, and anyone with an interest in how our world came to be the way it is."

John Authers, author of *The Fearful Rise of Markets: A Short View of Global Bubbles and Synchronised Meltdowns*

"*More* is a glorious sweep through economic history. Open any page and Philip Coggan gives us new insights on the global economic system. His new book is an undiluted pleasure."

Elroy Dimson, chairman of the Centre for Endowment Asset Management at Cambridge Judge Business School

**PRAISE FOR** *PAPER PROMISES*, **ALSO BY PHILIP COGGAN**

"[An] illuminating account of the financial crisis … convey[s] deep insights without a trace of jargon."

John Gray, *New Statesman*

"A remarkable book from one of the most respected economics journalists on the planet. Every page brings a fresh insight or a new surprise. A delight."

Tim Harford, author of *The Undercover Economist*

"By far the best analysis of the 'new normal'."

David Stevenson, *Financial Times*

"Bold and confident … Coggan covers the terrain with characteristic calmness and objectivity, avoids over-simplification, and laces his arguments with his trademark erudition … The alphabet soup of acronyms, from SIVs to CDO Squareds, is blissfully lacking … Finally, the book is free from the shrieking ideology that afflicts virtually all contemporary debates over money. Indeed, it offers a clear explanation of the fresh ideological divisions that have arisen over how to deal with the crisis … the book should be taken very seriously."

*Financial Times*

# MORE

# MORE

## A HISTORY OF THE WORLD ECONOMY FROM
## THE IRON AGE TO THE INFORMATION AGE

## PHILIP COGGAN

PublicAffairs
New York

PublicAffairs
Hachette Book Group—
1290 Avenue of the Americas, New York, NY 10104
www.publicaffairsbooks.com
@Public_Affairs

The Economist in Association with Profile Books Ltd. and PublicAffairs

Printed in the United States of America

Originally published in 2019 by Profile Books Ltd. in Great Britain.

First US Edition: March 2020

Published by PublicAffairs, an imprint of Perseus Books, LLC, a subsidiary of Hachette
Book Group, Inc. The PublicAffairs name and logo is a trademark of the Hachette Book
Group.

Print book interior Typeset in Garamond by MacGuru Ltd.

Library of Congress Cataloging-in-Publication Data has been applied for.

ISBNs: 978-1-61039-983-8 (hardcover), 978-1-61039-984-5 (ebook)

LSC-C

10  9  8  7  6  5  4  3  2  1

To Sandie
Always my inspiration

# CONTENTS

# PLATES

# CHARTS

# PREFACE

When we think about history, the temptation is to focus on revolutions, wars and kings – what was once described as "maps and chaps". And when we discuss economics, the focus is on the current measures of inflation and employment, and the complex equations and jargon that academics use to explain them.

It is easy to miss the big picture. Within the past 300 years, there has been an enormous change in human history, a change that has allowed the population to grow rapidly, and for many people to live longer and be taller and healthier than ever before. While there is still too much poverty, prosperity has extended even further in the last few decades, thanks in particular to the flourishing of the Chinese economy. This story is insufficiently told, and understood. Hence the motivation for this book.

Over 30 years ago, my first book, *The Money Machine*, was inspired by the need to learn about finance, and the discovery that there was no guide for the general reader. My idea was that I could do something similar for the world economy. Other, splendid, books on economic history exist, of course, but in general they exist to perpetuate the thesis that one factor or another was the crucial driver. This book is designed for those who want the full picture.

Had I realised, back in 2016, what an insanely difficult task this would be, I might never have started. As an *Economist* journalist, I have a full-time job to do, never mind the mountain of reading that was required for this task.

Let me say, straight away, that this is a book written by a journalist, and not an academic. There is original reporting in this book in the thematic chapters. But the bulk of the book relies on the distinguished scholarship of academics who have come before me. They are fully acknowledged in the notes and bibliography, but let me add my thanks here.

A word of caution is needed on the statistics. Historians like Angus Maddison laboured mightily to estimate the size of the global economy at various stages, and others have combed the data for information on prices, incomes and longevity. Inevitably, huge margins of error are involved, and even modern societies struggle to get the economic numbers right. So the figures in here are only a rough guess as to the level of economic progress (see the Appendix for a full discussion). As this is a global book, dates are recorded using the common era (CE) and before common era (BCE) notation, rather than BC or AD.

Thanks are also due to Ed Lake and Andrew Franklin at Profile Books for believing in the idea behind the book and for waiting patiently for me to finish. Paul Forty ran the editorial and pre-press team and Susanne Hillen was an expert copy-editor. My colleagues at *The Economist*, led by Zanny Minton Beddoes, Edward Carr and Andrew Palmer, have also shown forbearance while I work on the project; the same goes for my long-suffering office mates, Simon Long and Helen Joyce. Mark Johnson helped organise my trip to Asia and guided me safely through a Malaysian thunderstorm.

Extra gratitude is due to those who have read some of the chapters and made useful suggestions: Geoff Carr, Tim Cross, Patrick Lane, Charles Read, Callum Williams and Simon Wright. All mistakes are of course my own and not theirs. Other heroes were Alex Selby-Boothroyd, who drew the charts, and Sophia Bradford and Zoe Spencer who found the pictures.

Many people were helpful on my travels round the world: Daniel Brucker at Grand Central station; Frances Houle and her team at Berkeley; Caroline Katsiroubas at Freight Farms in Boston; Cheryl Lim at Iskandar Malaysia; Eugene Tay at the port of Singapore; ranger

Doug Treem at Ellis Island; Shu Yang at the University of Pennsylvania; and John Yates at the AMRC in Sheffield.

The biggest thanks are due to Sandie, and my children Helena and Catherine, for putting up with me through 30 months of research and writing. I am sorry for all the weekends that were not filled with country walks and cinema visits. Sandie made many helpful suggestions and corrected my foolish mistakes. As for Rosa, the cat, who sat on the keyboard at crucial moments, you should be ashamed of yourself.

Philip Coggan
*April 2019*

# MORE

# INTRODUCTION

## The urge to trade

Think small, at first. Take the most mundane consumer item in your house: a tube of toothpaste. Its journey to your bathroom involves thousands of people and hundreds of processes. The titanium dioxide that whitens your teeth has to be mined, probably in Australia or Canada, the calcium carbonate that acts as an abrasive has been extracted from limestone, and the xanthan gum used as a binding agent comes from grinding up plants. The toothpaste in my bathroom lists 17 different ingredients and that doesn't count the plastics that make the tube. All these materials must be brought to the factory where they are turned into the finished paste, and packaged into cardboard with a logo that experts have designed to catch your eye on the supermarket shelf. Then the product is sent by truck to distribution centres and eventually stacked on shelves by retail employees.

And then think big. Travel to a container port, like Felixstowe in Suffolk, on England's east coast, and you are in a land of giants. When I visited, a Maersk container ship, around 400 metres long, was ready to depart the dock. Its deck was filled with metal containers piled eight high; as many containers were below deck as above it. Three cranes, 80 metres tall, sat idly alongside. Their loading job was done. Within a few weeks, thousands of consumers would be using stuff taken from one of those containers.

The world economy involves this mixture of the big and the small on a daily basis. The monetary sums involved are so vast – trillions of dollars – that it is easy to forget that the items themselves are the ones we use every day: the food we eat, the clothes we wear, the devices we use. No man is an economic island.

Around 90% of world trade is carried by ship. In Felixstowe, metal boxes are piled along the dockside as far as the eye can see. In the course of a working day, 2,000 lorries arrive to deposit goods for export and then trek out again with imported materials.

The port also has three railway terminals, which carry about half of all the cargo. At the end of one line, I watch a feat of engineering magic as a traverser (the only one in the country) slides an engine sideways. This allows the train to reverse direction and pick up a new load at the end of a different line. These small triumphs of ingenuity are needed to bring the goods to your house, and they have deep historical roots.

There are huge ports like Felixstowe dotted across the globe. Singapore's deep-water harbour is one reason why Sir Stamford Raffles chose it as a base for British trading in 1819; another reason is its strategic location at the south-eastern end of the Strait of Malacca, between the Malay Peninsula and Sumatra. Any boat wanting to travel from the Indian Ocean to the South China Sea needs to go through the strait. Today the port is the second-busiest in the world and Singapore is one of the planet's most prosperous nations, thanks to its position at the heart of Asian trade and finance.

Shipping containers are so uniform in appearance that it is difficult to tell what is inside them. But in Singapore, it was possible to catch a glimpse of what the ships were actually carrying. Lined up on the quay were Toyotas and Hondas made in Asia (and on the way to Europe), Mercedes and BMWs made in Europe (and on the way to China) and Mitsubishi pick-up trucks en route to the Middle East. The biggest ships can carry up to 8,000 cars apiece, and 1.1m vehicles pass through the port each year.

The trade that passes through Felixstowe, Singapore and dozens of other ports every day keeps the global economy humming. And it forms part of an extraordinarily complex network. It is not just finished goods that are imported and exported, but components and raw materials. An iPhone includes displays made in Japan and South Africa, and sensors made in Taiwan, as well as other components made in Germany, France, Italy and the Netherlands. These parts are made from raw materials that come from Africa or South America and the whole thing is assembled in China. And yet the iPhone is widely thought of as a quintessentially US product.[1]

Humans have been trading for thousands of years. It is a different business from sharing, which, after all, wild animals do; a pride of lions will share a kill. It is also different from symbiosis; the pilot fish eats the shark's parasites and in return is left uneaten by the shark.

Trade requires the conscious recognition of a mutually beneficial exchange. You have something I want; I have something you want. Perhaps my apple tree bears more fruit than I can eat before it rots, and your hens lay more eggs than you can manage for breakfast. It makes sense to swap. This kind of deal seems uniquely human. As the great economist Adam Smith remarked: "Nobody ever saw a dog make a fair and deliberate exchange of one bone for another with another dog." (However, chimps will trade grooming for food, and, in one experiment, capuchin monkeys were given silver discs as a currency and used it to buy sex.)[2]

At the global level, trade occurs because resources are unevenly distributed. Some areas of the globe are rich in minerals; some have the sunny conditions required to grow fruit or cotton; others have the vast plains that can grow wheat. Over time some cultures have benefited from their expertise in making pottery, textiles or manufactured goods. They make what they are good at, and then exchange the surplus with other places that are good at making or growing something else.

Early trade may have started as mutual gift-giving, as still occurs in a modern society when we celebrate each other's birthdays, or bring wine when invited for dinner. Over time, this gift-giving might have become more systematic. Both parties would have realised that they gain from the process. In the case of the apples/eggs swap, each gets a more varied diet. Over time, this leads to specialisation. For some goods, this happens very quickly. Every medieval village had a blacksmith and a cobbler.

The same process leads to markets. These have existed at least since the time of the Phoenicians in the second millennium BCE, and have been found all over the world, particularly in small towns. Much of the trade will come from farmers bringing their surplus goods or livestock for sale. For specialists – those who sell wine, for example – markets will be a vital way of selling their goods. And once you have a market, buyers will compare prices. The cheapest producer will win. Over time, that will create the pressure for traders to become more "efficient" – producing more goods for a lower cost. Buyers and sellers must agree not just on the price of a good, but its quality, the place and time of exchange, and the nature and timing of payment. Innovations like markets, exchanges and financial instruments make this process easier.

Long-distance trade has also been around for thousands of years. The Visigoths refer in their laws to *negociatiores transmarini* – overseas traders. But for much of history, long-distance trade was both very expensive and risky. So trade only covered a small part of the economy, largely in luxury goods like jewels, spices or silk. Most of the stuff that people consumed was produced locally.

As ships grew larger and navigation became more reliable, it became possible to transport bulkier goods like timber, grain or slaves. In the last two centuries, trade has been transformed by the railway, the steamship and the internal combustion engine. So this book is in part a story of how trade became broader and deeper over thousands of years, to the extent that cross-border trade now encompasses more than half of everything the world produces every year.[3] The global economy has been formed by the complex interplay of competition, government intervention, consumer preferences and the distribution of natural resources. Change one part of it and we cannot be sure how the rest of the system will respond – something that voters should remember whenever politicians propose simple economic solutions.

### The state
The trader travelling by land could be robbed by bandits or his goods confiscated by local rulers as he passed through their territory. If he

travelled by sea he was at risk from storms or pirates. The ancients understood this risk and practised diversification. The Old Testament book Ecclesiastes advises: "Send your grain across the seas, and in time, profits will flow back to you. But divide your investments among many places, for you do not know what risks might lie ahead."[4]

Even at home, merchants might find that their local government had decided to seize their property. This certainly happened frequently in history and still occurs today. But this is a zero-sum game. If your crops are seized every year by the local bandit (or landlord), you will not bother to grow them next year. Long-term economic growth will not occur. As Thomas Hobbes, the gloomy 17th-century philosopher, wrote: "In such condition there is no place for industry; because the fruit thereof is uncertain."[5]

The existence of modern states, which protect the rights of private property and the peaceful settlement of disputes, was needed before economic growth could take off. A modern state provides courts that ensure that contracts can be enforced; that goods must be delivered when paid for, and payment made when goods are delivered; and that wages are paid when work is done. Businesses need public roads to deliver goods, schools to educate their workers, hospitals to heal them when they are sick, and so on.

Modern political debate all too often descends into a sterile debate along the lines of "capitalism is evil" and "government interference is wrong". In fact successful states have always benefited from a thriving private sector and the private sector has always benefited from the infrastructure provided by the state. The debate is where to draw the line; how to divide responsibilities between private and public sectors and how much of overall income should be claimed by the government.

The dividing line moved more in the direction of the government during the 20th century, but the move was not unidirectional. There were retreats in Russia and China and even in social democracies like Sweden. The first and second world wars showed that states need economic planning at moments of crisis. But it is unwise to rely on a few planners to foresee the future. Even a top industrialist can be caught out. Thomas Watson, the president of IBM for more than 40 years, thought that there would only be a market for five computers in the entire world.[6]

This book, then, is also the story of how governments have influenced economies, for good or ill, over the centuries. Many autocratic rulers realised that prosperous merchants were a good source of tax revenues and thus encouraged trade within and beyond the borders. Over the course of the last two centuries, governments have taken on a much broader remit, providing welfare for the old, sick and unemployed, and attempting to manage the economy so as to limit both inflation and unemployment. That shift has been good news for the population as a whole.

## Finance

Just as our ancestors traded, they also lent and borrowed money. This too is a form of trade. You have spare cash; I need cash to buy a new cow, or finance a trading voyage. If my investment earns a profit, and I pay you interest, we both gain from the experience.

Finance plays a very important role in the economy. It allows us to manage our lifetime expenditure. When we start work, we have little capital and need to borrow money to buy a house or consumer goods like cars. When we are middle-aged and earn a higher salary, the debts are paid off and we build up money for our retirement. When we are old, we live off the income from our savings. In aggregate, the old lend money to the young.

Businesses usually need to borrow money to start to expand their operations. Borrowing is needed to fund government functions (countries rarely raise as much in taxes as they spend on services).

The finance sector acts as a middleman in these transactions. Fund managers and pension schemes take our savings and invest them in interest-paying debts and the shares of companies. Insurance companies invest the premiums we pay to insure our lives and property; the extra income keeps the cost of insurance down. Charities invest the money we donate; the additional income they receive can be spent on good causes.

As economies grow, their financial sectors tend to get more sophisticated, and get used by more people. For all the faults of the modern financial sector (and there are many), it is worth reflecting on those economies where finance is underdeveloped; where citizens cannot get access to buy their own homes or start a small business. Better finance can help. In Kenya, for example, the rise of M-Pesa, a financing system that operates through mobile phones, has improved the lives of millions of people, making it easier for small businesses to operate.

It seems to be in the nature of financial sectors that they are subject to boom and bust. People need confidence to lend, and when they get nervous, the resulting squeeze on credit can cause economic havoc. In the run-up to the 2008 crisis, the financial sector clearly became too big for its Gucci boots, destabilising Western economies. Finance is a useful servant but a very poor master.

## The real meaning of progress

There is a school of thought that belittles economic growth and the obsession with GDP statistics. Of course, there is more to life than goods and services. But to understand how modern humans have benefited from economic growth, think back 600 years to the early 15th century.

If you were born in Europe back in 1420, your initial battle was to survive the first year or two of life: infant mortality was 30% or so. The typical European peasant in the Middle Ages would have very little in the way of furniture but the odd stool to sit on (no upholstered armchairs), and a straw bed to sleep in (probably infested with fleas and lice); no privacy (all would sleep together, close to the fire, the only source of warmth); little in the way of cutlery (knives but not forks or spoons); and very little light at night (candles were very expensive).

The food choice was extremely limited and there was no refrigeration to keep it from spoiling. In premodern China, millet, wheat, rice and corn supplied more than four-fifths of all energy. Europeans survived on coarse bread and vegetables made into stews and soups.[7] Meat and fish were occasional treats. Poor nutrition meant that people were smaller than they are today. There was no running water and nor were there flushing toilets. Any water had to be carried into the house, normally by women, from the village well, or from a river. In terms of entertainment, there were no printed books. In any case, few could read and many had poor eyesight, in the general absence of spectacles. Of course, there was no radio or television. People rarely washed and had very few choices of clothes.

Medicine and dentistry were primitive, so woe betide those who got ill. Women had to have several children to ensure that one or two made it to adulthood, but each pregnancy was a high-stakes gamble. More than one in three women died during their childbearing years.[8] Life expectancy was under 30. If your house was robbed or attacked, there was no police service to protect you, and if the wood, or straw, in your house caught fire, there was no fire brigade to rescue you.

If male, your working life would largely be spent on your own patch of land or the land of your social superiors. If female, you might be employed as a servant until old enough to get married. In marriage, as well as doing the housework, you would be expected to contribute to the crop- or livestock-rearing, or perhaps to earn a little money by sewing and spinning (hence the use of the term spinster for single females). Children would be put to work from a young age. Most people would spend their lives within a few miles of the place of their birth; roads were rudimentary and there were no railways or planes.

There were compensations, of course. Work was less intense. There were plenty of days off, although these were "holy days" rather than holidays; it was only in the last 100 years or so that most people, even in rich countries, could afford to head for the sun and stay in hotels. There was probably more of a sense of community than in modern societies.

The evidence is still strongly in favour of modern life. More children survive to adulthood and they grow up to be taller, better educated, and have many more choices over how to live their lives than they did in medieval times. They have a far greater chance of dying peacefully in their beds of old age (see chart). These advances would not have been made without economic growth.

As Steven Pinker recounts,[9] back in 1800 no country in the world had a life expectancy higher than 40. Now the world average is around 70; an African born today can expect to live as long as a European born in the 1930s. In 2016, 4.2m babies died in the first year of life.[10] That is a terrible number, but it has been steadily falling in

**Living longer**
Global life expectancy, years

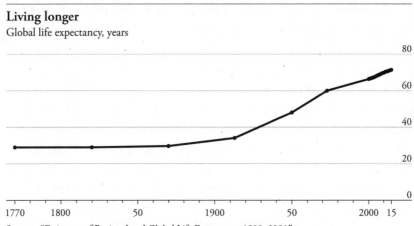

Sources: "Estimates of Regional and Global Life Expectancy, 1800–2001"
by James C. Riley; WHO; World Bank

recent years. Back in 1950, the number of infant deaths was 14.4m, at a time when the global population was less than half its current size. Around 97m children were born in 1950 but 141m were born in 2016 so the infant mortality rate has fallen from 15% to 3%.

Economic growth also helps all sections of society. A study of developing countries between 1981 and 1999 found that, in countries with the strongest economic expansions, poverty rates fell 6.1% a year; in those with the sharpest contractions, they rose 23%.[11] Thanks in large part to the "green revolution", the proportion of the world's population dying from famine in the last 50 years is 90% lower than in the first seven decades of the 20th century.[12] The number of people living in "extreme poverty" fell by a half, or 1bn people, between 1993 and 2011. The proportion of the developing world population living in extreme poverty dropped from 42% to 17% over the same period. Life expectancy in developing countries has risen from 50 in 1960 to 66 in 2011.[13]

Of course, this is not a totally positive story. Many people have borne a terrible price for economic development. Prominent examples include the slaves transported from Africa to the Americas, the indigenous peoples whose land was seized by European settlers, or the workers who lost their lives, or their health, in unsafe factories, mines and building sites. Their stories will also be told.

Economic change can also lead to environmental destruction. This is not simply the result of "capitalism", a word that tends to be used in a very slippery fashion. The deforestation of Easter Island in the middle of the last millennium was not the result of capitalism.[14] The megafauna of Australia (like the giant wombat) that were wiped out by early humans were not hunted to extinction in the pursuit of profit. Indeed, the same could be said of the North American passenger pigeon, which had flocks that could darken the skies but which proved no match for farmers with guns. One of the great environmental disasters of the 20th century occurred in the Aral Sea, which lost three-quarters of its volume thanks to mismanagement by the government of the Soviet Union in the name of communism.[15] Man is a voracious and destructive species.

But humans are also inventive and can find solutions to the problems they create. In the Western world, the smoke-filled air that left dirt on buildings and created London's "smogs" has largely been eliminated; rivers are no longer so polluted that they catch fire.

### Necessity's children

Innovation and technology are also two important themes in this book. It is easy to think, from a modern perspective, that technological advance is all about computers. But much simpler devices have proved vital: the plough, the watermill, the sextant. There have been inventions throughout the course of history; what marks out the modern era is the speed with which these innovations have spread around the world.

Economic growth comes mainly from two sources: having more workers and making those workers more efficient, in the sense of producing more each hour. Productivity can be enhanced by relatively simple new gadgets, such as the cotton gin developed by Eli Whitney, which removed seeds and waste from the cotton buds (although, by boosting the cotton crop, this invention perpetuated the US slavery system). But output can also be improved by new ways of organising production, such as the moving assembly line that allowed Henry Ford to produce cars more cheaply. Financial innovation, such as letters of credit, or legal reforms like the creation of the limited liability company, made it easier for traders to take risks and expand their operations.

Perhaps the most important area of innovation has been agriculture. Thomas Malthus, an 18th-century vicar, is famed for his gloomy forecasts about the dangers of population growth. He spotted the underlying problem of civilisation until that time: the limits on the ability to produce more food. New gadgets such as the seed drill may have helped escape this Malthusian trap, as it became known, but just as important were new crops, and new systems of field rotation that boosted output.

Specialisation – dividing work into tasks, with individual workers focusing on each one – is often the key to productivity improvement. It was one of the main insights of Adam Smith's famous book *The Wealth of Nations*. And its advantages had been noticed in ancient times. In the *Cyropaedia*, written by Xenophon in around 370BCE, it was noted that in Persia "there are places even where one man earns a living just by mending shoes, another just by sewing the uppers together, while there is another who performs none of these operations but assembles the parts. Of necessity he who pursues a specialised task will do it best."[16]

## The long sweep of history

This book tells the tale of how humanity moved from trading foodstuffs and the odd axe to developing a modern economy that produces both the giant ships in the port of Singapore and the ability to access much of the world's knowledge in a hand-held device. Many of the features that we think of as belonging to the modern "capitalist" economy – exchanging goods for money, lending and borrowing, enterprises that strive for profit, people who work for wages – have been around for thousands of years. What has changed over this long period is the scale of these operations and the number of people who are engaged in them.

It is the cumulative effect of one change after another that counts. For example, 17th-century Britain was short of wood. That encouraged the use of coal, which needed to be dug up from deep mines. Pumping water out of the mines was a priority, leading to the development of the steam engine. Steam engines, in turn, were put on rails as a form of locomotion. And the railway opened up the North American continent to trade, bringing cheap food to Europe

**The Great Enrichment**
World GDP, 2011 prices, international $trn

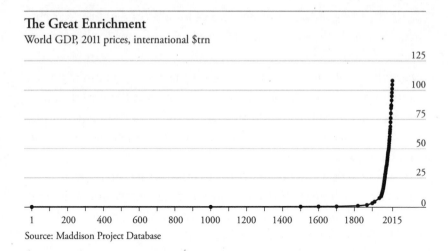

Source: Maddison Project Database

and freeing European workers for industry. But one can start the process of economic change from a different point (15th-century Portuguese exploration of Africa, for example) and develop a different chain of causation.

We have moved from the iron age to the information age. It has not been a uniform progression. The sudden surge in growth that occurred first in northwest Europe has been dubbed the "Industrial Revolution", but it was neither sudden nor solely about industry; Deirdre McCloskey's term "The Great Enrichment" is a better description (see chart).[17] The conventional narrative that we learn at school teaches us that this process happened, in Britain, around 1760, and involved a series of gadgets like the spinning jenny and the steam engine.

But, like a dog gnawing an old slipper, historians have worried away at this narrative. They have argued that signs of faster economic growth appear much earlier than 1760, while a decisive take-off to a more rapid growth rate was not really visible until the early 19th century. An even bigger debate concerns the causes of the Industrial Revolution, and why it appeared in a small corner of Europe and, in particular, Britain. Why not China, which had been the leading economy for much of recorded history? Explanations have ranged from exploitation of the colonies and the slave trade, the existence of better British institutions – such as constitutional monarchy and courts that enforce property rights – to arguments based on "culture" (Protestants favoured business more than Catholics; Britain was more appreciative of the "bourgeois" activities of hard work and trade). Historians have striven as hard to knock down alternative explanations as to build up their own.

This author inclines to the solution (spoiler alert) of Agatha Christie's mystery *Murder on the Orient Express*: they all did it. The failure of economies to achieve sustained growth before the period 1760 to 1820 was a sign of how difficult a task it was; it took a confluence of events to prompt Europe to take the lead.

But we should really talk about two revolutions rather than one. In the period from 1820 to the 1960s, this enrichment had only taken place in what we think of as the Western world: North America, Europe, Australia and Japan. In the last 50 years, more and more nations have made the breakthrough out of poverty, starting with Asian "tigers" like South Korea and Taiwan, and moving on to the giants of China and India.

Economic power is shifting away from Europe and North America, where it resided for the last three centuries, and back to Asia. This is a return to "normal" in some ways, since the Middle East, the Indian Ocean and the South China Sea were for a long time the heart of the global trading system.

Many economic changes that have led to long-term prosperity faced short-term opposition. Change means that some tasks must stop so that others may start, and that creates losers as well as winners. In the short term, the complaints of the losers may dominate the discussion. They lose their jobs or suffer cuts in pay and are understandably unhappy as a result. The gainers from the process tend to fall into two camps. Either they are the future workers who will be employed in the new system (and so are not currently around to lobby for their cause) or they are consumers who get a small benefit from cheaper prices or better services. The world economy may face this issue all over again in the next few decades as more jobs become susceptible to replacement by robots or artificial intelligence.

This will be a warts-and-all history of the world economy. But we need to remember how far we have come. In the first millennium CE, world population grew by only a sixth and per capita income fell.

In the second millennium, world population rose nearly 24-fold, per capita income 14-fold and GDP 338-fold.[18] One way to trace human progress is via the sources of our light. As humans switched from campfires to animal fat, sesame oil, candles, whale oil, kerosene and, eventually, electric bulbs, our sources of light became 143,000 times more energy-efficient.[19] Put another way, the cost of a given amount of light was around 12,000 times higher in the 14th century than it is today.[20]

To explain the development of the modern economy is a complex task. One way of telling the story is in strict chronological order. In economic history, the selection of time periods is even more arbitrary than it is for political history, which is punctuated by wars and revolutions. But a chronological story would be in danger of missing the huge thematic changes that have shaped the global economy. The timeline is thus interspersed with chapters that look at the biggest developments in economic history, such as agriculture, energy, manufacturing, transport, immigration, and technology, as well as chapters that look at the influence of central banks and the calculation of economic statistics.

My aim is for the reader to understand not just how the global economy developed, but how complex and interdependent it has become. Mankind started with simple tools like knives and axes, which many people could fashion. But even the most mundane modern items are beyond one person's wit to assemble. In 2008, Thomas Thwaites attempted to make a humble toaster from scratch. When he took one apart, he found 400 components made from 100 different materials. After nine months, and enormous effort, he created a rudimentary device that melted down within five seconds of being switched on. Few other people would have got that far.[21]

It is a salutary example. The everyday things around your house – the toothpaste, TV and toaster – have been assembled with materials from around the globe and have been handled, in some way, by many thousands of people before they reached your front door. This book will tell the story of how the global economy has reached this stage, wending its way from the mountains of North Wales through Grand Central station and the laboratories of Berkeley to the factories of Malaysia on the great web that connects the planet.

# THE ANCIENT ECONOMY

In the Welsh language, Penmaenmawr means "head of the great stone" and this mountain on the North Wales coast was long the site of a quarry. Ancient humans knew its worth as the repository of the kinds of stones that were useful as axe heads and, in particular, an arched blade known as an adze. Archaeologists have found blades from the site across the sea in Ireland and in England's Lake District, about 140 miles away.[1] The blades must have been exchanged, or traded, across substantial distances.

Such trade patterns were widespread in ancient times. Green slate adzes and chisels in north-western Russia have been found over a 500-mile radius. As far back as 7000BCE, obsidian, a black volcanic glass originally found in Cappadocia in central Turkey, was taken to Cyprus and the Zagros mountains on the borders of Iran and Iraq.[2] It was then shaped into blades to cut meat and reap plants.

Stones and tools are some of the best clues we have to economic life for much of human history. Early humans were hunter-gatherers and left no written records. But their lifestyle was remarkably persistent. If the history of *Homo sapiens* were fitted into a single day, farming only began after 10pm at night, and the Industrial Revolution did not occur until 11.57pm.

Archaeologists and anthropologists have a rough idea of our

early development. Our species was only one of a variety of hominids that emerged in Africa. Some hominids, including our ancestor
*Homo erectus*, used stone tools, perhaps as long ago as 2.5m years. As
far back as a million years ago, these early hominids may have made
the most important technological innovation of all time: the ability
to harness fire.[3] Fire allowed them to cook, and cooked food is a lot
easier to digest. This development meant that our guts shrank and
our brains expanded. (The chimpanzee, our closest modern relative,
has a colon three times larger than ours.[4]) It also gave us scope to
reshape the landscape in a form of agriculture called "slash and burn"
(see Chapter 2). The forest could be cleared so that the plants humans
favoured could be cultivated.

The first humans left Africa and migrated to other areas of the
world at least 100,000 years ago,[5] and by 60,000 years ago they already
had bows, arrows, fish hooks and needles, as well as ropes and sewn
clothing. Over the course of 90,000 years or more, humans walked
over land bridges (created by the ice age) to the farthest reaches of
Eurasia and the Americas; the southernmost tip of Chile was reached
around 12,000BCE.[6] The Pacific Islands were reached around 60,000
years ago, indicating that by that stage humans had learned to travel
long distances in boats.

Early humans played music; the oldest instrument in the world
is a 35,000-year-old flute carved from the wing-bone of a vulture.[7]
Grass pollen has been found in the famous caves of Lascaux, where
paintings of large animals have been found dating back 20,000
years. That probably indicates that Palaeolithic[8] humans used hay for
bedding.[9] And there is evidence that dogs were domesticated between
18,000 and 30,000 years ago, making them our oldest friend.

What was life like for those early hunter-gatherers? In the right
geographic locations, there was plenty of food: big game to hunt, fish
from rivers or the sea, fruit from trees and bushes, and wild grasses
that could be milled and baked. This food was shared widely around
the group; if modern hunter-gatherer groups are any guide, these
societies were egalitarian. And they did not have to work too hard. A
study of Bushmen tribes in southern Africa found that it took them
only 17 hours a week to find the food they needed and another 19 to
do chores.[10]

We can also assume that these groups traded with each other. This may have been a matter of ceremonial exchange, as with the Kula ring of necklaces and armbands in the Pacific Islands, which were part of a trade network. An exchange of gifts may have been a way of keeping the peace between rival groups, as well as asserting social status, like throwing a lavish party for your neighbours. But though the process is a matter of sometimes heated debate, it is not hard to see how modern trade could have developed from such origins; the gifts exchanged would tend to be of equivalent value or relations might break down. If the tribes happened to have a surplus of some types of goods, an exchange would clearly be to their mutual benefit. Those who lived by the sea might swap fish for fruit garnered by those who lived inland.

## Agriculture

The first great change in economic activity came with the move from hunter-gathering to full-time agriculture. It was a gradual and partial process that started around 11,000 years ago, probably because the retreat of the glaciers and a warming climate improved crop yields.

In the shorter term, this was a double-edged development. Yuval Noah Harari has described the shift to agriculture as "history's biggest fraud".[11] Farmers suffered from slipped discs and arthritis, had less varied diets, and were around six inches shorter than hunter-gatherers.[12] And they were at risk of famine through crop loss; a problem that mobile hunter-gatherers could avoid.

James C. Scott argues that a focus on the growing of cereal crops allowed the emergence of the early states, which taxed the population and created inequality as an elite grabbed a large share of the crop.[13] Cereals grew above ground and were harvested at set times of the year and thus were easy targets for the taxman; they could also be stored and doled out to the workforce as a form of wages. Surplus crops could be traded for goods with hunter-gatherers or nomadic pastoralists.

Agriculture was adopted independently in various places around the world, and it allowed the formation of the great civilisations in Mesopotamia, Egypt, the Indus valley, China, and eventually Greece, Rome and the Mesoamerican and Andean societies. It brought us "recorded history" in the sense of the first written documents.

Farmers may have started as a minority but they eventually outbred the hunter-gatherers, who may have practised infanticide to keep their numbers down. Estimates of the global population in 8000BCE are around 5m, and by the start of the common era (1CE) they range from 150m to 300m. The average density of foraging groups was 25 people for every 100km squared.[14] In contrast, China today has almost 15,000 people and the UK around 26,000 people per 100km squared. Without farming, the earth would never support more than 7 billion humans. In other words, it is probable that without the shift to agriculture, neither you nor I would be alive.

The great civilisations first emerged in river valleys where regular floods would deposit lots of fertile silt. Wheat was probably the first domesticated crop, around 10,000 to 11,000 years ago, although rice may have run it close.[15] It has changed immeasurably since humans first grew it (see Chapter 2). Wild wheat, when ripening, tends to shatter so that the seeds are blown away by the wind. Humans gradually selected the non-shattering types. But the wheat was initially grown as a sideline, a potential food reserve; there was plenty of fish, game and wild fruit to eat.

Eventually, cultivated food sources became sufficiently reliable that people settled in one area for the first time; sedentism, as it is called. The Natufian culture, which was in modern Lebanon from 12,500 to 9500BCE, established Jericho, perhaps the oldest city in the world. They also built stone houses. Settling down allowed a number of things to happen. Young children were less of a burden as they did not have to be carried from place to place, so the population could expand faster. In turn, this will have given farming populations an advantage in conflicts with hunter-gatherers. Animals could be domesticated rather than hunted. Sheep were tamed around 10,000 years ago, followed by pigs and cattle. This too was a very important moment in human history. As well as a ready source of food, domesticated animals were a potent genesis of infectious diseases.

Another reason why farming may have proliferated is that the growing population hunted all the big game of the area to extinction, as happened with megafauna in other parts of the world. Man arrived in Australia around 48,000 years ago, and within the next two millennia, the megafauna seem to have died out.[16] A variant on the same argument is that a growing population gradually depleted the wild resources and made people more reliant on wheat and domesticated animals. The causation might have gone either way; early farming may have allowed the population to increase or an increase in population might have required a focus on farming to support it. Examination of a site at Jerf el-Ahmar in northern Syria over the period 9500 to 8000BCE suggests that over time cereals and pulses (like lentils) became used more regularly than other plants.[17] A hectare of farm-land devoted to cereal crops like wheat, barley or millet can support a great many more people than is possible with hunter-gathering.

But the process appears to have taken place on a very slow and piecemeal basis. Archaeologists divide early history into a number of periods. The Epipalaeolithic lasted from around 18,000BCE, when the glaciers started to retreat, until 9600BCE (the Natufian culture is dubbed the late Epipalaeolithic). After that comes the Aceramic Neolithic, under which some farming occurs but pottery has yet to be developed. Then in around 6900BCE, the first pots emerge – a more sophisticated form of manufacturing than the creation of spears or axes. This era is dubbed the Neolithic and contained some remark-able feats of ingenuity, for example the erection of Stonehenge in around 3500BCE.

During this long period, as people moved from one area to the next, by land or sea, they took their seeds and livestock with them, spreading agriculture as they went. This movement may have been caused by climatic events, such as floods; by soil exhaustion, as areas were overcultivated; or simply when younger humans sought to establish their own independence away from the group.

It is not until around the fourth millennium BCE that we have the kind of societies that we associate with the term "civilisation". They have a government, towns and, crucially for our understanding, writing. Why the delay? For the first few millennia after adopting sedentism or agriculture, those populations must have been faced with continuous problems.

The first, given the sanitary conditions of the day, would have been the frequent outbreak of contagious diseases. Settled humans were much more likely to contaminate their water supplies with their own waste or that of their domesticated animals. Given what we know about the impact of the Black Death in the 14th century, or the devastating effect on the Americas of diseases brought by Europeans, many settlements must have been wiped out. Between 10,000BCE and 5000BCE, the human population may only have edged up from 4 to 5 million.[18] Second, natural disasters (particularly floods) must have destroyed some villages. Third, early settlements must have faced what economists call the "free rider" problem; it takes a lot of effort to grow the crops but less effort to steal them. Farmers were at risk of other groups taking their produce.

The idea of the "noble savage", of peace-loving tribes at home with nature, is quite persistent. But observations of modern hunter-gatherer tribes find that violent raids on their neighbours are quite common. Excavations in modern-day India uncovered the skeletons of one group of Stone Age hunter-gatherers; most were around 20 years old and none were over 40.[19] Steven Pinker tells the tale of Ötzi, a human found frozen in the Alps, who lived 5,000 years ago. He had an arrowhead embedded in his shoulder, unhealed cuts on his hands, wounds on his head and chest, traces of blood from two other people on one of his arrowheads, and blood from a third on his dagger and from a fourth on his cape. Estimates of war deaths from ancient sites, and from hunter-gatherers, are far higher than those from modern states.[20]

The first civilisations evolved to deal with some of these problems. Settlements could be defended with walls and forts; you were safer from violence (if not from disease) inside the walls. After the harvest, grain could be stored in a well-defended place. Water could be diverted and harnessed with the right kind of irrigation. This requires organisation. And the best-organised settlements will be the ones most likely to survive and prosper.

However, as James C. Scott points out, these advantages come with a big catch. If you store grain, someone has to be in charge of the store. If you dig ditches to channel water, someone has to be in charge of the construction work. That person (or people) may soon come to regard the communal goods as "their grain" and "their water" and act accordingly. Being in charge of the grain store gave the early bureaucrat enormous power; to grant or withhold food. Tombs from the era showed vast inequalities in wealth. Archaeologists found 990 gold objects in a grave in Bulgaria dating to the 5th millennium BCE; even the corpse's penis was sheathed in gold, indicating how long the metal has been seen as a symbol of wealth.[21] Graves in Mesopotamia dating to 5500BCE and China in 4000BCE also show huge differences in the value of goods buried with the dead.[22]

One early form of civilisation was centred on the temple. It makes sense that people would ascribe to the actions of a deity the arbitrary effects of the weather or the privations of disease. Appeasing the deity via worship or sacrifice was also logical if the result appeared to be a better crop. The source of power for temple priests was thus dual. They had the right to collect and distribute grain, but they were also the people with the knowledge of the rituals and practices needed to please the gods. In theory, the gods owned the lands but, conveniently, the priests acted as their agents. Perhaps this was the first example of George Bernard Shaw's dictum that "All professions are a conspiracy against the laity".[23]

The early civilisations may have had their faults but, like the switch to agriculture, their creation boosted the prosperity of the human species in the long run.

The great Mesopotamian civilisation lasted in various forms from before 3000BCE until conquest by Cyrus the Great of Persia in 539BCE. As well as writing, the civilisation developed numbers and uniform weights. It was based in an area dubbed "the fertile crescent", which had long attracted settlers. Excavation of a site at Abu Shahrein in modern Iraq, dated to the 21st century BCE, found another 17 layers of habitation, dating back to the beginning of the fifth millennium BCE.[24]

The emergence of cities (at its peak, Uruk had 50,000 to 80,000 inhabitants) required whole new forms of economic organisation. Even in the middle of the fertile crescent, Uruk (and other cities such as Ur) could not meet all their needs from within their boundaries. Stone, timber and metal ores all had to be imported, and Uruk traders established outposts in other sites round the region from which to organise the trade. The goods were transported into the city down canals via punts and basic boats. This trade involved a wide area, including what is now known as the Persian gulf, the peninsula of south-eastern Arabia, the Caucasus in the north and the Indus valley civilisation (of which more later).[25] Decorative seashells were a common find in Mesopotamian sites from the third millennium BCE, and their most likely provenance was the coast of India. Long-distance trade tended to focus on high-value items that were worth the risk. One example was lapis lazuli, a semi-precious stone found in modern Afghanistan.

This trade was recorded and categorised. The first written name in history is Kushim, who inscribed his name (or perhaps it was his title) on Sumerian tablets (the Sumerians were an early civilisation in Mesopotamia) that recorded transactions in commodities such as barley.[26] Those tablets have been dated to the period 3400–3000BCE. But they drew upon an earlier system in which different shapes and sizes of tokens represented different types and amounts of commodities. From this they made the crucial step of devising symbols to represent these commodities and etching them into wet clay tablets.[27] In the process, they invented numbers as well as writing.

For the first few hundred years of its discovery, writing seems to have been used exclusively for record-keeping. In a sense, writing was another technology with potentially vast consequences that humans were slow to develop fully.

At some point in the 4th millennium BCE, the citizens of Uruk built a stone temple that was larger than the Parthenon of ancient Greece. Building temples required a workforce, as did digging and maintaining canals. A workforce had to be paid, usually in the form of barley. The early symbol for food looks like a bowl, and bowls may have been handed out as wages or rations, of around 1 to 2 litres a day.[28] Barley was also used to pay rents and tax.

This was the era dubbed the Bronze Age, as humans discovered how to alloy copper with tin to form a metal that was easy to shape, and thus to form into tools. Such tools would have given their users an economic, as well as a military, advantage over other groups. Mesopotamia was lacking in metal ores, as well as in wood. This created an incentive to trade those goods with other areas such as modern-day Iran and Anatolia (in Turkey). The trading was undertaken, in some cases, by joint ventures of up to a dozen investors, funded by debt, a sign of increasing economic sophistication.[29]

Copper seems to have been smelted as early as the fifth

millennium BCE, an incredible achievement given the primitive technology of the time. It involved combining an ore with charcoal in some kind of kiln and heating the mixture to 1,200 degrees Celsius. The trade was extensive; there is a record of a single shipment to Ur of 20 tons of copper.[30]

Tools also helped another key economic development: specialisation. Someone had to create bronze and mould it into shape. Someone had to make the bowls in which Uruk's workers were served their grain. Someone had to brew the beer the worker drank. Beer was consumed widely by 4000BCE and was served in a thick, soup-like consistency. It was quite different from modern beer, did not contain hops, and seems to have had a low alcohol content.[31] Heating the water will have made it safer. Cities create both the need for, and the scope for specialisation. By crowding people together in a small area, a city ensures that they cannot grow or raise all their own food. By the same token, a crowded city makes it easy for everyone to visit a market of tradesmen who can fulfil their needs, and also creates the pool of demand that allows market vendors and tradesmen to earn their living. It is no coincidence that the sophistication of our modern economy has developed in tandem with the urbanisation of human life.

As cities became more complex, they developed more rules. The code of Hammurabi, a Babylonian king, dating from around 1754BCE, was not the first such code in history but it is one of the best known. The code contains 282 laws and a concept of judicial fairness (a presumption of innocence, the need for accused and accuser to provide evidence) that underpins modern legal systems. There are laws on trade:

> If a merchant give an agent corn, wool, oil, or any other goods to transport, the agent shall give a receipt for the amount, and compensate the merchant therefor. Then he shall obtain a receipt from the merchant for the money that he gives the merchant.

There are laws on legal liability:

If any one be too lazy to keep his dam in proper condition, and does not so keep it; if then the dam break and all the fields be flooded, then shall he in whose dam the break occurred be sold for money, and the money shall replace the corn which he has caused to be ruined.

While the code is hardly a feminist manifesto, women did have some property rights. If a husband divorced a childless wife, she got her dowry back. And if the wife had children:

Then he shall give that wife her dowry, and a part of the usufruct of field, garden, and property, so that she can rear her children. When she has brought up her children, a portion of all that is given to the children, equal as that of one son, shall be given to her. She may then marry the man of her heart.

And there are provisions for a minimum wage for workers and for debt cancellation in certain circumstances; what modern lawyers would call a *force majeure* clause:

If any one owe a debt for a loan, and a storm prostrates the grain, or the harvest fail, or the grain does not grow for lack of water, in that year he need not give his creditor any grain, he washes his debt-tablet in water and pays no rent for this year.[32]

In modern terms, this law (the 48th) gives the farmer a financial contract dubbed an option, giving him the right to walk away from the deal in certain circumstances. Thus the code has been hailed as containing the first financial derivative in history.[33] In a later era, the Mesopotamians used specific "futures" contracts in which, for example, a seller agreed to deliver a certain amount of grain at a certain price by a set day in the future.

The code also shows how the Mesopotamian economy had moved on over the space of 1,500 years. Sumerian and Akkadian empires had given way to the Babylonians. Monarchs had replaced priests as rulers. Land was held in private hands as well as by the temple, and could be bought and sold; the earliest evidence of land sales is from around 2700BCE.[34] There were markets; in the Akkadian language the word for street, *suqu*, may be the basis for the modern term for a market, a *souk*. There was money (in the form of silver) and it was borrowed and lent; the code sets a maximum interest rate.

There was also wage labour. Michael Jursa argues that, by the late Babylonian era, "the majority of the urban and rural workforce consisted, not of compelled labourers, but of free hirelings who were paid market wages in silver money."[35] A list of professions in Uruk cited 129 different types of job.[36] Governments dug canals and reclaimed land. Finance became more sophisticated. During the Assyrian era, 14 investors agreed to invest 26 pieces of gold in a fund run by Amur Ishtar, a merchant, who invested a further four pieces. Ishtar took a third of the profits, making him an ancient version of a fund manager. In short, Mesopotamia had many features of what we would call a modern economy.[37]

The Hammurabi code also describes a class of people called slaves, one of three types of resident, along with palace employees and private citizens.[38] Slavery was a feature of many societies right through to the 19th century; in ancient times, it was seen as perfectly normal. While we tend to think of the slave trade through the lens of the transport of Africans to the Americas, it was not exactly the same thing in ancient times. The Greeks did not have a single word for slavery, and the word *doulos*, often translated as slave, could also mean a person under the dominion of another (like a soldier in the army).[39] Slavery could also be temporary; if people failed to repay their debts, they were forced to labour until they paid it off, usually with a seven-year limit.

## Other civilisations

Mesopotamia was only one of several civilisations that emerged in river valleys. In Egypt, people had domesticated cereals and animals by around 5000BCE. An ancient Egyptian kingdom has been dated to around 3100BCE, based around the River Nile; the oldest legal document dates to around 2350BCE.[40] The rich flood waters of the Nile created fertile ground for crops (mainly wheat and barley) and helped to create a prosperous society by the standards of the time, with a high level of taxation and control. The Pharaohs conducted a census of all the land, cattle and gold under their control, and recorded the results on papyrus. Citizens were required to provide labour under the forced labour system that was used to build the pyramids; the pyramid of Cheops (or Great Pyramid of Giza) dates back to 2560BCE. Leaders regarded their workers as disposable; many workers will have died while building the pyramids and sometimes the Pharaoh's retainers were buried with the monarch.

The pyramids were an early example of what might be called the "monumental problem" – vast inequalities in wealth are generally needed for monuments to be created. Rich monarchs were needed to build the Taj Mahal or the Palace of Versailles; extremes of wealth were needed to create the English country houses that tourists like to traipse around. Many modern skyscrapers, built for Middle Eastern potentates and investment bankers, fall into the same category.

Egyptian farmers rented their land rather than owned it and paid a proportion of the crop to landlords. Records from 1950BCE show that rent was paid in barley, wheat and oil.[41] The Egyptians caught fish from the Nile and also kept cattle, goats, pigs and poultry. For textiles, they grew flax, which was spun into linen. They had textile workshops (with sophisticated heddle looms, developed as early as 3000BCE),[42] as well as artisans involved in trades like brewing, carpentry and pottery. Egyptians traded with other areas in the Mediterranean, importing goods like ivory and spice from other African areas to their south, and silver and wood from the Levant (modern Lebanon) to the east.

Cities emerged in the Indus valley (in modern Pakistan) in the 3rd millennium BCE. This civilisation spread over a wider area than either Egypt or Mesopotamia; it may have contained more than 2,000 settlements. Back in the fifth millennium BCE, the people of the area were using bricks and cultivating cotton. They made pottery with geometric patterns, and domesticated goats, sheep, cattle and buffalo. The Harappan culture built cities on a grid pattern, with streets of standard width. The culture may have been the first in the world to use wheeled transport in the form of ox-drawn carts (hence the need for wide streets),[43] and they were pioneers in the spinning and weaving of cotton. They also traded with Mesopotamia and Egypt. The Pharaoh Ramses II was buried in 1224BCE with a peppercorn (presumably from Asia) in his nostrils,[44] while Harappan seals have been found at Sumerian sites.[45] But the Indus culture seems to have suffered a disaster around 1800BCE, perhaps because the Indus and Punjab rivers shifted their course.[46]

The Chinese were growing millet and rice in the Yellow River valley and rice in the Yangtze river valley from around 8000BCE. Knowledge of rice cultivation seems to have spread from China to Vietnam, Thailand and Korea. As in Mesopotamia, a sophisticated culture developed. In the Longshan era, lasting from around 3000BCE to 1900BCE, the Chinese were the first to develop silk. In the third millennium BCE, the Chinese were using bronze and may have been the first to cast iron, in around 500BCE. It seems to have taken longer to develop writing. The earliest form of Chinese script dates back to around 1500–1000BCE.

Excavations in New Guinea have also uncovered drainage ditches dating back 9,000 years, and the people of the region grew sugar cane and bananas; chickens and pigs arrived from the rest of Asia in around 1600BCE.[47] Over in the Americas, a wide range of plants, including maize (corn) and the potato, were domesticated around 3500BCE, along with a few animals such as turkeys and llamas. In short, agriculture and complex civilisations were widespread around 5,000 years ago, indicating that humans in many areas had independently devised similar structures.

## The classical era

The focus of ancient history starts to shift to the west in the second millennium BCE with the development of the Mycenaean civilisation in Greece, along with the Minoans in Crete. Tales of these two civilisations still resonate today. It was from Mycenae that Agamemnon led an expedition to recover Helen from Troy, while the Minoans gave us the story of the labyrinth and the minotaur. The Minoan civilisation faced several setbacks in the face of what were probably earthquakes or volcanic eruptions, but its influence spread from mainland Greece to Egypt and Israel.

Excavations indicate that Mycenae became prosperous from around 1600BCE, with a great palace built around 200 years later. The city suffered a sharp decline after around 1200BCE, probably in the face of invasion; during this period, civilisations around the Mediterranean were being attacked by mysterious "sea peoples". This seems to be one of the first instances of a recurring pattern in which a wave of peoples (usually stemming from Asia) caused huge upheaval as they moved west; the end of the western Roman empire, the great Arab expansion of the seventh century CE, and the Mongol invasions of the 13th century CE are other examples. In this case, the period from around 1100BCE to 750BCE is known as the "dark age" of ancient Greece – the written records sputter out.

There were interesting developments elsewhere. The Phoenicians were the first people to establish a trading network across the Mediterranean in the first millennium BCE, from an original base in modern Lebanon. Although we call them Phoenicians, that wouldn't have been the name they used; they thought of themselves as hailing from one of their coastal cities, such as Tyre, Sidon, Berot (modern Beirut) or their most famous outpost, Carthage, established in 814BCE. The word Phoenician comes from the Greek and is related to the colour purple (or dark red); one of the culture's best-known products was a valuable dye made from sea snails. The Phoenicians left very little written record of their own activities; we know about them from the works of Homer, Herodotus and from the Bible (the name of which comes from Byblos, a Phoenician city associated with the paper business).

At an early stage in the second millennium BCE, the Phoenician cities were subject to the authority of the Egyptian Pharaohs. But they spread their influence across the Mediterranean, thanks to their great skill as sailors. They set up bases in the Aegean, North Africa, southern France and southern Spain, where they mined silver near Cadiz. These bases were used mainly as trading sites rather than as footholds for future colonisation. Herodotus reported, with scepticism, that the Phoenicians might have circumnavigated Africa. As well as their dyes, the Phoenicians were known for their olive oil, wine, cedar wood, metalwork, ivory and wood carving, and for glass-blowing (which they may have invented). They also acted as middlemen, trading in spices, linen and slaves that originated elsewhere. As traders, they spread their ideas and culture across the region, including their 22-letter alphabet, which was adopted by the Greeks and adapted by the Romans (aleph and bet are the symbols for ox and house).

Trade helped these early civilisations to flourish. One study looked at the correlation between the presence of archaeological sites and the potential connectedness (as judged by the shape of the coast and the location of islands) in the Mediterranean. The link emerged most strongly after 1000BCE when sea travel became more common and trade grew.[48]

After 750BCE, the golden era of ancient Greece began. Its hold on the modern imagination remains strong, not least in the language we use: democracy (rule by the people), phobia (fear), and prefixes such as homo-, hetero-, mono- and pan-. As well as the word *oikonomikos* (or oeconomicos) for economics, the Greek word for an open market, agora, gives us the term agoraphobia, a fear of open spaces.

Just as Babylon needed to import wood and metal, Greece had to bring in wheat from outside in order to feed its population, which grew around fourfold between 750BCE and 300BCE.[49] It did produce its own foodstuffs, of course, in the form of wine and olives. But it also had something very precious to export as well: silver from the mines of Laurion, near Athens.

The use of precious metals for money in the form of coins was another significant economic development. The first coins with a human image were struck by Alyattes of Lydia (in the western part of modern Turkey) around 650BCE, but the Greeks took up the idea quickly; by 480BCE, they had opened nearly 100 mints.[50] The Athenian owl was perhaps the first coin used across a wider region. Stamping the coin with the image of the monarch or a symbol associated with the state, like the owl, had two functions: the first was to reassure users as to the quality of the coin, while the second was to assert the power of the monarch or state.

Other tokens were used. Around the time that the Greeks were developing silver coins, the Indian civilisation started to use punched metal discs, and the Chinese were using bronze coins with a hole through them so that they could be strung together. Seashells (cowrie) were used in some parts of the world, as were beads. And as already mentioned, the Babylonians and Egyptians used tokens as a way of recording stores of grain; these same tokens could be used to represent the ownership by a particular individual of part of these stores, a kind of certificate of deposit.

One can think of these tokens as a system of credit. Anthropologists now doubt that any society operated solely on a system of barter. Somehow they kept a record of who owned (and owed) what, rather as shopkeepers used to chalk on a board which of their customers still needed to pay for their purchases. The giant stones of Yap in the Pacific Ocean, or the tally sticks used by the British Treasury until 1826, are two ingenious examples of the concept.[51] (A tally stick would be cut in half, with the lender and borrower keeping the separate parts. The transaction could be settled by matching up the two pieces.)

So why were coins useful? Money has various functions: as a means of exchange, as a store of value, and as a unit of account. The rarity of silver and gold gave them clear advantages as a store of value over shells and beads. And coins with set values were a good unit of account, as they remain today. People were also willing to accept them as a means of exchange across a wide area; this made coins very useful for cross-border trade. But they were almost too valuable; it was hard to use them for small transactions, and people were tempted to hang on to them and to offer something else as a means of exchange. It was tempting to bury coins to keep them safe, a practice that reduced the money supply but has proved very useful for historians. The supply of gold and silver also depended on new discoveries, something that bore little relation to economic development. For much of human history, there were never really enough coins around to transact everyday business. In quite recent times, in fact, many farm tenants still paid their rent in grain or other produce (for example, the sharecropping system that applied to many former slaves following the US Civil War).

Like the Babylonians before them, the Greeks devised a form of options contract. Aristotle tells the tale of Thales of Miletus, who predicted a particularly large olive harvest, and negotiated a deal with olive-press owners that gave him the right to hire all their presses during the following autumn.[52]

While we may associate the ancient Greeks with highbrow philosophy, their economy depended on the use of slaves of various kinds. Slaves dug up the silver in the mines of Laurion, and built the temples. Those who acted as servants in Greek houses had a less arduous life than the miners, of course. There were many freeborn Greek farmers (it was a largely agricultural economy) and some artisans in the towns.

Women in Athens had few rights, but Aristotle estimated that they owned two-fifths of all land in Sparta, its main rival. Some modern scholars think that every Spartan woman received some land from their parents, and that female ownership of property was on the same basis as that of males.[53]

The practical side of Greek thinking showed up in a myriad of inventions: the gear, the screw, the connecting rod, and the piston. They even managed to develop a simple steam engine. Another two very significant long-term innovations were the watermill (for grinding corn) and the use of cranes to unload ships.

The Persians under Cyrus the Great conquered Babylon in 539BCE and maintained the sophisticated infrastructure of canals and roads that allowed 1,600 miles to be covered in a week.[54] Darius the Great even attempted to build a version of the Suez canal, although the sources disagree on whether he completed it.[55] As with many other civilisations of the time, the Persians under Darius had a dominant royal sector, which employed around 16,000 workmen, including stone masons, carpenters and blacksmiths. Under the Sasanian dynasty, which emerged around 220CE, traders were organised into guilds and allocated specific spaces in bazaars. Some land was worked by hired labour, but other properties were let out to tenants. Barley was the main cereal crop.

## Two great empires

When we turn to the economic influence of the Romans, who replaced the Greeks as the dominant power in the Mediterranean by the second century BCE, it is tempting to think in terms of John Cleese's speech in Monty Python's *Life of Brian*: they brought the aqueduct, roads, sanitation, public baths, etc. The Romans were amazing builders and engineers; their roads were not equalled in Europe until the 18th and 19th centuries. They invented a form of concrete and used it to build arches far greater than any civilisation had previously achieved.[56] The 43-metre dome of the Pantheon, held together with lime mortar, was not surpassed until the modern era either.[57]

As well as being great engineers, the Romans were shrewd enough to take advantage of technology developed by others; they built large numbers of watermills, for example, even though the Greeks were the first to think of them. Given the time and effort needed to grind wheat, this was no small advance. But perhaps only 1% of the power the Romans used came from watermills; the rest came from human and animal power.[58]

The Romans also made a big contribution through the spread of their empire, and the freedom this created to trade within it. The risk of losing goods to theft was not entirely eliminated but merchants were safer under the *pax Romana*, or Roman peace, as it was known, than they were before or afterwards.

The political scientist Mancur Olson took a fairly cynical view of this process. A roving bandit is inclined to confiscate as much property as he can find and then move on to another location. A monarch or tyrant is a "stationary bandit": ruling a set amount of territory, he takes only a portion of wealth every year, since that is the most lucrative strategy in the long run.[59] But as well as stability, the Romans also brought their legal system, which protected its citizens' economic rights. The law "guaranteed private property, discouraged dishonesty in business and made it relatively easy to enforce contracts".[60]

There was also an early version of a "universal basic income", in the form of a corn distribution that began in 58BCE (it was granted to every citizen rather than being focused on the poor). The Romans had to import 150,000 tons of grain a year to feed the city's population; some of this came from the rest of Italy but a lot of it was from Egypt.[61] The annual tribute from Egypt in the reign of Augustus may have covered 70% of the city's grain consumption.[62] The emperor Claudius built an artificial harbour near the port of Ostia to cater for the larger ships needed to import the grain – a useful example of strategic planning.

Waterborne trade was just as vital then as it is today in the era of the giant ports of Singapore and Felixstowe. To transport goods by land was slow and required a huge amount of costly animal power; edicts issued by the emperor Diocletian suggest that the price of a wagon-load of wheat would double over 300 miles. It cost less to take grain from one end of the Mediterranean to another than it did to transport it 75 miles by road.[63] That explains why ancient cities were built by rivers or the sea; they simply could not have conducted their trade any other way.

But despite their willingness to invest in infrastructure, neither the Greeks nor Romans seemed to have believed that it was their duty to try to expand the economy as a whole. They viewed raising livestock and growing crops as "natural" ways of generating wealth. Rather like the English aristocracy of the late 19th century, they looked down their noses at people who were involved in "trade", although they were not above benefiting from it through intermediaries.

Nevertheless, the Romans did produce important business developments. They created the basis of corporate law in the idea that an association of people could have a collective identity separate from its individual members. Some individuals acted as tax "farmers"; they paid the state upfront and then collected the taxes from other citizens. (Tax farming lasted well into the modern era, most notably in pre-revolutionary France.) Roman traders banded together in partnerships known as *societates*, a primitive version of the modern company. One structure that proved long-lasting was the *societas publicanorum*, an organisation that could survive the death of its founder. These bodies could raise funds from shareholders and own property. They were mainly used to build and maintain public buildings, and to collect taxes.[64]

Roman craftsmen formed guilds known as *collegia* and *corpora*, another development that would have exceptional longevity.[65] The Romans can in addition be credited with starting the fashion for brand names. Factory-built lamps, with brands like Fortis and Strobili stamped on their bases, have been found in northern Italy. The Fortis brand was even pirated.[66]

Invasion and conquest brought the Romans treasure, and captives who could be put to work; successful generals like Julius Caesar could translate the resulting resources and prestige into political power. The conquered provinces would be a source of extra taxes. Generals could also parcel out land to their retired soldiers, securing their loyalty. In the long run, of course, this expansion brought the enormous danger of "imperial overreach" – a longer frontier to defend, long lines of communication, and a bigger band of enemies.

Over time, the tax burden grew and Roman emperors were tempted to debase the currency in order to raise money, particularly in the third century CE. The same amount of precious metal could be turned into many more coins. The currency went from pure silver to a silver content of just 4% in the course of two centuries.

The expansion of their empire brought the Romans into contact with other areas of the world; here were the first inklings of a global economy. Trade with India was possible in part because the Romans were able to subdue the pirates that operated in the Red Sea, and wealthy Romans were eager for the luxuries produced in the rest of the world, such as Indian spices and Chinese silks. Pliny the Elder complained of the fortunes that were lost from the empire annually to purchase Asian products, "so dearly do we pay for our luxury and our women".[67] The Romans were not the only ones to appreciate Asian spices. The Visigoths demanded pepper as part of the ransom for relieving the siege of Rome in 408CE.

Roman coins bearing the heads of Augustus and Nero have been found in the south of India, along with amphorae (jugs), mirrors and statues. Roman and Greek wine was also exported to India; there was even evidence of trade in counterfeit wine from the Greek island of Kos. A Roman gold medallion with the head of the emperor Antonius Pius from 152CE, along with other goods, has been found in modern Vietnam.[68] Conversely, a statue of a Tamil heroine was found in the ashes of Pompeii.[69]

In the first century CE, a Greek merchant wrote a book called *The Periplus of the Erythraean Sea*,[70] which was a sailing guide for merchants hoping to make the trip to India. The trick was to take advantage of the monsoon winds. Between April and August, the Himalayas drew winds from the south, bringing monsoon rain with them, but allowing sailors to head north; between December and March, the winds blew south again. Time it right and it was possible to get from the Red Sea to south India in around six weeks.[71]

While Rome was starting to dominate the Mediterranean area, China was consolidating under various emperors. The first, short-lived Qin dynasty had a single emperor, but his rule was highly significant. He standardised weights and measures and the written language, set up a tax register, and decreed which crops should be sown in a given area. When he died, he was buried with his terracotta army of more than 8,000 soldiers and 130 chariots: a farmer discovered the site in 1974 and now the terracotta soldiers are a popular tourist destination.

Qin's rule was followed by the Han empire. At first it struggled to maintain control but by the first century BCE, it was in charge of a territory equalling that of the Roman empire: around 5.2m square km.[72] This was a *pax Sinica* equivalent to the *pax Romana*. The population of Han China, at almost 60m, was around that of the Greco-Roman world; each may have made up around a fifth of the global total. Rice production was a vital part of Chinese agriculture and even today it generates almost three times as many calories per acre as wheat.[73] Well before the Han dynasty, in around 500BCE, the Chinese were using draught animals for ploughing and their faeces as fertiliser. The adoption of the paddy-field system, in which the rice was flooded, may have doubled or trebled rice yields.[74]

This was a sophisticated society with a structure of hamlets, communes, districts, and prefectures or commanderies. The Qin emperor set up 36 commanderies in total, although this was expanded to 42 by his successors.[75] Adult males were conscripted into the armed forces and required to do a month's hard labour each year. State monopolies on iron, salt and alcohol were vital sources of revenue for the Han dynasty, which may have employed as many as 130,000 officials across the whole empire.[76]

Chinese emperors came and went rapidly, rather like their Roman equivalents. Under Wen, the fifth emperor of the dynasty, peasants facing high rates of interest who lost their land were forced into extreme measures. A slave market existed well before the Han dynasty and may have developed in part from the use by the state of convicts as forced labour; some of those convicts were sold to private owners. One study found "plenty of evidence that, in times of economic distress, people sold their children, their wives and even themselves into slavery, and that these slaves were known as nu-pi".[77]

There were 11 attempts to redistribute land to the peasantry between 140BCE and 9CE.[78] The last of these, by Wang Meng, also involved the reformation of the coinage and reintroduced cowrie shells. But bad harvests and floods undermined his rule, as they were to undermine many of his successors.

There does not seem to have been any significant direct contact between Rome and China, though Roman delegations may have reached China on a couple of occasions. Chinese sources mention a delegation from the emperor Marcus Aurelius Antoninus in 166CE and a later delegation may have arrived in the third century, after the fall of the Han dynasty.[79] But most documents from the Han era mention no place any further west than the Kushan empire (in modern-day Afghanistan and Pakistan).[80] Knowledge of the Chinese empire did circulate in Europe; a Greek merchant living in Egypt in the first century CE wrote of "Thina", a land that produced silk. The silk that clothed Roman aristocrats came through India or the Parthian empire, which then ruled the Mesopotamian region.

The combination of Roman and Han rule created the most prosperous global economy the world had yet seen. People of the time did not measure economic output, but historians have a number of indicators that show this era to have been highly active. The first is the production of lead. It is possible to measure the lead content of ice layers in Greenland and Antarctica, and of sediments in Swedish lakes.[81] This allows us to estimate the lead concentration in the atmosphere in past eras and thus to assess the level of economic activity.

Lead was used in the production of coins; 400 parts of lead were needed to extract one part of silver. It was also used to make baths and pipes. The Latin word for lead, *plumbum*, is reflected in both the chemical symbol for lead, Pb, and the English word plumber. Up until around 1000BCE almost all lead in the atmosphere came from natural sources. Lead traces then started to increase and reached a peak in the last two or three centuries BCE and the first two centuries CE. Traces of copper have also been found in the ice sections, with a peak at around the same point.

A third measure relates to the discovery of shipwrecks in the Mediterranean; these can be dated from their cargoes. The peak in activity occurred between 200BCE and 200CE and tailed off pretty quickly after that point. Angus Maddison, the economist, reckoned that the zenith for Roman income, urbanisation and population occurred around 164CE; after that a smallpox plague killed around a sixth of the citizens.[82] The empire's power briefly revived under

Diocletian and Constantine in the late third and early fourth centuries, but the focus of the empire (including the wheat tribute) shifted to the city of Constantinople or Byzantium. Rome was sacked in 410CE and the last western emperor gave up in 476CE. Europe's significance as an economic power declined with it, although, as we shall see, the Asian market still thrived.

## From stone axes to silk clothes

Mankind's move from hunter-gathering eventually delivered the sophisticated societies of the Mesopotamians, Greeks, Romans and Han Chinese. Writing may have initially only been used for recording the details of transactions and the records of grain stores, but it gave rise to the stories of Homer and the histories of Herodotus. Some of the great thinkers in human history emerged in the first millennium BCE: the Buddha, Confucius, Lao Tzu, as well as the Old Testament prophets and the Greek philosophers.

These societies were not primarily "market economies". Most people, for most of the time, met most of their needs from their own resources. To the extent that they used the market, they may have brought some surplus food to exchange for things they could not make themselves, such as tools or pots. Some people did work for wages, although these could be in the form of food rather than money. Such work was often seasonal (harvesting), occasional (construction), or forced (the system imposed by the state).

But what was innovative about these civilisations was the creation of cities, which required a different kind of economic organisation. Rome may have had one million citizens at its peak. The result was the development of artisan trades, shops and markets. There were no factories in the modern sense but there were workshops; the shield factory of Cephalus in Athens had more than 100 workers.[83] There was a global trading network with Roman soldiers serving on Hadrian's Wall in northern England using Indian pepper while Asians used Roman coins and bowls.[84]

These societies may not have planned their economies deliberately but did pursue policies that boosted output. The primary purpose of Roman road-building may have been military but the 78,000km of roads they built could also bring goods to market.

Military conquest brought back booty, which expanded the money supply and stimulated consumer demand.

Nor should we belittle their longevity. Mesopotamian and Egyptian civilisations survived for thousands of years; the western Roman empire existed for longer than America has been an independent state, and the eastern version lasted another thousand years after that. The Han dynasty may have collapsed in China but the "middle kingdom's" glory years were yet to come.

James Scott argues that it is a mistake to think that the collapse of ancient civilisations was a tragedy; it is wrong to confuse the welfare of the people with that of the elite.[85] The ordinary person may have been happy to escape the forced labour, taxes, harsh punishments and diseases caused by ancient city states.

But the pessimism should not be overdone. Ian Morris, a historian, reckons that per capita income in provinces conquered by the Romans rose around 50% in two centuries; house sizes, food consumption and human height all increased.[86] Maddison estimated that per capita income in the Roman empire was around $540 in 1990 dollars, figures that may not have been surpassed until the rise of England and the Netherlands in the 17th century BCE. After the fall of Rome, the Italian population fell by a third and per capita income by more than half.[87] Towns fell into disarray and peasants faced the constant threat of losing their crops, or their lives, to armed raiders. As ages go, that sounds pretty dark.

Through it all, of course, most people were still involved in producing their own food. In most societies they would remain so until the late second millennium. And so we cannot possibly understand the ancient economy without understanding agriculture, the subject of the next chapter.

# AGRICULTURE

## The Hanging Gardens of Boston

A snowy car park off interstate 93 in the south end of Boston is the last place you would expect to find a farm. It is admittedly a very small farm; a converted container of the kind that fills the world's merchant ships. Inside the box you can find lettuce, kale, flowers, even wasabi; all growing in a carefully temperature-controlled environment.

As you enter the container, the first thing you see is a set of trays. Seeds have been planted in them, inserted into small plugs of peat moss. Above the trays are a series of plastic containers filled with nutrients that are being drip-fed to the plants through pipes. The seeds grow in these trays for two to three weeks before moving to the back half of the container where they hang vertically. This arrangement saves a lot of space; a container can grow as much produce as two acres of farmland. The concept is known as hydroponics, whereby plants grow in water with the help of artificial light.

The whole exercise is designed to be as efficient as possible. The apparatus within the container captures moisture from the air and uses less than 5 gallons of water a day. On a traditional farm, a head of lettuce requires 3.5 gallons of water to grow; in the container, a lettuce requires just 0.1 gallons. Electricity use is 125 kilowatts a day, or about the same as that used by one to two local houses.

Freight Farms, the company behind the idea, was dreamed up in 2010 by Brad McNamara and John Freedman. It sells its wares to small farmers, but also to non-profit customers like food banks and shelters that have mandates to provide employment for the people they help. Universities and schools use the container farms for student engagement. And it is the kind of company that creates enthusiasm in its employees; hence the willingness of my guide, Caroline Katsiroubas, to drive through a blizzard to show me round on such a dismal day.

Hydroponic farms are a mini-wonder of the world. Although not quite the Hanging Gardens of Babylon, the Hanging Gardens of Boston are still a technological marvel. They can be used to grow food in some very inhospitable climates – a similar venture operates in Alaska, north of the Arctic circle, where fresh produce can take a week to arrive.[1] At the moment, the cost of power means vertical farms are suitable for producing only high-value produce. But the cost may come down.

For much of recorded history, most people farmed and most economic activity involved crop-rearing or the raising of livestock. Over the last 200 years, however, the sector has become steadily less important in economic terms. In 1995, according to the World Bank, agriculture contributed around 8% of global GDP; by 2015, it was just 3.8%.[2]

But that apparent decline is, in fact, a measure of agriculture's success. Without enormous improvements in productivity, it would never have been possible to shift so many workers out of farming and into manufacturing and services. And without those same productivity improvements, the planet would never be able to support the 7.7bn humans who are alive today. In the first seven decades of the 20th century, an average of 49 people per 100,000 died from famines somewhere in the world; in the subsequent four decades (up until 2010), the average was just 4.5.[3] Thomas Malthus, the cleric and scholar whose 1798 essay predicted that food production would never keep pace with population growth, has been proved wrong time and again.

As recently as 1950, farming still employed two-thirds of the global workforce.[4] We can classify the countries of the world by the proportion of the workforce involved in agriculture. If the figure is under 20%, then it is probably a developed country. In Greece, the level is 13%, in France 3% and in Germany 1%. At the other end of the scale you have countries like Burundi (91%), Ethiopia (71%) and Afghanistan (62%). China's incredible pace of development saw agriculture's share of the workforce fall from 55% in 1991 to 27% in 2017.[5]

Although it now employs a minority of the world's workforce, agriculture still takes up a large proportion of our land. Out of a global land mass of 13bn hectares,[6] arable and tree crops occupy 1.7bn hectares and pasture (for livestock) takes up another 3.5bn hectares.[7] As the population grew in the 19th and 20th centuries, more and more land was set aside for farming at the expense of forests or wilderness. In 1850 there were 118m hectares of American farmland, but by 2012 there were 370m.[8]

There have been four (or perhaps five) structures of land ownership through history. The first is for land to be held in common. The second is for land to be owned by the monarch and various nobles, and to be farmed by peasants or serfs in return for services given to the upper classes. The third is for land to be rented from larger landlords, in return for cash or a share of the crop. The fourth is for the land to be owned by individual farmers. In America and elsewhere, this has evolved into a fifth type where the land is owned by large agricultural companies.

Systems where the individual farmer or peasant has strong ownership rights over his or her land seem to be the best for agricultural productivity; only then will they make the long-term investments needed to improve yields. A study of land rights in three developing countries concluded that "if property rights are absent and if land tenancy is insecure, farmers do not care much about the land use".[9] Instead, they "concentrate on short term profit maximizing at the cost of accelerating the degradation of land". Some of the worst famines in the 20th century were related to the collectivisation of farm land in China and the Soviet Union.[10] Between 1973 and 1992, when Peru's farming was collectivised, its agricultural production rose 24%. Don't be too impressed: once the collective farms were dismantled, it rose 170%.[11]

The land structure of earlier eras was probably one of the most important reasons why economic growth was so slow to get going. When landlords were able to impose excessive rents or fees, or when the peasants' long-term right to the land was in doubt, there was little incentive to improve crop yields. The break-up of the old aristocratic estates was a precursor to an enormous improvement in agricultural productivity. And better yields were a necessary condition for industrialisation.

## Changing crops and livestock

Over the last 12,000 years, agriculture has changed our environment enormously. In its name, forests have been cleared and vast areas of land have been devoted to specific crops. In most developed countries, the landscape is criss-crossed by man-made features like roads, railways and canals. Even where we feel that "nature" exists, it is shaped by humankind in the form of parks, gardens and managed woodlands.

Humans favour some species a lot more than others. The world has around 250,000 plant species of which around 50,000 are edible; humans regularly eat only 250.[12] The most important are the cereals – wheat, rice and corn (or maize), which comprise the bulk of our calorie intake. Further back in time, other crops such as barley and millet played significant roles in the human diet.

These crops have been altered by thousands of years of human cultivation and selection. As Tom Standage writes, they are "deliberately cultivated technologies that only exist as a result of human intervention".[13] Take corn or maize, for example. Its ancient ancestor was teosinte, a Mexican wild grass. Back then, the yellow kernels that we enjoy eating were encased in a tough shell called a glume. That glume was hard to break down in an animal's stomach. It thus emerged in the droppings, giving the kernels a nutrient-rich environment in which to grow.

In some cases, a genetic mutation meant that some kernels lacked their casing. Before humans came along, that would have been an evolutionary disadvantage. As it was, the mutation was a boon. The Aztecs, Mayans and Incas who cultivated the plant preferred unprotected kernels and sowed them as seeds. They also preferred larger ears on the plant so selected for that characteristic. The modern plant is a giant compared with its ancient predecessor (the oldest remains of a maize cob date back to 5400BCE).[14] It could not exist in its current form without human cultivation. Wheat too was selected so that its seeds did not scatter in the wind and its crop ripened at the same time.

The pattern has been repeated at many times, in many places and with many crops. Rice has been such a key dietary component in Asia that rulers were determined to improve their supply. Zhenzong, a Chinese emperor from the Song dynasty, learned of a rice variety, grown in what is now Vietnam, that was drought-resistant and quick to mature. Seeds were brought back to China, helping to spur a near-doubling of the population between 1000 and 1200CE.[15]

A similar process has happened with livestock. Herbivores like sheep and goats were the first grazing animals to be domesticated because they could feed themselves. All that was needed was a large enough patch of ground.

A domesticated animal makes (unknowingly, of course) a Faustian bargain. Its needs are well provided for, and humans offer protection against other animal predators. It is encouraged to reproduce and pass its genes on to other generations. But the price is a loss of freedom and a foreshortened life. Over time, these animals grow more placid, less wary of humans, and they develop smaller brains. A domestic pig has a brain 33% smaller than that of a wild boar; sheep have brains 24% smaller than that of their wild ancestors.[16]

The process of domestication may have been remarkably swift. A Soviet scientist Dmitry Belyaev began an experiment with silver foxes in the 1950s. He selected the foxes that were the least aggressive towards humans and bred them. The cubs were hand-fed by humans and also petted. Within four generations, some fox cubs were wagging their tails in response to humans, just like a domesticated dog. By the sixth generation, some cubs were whining, whimpering and licking in dog-like fashion. The study was continued after Belyaev's death by Lyudmila Trut who found that by the 30th generation, and after only 50 years, around half the fox cubs had domesticated traits.[17]

The success in taming foxes gives us a clue as to how mankind turned the wolf into the domesticated dog.[18] The dogs would have been highly useful as guards as well as hunting companions (doubtless some were eaten as well). But there turned out to be only a limited number of animals that were suitable for domestication.

The Food and Agriculture Organization of the UN lists just 39 kinds of livestock. Only 14 types of mammals weighing over 100 pounds were domesticated and Jared Diamond points out that these were unevenly distributed; South America had just the llama and its close relative, the alpaca.[19] North America, Australia and sub-Saharan Africa had no qualifying mammals at all. This must, Diamond argues, have held back economic development in those continents.

As humans moved around the world, they took their plants and animals with them, with devastating effects on the indigenous flora and fauna. The clearest example of this was the "Columbian exchange", which followed the European "discovery"[20] of the Americas in the late 15th century. Corn was being grown in Spain and Portugal by the 1520s, and reached China by the 1550s. It produced 100 to 200 times as much grain for every seed that was sown, compared with a multiple of four to six for wheat. Corn was accompanied by the potato, which produced two to four times as many calories per acre as wheat, rye and oats, and was suitable for growing in many different types of soil.[21]

Plenty of crops went the other way, including wheat, rice and olives. Europeans also brought their livestock, including horses, sheep, cattle, pigs and chickens, to the Americas, and remade the landscape to suit their style of agriculture, destroying the lives of the native inhabitants in the process. (Disease was by far the biggest killer, followed by warfare, reducing the pre-Columbian population by around 50% within a short period.)[22] Terrible though this was, the exchange of crops made it possible for the world to support a much larger population in the long run. In China, for example, the arrival of maize and sweet potatoes gave people a crop to grow in areas that were too dry for rice. That helped the population rise from 160m in 1600 to 380m by 1820.[23] (The chilli pepper, now seen as a staple of Asian cuisine, also came from the Americas.)

Another way in which crops were spread round the world was when they came under the same political, or religious, authority. The spread of Islam meant that sixteen food crops, like rice, bananas and spinach, as well as cotton fibre, were diffused from India all the way to Spain. Growing many water-hungry crops required the creation of extensive irrigation systems; what has been dubbed an "Arab agricultural revolution" brought more marginal land into cultivation.[24] The

Mongols were also keen diffusers of new crops and even had a "cotton promotion bureau" to encourage the use of the plant in their possessions.[25] Much later, the British, whose empire spanned the globe, were eager to get their hands on sources of rubber. In 1876, Henry Alexander Wickham smuggled 70,000 seeds out of Brazil. Botanists at Kew managed to grow plants that were then shipped to colonies in Sri Lanka and Malaya (modern Malaysia), which by the 1920s was the world's biggest rubber producer.[26] This turned out to be a fortunate shift since Brazilian rubber production was wiped out by a leaf blight from the 1920s onwards.

## The nutrient problem

Crops take nutrients from the soil, which need to be replaced. This was not a problem for hunter-gatherers, or for those who used slash-and-burn agriculture, where an area would be cleared by fire, with the ashes fertilising the soil. Once the crop had been harvested, the tribe would move on to another site. But it became a problem for settled farmers. They soon discovered that planting the same crop every year exhausts the soil. The Greeks and Romans dealt with this problem by leaving their land fallow every other year. The fallow land would be turned over to animals and their droppings would act as fertiliser.[27]

This system meant that 50% of the land was not producing crops on a regular basis, leaving plenty of scope for efficiency gains. By the early Middle Ages, much of northern Europe had adopted the three-field rotation system (in southern Europe, a lack of rain and thin soils made the switch more difficult).[28] Under this, one-third of the land was planted with a cereal (wheat, barley or rye) in the autumn; another field was planted in the spring with oats, barley and legumes (peas, beans and lentils). The third field was left fallow. This used two-thirds of the land rather than 50% and produced two crops a year, rather than one. And the oats could be fed to the horses, which helped with the ploughing.

Humans were also able to boost crop yields by adopting new technologies. In around 4000BCE, for example, the Egyptians started to use wooden ploughs. These could break up the soil, making planting easier, bringing up fresh soil (with nutrients) and pushing weeds under the surface. The Chinese had a heavy, or mouldboard, plough made from iron as early as the third century BCE; this was one of the reasons that their agriculture was more efficient than that of Europe. The Chinese also used the seed drill, weeding rakes and wheelbarrows well before they were introduced in the west.[29] The iron plough became widely used in Europe by around 1000CE, making it possible to farm the heavier clay soils in the north. These heavy ploughs needed animals to pull them. Ancient horse collars had a tendency to restrict a horse's breathing, and thus its pulling power. In the fifth century CE, the Chinese developed a collar harness, which allowed the horse to use its full strength.[30] The collar spread to Europe in the tenth century as tribes migrated.

These improved agricultural techniques, along with a warmer climate and the expansion of farming in eastern Europe, seem to have allowed a population rise in the "High Middle Ages" from 1000 to 1250CE. But the 14th-century Black Death, or plague, caused huge declines in affected areas, and widened a division between western and eastern Europe. In the west, serfdom declined in the 12th and 13th centuries as prosperity caused more landlords to produce food for the market, and to convert feudal obligations into money rents; in the 14th century, the loss of population made landlords desperate to recruit tenants. By the 16th century, serfdom in western Europe had virtually disappeared.

Eastern European peasants started to enjoy more freedoms in the 12th and 13th century, particularly as German settlers moved into the area. But in the 14th and 15th centuries, eastern European landlords reacted to hard times by imposing more and more obligations on the peasantry, reducing them to serfdom. The political power of the nobility, and the relative lack of cities to which peasants could escape, seems to have contributed to this development. Serfdom would last for several centuries more.[31]

Perhaps this divide was crucial in economic history, paving the way for improvements in agricultural production and industrialisation in the west of the continent and leaving the east behind. The traditional explanation focused on an "agricultural revolution" in 18th-century Britain, which in turn paved the way for the Industrial Revolution. Tribute was paid to pioneers like "Turnip" Townsend, Jethro Tull and his seed drill,[32] and Coke of Holkham Hall. Since then, however, the achievements of such people have been downgraded.[33]

However, it still seems clear that agricultural productivity in England did improve over the period, and this not only helped the population to grow but allowed workers to move off the farm and into the textile factories. Part of this was a further expansion in the amount of land devoted to productive use; the amount of fallow land fell from 20% in 1700 to 4% in 1871. The extra land was planted with new fodder crops, notably turnips and clover.[34] Some of this was the result of the "enclosure" movement, whereby open fields, previously farmed in common, were hedged off and cultivated by larger landowners; it has been estimated that crop yields were around 20–25% higher on enclosed land than in open fields.[35]

We now know why it is that land needs time to recover before being replanted. Plants need nitrogen. There are microbes in the soil that capture nitrogen from the air and make it available to the plants. But they cannot do so year in, year out. Legumes have nodules on their roots that attract bacteria (known as rhizobia) and fix nitrogen to them; some of this ends up back in the soil, which is why adding legumes to the crop cycle is helpful. English farmers were planting legumes in the 18th century and were more systematic about collecting manure for use as fertiliser than their neighbours on the continent.

The Chinese used both animal and human waste, the latter known as "night soil". They were rather more effective than the Europeans; in the 13th century, fields around Paris were only fertilised with manure once in every nine years.[36] Adding manure to the soil is useful because the waste includes nitrogen, but the concentration is only 1–2%. That is why there was such excitement in the 19th century about the discovery of the Chincha Islands off Peru, which had been home to seabirds for thousands of years. Their droppings, or guano, reached a depth of 200 feet at some points. This guano contained 20 to 30 times more nitrogen than animal manure.[37] In the 19th century, there was the equivalent of a gold rush in Peru. Prisoners, slaves and indentured Chinese workers dug out the guano and transferred it into waiting boats. Up to 300 ships a year waited for the smelly cargo, and, by the late 1870s, the guano mountains had been exhausted.[38] In total, Peru exported some 10.4m tonnes of bird shit and enjoyed, for a while, economic growth of 9% a year.

When the guano ran out, alternative fertilisers were needed. Agriculture turned from birds to the boffins. The key to producing artificial fertilisers was to harness nitrogen, which makes up about 78% of the atmosphere. The difficult bit was extracting it from the air; nitrogen is not a very reactive substance. A German physicist called Fritz Haber worked out that a combination of heat, high pressure and a metal catalyst could convert nitrogen and hydrogen into ammonia. The process was bought by BASF, a German company, where another chemist, Carl Bosch, figured out how to industrialise the process. This ammonia was turned into fertiliser of various kinds, including ammonium nitrate and urea. Without it, the current level of global population could never have been reached.

The Haber-Bosch process could be put to more deadly purposes, such as the manufacture of explosives and chlorine gas, which the Germans used in the First World War. On the night that Haber celebrated a German chemical attack at Ypres in 1915, his wife committed suicide with her husband's gun (although her motives were not completely clear).[39] When Germany lost the war, the patents for the process were confiscated and other countries were able to exploit it. But it is an expensive business and widespread adoption did not take place until after the Second World War; production rose from 3.7m megatonnes in 1950 to 133 megatonnes by 2010.[40] The process requires 1–2% of world energy use each year.[41]

Another huge boost to agricultural output came from the opening up of the Americas. The plains of North America and the pampas of Argentina were rapidly exploited in the late 19th century. And thanks to the railway, the steamship and refrigeration, these goods could be shipped back to Europe. The result was an "agricultural depression" in some parts of the continent because Old World farmers could not compete with the produce of the new. In turn, this may have spurred the emigration of many European farm workers to North and South America.

## The seeds of success
New fertilisers and the addition of more cultivated land were two of the four big factors in agriculture's 20th-century success. A third was the use of mechanisation – tractors, combine harvesters and the

like. This was more efficient than horsepower, and freed the quarter of arable land that was needed to feed the horses. The effect was to boost the amount of food that was available to feed the human population.

The fourth development was the creation of new seed varieties. This was driven by the need to tackle a big problem. Covering the earth's surface with vast quantities of a single crop creates the risk that disease will devastate production, as with potato blight in the 19th century. Wheat, for example, is attacked by a fungus dubbed wheat leaf rust.[42] In 1942, at a research station in Sonora, Mexico, a scientist called Norman Borlaug began painstakingly to test various strains of wheat in an attempt to create a higher-yielding version that was resistant to rust. This involved a dwarf version with a shorter, stronger stem to support a larger seed head. It took time for farmers to accept the new seeds and there were setbacks along the way, including the emergence of a new form of rust. But by 1959 Mexico was raising 14 times more wheat than before Borlaug's arrival. By 1964, it had become a net wheat exporter.[43]

Mr Borlaug then headed to Asia and tried to convince the governments of India and Pakistan to adopt the new strains. Both countries' governments were very suspicious of the motives of foreign suppliers, but some disastrous harvests and a reduction of American aid tipped the balance. Planting the new seeds was not enough. In 1968, Borlaug also persuaded Ashok Mehta, India's deputy prime minister, to increase fertiliser production so that the seeds could flourish. In Pakistan, wheat production rose from 4.6m tons in 1965 to 7.3m tons in 1970; by 2000, the country was producing more than 21m tons. By 1974, India was self-sufficient in cereal production. By 2000, new seed varieties contributed 86% of wheat output in Asia, 90% in Latin America and 66% in the Middle East and Africa, showing the importance of Borlaug's work.

Separately, the International Rice Research Institute improved yields by cross-breeding dwarf varieties. One variety known as IR8, or "miracle rice", could produce 5 tons per hectare or 10 tons with fertiliser, where only one ton was produced before. It also had a shorter growing season and was more resistant to pests. Nekkanti Subba Rao, the first farmer to plant the seeds in the Andhra Pradesh region of

India, became known as Mr IR8 and later pioneered a flood-resistant rice strain.[44]

This "green revolution" transformed a region that had been repeatedly blighted by famines. The new wheat plants could be grown twice a year or alternated with rice; it became possible to get 2 tons of wheat and 3 tons of rice from an acre that had previously produced only half a ton of either. Borlaug received both the Nobel peace prize and the Congressional gold medal for his work, a combination reserved for the likes of Martin Luther King and Nelson Mandela.[45] Without the green revolution, Paul McMahon reckons that 2bn people might not be alive.[46] In the late 1960s, doom-mongers were warning of world famines and "population bombs", but while Asia's population more than doubled from 1.9bn to 4.4bn between 1965 and 2015, cereal production tripled. As well as cereals, farmers were able to improve the yields of roots and tubers by 40% between 1980 and 2005.[47]

Avoiding famine was benefit enough. But the green revolution also brought wider prosperity. A study of 84 countries by the Centre for Economic Policy Research (CEPR) found that a 10 percentage point increase in the share of agricultural land taken up by high-yielding crop varieties boosted GDP per capita by around 15%.[48] Part of this increase is because a more efficient agricultural system allowed workers to move into manufacturing and other, more productive, areas of the economy.

The green revolution seems to have slowed the process of agricultural expansion. "Improvements in the productivity of food crops lead to intensification of agriculture on a smaller land area", the authors of the CEPR study conclude. And there was no sign of a Malthusian effect in which more food generated a larger population, which would exhaust the bigger food supply. Fertility declined, perhaps because parents were more certain that their existing, better-fed children would survive.

Of course, the green revolution is not without its unpleasant side effects. Irrigated farmland uses 70% of the water extracted for human use, a problem for areas like California or Australia, which suffer from periodic droughts. Nitrogen and other fertilisers are washed off the land and into rivers; this can upset the ecology of the ocean. Algae, which feed off the nutrients, can then spread into a "bloom" that kills off other life. A regular bloom, with an area of 6,500 square miles, forms every summer in the Mississippi delta.[49]

Technology can be used to reduce the impact. In California, farmers use sensors to detect moisture in the soil and thus calibrate the amount of irrigation needed; this reduces water use by 20%. Farm equipment like tractors are now fitted with global positioning systems, which means that they are much more efficient at covering a given area of ground; this reduces fuel use.[50]

Farming is also now an industrial process. In 2016, there were almost 23bn chickens in the world,[51] up from 4bn in 1960.[52] While wild chickens can live for six years, caged chickens are slaughtered before they are 12 weeks old. They live in hot polluted conditions and are too heavy for their legs to support them, causing painful disorders.[53] This is a brutal system.

If the problem on land is the cruel treatment of livestock, the problem at sea is overfishing. Industrial trawlers can process 1,200 tons of fish a day and global fish stocks are under threat. The UN's Food and Agriculture Organization estimates that, of the fish stocks it monitors, 52% are fully exploited, 17% are overexploited, and 8% are depleted or recovering from depletion.[54] Thanks to aquaculture, or fish farming, global consumption of fish is higher than ever before, at 20 kilos per person. In China, aquaculture supplies almost half the fish that is eaten. But farmed fish tend to be fed on smaller fish, and they are subject to supply pressures. Global warming is causing oceans to become hotter and more acidic, making life more difficult for species like crabs and oysters, which build their shells from carbonates. In the face of these difficulties, countries get more defensive about fishing rights in the areas around their coasts, and more aggressive about the rights to fish on the high seas.[55]

Agriculture cannot afford to stand still. There may be an extra billion people on the planet by 2035, and another 100m tonnes of rice will be needed to feed them, or around 30% more than current production levels. That would require an increase in rice yields of 1.2–1.5% a year, but yields are only rising at half that pace.[56] Many scientists pin their hopes on genetically modified crops, although the idea is politically controversial and is banned in some countries. Crops may be genetically modified to resist pests, or tolerate pesticides; they can be flood-resistant or drought-resistant; and they can be modified to help people with vitamin deficiency. A report from the National Academies of Science, published in 2016, found that genetically modified crops had caused no harm to human or animal health.[57] A different meta-study of GM crops between 1995 and 2014 found that both yields and profits for farmers were enhanced.[58]

The ghost of Malthus could still come back to haunt us. Global warming may reduce crop yields by 3.1–7.4% for each degree rise in temperature, according to a 2017 study published in Proceedings of the National Academy of Sciences. Some areas may get too much rain. Other areas may get too little. Warmer weather may increase the number of pests.[59]

History should teach us to be cautious about making apocalyptic forecasts about food supplies. The container farm that began this chapter shows that human ingenuity can find new, and more efficient, ways of producing food. But the more people that crowd this planet, the greater the danger that might come from an unexpected direction – a decline in pollinating insects, the pollution of water supplies, or the emergence of a new fungus, virus or bacterium that attacks the plants on which our ecosystem depends. The best hope is that humanity muddles through, as it has in the last 300 years. But as the next chapter shows, we haven't always been so lucky.

# THE ASIAN MARKET: 200–1000CE

Economies can be disrupted by climatic disasters – volcanic eruptions or cooling temperatures. But they also struggle when central authority is breaking down, and it is hard for people to trade or keep their crops safe from warring armies. Sometimes these factors can interact.

That seems to have been what happened in the period from 200 to 600CE. There was great political turmoil. The fall of the western Roman empire, marked by the sack of Rome in 410 and the abdication of the last emperor in 476, was only part of the story. China took a long time to recover from the demise of the Han dynasty. For a period from 220 to 280CE, the country was split into three kingdoms, known as the Wei, Shu and Wu. Briefly reunited under the Jin dynasty, the kingdom then suffered a further period of turmoil thanks to invasions by peoples known as the "five barbarians". The sack of Luoyang in 311CE by the Xiongnu was the equivalent of Rome's fall.[1]

Peoples were on the move across the Eurasian continent. Perhaps this was due to climate change, which forced people to travel in search of new crops to farm or pastures for their livestock. After 400CE, the weather cooled – climatologists refer to this period as the "Vandal Minimum" – and this lasted into the eighth century. In 536CE, both tree rings and written records suggest that there was some event – either a volcanic eruption or an asteroid strike – that had a prolonged adverse impact on harvests.[2] Further eruptions may have followed in 540 and 547CE, while an outbreak of the bubonic plague was recorded in 541CE. It seems to have taken a century for Europe to recover from the cumulative impact of these setbacks.[3]

Population movements had a ripple effect. As one tribe shifted into the lands occupied by another, the latter tribe was forced to fight, be conquered, or to move itself. Broadly speaking, the shift was westwards. Persia built a 125-mile wall to keep the invaders out and Rome helped to finance it. But it was a sandcastle against the advancing tide.[4]

As it turned out, the Persians under the Sasanian empire survived the period in much better shape than did the Romans. In the late fifth century, the empire was defeated by the Hephthalites, or "white Huns", a people from the steppes of Asia, who also conquered northern India. But the Sasanian dynasty survived until the middle of the seventh century.

The Byzantine or eastern Roman empire, with its capital in Constantinople, probably reached its peak in the sixth century under the emperor Justinian, who managed to reconquer much of Italy and North Africa. This Greek-speaking regime survived until 1453, although in much diminished form in its final centuries.

India, meanwhile, enjoyed what was described as a "golden age" under the Gupta empire, which managed to rule much of the subcontinent from the early fourth to the middle of the sixth centuries CE. The Gupta regime had the equivalent of both guilds and chambers of commerce, which attempted to control quality, prices and training regimes for certain occupations. It was during this period that Indian mathematicians developed the concept of zero as well as our modern system of numbers.[5] Arab traders later picked up the system, and when their knowledge was passed to Europe, the symbols were called "Arabic numerals".

There was an Asian trading system that linked the Middle East (the Persians and the Byzantines), the east coast of Africa, India under the Guptas, and China, which was economically important even during political turmoil. No Roman coins have yet been found in

China, but Byzantine coins, dating from the sixth century, have been discovered, along with Sasanian coins from the third to the seventh centuries.[6] Chinese coins from the eighth and ninth centuries have been found on the east African coast.[7] One of the key conduits of trade in this period was the Sogdian empire, an Iranian civilisation that lived in what is now Uzbekistan and Tajikistan. The Sogdians created the great trading centre of Samarkand, and dealt in goods like musk, silk, silverware and slaves with the Byzantine empire, the Indians and the Chinese. Their activities seemed to reach their height in the fifth and sixth centuries CE.[8]

The Sogdians were early traders on what has become known as the "Silk Road", although the term was not coined until 1877 by Baron Ferdinand von Richthofen. The terminology makes the route seem a lot more substantial than it was in real life. Valerie Hansen, a historian, wrote that "Over a hundred years of archaeological investigation have revealed no clearly marked paved route across Eurasia but a patchwork of drifting trails and unmarked footpaths."[9]

The land route from China to Persia and the Middle East was arduous. It needed to pass through the Ganzu corridor between the Qinghai mountains to the south and the Gobi Desert to the north, then round or through the Taklamakan Desert (in modern Xinjiang) and past the Pamir knot, where several mountainous ranges meet (a spot known as the "roof of the world"). Most merchants' business was probably local in scale, passing on goods to someone else along the route. An analysis of seventh-century trading caravans found that most contained fewer than ten men.[10]

Silk was a significant part of the trade. The textile was highly valued and used as a currency – Chinese soldiers were paid in rolls of silk, which proved very useful on their travels. In 1118CE, 3.9m bolts of silk were produced in China for tax purposes.[11] According to one estimate, over 5m pieces of silk went down the road in the first half of the eighth century.[12] But gold, silver and metals were also valued items, and the Chinese were keen to get hold of the horses that could be found on the central Asian grasslands. There was very high Middle Eastern demand, particularly in the Abbasid caliphate, for Chinese ceramics, which were fashionable items to own.

While the term "Silk Road" is now commonplace, it is worth

noting that most goods will probably have been transported by sea. (Indeed, in the terminology of the current Chinese government's Belt and Road initiative, the sea route to Africa and the Mediterranean is the road element.)[13] The overland route was vulnerable to disruption by raiders and suffered a decline after around 750CE before reviving again at the time of the Mongol empire.

Shipwrecks in the South China Sea have shown vast cargoes of pottery, with 55,000 pieces in one wreck and 500,000 in another. Such cargoes were far too bulky to have been carried by pack animals. One of the most remarkable finds in recent years was the Belitung shipwreck, found off the coast of Indonesia. This Arab dhow was on the way back from China in the ninth century CE and contained the largest ever hoard of Tang dynasty artefacts. It also had a lateen, or triangular sail, which allowed a vessel to make forward progress when the wind was in the wrong direction, by "tacking" from side to side. This was a great advantage over square-sail ships.[14]

This Asian trading market was truly a melting pot, with Malays, Tamils, Arabs and Persians, as well as Chinese, all participating.[15] By the ninth century CE, the sea route between the Persian Gulf and China was well established – via the Malabar coast of India, Sri Lanka, the Nicobar islands (north of Sumatra), the Malay peninsula, the strait of Malacca, and past Cambodia and Vietnam to Canton. Ships sailing to China from Mesopotamia and Persia left the Persian Gulf and then skirted the coast of Pakistan and India.[16]

China was far more rich and sophisticated than Europe in this era. Chang'an was the capital of the Tang dynasty and boasted markets in both the east and west of the city. The former had 220 different groups of shops including restaurants and inns. An inventory of goods found at a monastery included lapis lazuli from Afghanistan, agate from India, amber from Europe and pearls from Sri Lanka.[17] Any ambitious merchant of the era would have been told to "Go east, young man".

## The rise of Islam

In a period of population movements, one shift outranks all the others. The Prophet Mohammed and his followers left Mecca for an oasis called Yathrib (now Medina) in 622CE. In one of the most successful campaigns in history, by 644CE the group had conquered the whole of Arabia, part of the Sasanian empire, and the Syrian and Egyptian provinces of the Byzantine empire. In the late seventh century, the Arabs extended their control across much of North Africa, and in the eighth century, they conquered much of Spain and the Indus valley (in northern Pakistan). In 751, an Islamic army defeated the Chinese at the battle of Talas, somewhere near the border of modern Kazakhstan and Kyrgyzstan. It is possible that this battle led to the Arabs adopting paper, which the Chinese were already using.

As well as spreading Islam as they went, the Arabs also took with them their trading culture (Mohammed himself was a merchant). Over time, as they traded further and further afield, they tended to establish settlements along the route – on the coast of India and in South-East Asia, for example. Naturally enough, those early merchants set up the mosques, legal institutions and bazaars they needed to maintain their culture and sustain their business.

This was a vast common market with its own institutions and traditions. Families would organise themselves into partnerships, under which the risks and profits would be shared in proportion. Another arrangement was the *qirad*, which saw an investor entrust his capital to someone who used it in trading venture, in return for an agreed share of the profits. Merchants would have agents in cities with which they traded; this would allow credit to be granted, via the use of bills of exchange, a written order instructing the recipient to make a payment. A *hawala*, or order to pay, was very similar to a modern cheque. In the upper left corner was the amount to be paid; in the lower left corner of the order was the date and the name of the payer.[18] The *hawala* system is still widely used in the Islamic world as a system of cross-border payment.

Trust was vital to this system as traders believed that their fellow Muslims would not break their word.[19] Buying and selling on credit was widespread. While interest was avoided, bankers charged fees for lending money, for changing money, and for issuing bills of exchange.[20] The goods traded were the typical high-value items of the day. The Arabs bought pepper and other spices, jewels, cloth (including silk) and porcelain from India and China, and sent coral, ivory and textiles in return.[21]

Taxes were levied on land and on non-Muslims; an approach that encouraged conversion. Import duties were also imposed. Under the Umayyad caliphate, gold coins called dinars were minted in 691CE. The coins had an Arabic inscription, proclaiming the truth of Islam.[22] They were a rival in international transactions to the Byzantine solidus, another gold coin. Dinars have been found buried in Scandinavia and England.

As well as their growing commercial sophistication, the Islamic empire of this period had high rates of literacy and a record of technological innovation. They were eager to learn from other cultures. In Baghdad, an institute translated the works of Aristotle, Plato, Hippocrates and Galen (helping to preserve them for modern readers). There were specialist schools in medicine, astronomy and maths.[23] The work and name of Persian mathematician Muhammad ibn Mūsā al-Khwārismī gave us the words algebra and algorithm. Jabir ibn Hayyan, an early chemist, developed distillation, a way of separating liquids through differences in their boiling points.[24] Ibn al-Haytham, who lived in the late tenth and early 11th centuries, was a pioneer in the field of optics and his empirical approach made some dub him "the world's first true scientist".

The Arabs eagerly adopted paper, and by 1000CE bound books made of paper circulated widely in different parts of the Muslim empire. Gunpowder, also taken from the Chinese, was used for weaponry. The Islamic empire also developed the horizontal windmill for grinding corn and the sextant for navigation.

Another important area of innovation was agriculture: the Arabs picked up a number of crops on their travels and started growing them at home – rice, sugar cane, cotton, melons, aubergines and citrus fruit.[25] In turn, this required advances in irrigation, such as the waterwheel. And higher food production made it possible to sustain a bigger population.

All this created a large, sophisticated and prosperous civilisation by the standards of the era. Baghdad was only founded in 762CE but by the ninth century, its caliph was boasting to the Byzantine emperor that "The least of the territories ruled by the least of my subjects provides a revenue larger than your whole dominion."[26] By 900CE, the city had a population of around 500,000; one tenth-century book described Baghdad as the most prosperous city in the world.

Whether that was true may be a matter of timing. In the eighth century that claim would have been reserved for Chang'an, which was the Chinese capital and had a population that has been estimated at anywhere between 600,000 and 2 million. But the city was ransacked by the Tibetans in 763. By the tenth century, China was suffering another period of turbulence, being split into ten kingdoms.[27] Under the Song dynasty (960–1279) Kaifeng became the leading city with an estimated population of one million.[28]

Despite the turbulence, China continued to be the centre of much technological advance. Under the brief Sui dynasty, the Chinese joined a series of canals, along with arms of the Yangtze river, into a Grand Canal that connected the south, a key rice- and grain-producing region, with the north of the country. It built on an earlier Han Gou canal that dated back to the fifth century BCE. The canal system could be used to transport grain to famine-hit areas and to supply military garrisons. In the late tenth century, Chinese use of locks allowed the Grand Canal to reach 40 metres above sea level.

As Chinese traders fanned out across Asia by land and sea, they improved their navigation skills – inventing the magnetic compass, the sternpost rudder (for steering) and watertight bulkheads. On land, the Chinese had developed the stirrup and the wheelbarrow in the early centuries CE. And they developed printing in the eighth century, 700 years before Gutenberg. As already noted, their invention of the collar harness allowed horses to pull a greater load without choking themselves. In the 11th and 12th centuries, new rice grains helped the population to double.

And what of Europe during this long period? As we saw in Chapter 1, archaeological records of lead traces and shipwrecks suggest a collapse in economic activity from the second century CE onwards. Manufactured goods like pottery and roof tiles were also much less common.[29] For many people, this may not have made that much of a difference to their lives. They did not rely on coins and could not afford many of the items that were then the focus of international trade. But there were other signs of decline; forest areas grew, which implied that the area of cultivated land declined. Rome's population fell to 5% of its 2nd-century peak of one million or so under the emperors.[30] And the resettlement of Europe by new peoples meant violence and misery for the original inhabitants. In 14CE, Italy had an average income of 2.2 times the subsistence level, almost twice as high as Britain's; by the year 700CE, average income in Italy was only 20% above subsistence.[31]

Some kind of order was restored by Charles the Great (Charlemagne), a Frankish king who managed to unite much of western Europe, including Saxony, Bavaria and northern Italy. In 800CE, he was crowned as Holy Roman Emperor, a title that lasted a thousand years, and revealed a certain hankering for a previous era of stability. Charlemagne also established a uniform currency in which a pound of silver was divided into 240 pennies and 12 pennies were called a solidus or shilling, used as a unit of account. Older Britons will recognise this system as the basis for the pre-decimal currency that survived until 1971. The ninth century saw Europeans adopt the stirrup (which, as mentioned above, originated in Asia) and, in the tenth century, the nailed horseshoe, vital precursors for an age of mounted knights. A knight with his feet in stirrups was much harder to knock off his horse.

The unity of the Carolingian empire (as we now call it) did not last long. It was divided into three in 843, into, broadly speaking, western France, western Germany, and a middle kingdom of the Low Countries, eastern France, Switzerland and northern Italy.[32] Europe was still dogged by raiders and bandits, most notably the Vikings who attacked by sea and river, and the Magyars, who invaded from the east, before settling in modern Hungary.

In this insecure world, it made sense for peasants to settle near a monastery, which had weapons and walls behind which to shelter, or to accept the protection of a local military leader or lord. The manorial system, or demesne (hence the modern word, domain), developed from this route, under which peasants offered services and part of their crop and received security in return. For the peasants, the exactions of the lords were probably lower than the potential losses to bandits.

But agricultural improvements were achieved in this era and the amount of cultivated land expanded again, especially as German settlers moved into eastern Europe. The centre of power shifted east when Otto the Great of Saxony defeated the Magyars in 955, conquered Italy, and was crowned Holy Roman Emperor in 962. Towards the end of the period, European merchants began to re-establish trading contact with Egypt and the Middle East. But the continent was still something of a backwater.

### Slow progress

Asia was very much the centre of the world, both economically and politically, during this period. But the prosperity gap between Asia and the rest of the world was not on the scale of the gap between Europe, America and the rest of the world in 1900CE. Humanity made some technological advantages in the first millennium CE, especially in agriculture, but progress was slow. Indeed, Angus Maddison estimated that world population rose by a sixth in the millennium to somewhere between 250m and 345m; per capita income rose by around 10% in Asia but fell in the area covered by the western Roman empire. Life expectancy in 1000CE was just 24, and a third of babies died in the first year of life.[33]

Life for most people carried on much as it had for several thousand years: back-breaking toil to produce a subsistence crop on their land, a crop that was vulnerable to seizure by bandits or some form of taxation by local magnates. Few people could read or write, so knowledge was very slow to diffuse. Those who were born poor were likely to die poor. When the population is barely able to feed itself, there is neither the spare labour force to make other types of goods nor the demand to buy them. The "Malthusian trap" was still in place. Any gain in population would cause living standards to fall and eventually outrun the food supply.

There were just a few inklings of the enormous changes that would take place in the second millennium. Chinese and Arabic innovations in science, technology and business models were spreading, and would be copied with great success by Europeans, the magpies of global economic history. A thousand years later, in a nice irony, the Europeans and Americans would complain that the Asian powers were copying technology from them.

# EUROPE REVIVES: 1000–1500

Why are we so much more prosperous than our ancestors? The most dramatic changes in the world economy have occurred since 1820 or so. But it is still possible to see some of the roots of that development in the first half of the second millennium CE.

During that period, navigational advances were made in shipping, cities grew, and commercial activities developed. The arrival of Europeans on the shores of the Americas just before 1500 and the efforts of Europeans to break into the Asian trading markets meant that, for the first time, most parts of the globe were linked.

One necessary condition for rapid economic growth, though not sufficient alone, is that the population can feed itself. In the first three centuries of the second millennium, as already noted, new rice varieties enhanced yields in China. The Mesoamerican cultures domesticated corn, peppers and tomatoes, and may have been the first to domesticate cotton. They developed a sophisticated system of agriculture, with terracing on the uplands and canals in the lowlands; corn supported a high population density. But they lacked draught animals or the wheel.[1]

In Europe, along with technical advances like the iron plough and heavier horse collar, there was a systemic change from a two-course to a three-course crop rotation, which reduced the proportion of fallow land from 50% to 33%. More land was also brought into cultivation from forest and wilderness, particularly in the eastern half of the continent. Europe was at this stage an exporter of raw materials to the rest of the world, and an importer (when it could afford them) of luxury goods.

At the start of the period, Europe was rediscovering its political strength. Its borders were expanding. From the 11th century onwards, various Christian kings (of Leon, Castile, Aragon, etc.) took back more of the Iberian peninsula from the Muslim rulers of Al-Andalus. This was good news for early settlers. In the 1150s and 1160s the archbishop of Toledo was offering land in return for rents of just one-tenth of the annual grain harvest or one-sixth of the grapes, a much lower burden than in established areas.[2]

Much more ambitiously, the First Crusade led to Christian kingdoms in the Middle East, some of which lasted nearly two centuries. This occupation seems to have sparked European demand for new goods, particularly sugar. Christian merchant ships were trading in Alexandria and Damietta even at the height of naval battles between the crusader states and Saladin, the Muslim leader.[3]

There was still plenty of conflict within Europe, of course – the battle for control of England, which had involved the kingdom of Denmark and Norway, was settled in 1066 when William of Normandy launched a successful invasion. In essence, this was a world where strongmen were able to conquer vast swathes of territory, and only strongmen were able to protect land against raiders from outside.

The structure that emerged from this process has become known as the feudal system. In the classic model, familiar from school textbooks and films about merry England, there is a formal hierarchy: king, barons or nobles, knights, and peasants, with each layer of the structure having its own rights and duties. In theory, this system would be unchanging: "the rich man in his castle, the poor man at his gate, God made them high and lowly, and ordered their estate."[4]

But it was far from universal. Modern nation states had yet to emerge. Kings might claim ownership over extensive areas of land but did not always have control over them. Cities were outside the feudal land structure, as to some extent was the church. In certain areas, and in times of turmoil, the manorial system might not operate at all.

## Medieval life in Europe

The manor is the English term for an area of land owned by a feudal lord. He would farm part of this property himself (the demesne) and the rest of the property would be farmed by peasants. Some of these peasants would be outright slaves, although in England this declined pretty quickly after the Norman Conquest. Serfs were not technically slaves but their status was weak. As well as labour service, they owed their landlord rent, a death duty, a payment on marriage and a poll tax. They had little option but to pay up since the landlords also ran the local courts. Other peasants had more rights, but still had duties to their landlords. The Domesday Book found that English serfs were 40% of the population, smallholders were 32%, freemen 14% and slaves around 10%.[5]

Barbara Hanawalt gives a picture of life in a medieval English village in her book *The Ties That Bound: Peasant Families in Medieval England*. The frame of a typical house would be made of wood, with the walls consisting of turf or "wattle and daub" – sticks mixed with mud. The hearth with the fire would be kept in the middle of the room, and fuelled with wood gathered from the countryside. For firewood, peasants were entitled to any twigs they could pull off hedges and trees with tools known as hooks and crooks (hence the phrase "by hook or by crook"). The floors would be covered with straw, the bed would be a straw pallet, and the windows would lack glass. Household goods would be limited to a few pots or a bench and even these were often borrowed from the landlord.

If they lived in a village, the peasants would keep a small garden, known as a croft, attached to the house, in which they could grow vegetables or keep chickens and other livestock. The diet would have lots of bread, butter and cheese, vegetables such as peas, beans and cabbages, fruit when available, fish from the river, and some meat, particularly mutton. They would keep most of the food they grew but some would be sold in exchange for goods they did not make themselves, such as tools. Villages would have their own artisans, such as carpenters and blacksmiths; households would earn extra income by spinning, or brewing, or by working as servants in the lord's house. Women bore a heavy burden, fetching the water and the wood for the fire, looking after the poultry, doing the spinning of textiles (and the mending of clothes), picking the wild fruits and nuts, and overseeing the garden, making butter, cheese and beer, as well as all the cooking and cleaning.

The crop details changed from country to country but similar lifestyles were lived across Europe. Most people spent their lives just getting by. They had very little income left after their food, rent and taxes were paid. Famine or disease could carry them, or their children, off at any time.

At the start of this period, medieval Europe was still poor, relative to Asia. Whether or not we believe all his tales, Marco Polo, the Venetian who travelled to China in the late 13th century, described how he marvelled at the riches he saw displayed along the route, from Turkish carpets to Chinese silk clothes. Chinese pottery was far more sophisticated than anything produced in the west, which took centuries to catch up. Chinese metallurgy was also much more advanced.[6] European travellers were subsequently inspired to travel to Asia to make their fortunes.

Indeed, one of the most striking things about European culture at this time was its willingness to learn from elsewhere. Asian goods, such as spices, were in high demand; technology was imported from China and the Arab world; and, perhaps most crucially, in this period, Europeans adopted some Islamic commercial practices.

In part, this was driven by the desire to trade with the Islamic world. Trade in bulky goods meant sea voyages (in the 13th century, the price of grain increased by 15% for every 80km travelled by land in Britain).[7] Sea voyages involved the risk of shipwreck and loss of cargo through pirating, so merchants looked for ways to reduce that risk. One such vehicle was the family partnership or *compagnia*: literally, those who come together to take bread (*panis* in Latin). Where non-family members were involved, the structure would be a *collegantia* or *commendia*.[8] One partner would lend money to the travelling merchant and would take the bulk of the profits if the voyage was successful but suffer all the losses if it were not.

Modern companies and corporations stem from these roots. The key concept was the division of risk. A merchant might have the idea, and the gumption, to undertake a risky trading voyage, but lack the capital. Another person might not have the time for such a trip, or the inclination to endanger his person, but have the capital to put at risk. By bringing the two people together, these structures allowed more voyages to occur than would otherwise be the case. The result was that European citizens were able to buy a wider range of goods than before, and that Byzantine, Islamic and Asian merchants earned higher prices because of this new source of demand. Trade between regions enhanced general prosperity.

## Italian cities

The Italian root of words like *commendia* shows where the "commercial revolution" developed. A group of Italian cities led the way – Venice, Genoa, Amalfi and Bologna. Venice benefited from its ability to trade with both the Byzantine empire of Constantinople and the Islamic caliphate in Egypt. The city gave naval aid to Byzantium in 1080 and was rewarded with a special charter called the Golden Bull, which gave the city trading privileges and exemptions from tolls.[9] Venice also seized control of Constantinople in 1204 under the Fourth Crusade, and its Latin empire lasted until 1261. Constantinople was a great prize because of its wealth and its trading links with the Middle East and Asian markets. Genoa on the northwest coast of Italy was able to trade with the Muslim rulers of southern Spain and North Africa.

The Venetians tended to exchange bulky goods like iron and timber, plus human slaves, for the spices and textiles desired from the east. It was also able to sell its glass products, whose manufacture was shifted to Murano in the lagoon area from 1291 onwards because of the fire risk. (The first eyeglasses appeared in the late 13th century, an unsung advance in human wellbeing.) Murano was the leading European centre for glassmaking for the next three centuries.

Trading trips were famously risky operations. A failed voyage is the centrepiece of the plot of Shakespeare's *The Merchant of Venice*, while the phase "when my ship comes in" stems from the idea that the safe arrival of a cargo was a welcome bonus. For the investor, the answer, where possible, was to split one's capital among as many voyages as possible. In Venice, ownership of the ships and cargoes were divided into shares called *loca*. A wide range of citizens could invest; individuals could hold one-24th of a *locum*.[10] Ownership of a *locum* could be pledged as security for loans.

Another Italian financial innovation was public debt. Venice set up a loan office called the Monte Vecchio in the 13th century. Rich citizens were compelled to make loans to the city but they received an annual interest rate of 5% in return. The debt was tradable and citizens bought the loans as a home for their savings; a 5% yield at a time of zero long-term inflation was a pretty good deal. The bonds were traded (along with commodities) at an exchange in the central area called the Rialto. The Venetian state paid interest regularly even during the Black Death. But, in a telling sign of Venetian decline, interest payments were suspended for the first time in 1379 and the yield was reduced to 4% in 1383. The state was never able to catch up on interest payments and by the late 1470s was 20 years behind schedule.[11]

Monarchs had borrowed money before, of course. But for the lender, this was far from a risk-free investment. If the monarch decided not to repay, the lender had no recourse, as the monarch had effective control of the legal system. Venice paid its debts regularly for more than a century precisely because many of the people governing the city were also investors in the loan; they had no desire to default. The same idea was adopted by Britain and the Netherlands in the 18th century, giving them the financial firepower to take on the European absolute monarchies of France and Austria.

Another aspect of the commercial revolution was the development of the credit market, and in particular the bill of exchange. The idea had been common in the Islamic world and depended on the existence of merchants who had links or agents in other cities and empires. Say a merchant in Florence wished to buy goods from another in Constantinople. Sending gold or silver coins by boat was risky; even if the money got there, the Florentine might not feel confident that the goods would arrive by return. So he would give an international merchant a promissory note (the bill of exchange), which would be sent to the seller. The seller would hand over the goods and get payment from the agent of the international merchant in Constantinople. The buyer would then make his payment in Florence and the international merchant would get a healthy cut by being the middleman. The greater availability of credit meant that interest rates fell from the high rates typically charged in ancient times; in the early 14th century, annual rates in Italy were around 8–12%.[12]

It is a good rule of thumb that a higher risk demands a higher reward. Poor people struggle to get cheap credit because they lack the collateral (such as a house) that can back the loan, and lenders worry that they will fail to repay; they need a higher interest rate to compensate for those who default. By the same token, when societies are stable and the rule of law is trusted, interest rates tend to be lower than in times of war or anarchy.

## The great fairs

A further area of development for credit markets occurred at the international trade fairs that developed in Champagne in the 12th century. The fairs came under the protection of the counts of Champagne and Brie, who benefited from tolls and fees when merchants travelled to their areas and who offered protection in return. There were six fairs a year, each lasting around two months; cloth was the most important commodity but spices were also popular. These were sophisticated events, with a set timetable for trading and officials called "Guards of the Fair" who intervened to hear complaints and enforce contracts.[13]

Each trader could have arrived with bags of gold and silver from their home towns, but that was a risky strategy in 12th- and 13th-century Europe. Indeed, many traders would be both buying and selling, so they would probably have to lug their coins back on the return journey. So bankers operated at the fairs, acting as clearing houses for all the trades; a merchant would end up with a credit or debit that could be settled later, or simply rolled over to the next fair. In this way, credit allowed more trade to occur; as one author wrote, "credit enabled a small investment of hard cash to go to work simultaneously at more than one place".[14] Financial innovation thus lowered transaction costs, allowed cash that would otherwise be hoarded to be put to work, and allowed merchants to take more risk. Without it, trade would not have flourished as it did.

There was a general shortage of coins in Europe in the Middle Ages. At the start of the period, Europe was surviving with the help of coins from the Byzantine and Islamic worlds. Eventually the Italian cities developed the wealth and confidence to issue their own gold coins, starting with Genoa and Florence in 1252,[15] while Venice followed with the ducat in 1284. Silver was discovered in various parts of central Europe between the 960s and 1160s and this also eased the currency shortage.

## The Hanseatic League

Italy was not the only centre of commercial activity in medieval Europe. Towns on the coast of the Baltic and North seas banded together in commercial organisations called *hansa* (from an old German word for a convoy). The first organisations seem to have emerged in Lübeck in northern Germany and in Gotland, an island off Sweden in the middle of the 12th century. Over the course of the next three centuries, 200 towns and cities joined the club.[16] The cities acted as a cartel, using their economic and military power to demand trading privileges and lower taxes from other rulers. They had a firm grip on trade in herring and cod in the seas where they operated; the fish was salted on board and could thus be kept for future consumption. They used sturdy boats called *kogge*, or cogs,[17] and flat-bottomed boats called hookers for heavy cargoes.[18] News travelled over the trade network. The first inkling the British had of the Mongol invasion of Europe was when the price of fish at Harwich rose sharply because the sailors in the Baltic fishing fleets had been diverted to fight the invaders.[19] Discipline in this trade was ruthlessly enforced; any captain who lost his cargo would have his ears cut and would spend time in jail.[20]

Another centre of urban development was Flanders, where a textile trade had developed as early as the ninth century. The area was good for raising sheep although wool was also imported from England and Scotland. At some point in the 11th century, Flemish weavers switched from a horizontal to a vertical loom, a shift that improved productivity three- to five-fold. Spinning also became more productive with the adoption of the spinning wheel.

By the 13th century, Flemish textiles were traded as far away as Syria.[21] In 1277, the first Genoese ships arrived in Bruges, and Venetian galleys followed in 1314; the Italians swapped spices for textiles.[22] Between a third and a half of the labour force of Ghent worked in textiles in the late 13th and early 14th centuries.[23]

## The importance of towns and cities

Towns and cities are usually in the forefront of economic development. The sophistication of China under the Song dynasty was in part due to its city network; around 6m Chinese people lived in cities during that era, representing around half the global urban population.[24] The major city of the time was Kaifeng, but under the Ming dynasty (1368–1644CE), Beijing gained primacy.[25] Cairo had a population of 600,000 in the 14th century, and the cities of Oman, Bahrain, Aden and Jeddah were all important trading points in the Islamic world.[26]

Cities do not produce all their own food; they need to earn enough income to buy food from elsewhere, and that in turn encourages the development of new trades and industries. Markets can be held in towns, where large numbers of consumers and merchants can gather together. And cities were places where people could escape from their fixed roles under the feudal system. Cities could also provide some food security; Venice kept stocks of millet, which fed its citizens when besieged by Genoa in 1372.[27] At this stage, however, cities did not have the critical mass to transform the economy completely: in 1500, only around 15% to 20% of Europeans lived in them.[28]

Many trades were organised into guilds, a tradition that stemmed back to Roman times. Historians are divided about whether guilds helped or hindered economic development. On the one hand, they provided a route for craftsmen to be trained, first as apprentices and then as journeymen, before becoming masters. Guilds also acted to maintain quality standards. By the same token, they could act as cartels and keep out people who had new ideas. The more narrowly defined the guild, the greater the power it had to act as a cartel. There were 101 guilds in Paris in the 1260s, including three separate groups that made buckles.[29] So it would be a mistake to think of medieval Europe as a free-market paradise. In Toulouse, for example, the city set limits on the profits made by millers and bakers. Sumptuary laws were passed to restrict the type of clothes and jewellery worn by certain social classes; the poor were not allowed to get ideas above their station. The main focus of the ruling classes was maintaining their position, not growing the economy.[30]

## Asian developments

This chapter has focused on Europe so far, but much was happening in Asia in the first half of the second millennium. At the start of the period, China under the Song dynasty was the most sophisticated civilisation on the planet. Their technology was streets ahead of Europe. Chinese astronomers calculated the world's circumference to within a few metres, and emperors kept their own academies of scholars and artists.[31]

The most dramatic political shift was the emergence of the Mongol empire in the 13th century, a development that may have been due to mild and wet conditions on the steppes, which increased the number of horses and other livestock on which the tribes depended. The military strength of the Mongols, including archers mounted on horseback, powerful siege engines, and rapid movement, prevailed over almost any enemy they met. Inhabitants of captured cities were slaughtered and tales of barbarian savagery prompted many targets to surrender rather than resist. In the course of the 13th century the Mongols conquered the whole of China. Their empire stretched the width of Asia; it covered a sixth of the world's land mass and contained a quarter of its people.[32]

History has awarded the Mongols a reputation for slaughter. But like many empires before and after them, they recognised the importance of trade. They encouraged arts and crafts in the cities they conquered, kept taxes low and were relaxed in matters of religion.[33] They also had a highly efficient postal service, with messengers able to travel 250 to 300 miles a day with the help of fresh horses. Thanks to their fearsome reputation, banditry was much reduced; and a series of posting houses monitored the arrival and departure of trade caravans. A chronicler of the day boasted that "a maiden bearing a nugget of gold on her head could wander safely throughout the realm".[34]

The trading routes of the era may have helped to spread the Black Death from Asia to Europe in remarkably quick time. The first signs of the disease are now thought to have occurred in Astrakhan on the Caspian Sea in 1346. By the following year, it had hit Constantinople, and the rest of Europe was ravaged in 1348 and 1349.[35] The route of the disease may have been via a Mongol siege of Kaffa in the Crimea, a base for Italian merchants – the merchants fled back home, taking it with them. And the speed of its spread suggests that it was ship-borne rather than travelling over land.

Most people think the disease was the bubonic plague, caused by the bacterium *Yersinia pestis*, which has been found in mass graves from the Middle Ages.[36] However, scientists have moved away from the theory that the disease was carried by rats. Regular human fleas and body lice were to blame.[37]

The effect of the plague was catastrophic. In some cities, such as Florence and Siena, as much as 60% of the population may have died within a few months. The total death rate could have been a third to a half of Europe's population. The Middle East was also affected badly, with Alexandria, Baghdad and Damascus all succumbing to outbreaks; perhaps 40% of Egypt's population died. Between 1330 and 1420 the population of China fell from 72m to 51m. All told, at least 75m people died and the total may have been more than twice as high. An epidemic that had the same impact today would kill between one and two billion people. The world population took two centuries to recover, not least because the disease kept returning; England suffered another 14 outbreaks before 1500.

For anyone who has seen a post-apocalyptic drama like *The Walking Dead* or *The Stand*, it may seem remarkable that medieval society functioned at all in the face of such a death toll. For those who survived, however, the effects were actually quite positive. With fewer people, and the same amount of land, it was natural for rents to fall and wages to rise (although prices rose too). A contemporary chronicler complained that the shortage of labourers was so acute that "the humble turned up their noses at employment, and could scarcely be persuaded to serve the eminent for triple wages".[38] The gap between skilled and unskilled wages dropped. In the early 14th century, an English carpenter earned twice as much as a labourer; by the early 15th century, only a quarter more.[39]

This shift in favour of labour did not go down well with the rulers of the time. In 1349 and 1351, Edward III of England tried to limit wages to the level prevailing in 1346, before the plague had struck. It didn't work. In France, King John II allowed for a more realistic one-third increase in wages in 1351. Real wages had their longest and most significant rise in premodern European history.[40]

The Black Death is one of the examples cited by Walter Scheidel whereby shocks to society led to a reduction in inequality.[41] As well as earning more, workers had a better diet. Bread formed half the intake of harvest gatherers in Norfolk in the late 13th century, but only 15–20% in the late 14th, while the share of meat rose from 4% to 25–30% over the same period. Serfdom was already in decline in western Europe, with feudal duties being converted into money rents; the Black Death helped to finish it off. In eastern Europe, by contrast, serfdom remained in some places until the 19th century, a division that may still have significant effects today.[42] Landlords in eastern Europe seemed unable to earn a profit unless they could compel peasants to work. Strong states were happy to collaborate with the landlords in enforcing their power, and eastern European peasants did not have the option of escaping to cities as their counterparts in the west did.[43] In western Europe, by contrast, power was more diffused between a number of states, and there was always the option to move off the land and find work in industries such as textiles.

## China's retreat

In the early 15th century, China was still by far the world's most powerful state. That was demonstrated by Zheng He, a Chinese admiral, who commanded seven great voyages, with 100 to 300 ships and up to 27,000 men, which reached Vietnam, Indonesia, Sri Lanka, India and even Africa. The ships were huge by the standards of the day, 20 times larger than Columbus's *Santa Maria*. History might have been very different had the ships sailed across the Pacific to the Americas. But the aim of the journeys was not conquest, or even trade, but a show of prestige. The trips were expensive, and the Chinese were also at that time facing a renewed threat on their northern borders from the Mongols (the capital was moved from Nanking to Beijing, much nearer the northern border, in 1421). By 1436, the voyages were abandoned.

If that decision was unsurprising, what happened next was remarkable. The Chinese turned in on themselves. By 1500, the death penalty applied to anyone who built a ship with more than two masts; in 1525, coastal authorities were ordered to destroy ocean-going ships.[44] It was at precisely this stage that European nations were starting to expand round the world. Under the sponsorship of

Prince Henry the Navigator (who was neither a sailor nor a navigator), the Portuguese started to explore the west coast of Africa in the 15th century. With the help of a new ship design called the caravel, the Portuguese reached Madeira in 1419 and the Azores in 1427. Fatefully, they started to trade slaves and to grow sugar on plantations. But they were also looking for a route round Africa to the "spice islands" of Asia.

Spices were a very lucrative business, with prices in Europe many times those in Asia. The medieval spice trade was quite closely controlled by guilds in modern Sri Lanka, and the Malabar coast of India.[45] From there the spices were shipped via the Middle East, where further costs were added and middlemen took another cut. The Turks captured Constantinople, ending the 1,000-year-old Byzantine empire in 1453, which seems to have cut off, for a while, one of those trading routes. So there was a big incentive for anyone who could find a sea passage to Asia. Bartolomeu Dias managed to round the southern tip of Africa in 1488, which he called the "Cape of Storms", later renamed, in a classic example of the power of advertising, the "Cape of Good Hope".

Europe's exploration drive was made possible by various improvements in shipping that occurred in the Middle Ages, including, as has already been noted, the lateen or triangular sail, taken from the Islamic world, and the sternpost rudder and the compass, which improved steering and navigation and were taken from the Chinese. By the late 15th century, European fishermen were exploiting the great cod shoals off the coast of Newfoundland; the Vikings had earlier learned how to preserve the fish by freezing it.[46]

Food was not the only reason for exploration. Europeans were well aware of the wealth and power of the Chinese state. When Columbus set sail in 1492, he was hoping to meet the "Great Khan of Cathay" and to involve him in a hare-brained plan to recapture Jerusalem.[47] Finance for his voyage came from Spain, which was eager to compete with the Portuguese. Of course, as mentioned earlier, Columbus did not "discover" the Americas, which were occupied already, and he did not land on the North American mainland, stopping only in the Bahamas, Cuba and Hispaniola (modern Haiti and the Dominican Republic).

There is an energetic debate about the causes of the "great divergence" that saw the Chinese standard of living fall way below that of Europe by the middle of the 19th century. But one factor must surely have been the vigorous competition between European states, which both spurred them on and prevented the kind of edict against seaborne trade that restricted Chinese growth. While the Europeans still adopted Chinese technology during the Middle Ages, they started to improve on it towards the end of the period. The Chinese had developed gunpowder, but in the 15th century the Europeans built bigger and better cannons; and the Chinese developed printing, but the Europeans turned this into a publishing industry via the adoption of movable type.

The 15th century marked the end of another era in Chinese economic history – that of paper money. It was hardly surprising that this emerged first in China, which developed both paper and printing. Relying on paper money required a fair degree of trust: Marco Polo thought it testament to the authority of Kublai Khan that his mere promise on paper carried the same value as gold or silver. Certainly, Chinese paper money was in part a government initiative; merchants were encouraged to exchange their coins with the Treasury in return for compensation notes, called Fey-thsian, or flying money. By the Yuan dynasty (1279–1367), paper money was the only legal tender.[48]

Given the general shortage of metal, paper money certainly made sense as a currency, and its existence may have stimulated the Chinese economy. But, over time, the ability to issue paper money was so tempting that too much was created and inflation set in. From being worth 1,000 copper coins in 1380, a kuan note was worth less than a quarter of a coin by 1535.[49] By that stage, coins had come back into use. New note issues had been abandoned in 1450.

Back in Europe, there was a "great bullion famine" in the mid-15th century, which probably resulted from the leakage of coins to Asia (to buy luxury goods), and from a decline in production in the continent's silver mines. This did not lead to the adoption of paper currency but, rather, to an enthusiastic search for new sources of precious metals, spurring first the voyages to Africa and, as the 16th century dawned, the exploitation of the Americas.

India was also a prosperous area in the Middle Ages. Marco Polo visited the Coromandel coast in the south-east of India, and Tanjore (now Thanjavur), which he described as the "richest province on earth", thanks to its high production of pearls and gems (although he was surprised that the king sat on the ground). At the time it was part of the Cholan empire, which dominated southern India from the tenth to the 13th centuries.[50]

## A turning point

Apart from the roundness of the number, there is nothing magical about the year 1500, this chapter's chosen endpoint. But by the end of the millennium's first half, European sailors had reached the Americas and Asia, with devastating consequences for both. China was no longer dominant. Western European incomes rose around 80% in the first half of the millennium; incomes in Asia and eastern Europe just 20%.[51] Precise comparisons are dogged by the lack of accurate statistics. Angus Maddison argued that western Europe had already caught up with China in the 14th century,[52] while Kenneth Pomeranz[53] contends that the real gap did not emerge until the middle of the 18th century.

But the tide of history had turned. Timur-the-lame, or Tamerlane (1336–1405), was the last of the great conquerors from the Eurasian steppes. Instead of an invading force coming from the east of Eurasia, as had been seen with the Mongols or the Turks, the Europeans who came from the west to Asian markets in the late 15th and early 16th century were better armed and more ruthless than the natives. Europeans had adopted many technologies developed in China, such as gunpowder and printing. But from 1500 onwards, technological development tended to flow the other way.

A global trading system may have been essential for the development of the modern economy, but it was not sufficient to transform the standard of living dramatically. For that, humans needed new sources of energy to exploit. And that is what we turn to in the next chapter.

# THE QUEST FOR ENERGY

The search for new energy sources has taken people in many directions over the last 500 years, to the depths of the oceans in the search for oil and gas, and to the building blocks of matter in order to generate nuclear power. And sometimes it can head in an unlikely direction.

Take the humble clam, for example. Some clams emit a yellowy-green light from their mouths. This is due to iridocytes that reflect yellow and green light, but absorb the red and blue light that is useful for photosynthesis. But that is not all the iridocytes do. Inside each clam are columns of algae, plant-like organisms that help with the photosynthesis process. The iridocytes act like lenses, scattering the light widely among the algae.

That process could be very useful for humans too. One obvious source of cheap energy in the future is sunlight, and perhaps there is a way to exploit the natural processing of light that plants depend upon. One idea is to use algae, but algae tend to sit on the surface of ponds: you would need a very big surface area to generate energy this way. Stacking the algae vertically would take up less space but the sunlight would only hit those at the top of the stack.

So perhaps we can learn a lesson from the clam and create artificial iridocytes that scatter the sun's rays more effectively. Or at least that is the idea of Shu Yang, professor of materials science, and her team at the University of Pennsylvania. Like many pioneers before her, she is trying to take energy use in a new direction. Together with student Hye-Na Kim, she has developed a way of synthesising nanoparticles to form microbeads that could mimic the actions of the iridocytes.[1]

On the other side of America, in a hillside campus overlooking the Golden Gate bridge, Frances Houle, deputy director of the joint centre for artificial photosynthesis at the University of California, Berkeley, is working on a different approach. Her team is trying to find the most efficient way to use sunlight to separate water into oxygen and hydrogen, so that the latter can be captured and used for fuel. It is a painstaking process: first, trying to find the right chemicals to act as a catalyst; then combining the catalyst with a transparent coating so that the sunlight can get through; and finally scaling the process up to a sufficient (and efficient) size.

An atomic force microscope looks at the nano scale of the material to see how every grain is performing. It can go down to 10 nanometres, or a hundred-millionth of a metre. The microscope shows that the current flows along the edges of the material, so you want a substance with lots of edges. In a lab, wearing safety glasses, I am shown a lamp shining on a small chip from which bubbles of hydrogen emerge. These bubbles are only a start. The trick will be to scale up the process and make the chips last ten years or so.

Maybe this research will prove successful; maybe it won't. But the prize is so great that people will keep trying. Fossil fuels, such as coal, oil and gas, formed from dead organisms, provide an enormous amount of energy, but they are the largest single emitters of the greenhouse gases that contribute to global warming. And digging up these fuels is an expensive and invasive task. So scientists are searching for ways to get energy from renewable sources like the sun, the wind and the tides.

It is hard to overstate the importance of energy to the economic transformation of the planet. Between the years 1500 and 2000, the real cost of energy use fell dramatically; 90% for domestic heating, 92% for industrial power, 95% for freight transport on land, and 98% for sea freight transport.[2] Without this energy, we could not power the machines that perform our household chores, nor enjoy the many types of goods brought to us from all over the world. Our lives would be literally and figuratively less rich.

## The fuel of life

Humans need energy for four main tasks: to provide heat; to generate light; to power machines (from the humble plough to the computer); and for transport. Until quite recently, we used wood for heat; candles and reeds for light; and animals to power machines and for transport. Before 1700, water and wind power were widely used to power machinery (particularly for grinding corn). But neither watermills nor windmills could produce power on a sufficiently large scale to transform the economy. Coal made all the difference. As Britain exploited its reserves, its energy usage and output rose 15-fold between the 1650s and 1850s. The increased output represented a direct expansion of the economy by itself and allowed other industries, like iron and railways, to flourish.

Improved energy sources not only make our homes warmer and lighter, they enable speedier travel and vastly expand the range of devices we can use. More efficient energy sources enhance economic growth. Humans and animals need to be fed in order to expend energy. The draught horses needed to pull vehicles in late 19th-century New York required the equivalent of four acres of farmland to feed each one every year.[3] That placed a limit on the economy's ability to grow. An economy that relied on burning wood needed a large land area devoted to forest – land that could not be used for growing the oats needed for feeding horses, or the wheat needed to feed humans. More land could be brought under cultivation but eventually only marginal, and unproductive, land was left.

The key measure is energy return on investment (EROI), or "the ratio between the energy delivered by a particular fuel to society and the energy expended in the capture and delivery of this energy".[4] The earliest uses of fossil fuels had very high EROIs; in 1919, the ratio for US oil and gas may have been 1,000:1.[5] That explains why coal, and then oil, transformed the global economy. But as time has gone on, fossil fuels are being exploited in more difficult places: under the North Sea, for example, or locked in rock (requiring fracking), and EROIs have declined. Getting oil from deep-lying Canadian tar sands, for example, may have an EROI of under 3:1, and even less if the full cost of transport and refining is included.[6]

The first fossil fuel to be exploited was coal, the remnants of plants that lived in swampy forests millions of years ago. The Chinese developed coal from the fourth century CE onwards.[7] England was lucky enough to have substantial coal deposits, some of which were close to the surface and thus easy to develop; in the 1560s, they were producing around 177,000 tons a year.[8] But the English had also cut down large areas of woodland and were short of timber, which was needed for constructing houses and ships as well as for fuel; the cost of firewood in London more than doubled between 1500 and 1592. Londoners turned to coal instead, increasing their consumption from 35,000 tons a year in 1591 to 467,000 tons by 1700.[9] By that stage, total English production was 2.2m tons a year.

The biggest deposits of coal were buried far beneath the surface, requiring pits and tunnels to be dug, and men, women and children to undertake dirty, dangerous and back-breaking work to bring it to the surface. Gas or "damps" (related to the German word for vapour) was one great danger, and the miners had terms for all the different kinds: chokedamp, firedamp, stinkdamp, whitedamp and methane. To deal with pockets of methane, or firedamp, one unlucky soul, called the fireman, would be sent ahead of the others with a bunch of lit candles at the end of a long pole. The candles would ignite the gas and the fireman would dive to the floor, allowing the flames to pass over his head. Water-soaked clothes were his only protection.[10] Carbon monoxide, or whitedamp, is both odourless and colourless but toxic; the miners would carry a caged bird with them, as birds are more quickly affected by the gas than humans. So the birds would act as an early warning system, hence the phrase "canary in a coalmine".

Water was perhaps an even greater threat to miners; underground passages can quickly flood. So there was a need to pump water out of the mine, using human or horsepower. But that was only effective at raising water from a maximum depth of 45 to 60 metres. A French engineer called Denis Papin created an engine in the late 17th century that used the energy released when water turned to steam. The design was improved by Thomas Newcomen, who created a steam engine pump for mine use; his machines were used for the next 200 years.[11]

The engine was barely efficient, but that made little difference as it was powered by coal, a material in plentiful supply at the mine. Indeed, because deeper mines could be dug, coal was even more abundant. In economic terms, Newcomen's engine reduced the cost of pumping, relative to horses, by five-sixths.

By the time Newcomen built his engine in 1712, many English industries had switched from wood to coal, from brewing and brick-making through glassmaking to soap production.[12] So the exploitation of additional coal supplies made it easier for such industries to expand in the 18th century. Furthermore, the need to transport coal over long distance spurred the development of canals, railways and shipping routes. The use of coal for heating also led to the redesign of houses, with chimneys needed to carry the smoke away from the living area.

The other areas of Europe that industrialised early, such as Belgium, northern France and the Ruhr district in Germany, were also close to coal deposits. One study has found that cities located close to coalfields grew faster after the Industrial Revolution (but not before it) and that the introduction of coal-using technologies can account for up to 60% of European urban growth between 1750 and 1900.[13] Not all historians agree on the importance of coal to the Industrial Revolution but it is hard to see how sufficient energy could have been generated any other way. E. A. Wrigley estimates that a third of England would have had to be covered in trees to supply the energy created by coal in 1800.[14] The ability to exploit coal, a present from the primeval past, was like one of those fortunate bequests that restored the wealth of the heroes and heroines of Victorian novels.

James Watt developed a more efficient form of steam engine that used a separate condenser, allowing the cylinder to be kept hot, thereby saving energy. Watt's engines made rotary motion possible and thus allowed for more sophisticated uses than simply pumping water. But Watt's fierce defence of his patent rights (along with his partner, Matthew Boulton) limited the widespread adoption of engines before 1800. By that date only 2,200 steam engines had been built in Britain, some two-thirds of which were Newcomen engines, and only a quarter Boulton and Watt engines.[15]

Water power was still very important and, as late as 1830, industry generated equal quantities of power from steam and water.[16] Gradually, in the first half of the 19th century, steam engines became adopted by the cotton business, one of Britain's leading industries. Railways powered by coal (and transporting it as well) transformed the nature of distance and time (see Chapter 11). Coal, or rather its purified form, coke, replaced charcoal as the source of heat for iron production in the 18th century, and advances in iron manufacturing allowed better machines (including steam engines) to be built from the 1780s onwards.[17] A virtuous circle was at work; improvements in one industry led to developments in another. Trains on their iron rails brought coal to the cities to power the cotton mills. And cotton, rail and iron were the three leading industries of the 19th century.

Coal also played its part in the rising power of the trade union movement. It was natural for coal miners, working as they did in dangerous and arduous conditions, to develop camaraderie. The mine owners showed little compassion for their workers and, quite often, a ruthless determination to crush union action. But the concentration of coal production at a small number of sites (compared with farming or woodcutting) gave the miners the power to disrupt production. Between 1881 and 1905, American coal miners were involved in strikes three times more often than other workers.[18] Miners, along with railway workers (who also had the power to disrupt coal supply), formed some of the most powerful unions in Europe and America in the late 19th and 20th centuries. This led to faster wage gains for the workers concerned.

There was a dark side to the new energy source. The coal that powered the "dark satanic mills" of northern England, and heated the workers' homes, polluted the city air, covering buildings in grime and shortening lives through the effect on residents' lungs. It was not until the 1950s that Britain passed a Clean Air Act, after the deadly London smog of 1952 had killed thousands of people. In modern times, the air quality in Chinese cities has been blighted by the country's heavy coal use, prompting substantial anti-pollution measures in 2013.

### Light of the world
As a solid fuel, coal was a very useful source of heat but not of light.

Until 1800 or so, the world was a pretty dark one when the sun went down. Humans were still dependent on ancient technologies like wax candles and rushes for illumination. Only one ten-thousandth of the energy of candles is turned into light.[19]

Oils were a more promising option. The shipping fleet of Nantucket, Massachusetts, roamed the ocean in search of the sperm whale, the best source of whale oil. In 1774, Nantucket's 150 ships killed 3,000 whales.[20] Turpentine, derived from pine trees, was also used as a light source, although it had a pungent smell.

Neither of these fuels was ever going to be sufficient for mass usage. Once again, the coal industry provided an answer, in the form of coal gas. The flammability of coal gas was understood in the 18th century and the first practical uses were developed in its later stages. Alessandro Volta, the inventor of the battery, developed a lighter powered by coal gas, and William Murdoch, who worked for Boulton and Watt, managed to light his own home with gas in 1792, and the Soho foundry (which manufactured steam engines) in 1798. Others were quick to see the potential and Pall Mall in central London became the first street to be lit by gas in 1807.[21] Gas lighting was adopted in Paris and Rhode Island (in America) at around the same time.

Factory owners also appreciated the advantages of gas lighting; it was used in mills in Salford (Lancashire) and Sowerby Bridge (Yorkshire) in 1806 and in New England textile mills during the following decade. Gas lighting was less likely to cause fires than candles or oil lamps. And the owners (but not the workers) were delighted that the lights made much longer working hours possible. Gas light, with its distinctive smell, was used well into the 20th century.

Oil was formed when tiny animals such as algae and zooplankton died and fell to the bottom of the sea (it is found in landlocked areas where seas once existed). Its usefulness has been known since ancient times; it was found near the earth's surface in areas such as tar pits. Bitumen, as the sticky substance was known, was used as mortar in walls, to waterproof ships, and by the ancient Egyptians for embalming. It is thought that bitumen was a key component in the Byzantine secret weapon known as "Greek fire", which would burn on the surface of water and could thus devastate enemy shipping.

In 1853, a British physician called Abraham Gesner managed to distil a flammable liquid from bitumen, which was called kerosene, from the Greek for wax. It quickly became clear that kerosene was ideal for lighting; it burned six times more brightly than sperm whale oil and four times more brightly than gas light. That sparked a search for sources of kerosene. The modern oil era began in 1859, when an engineer called William Smith, using a method for extracting salt, found oil under the ground in Titusville, Pennsylvania. Under the American rule of capture, landowners were entitled to all the oil they could drill from their land, even if this drained a reservoir that sat under someone else's property. This caused a race to produce oil as quickly as possible.[22] A boom-and-bust process followed: Titusville once had more millionaires per capita than any other city. Now it is a town with fewer than 6,000 people.

By 1862, Pennsylvania was producing 3m barrels of oil a year, and kerosene's competitive advantage was boosted by the disruption to whaling caused by the US Civil War. Eager fortune-hunters swarmed into the state, creating the tradition of "wildcatting", whereby a lone prospector hoped to strike it rich. Between 1880 and 1920, the amount of oil refined in the US grew from 26m barrels a year to 442m.[23] There was successful oil exploration elsewhere; the Baku oil fields were developed in modern Azerbaijan, then part of tsarist Russia, while oil was also produced in Peru, Poland, Romania and Sumatra.

Kerosene was dangerous and prone to fires and explosions. A safer source of light was needed. In the first half of the 19th century, scientists were beginning to understand the properties of electricity and electromagnetism. Humphrey Davy had demonstrated an arc lamp in the early 1800s but it wasn't until the 1870s that they came into commercial use in public areas such as the Gare du Nord (a Paris railway station) in 1875, and the Wanamaker department store in Philadelphia in 1878.[24]

But the arc light was too bright and powerful for domestic use. Something much smaller was needed. Thomas Edison filed his first patent for an incandescent light bulb in 1878, but it was only later that he discovered a carbonised bamboo filament that could last for 1,200 hours. The product was first marketed in 1880.[25] Light bulbs were all very well, of course, but they were of no use unless homes had a source of electric power. Edison opened a generating station in Pearl Street in Manhattan in 1882.

His plans relied on direct current, which is only effective over short distances. That meant that each neighbourhood would require its own generating station. The other option was to use a rotating magnet turning within a set of conductors wound in coils; this produced alternating current (AC). AC could be used to send high voltage (and thus a low-amp current) on small wires over long distances without losing energy. Transformers could then turn the high voltage back down to the low voltage (and higher current) needed for home use. Edison warned of the dangers of AC, even creating the first electric chair for the state of New York to demonstrate the risks. But the battle was won by the rival AC system of Westinghouse (the founder George Westinghouse had developed the railway brake). By the summer of 1888, the company was powering electric light in cities across America's eastern seaboard.[26]

Those generating stations were mostly powered by coal, although the great waterfalls of Niagara were also harnessed and, by 1905, the Niagara plant was producing 10% of all America's power.[27] In time, electric power would change the economy. Between 1902 and 1929, the amount of electricity used in the US rose 16-fold while the nominal price fell 60%.[28] Factories were redesigned because of electricity; each machine could have its own power supply rather than rely on an elaborate system of belts and pulleys from a central power unit. Streets became much more brightly lit.

Electricity was a "general purpose technology" in that it made many new devices and activities possible. Our houses became full of gadgets, both labour-saving (washing machines and irons) and entertaining (record players and TVs). Skyscrapers became possible as electric-powered lifts allowed people to get to the highest floors.

One of the great stories of the first half of the 20th century was the electrification of large parts of the developed world. In the first volume of his great biography of Lyndon Johnson,[29] Robert Caro recounts how LBJ cajoled and wheedled the government to lend enough money to bring power to farmers in the dirt-poor Texas area he represented. When it finally happened, in 1939, families started to name their kids Lyndon. An opera called *The Electrification of the*

*Soviet Union* was inspired by the sheer scale of the massive communist-era project, Lenin having declared that "Communism is Soviet power plus the electrification of the whole country, since industry cannot be developed without electrification." The plan, launched in 1920, involved the construction of 30 power plants across the country, with the aim of more than quadrupling the power capacity inherited in the tsarist era. The targets were achieved by the early 1930s.

### Churchill's gambit

Another great 20th-century story was the shift was from coal to oil. The development of the petrol-fuelled internal combustion engine was a major driver of oil demand but it would be a mistake to ignore the switch of steamships from coal to oil. Before the First World War, Winston Churchill and Admiral Fisher decided to convert the British navy to oil. It made ships faster, required fewer personnel, and allowed them to stay at sea for longer. In turn, however, dependence on oil made the British determined to secure a reliable supply, so they made arrangements for a British company, Burmah,[30] to take over a concession in Persia. A new company called Anglo-Persian was formed in which the British took a stake; eventually Anglo-Persian became the modern British Petroleum (BP).

The importance of oil in fuelling ships, planes, trucks, cars and motorcycles during the First World War was clear. As a result, the big powers developed an obsession with having control over oil supplies. Japan's expansionist plans in South-East Asia in the 1930s (and the attack on Pearl Harbor in 1941) were driven, in part, by the country's lack of domestic oil reserves. One of Germany's objectives in invading Russia was to gain control of oil supplies in the Caucasus. And Saddam Hussein's invasion of Kuwait in 1990 triggered the first Gulf war because the West did not want to see him control more Middle Eastern oil reserves.

For much of the first half of the 20th century, oil production was controlled by Western companies: the "seven sisters" of Anthony Sampson's 1975 book (BP, Chevron, Exxon, Gulf, Mobil, Shell and Texaco).[31] Often these companies had generous concessions from local governments, granted during the colonial era. But many developing-world governments seized back control via nationalisation after the Second World War; by 2014, 15 of the world's largest 20 oil companies were state-owned. Saudi Arabia's Aramco and China's Sinopec are the two largest examples.

The Middle East's importance as an oil-producing centre steadily increased through the twentieth century. Serious production of oil in Iraq began in 1934; and the first successful well in Saudi Arabia started pumping in 1938 and eventually produced 32m barrels.[32] Before the Second World War, the Middle East produced 5% of the world's oil; by 1959, it was 25%;[33] and by 1970 it was 30%.[34] The Arab countries demonstrated their power in the wake of the Yom Kippur war of 1973 when the Organization of Petroleum Exporting Countries (Opec) cartel embargoed supplies to countries that supported Israel and pushed through a quadrupling in the price of crude (see also Chapter 12).

But higher oil prices spurred a greater focus both on energy saving in the Western world and on the search for oil in more remote places. In the 1970s, Britain and Norway were able to develop drilling rigs in the deep and stormy North Sea, and a large oil field was found in Prudhoe Bay, off the Arctic coast of Alaska in 1967. Neither Britain nor Norway are members of Opec and the proportion of the world's oil produced by the cartel fell from 55% in 1973 to 30% in 1986. But by 2017, Opec's share of global production was back up to 40%; even more significantly, member countries had more than 80% of proven reserves. More than a third of those reserves were in Venezuela and Iran, two countries with which the developed world has problematic relations.[35]

America remained an important producer throughout the century, with California, Indiana, Ohio and Texas all enjoying booms at one stage or another. But as production elsewhere grew, the US share of the global market fell from 64% in 1948 to 22% in 1972.[36] In the 1950s, an American geologist called M. King Hubbert predicted that US oil production would peak in the 1965–70 period and then start an irretrievable decline. Production did indeed peak at 10m barrels in 1970 and Hubbert's theory led to worries that world oil production might peak in the first decade of the 2000s.

## The fracking fracas

Before that could happen, a new and controversial method of finding fossil fuels was developed. In the 1990s, a few enterprising wildcatters had attempted to release gas from rock formations deep below the ground in America. Vertical drilling did not work on these formations so the wildcatters worked out a method of horizontal drilling, with the drill entering the ground at an angle and then gradually curving round. The rock is then fractured, or broken up, by blasting it with various liquids. The term hydraulic fracturing became shortened to "fracking". One of the pioneering groups was Mitchell Energy, which found vast gas reserves in the Barnett field in Texas.[37] Other fields, like the Marcellus shale in the north-east region and the Caney field in Oklahoma, were developed in the 2000s.

Fracking made an enormous difference to the US energy market, after a long period when the country was dependent on imported fuels. America became the world's largest producer of natural gas. In 2005, it produced 19m cubic feet; in 2017, nearly 29m.[38] That production boom caused natural gas prices to fall – from a peak of $12.7 per million BTU (British Thermal Unit) in June 2008 (and $8 at the start of the year), they dropped to $2.8 by April 2018.[39] That reduced the cost of energy for businesses and consumers.

The technique worked for oil as well as gas. Thanks to fracking, US oil production rose from 5 million barrels a day (mbd) in 2005 and 7.5mbd in 2013 to 10mbd by 2018.[40] That was more than was produced in the Hubbert peak of 1970. Shale oil is more expensive to get out of the ground than "conventional" oil supplies and has a lower EROI. Still, it is highly valued in America as a way of avoiding energy dependence on overseas producers in the Middle East and Venezuela.

Fracking is far less popular elsewhere, with France, Germany and Ireland all imposing moratoriums. There are concerns about pollution of water supplies, the earth tremors associated with the technique, and the noise and congestion that can occur in rural areas.[41] In terms of climate change, the gas produced by fracking has tended to replace dirtier coal, but it is, of course, still a fossil fuel.

The world remains heavily dependent on fossil fuels. As of 2015, 32% of the world's energy needs came from oil, 28% from coal, and 22% from gas. Compared with 1973, there has been a reduction in fossil fuel dependence (in oil and coal, not gas) but they still provide more than four-fifths of the total.[42]

For people in the rich world, access to electricity is taken for granted and anything more than a temporary supply cut is a massive inconvenience. But that is not true for everyone. The proportion of the global population with access to electricity rose from less than 72% in 1990 to almost 88% in 2016, which still leaves around a billion people without power.[43] And many people who do have an electricity supply face problems with reliability; fewer than 20% of citizens of Lagos report that their electricity works all or most of the time.[44] In March 2019, Venezuela suffered a blackout that lasted a week and left hospitals without power. A fortnight later, the power failed again.[45]

Wider usage is not positive for those worried about carbon emissions. The world generated almost 25 terawatt hours of electricity in 2016, more than double the 1990 level (a terawatt hour is a billion kilowatt hours, or a trillion watt hours). Much of that increase is down to Asia: China generates around a quarter of global electricity, with America producing around a sixth.[46]

Nuclear power produces around 5% of global energy, a far lower proportion than many would have hoped in the 1950s when the technology was first introduced. The accidents at Three Mile Island in America and Chernobyl in Ukraine raised fears among the public, and just when those concerns were subsiding an earthquake and tsunami caused a nuclear release at the Fukushima Daiichi plant in Japan in 2011. Germany accelerated plans to close its nuclear reactors in response. Nuclear power has very low carbon emissions, once built, but the costs of construction are substantial, delays have been common, and few places want to house the resulting nuclear waste.

A switch to renewable energy sources would cut carbon emissions substantially. Governments have, accordingly, subsidised the development of the two most promising green technologies – wind turbines and photovoltaic cells (PV). Around $800bn was pumped into these industries between 2008 and 2016.[47] Once these energy sources are installed, they cost very little to run. For a while in June 2018, more than 70% of Britain's electricity was being generated by renewables. The problem is that both wind and sun are intermittent.

That means traditional energy sources – coal, oil, gas – will still be needed as a back-up.

A move to renewable energy may require a similar transformation of the global economy to the one that accompanied the rise of coal and oil. It may need special taxes that focus on the carbon footprint of traditional energy sources. Renewables will only be able to capture a large share of the energy market if a way is found to store energy on sunny and windy days, so it can used in cloudy, calm periods. That will require better, cheaper batteries than we have now. Or perhaps the scientists studying clams and artificial photosynthesis will crack the problem. The trick is to find energy sources that are both cheap and reliable enough to keep the economy functioning without damaging the environment. In late 2018, the amount of renewable energy capacity in Britain exceeded that of fossil fuels for the first time.[48] Such an outcome looked very unlikely just ten years previously and shows what is possible. The energy pessimists have been proved wrong before.

# THE GREAT CHANGE: 1500–1820

Everyone can agree that the global economy changed enormously in the latter half of the second millennium. What is not universally agreed upon is exactly when it did so, or why. Arnold Toynbee, a historian, popularised the term Industrial Revolution in a series of lectures (and a subsequent book) in the 1880s. When this author was at school, the revolution was dated to around 1760, largely based in England, and was linked to a series of inventions including textile machinery like the spinning jenny and the steam engine developed by James Watt.

But the picture is a lot more complex and uncertain than the school textbooks suggested. In the mid-18th century, around 70% of humans were still living in "agrarian empires" of one kind or another, whether in China, India, Japan, Russia, or under the Habsburg monarchy.[1] The term "revolution" implies a sudden change but that is not what the numbers (such as we have) appear to suggest. British economic growth per capita did not rapidly accelerate in the years after 1760 and may even have slowed (the country had already made a significant switch from agriculture by this stage).[2] Adam Smith, whose book *The Wealth of Nations* appeared in 1776, knew about the steam engine but did not seem to think it heralded a new era. Few steam engines were in use before 1800, as noted in the previous chapter. Nor was change confined to Britain. Other parts of Europe (and some parts of the US) were showing signs of industrialisation in the late 18th century, such as the setting up of textile factories, ironworks and the greater use of coal.

So this chapter will take events from the European incursion into Asia and the Americas around 1500 up until 1820, a point at which industrialisation started to become more widespread. The great historian Angus Maddison, who compiled the best estimates of economic development, spotted a break in the data at around 1820. The increase in global per capita income between 1000 and 1820 was just 50%. Between 1820 and 2000, the growth rate of per capita income rose 24-fold. By 1820, it was also pretty clear that western Europe and North America were pulling away from China and the rest of Asia in economic terms. In the 11th century, income levels in the West were below those of Asia. By 1820, they were twice as high.[3]

The earliest phases of industrialisation were a mixed blessing as far as mankind was concerned. The process that Deirdre McCloskey dubbed "the Great Enrichment" had not really started.[4] Most people did not see the full benefits, in the form of higher living standards, until the second half of the 19th century (see chart). What was unprecedented about the period, however, was that countries were able to support a much higher population than before without a *collapse* in living standards. Malthus had written that the eventual result of rising populations would be that "sickly seasons, epidemics, pestilence, and plague, advance in terrific array, and sweep off their thousands and ten thousands. Should success be still incomplete, gigantic inevitable famine stalks in the rear, and with one mighty blow levels the population with the food of the world."[5] It didn't happen.

In the course of the three centuries covered by this chapter, there was a significant population increase. In England, the population rose from 5.7m in 1750 to 10.4m by 1821, the end of our period. Many lived in misery, but they were alive. European famines became less and less frequent, while the plague (or Black Death) seemed to lose its impact. Global population in 1820 was more than double its level in 1500, according to Maddison.[6] Global per capita income rose 18% in that period, although the gain in western Europe was more impressive at 56%. By this stage, European incomes were 80% above the global average. Life expectancy in western Europe was around 36,

**Healthier and wealthier**

England*, GDP per person, 2013 prices, £'000

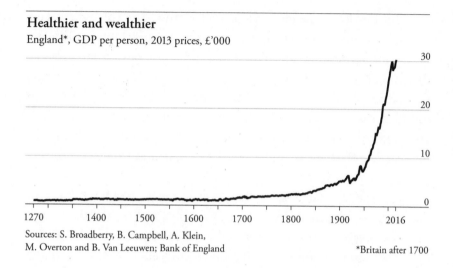

Sources: S. Broadberry, B. Campbell, A. Klein,
M. Overton and B. Van Leeuwen; Bank of England     *Britain after 1700

compared with 26 for the global average. And Europe was also more urbanised. The share of the European population that lived in cities doubled during this period.[7]

Something remarkable was happening and, by 1820, people realised it. In a sense, understanding the beginnings of the great economic change is like the plot of a mystery novel. There are a number of potential suspects and a good detective needs to assemble them all in the library, before revealing whodunnit.

## European expansion

In global terms, the most startling development post-1500 was the emergence of Europe as the dominant power. This was true of trade as well as of politics. Between 1470 and 1820, Europe's merchant shipping fleet rose 17-fold in size.[8] After 1500, the transport of heavy goods, such as Baltic timber, made larger ships economical. The Dutch developed the flute (or fluyt), which had more cargo space and needed smaller crews.[9]

The arrival of European settlers and expropriators in the Americas linked the world together for the first time. It resulted in the Columbian exchange, whereby American crops were brought to Europe and Asia, and European crops and livestock headed the other way (see Chapter 2).

But Europeans headed east as well as west. The Portuguese were the first to break into the Asian markets and quickly established a protection racket over shipping in the Indian Ocean. What attracted the Europeans to Asia were spices. These were largely produced on very small islands, part of modern Indonesia, which the Europeans found it easy to dominate. The profits made from the spice trade attracted competitors – first the Dutch and then the English and the French. The Portuguese bully found itself outmuscled by even bigger bullies.

In the Banda Islands, the source of nutmeg, the Dutch killed or deported the vast majority of the population and turned the islands into slave plantations. They centred clove production on the islands of Ambon and Ceram by cutting down trees elsewhere.[10] If a trader could get a ship back to Europe, avoiding the dangers of shipwreck and piracy, the rewards were huge; a kilo of pepper cost 1–2 grams of silver in the Indies but fetched a price of 20–30 grams in Europe.[11]

In Latin America, the Spanish found the gold and silver they were looking for. The most developed site in South America was Potosí, a city built 13,000 feet above sea level in the Andes. At its peak, in the first half of the 17th century, the city had 160,000 inhabitants. The workers were drawn largely from the indigenous population and it was a dirty, dangerous job, not least as mercury (a poison) was used to refine the silver. After the ore was dug out of the mountain, it had to be carried down to sea level on the back of llamas and then transported across the oceans, either back to Spain or across the Pacific to Manila to exchange for Asian goods. It was all very profitable for the Spanish monarchy, which took a fifth (the *quinto real*) of all the bullion.

As the silver resources of the Americas were depleted, the European focus moved to the plantation system, whereby raw materials like cotton and sugar were developed with slave labour, taken from Africa (see Chapter 9). Conquerors have exploited subject peoples for thousands of years. What was unusual about the European exploitation was its nakedly commercial nature. Both Dutch and British expansion in Asia was spearheaded by companies in the form of the VOC (*Vereenigde Oostindische Compagnie*) and its equivalent, the East India Company. These firms were vehicles for making their Dutch and British employees rich, largely at the expense of the local people. In Bengal, for example, the British East India Company took over the tax system, and their demands pushed many peasants into becoming forced labourers.

In the long run, Europe's expansion created a global system in which silver from the Americas was used to buy spices from the Indian Ocean, with the silver eventually finding its way into the Chinese economy, which was desperately short of coins. The *San Francisco Javier*, a ship that sank near Manila in 1733, had a staggering 1.2m pesos (silver coins) on board.[12] The flow of silver into the European economy is often fingered as the culprit for 16th-century inflation but it may well have acted as a monetary stimulus to the global economy by boosting demand for all kinds of goods. There was a "bullion famine" in the 15th century, which may have restricted trade; the American inflow solved that problem.

In his monumental work *The Great Divergence*, Kenneth Pomeranz argued that Europe's global expansion was the key to its ability to overtake China in the modern era.[13] The colonies eased ecological constraints on Europe, in the form of extra timber and new crops, and relieved population pressures (and thus avoided the Malthusian trap) by allowing settlers to move overseas. By 1790, the population of the US was around 3.9m, of whom almost two-thirds had come from the British isles and almost a fifth were African slaves.

Some argue that Europe's growth was largely dependent on the exploitation of those in other continents. In his book *Empire of Cotton: A New History of Global Capitalism*, Sven Beckert argued that the 16th century saw the emergence of "war capitalism" marked by "slavery, the expropriation of indigenous peoples, imperial expansion, armed trade and the assertion of sovereignty over people and land by entrepreneurs". In *Capitalism & Slavery*, Eric Williams said that profits from slavery were recycled into the textile industry; the British cities of Bristol and Liverpool owed much to the slave trade.[14] In Asia, Shashi Tharoor states, "Britain's Industrial Revolution was built on the destruction of India's thriving manufacturing industries", in particular the wholesale transfer of textile production.[15]

There can be no doubt that the arrival of Europeans in the Americas had a catastrophic impact on the indigenous population. In Mexico, the population fell by an estimated 90% and in Peru by

40%. Some of this was the result of military action or brutal treatment in places like Potosí. But most damage was caused by disease. The American population had never experienced the viruses that cause smallpox, influenza or measles, or bacteria that lead to tuberculosis and cholera.[16] This was the stark downside of the Columbian exchange.

It is important not to romanticise the pre-European societies of Latin America. Several civilisations had come and gone, with ecological decline probably playing a part in the collapse of the "classic" era in the first millennium CE. In 1500, both the Aztec and Inca societies were relatively recent developments and were technologically unsophisticated. They had not developed the wheel, ships or discursive writing.[17] They practised human sacrifice and depended heavily on the labour of subject peoples. As a consequence, the Spanish found plenty of allies willing to rebel against their overlords. In a bitter irony, of course, the local tribes simply exchanged one set of masters for another, with the Spanish also demanding forced labour under the *encomienda* system. By and large, Spanish and Portuguese colonists did not settle as small farmers as they did in North America, but as plantation owners. This had long-term effects on South American economic development.[18]

In economic terms, the European expansion was extremely significant. The connections that formed between the Americas, Europe and Asia meant that world trade grew 20-fold between 1500 and 1820, three times faster than GDP, laying the foundations for today's global trading system.[19] Just as European cities like Bristol and Liverpool flourished from international trade, so did Asian ports like Singapore and Manila.

## Cultural change

The period around 1500 was marked not just by European exploration, but also by the Renaissance, a great flowering of art, architecture and philosophy. In part, this represented a break from the narrowly Christian focus of much medieval culture. The 16th century also saw the Protestant Reformation, in which the ideas of Martin Luther and others were spread more easily thanks to the European adoption of the printing press.

These developments had a significant psychological impact. Medieval Europeans tended to assume that the ancient philosophers in Greece and Rome had discovered pretty much all there was to know. But the ancients knew nothing of the Americas, including the many strange plants that grew there, some of which would change European agriculture. In short, there were new things to discover and ordinary people could benefit from those discoveries.

Traditional sources of power came under challenge. Protestantism asserted that the Catholic Church was not an infallible authority on religious doctrine. Scientists also understood more about the universe; Copernicus, Kepler and Galileo helped establish the principle of heliocentrism, that the earth revolved around the sun.

As David Wootton, a scientific historian, noted: "It is this assumption that there are new discoveries to be made which has transformed the world for it has made modern science and technology possible."[20] In the 17th century, philosophers like Francis Bacon introduced a systematic way to think about scientific research, while Isaac Newton changed the way people thought about the universe. In the 18th century, the ideas of the Enlightenment favoured liberty, tolerance and reason over faith and appeals to authority.

What did all this have to do with steam engines or textile production? There are only a few direct links between scientific advances and the technological changes of the 18th century. Those who created the first steam engines benefited from an understanding of the concept of atmospheric pressure and the nature of a vacuum. Many industrial pioneers, however, lacked a formal education and owed their success to their ingenuity and a trial-and-error approach.

Nonetheless, European society was open to the possibility of change, and to the idea that change might lead to material advance. Deirdre McCloskey argues that the "bourgeois values" of individual betterment and personal liberty were the underlying drivers of economic change.[21] Joel Mokyr says that the bourgeois ethic "involves an implicit recognition of the value of progress: hard work and education can make one better off."[22] The crucial difference from the Middle Ages was that people thought they could rise up the social structure, and that their route to success was via business or trade.

## Institutions

One school of economists, led by Douglass North, argues that sound institutional arrangements were necessary for the Industrial Revolution to take place.[23] Economic growth requires both risk-taking and long-term capital investment. Such things are unlikely if entrepreneurs fear that their gains will be confiscated.

In small economies, individuals will trade with people they know. Those who break the trust of their partners will find themselves ostracised from future deals. Overseas trade, where it occurred, could be conducted through close relatives. But as economies expanded, and people moved into towns and cities, it was impossible to rely solely on personal contacts.

Legal contracts were created, but depended on impartial courts to enforce them. In turn, this required the existence of governments that recognised the advantages of commerce. As North noted: "Establishing a credible commitment to secure property rights over time requires either a ruler who exercises forbearance and restraint in using coercive force, or the shackling of the ruler's power to prevent arbitrary seizure of assets."[24]

In the Middle Ages, during the commercial revolution, Europe had developed (or copied) a range of business and financial structures that allowed merchants to trade internationally. Over the centuries, these instruments became more widely used; by the time of the French Revolution, the volume of trading in bills of exchange was five to six times the circulation of metal money.[25] The creation of the Dutch and British East India companies made it easy for merchants to finance a global trading network.

In Britain, the Glorious Revolution of 1688 removed the absolutist James II from the monarchy and briefly united Britain and the Netherlands under the rule of William of Orange. The Dutch Republic had been enormously successful, in economic terms, in the 17th century. From 1688 onwards, the powers of the British monarchy were constrained and Parliament had significant sway over the nation's finances. The contrast with absolutist France, dogged by financial problems throughout the 18th century, was clear.

Britain developed a range of economic institutions over the next two centuries that boosted its economic growth: a central bank that safeguarded the currency; commercial banks and capital markets that allowed businesses to raise money; a strong insurance market; and limited liability companies. The country may have been ruled by an aristocracy but many noble families were alert to the economic opportunities that could arise from trade, particularly where coal was found under their estates. The British parliament was generally in favour of industry, and entrepreneurs were free to innovate. In France, by contrast, state regulation was such that 317 articles governed the dyeing of cloth, largely focused on maintaining medieval production techniques, and each piece of material required at least six inspections. New inventions were restricted because they would clash with existing monopolies.[26]

## Energy

The last chapter emphasised the importance of coal. Britain was an early industrialiser because the country had abundant supplies of coal and was running short of wood. In the iron industry, coke, a high-carbon form of coal, was used by Abraham Darby to refine iron. It was a replacement for charcoal, a purified version of wood. Iron output could never have expanded as it did in the 19th century if it had been forced to rely on charcoal as a fuel source.[27]

Cast iron allowed for the construction of better steam engines, and for structures like the bridge over the Severn at Coalbrookdale in Shropshire, built by Abraham Darby's grandson.[28]

Coal, oil and gas are used for heat and to power the machinery for making goods and transporting people, and these energy sources power the electrical devices that fill our homes. Without such sources, industrial transformation would not have been possible.

## Technological change

Technological change is the "X factor" of economic growth (see Chapter 17). The economy could not have advanced without new ways of making things, and of organising production. There were many technological advances in mankind's history before 1500, from control of fire through the wheel to the iron plough, the compass, and even eyeglasses. What has been unprecedented about the modern era has been the sheer number of innovations and the speed with which they have been spread.

In part, this has been down to the self-reinforcing nature of these changes. For example, invention of the "flying shuttle" improved the productivity of weavers. That created the demand for more raw material in the form of spun thread. Sure enough, the spinning jenny, the water frame and the mechanical mule all emerged in the 1760s and 1770s, massively improving the productivity of spinners. As the efficiency of textile production improved, the price of finished goods fell and this increased demand for the product. Manufacturers were able to benefit from economies of scale.

Steam engines were introduced to pump water. But producers had long used water and wind power for other purposes like grinding grain or treating textiles. There was every incentive to try to adapt steam engines for similar purposes. At some mines, the coal that powered engines was transported from the pithead on rails; again, this led to the adaptation of steam engines to run on those rails. Iron rails were better than wooden ones and this boosted demand for the iron industry. Even more fundamentally, the introduction of printing (another technological advance) made it easier for knowledge of the new techniques to spread more quickly than in the past.

## Sorting out the suspects

Attributing economic change to any single factor is hampered by either the data or the timing. Take the thesis of Eric Williams, that slavery created the wealth from which Europe industrialised. Portugal transported two-thirds as many slaves as Britain over the course of the trade but did not develop a manufacturing sector; the French were much more successful in exploiting the Caribbean than were the English; and sugar contributed a bigger proportion of Spanish national income in the 18th century than it did in Britain.[29] Other regions, such as Belgium and Germany, managed to industrialise without any significant colonial possessions at the time.[30]

What about coal? While many of the earliest industrialisers had coal resources, very few steam engines were in use by 1800 and the majority of textile mills were still water-powered by 1820. Cotton manufacturing played a huge part in Britain's expansion, going from less than 3% of economic output in 1770 to more than 20% by 1830,[31] but other economies managed to industrialise without such a dependence on the textile industry.

Believers in free markets as the main driver of expansion need to explain why high British taxes (in relative terms) and restrictive legislation, such as the 1720 Bubble Act that made it difficult to form joint-stock companies, did not hold the country back. British institutions were far from perfect; property rights were just as good in France or China.[32] And Britain suffered plenty of political turmoil, including a civil war in the mid-17th century.

So it seems more likely that all of these factors had to come together for industrialisation to occur. Earlier societies either lacked the energy supplies, technical expertise, free labour force or institutional acceptance for change to take place. It was only in the 18th century that this concatenation could start to happen.

What adds lustre to the "Orient Express" explanation for the shift (they all did it) is that it allows the various factors to interact. Take, for example, the idea of an "industrious revolution", as coined by Jan de Vries,[33] in which the availability of new products such as tea or pottery encouraged people to work longer hours in order to earn the income to pay for such goods.[34] It is, of course, very difficult to estimate working hours so far in the past. But England abolished 49 holy days in 1536, and over the next two centuries, similar cutbacks of feast days occurred in the Netherlands, France and Austria. The practice of taking "Saint Monday" off to recover from the excesses of the weekend also declined.[35]

De Vries cites the example of the watch, a newish technology that might have seemed an expensive indulgence to earlier generations. As early as 1700, 13% of domestic servants owned a watch and 5% of general wage earners. By the end of the century, as judged by inventories of their estates, 40% of those deemed paupers owned either a watch or a clock. That created demand for the product – nearly 400,000 watches a year were being made in the late 18th century – and thus employment. There were signs in the 17th century that British life was getting more commercial; the number of shops in London rose from 50 to 60 in 1663 to 300 to 400 by 1700.[36]

The same trend was developing elsewhere in Europe. A survey of French wills showed that there was a big leap in ownership of a range of household goods between the 17th and 18th centuries, including saucepans, dishes and chests of drawers. In addition, there were new foodstuffs, particularly tea, sugar, and spices like nutmeg, which had become more widely available thanks to European expansion.

But why Britain? The country would not have been many people's pick as the hub of economic dominance in 1500. A well-informed gambler betting on the future at the time might have picked Spain as the coming economic power, as it was well placed to exploit the American colonies. Or they might have selected the existing centres of European economic activity in 1500, the Low Countries and northern Italy. Some of these economic rivals were scuppered by politics. The northern Italian cities suffered in the wars of the early 16th century and lost some of their trading advantages with the disappearance of the Byzantine empire. The British and Dutch textile industries outcompeted the Italians in the 17th century. And Spain wasted its colonial wealth, failing to develop a manufacturing sector.

Britain had a colonial empire with access to raw materials, an institutional structure that protected merchants, a culture of innovation, and plenty of coal. In the course of the 16th and 17th centuries, Britain moved steadily away from being a purely agricultural economy. It helped that British farming had become more efficient with the help of new crops, and new techniques (like adding lime to soil) and forms of land use. During the Middle Ages, British farmers had steadily obtained more freedom to use their land as they wished (at least in comparison with other countries). This freed labour for other roles. By 1700, only around a third of the population worked in agriculture; almost as many were merchants, shopkeepers or craftsmen.[37] In contrast, more than half of continental Europeans still worked on a farm in 1840.[38]

English people became more educated; the proportion who could sign their name rose from about 6% in 1500 to 53% in 1800. And a sign of their prosperity was that British males were taller in the mid-18th century than their French and Italian counterparts, judged by military records.[39] The English also benefited more than other countries from skilled immigration, starting with Flemish weavers back in the 14th century; of the 55 grants of monopolies made by Elizabeth I, 21 were issued to aliens or naturalised subjects.[40]

Britain's biggest export in the 16th and 17th centuries was wool. It had moved from simply exporting the raw material to weavers in Flanders to producing woollen textiles, such as worsted, a high-quality yarn. That industry used the "putting out" system, with merchants subcontracting the manufacturing to domestic workers, often women. This gave many agricultural workers an extra source of income. It also provided a model that was easily adapted in the 18th century when British factories started producing cotton goods. By the middle of the 18th century, over half of the adult males in Lancashire derived most of their income from textiles.[41]

The British were aware of the competition for wool textiles from cotton clothing. India's printed textiles, or calicoes, were highly attractive to European consumers, being lighter and less scratchy than woollen wear. In 1700 and 1721, Britain passed the Calico Acts, banning the import of printed cloth but not the raw material. That created an incentive for home production to fill the gap.

But it was not all about protection. The British success in revolutionising the production of cotton textiles should not be overlooked. The time taken to spin 100 pounds of cotton fell from 50,000 hours to 135.[42] Some of this was built on existing skills. Watchmaking skills could be transformed into making the gears that went into much textile machinery and Britain had a thriving watch industry.[43]

Not only did the country produce inventors who were able to get round the technical difficulties of machine production, they were able to get finance for their plans. Much of this came from local sources but in the course of the 18th century, a banking system developed. A Birmingham ironmaking family set up Lloyds, a brand name that survives today. The number of banks outside London rose from 119 in 1784 to 800 by 1808.[44] Merchants created their own credit system by using bills of exchange as a form of currency. British prosperity gave the government a strong tax base, and thus avoided some of the problems faced by other regimes. In 1788, British taxes took 12.4% of national output, compared with just 6.8% in France.[45] When the cash-strapped Bourbon monarchy recalled parliament in 1789 in an attempt to raise money, a revolution quickly followed.

Britain also had an active capital market for those who needed it. In 1701, Daniel Defoe was sufficiently exercised about speculators to write a book called *The Villainy of Stock-Jobbers Detected*. The rapid rise to wealth achieved by some pioneers, such as Sir Richard Arkwright, encouraged others to follow the same path. The South Sea Bubble, in which a company issued shares and promised to repay the national debt, set back the development of the corporate structure for more than a century. The bubble's collapse was the scandal of the age. Yet it did not taint British attitudes to commerce in the same way that attitudes were changed by the Mississippi bubble of the same era.

In institutional terms, the powers of the monarchy had been constrained in the course of the 17th century; Britain never enjoyed the inflow of precious metals that sustained the Spanish kings.[46] The country was happy to indulge in foreign trade, the value of which increased around 150% between the 1660s and the 1750s. This trade helped to build the shipping fleet, and the tonnage of English merchant shipping rose by two-thirds between 1660 and 1702.[47]

Another argument that has been made for British primacy is that wages were higher than those in other countries, giving employers an incentive to replace expensive workers with machinery. However, recent work by Judy Stephenson of the LSE suggests that previous estimates of British wages in the building trade may have been overstated.[48] The argument is hard to settle, in part because the information on standards of living in the 18th century is limited. Economists also point out that many of the other factory labourers were low-paid women and children.[49] Whatever the reason, the British were much quicker at adopting new technology than were other countries. Steam engines were used in the Netherlands, Russia and Germany in the 1770s but no one came close to the British in terms of scale. In 1800, the British had 25 times as many engineers as the Belgians, the next-biggest users.[50]

Britain was quick to exploit its coal resources for heating, in part because wood was getting scarce in the area round London, where the population was growing rapidly: the capital housed 500,000 people in 1700, up from just 55,000 in 1520.[51] Between the 1580s and 1640, coal shipments from the north-east of England to London rose from 50,000 tons a year to 300,000.[52]

In short, there was plenty of change in Britain, and indeed economic growth, before textile machinery was invented and the factory system developed. Call this commercialisation, or proto-industrialisation, but the economy of Britain in 1700 looked quite different from its medieval counterpart.

## Why not elsewhere?

Could widespread industrialisation have occurred in earlier times or other places? Or, to put it another way, why didn't it? Song China in the 11th and 12th centuries used water power to drive textile machinery, had coal resources, and had developed woodblock printing (allowing the creation of paper money).[53] It was clearly well ahead of Europe in terms of technology, while the Muslim world was also richer and more learned than its Christian counterpart.

China had a good education system, a developed merchant class and a large internal market that could have generated economies of scale for any nascent industries. It also had a very productive agricultural sector, which fed a much denser population than was possible in Europe. But there does not seem to have been quite the same enthusiasm for overseas adventures, or for novelties, as there was in Europe. The abandonment of Zheng He's voyages was mentioned in Chapter 4; and another famous case was the emperor's letter to Britain's George III, in response to a commercial mission, that "Our Celestial Empire possesses all things in prolific abundance and lacks no product within its borders".[54]

In Europe, there were lots of competing nations, all of whom might hope that technological change would give them an advantage over their rivals, and might fear that the same change, if adopted by other countries, would leave them behind. China had no obvious local rivals and its leadership perceived the idea of economic change as destabilising. There was no sign of the same drive for technological advance in 18th-century China that was seen in Britain. Indeed, ancient infrastructure like the Grand Canal and irrigation systems were showing signs of decay in 1800.[55] China was as agrarian in 1850 as it was in 1750.[56] Perhaps, as Robert Allen argues, this was because labour was relatively cheap and energy was dear.[57]

There was little interest in overseas trade and no attempt to boost the interests of Chinese merchants along the lines of the Dutch and British East India companies. A further problem for China was that, while it had coal reserves (which it is still exploiting), they were in the north, while the richest region was in the south. The country had some of the pieces of the jigsaw, but not all.

Like China, the Islamic world in the early modern period showed little sign of economic change. The political power of the Ottoman empire peaked in the 16th and 17th centuries and began its long decline. Tax revenues were farmed out to investors, a practice that weakened the financial power of the state in the long run. There was little interest in assisting those merchants who wanted to trade overseas, a factor that Sevket Pamuk, a historian, believes was more important than geography, resources or culture in explaining why the Islamic world fell behind western Europe.[58]

In 1700, India had 140m people, compared with 40m in western Europe. It had a flourishing textile industry, as already noted, and important trading links with the Middle East, South-East Asia and China through its coastal ports. On one estimate, Indian weavers in the mid-18th century had a higher standard of living than their British equivalents.[59] India had a centralised authority in the form of the Mughal emperors. But the Europeans had been nibbling away at the subcontinent, with the British acquiring Madras in 1640 from a local ruler and Bombay in 1661 when Charles II married Catherine of Braganza. The British got their first permit to trade from the emperor Jahan in 1657 and took advantage of the divided nature of Indian policy; there were more than 650 princely states.[60]

British rule was focused on the East India Company, which was the source of many a fortune over the following two centuries, including that of Thomas Pitt, the father and grandfather of two 18th-century prime ministers.[61] Mughal authority was weakened by an attack from Nadir Shah of Persia, who sacked Delhi in 1739, and a contest of supremacy between France and Britain in the Seven Years War of 1756–63. The British destroyed the Indian textile industry, which produced 25% of global output in the early 18th century.[62] Indian export markets were blocked, and its domestic market was flooded in the 19th century with cheap British imports.

Whether or not the British owed their economic success to colonialism, they undoubtedly damaged India's economic development. As Shashi Tharoor points out, India made up 25% of global GDP in

1700, before the British arrived, and just 4% in 1950, after they left. After 200 years of rule, Britain left India with a life expectancy of 27 and a literacy rate of 16%, and with 90% of the population living below the poverty line.[63] The railways (funded by Indian taxes, in any case) were paltry recompense.

In Europe, the Netherlands might plausibly have beaten Britain to the punch. The Dutch had a limited supply of land and had thus been forced to make their agriculture very productive. They had a highly developed financial sector and an urbanised population. The Dutch were quicker to grab the Asian market than was Britain, and they had a powerful navy, which humiliated the English in 1667 by burning their docks, and an army that was called in to chase out the English king in 1688. But the small size of the Dutch nation may have made it difficult for them to develop an internal market of sufficient size. They lacked Britain's coal resources and depended on peat, and were worse affected than Britain by the expansionary ambitions of the French monarchy.

Industrialisation did occur in the southern Low Countries (modern Belgium) but the area was dogged by historical conflict. In the first half of the 16th century 40% of the world's trade was channelled through Antwerp.[64] But the city suffered during the long Dutch war of independence against the Spanish monarchy. It was sacked in 1576 and never recovered its earlier position. Flanders, however, retained its textile industry and it started to mechanise after a British machine was smuggled into the region in the 1790s. By 1810, there were 10,000 workers using 115,000 machines. Cast iron production also expanded in the first two decades of the 19th century; Belgium was rich in both iron and coal.[65] This was an early sign that Europe could catch up with Britain.

Germany, which would become a great economic and political power in the 19th century, was still not a unified country in the 18th century. Its economic progress had been set back by the Thirty Years War of 1618–48, which may have killed a third or more of the population,[66] and the countryside was ravaged by invading armies.

North America would become the world's great industrial power in the course of the 19th century but it did not lead the way. The first wave of settlers established themselves on the east coast, and devoted themselves to farming and fishing. As the population grew, they gradually encroached on the land of the indigenous population, forcing them west. Tobacco was the first great export crop, accounting for around 80% of exports by 1700.[67] The colonies depended on Britain for almost all their luxuries and manufactured goods. Many of the early planters lived beyond their means, ending up in debt to British merchants and creating one source of grievance with the colonial power.

Another problem was tax. The colonies were expensive to defend, particularly during the Seven Years War between England and France of 1756 to 1763, which pushed up British government debt by almost 70%. Americans were around 50% better off, on average, than their British counterparts in the 18th century.[68] That explains why so many Britons wanted to emigrate and why Britain thought the colonists could afford to help with defence. But attempts to defray the cost by taxing the colonists met with fierce resistance. Oddly enough, the Boston tea party protest was sparked, not by a tax, but by the import of cheaper tea after a monopoly was given to the East India Company; this was a threat to the income of those who had smuggled tea from elsewhere.

After independence, there was a battle between the founding fathers over the economic direction of the country. Thomas Jefferson and James Madison favoured a rural state; they were suspicious of banks and government spending. In the opposite camp was Alexander Hamilton, who wanted to make the country less dependent on foreign capital. He favoured the assumption of state debts, and the establishment of a national bank. He argued that a successful economy "must establish a rule of law through enforceable contracts, respect private property, create a trustworthy bureaucracy to arbitrate legal disputes; and offer patents and other protections to promote invention". Hamilton may have lost power and influence with the retirement of George Washington in 1797, and died later in a duel with Aaron Burr, but his economic vision won the day.[69]

The first US textile mill was set up in 1790 by Samuel Slater, a British expat who had learned the designs of the vital machines at home. By 1808, around half of the country's mills belonged to Slater, his associates, or former employees. An embargo on British goods imposed by Thomas Jefferson in the course of the Napoleonic Wars, followed by the war with Britain of 1812–15, disrupted the supply of textiles across the Atlantic. By 1814, there were 243 mills operating in 15 states, employing a quarter of the workforce in New England and mid-Atlantic states.[70]

American ingenuity was already showing itself. The invention of the cotton gin by Eli Whitney in 1793 vastly increased the supply of cotton, while the first commercial steamboat service was launched by Robert Fulton and Robert Livingston in 1807.

Thomas Jefferson's purchase of the Louisiana territories from Napoleon in 1803 for the bargain price of $15m doubled the size of the nation and set the stage for the country's meteoric rise. Just as the Italian city states had been overtaken by the national states of England, France and Spain, so the European countries would eventually be surpassed by a continent-wide superpower.

## Divergence

Whether or not there was an Industrial Revolution in the strictest sense, the foundations of modern prosperity were laid in the period from 1500 to 1820. The greater use of machines, the substitution of coal for wood and other forms of energy, the emergence of the factory system – all these occurred in this era. Western Europe accelerated away from the rest of the world, with the US catching up rapidly.

Other eras had seen technological change. But this period saw the emergence of a self-sustaining process in which changes in one industry were linked to conditions in another. As we have seen, steam engines were needed to pump water out of coal mines; the use of coal (in the form of coke) improved the production of iron; better iron improved the manufacturing of steam engines; and so forth. A bigger and more prosperous population created demand for more goods, which allowed economies of scale and stimulated innovation. The need to shift coal led to investment in canals and eventually railways. And so on.

Another change was the emergence of systematic thought about the economy. There had been plenty of debate in the Middle Ages about the nature of money and about the definition of usury. The inflation that resulted from the import of silver from the Americas reignited this debate, as did the debasement of the pound by Henry VIII. The concept now known as Gresham's Law,[71] that "bad money drives out good", was beginning to be understood; people will pay for goods in a currency that has low intrinsic value and hoard the coins that are closest to pure gold and silver.

But commentators started to think more broadly about economic activity. The philosopher John Locke argued that there was a "natural" rate of interest, a rate needed to encourage savings, and also suggested the concept that the speed of circulation of money, not just its quantity, was important.[72] These issues were more than a matter of theoretical debate. From this point onwards, what people thought about the economy started to affect actual policy. Any history of economics must thus reflect what economists thought at the time.

The person who can best claim credit for founding the discipline is Adam Smith. His modern reputation is of a narrow believer in the free market, but that is a distortion of his views. In *The Theory of Moral Sentiments*, he writes: "How selfish soever man may be supposed, there are evidently some principles in his nature, which interest him in the fortunes of others, and render their happiness necessary to him, though he derives nothing from it, except the pleasure of seeing it." And in *The Wealth of Nations*, he wrote that "No society can surely be flourishing and happy of which the far greater part of its members are poor and miserable."

Adam Smith's real target was the use of state policy to favour certain industries in the form of monopolies. In *The Wealth of Nations*, he wrote: "Consumption is the sole end and purpose of all production; and the interest of the producer ought to be attended to, only so far as it may be necessary for promoting that of the consumer." He attacked the notion of mercantilism, which believed that trade was a zero-sum game in which the aim was to get more gold than other nations. On the contrary, the aim of trade was to import goods that one needed or desired.

He emphasised the benefits of specialisation. One example was the pin factory, where the separation of tasks into discrete steps, handled by different workers, enabled pin production to soar. And the same was true of trade. No sensible person would spend time constructing products at home for a price far higher than they could be obtained in a shop. "What is prudence in the conduct of every private family, can scarce be folly in that of a great kingdom", he wrote. Scotland could, with the help of greenhouses and hotbeds, produce its own wine at cost 30 times higher than it would pay for imported wine from Portugal or France, but what would be the point?

Instead, Smith emphasised the benefits of competition. In the absence of monopoly, producers will always be under pressure to meet the needs of consumers. Hence his famous line that "It is not from the benevolence of the butcher, the brewer, or the baker, that we expect our dinner, but from their regard to their own interest."

Adam Smith tackled the economic issues that were relevant at the time: the growing importance of international trade and state intervention in favour of certain industries. He did not deal with issues like unemployment, the economic cycle, or a general deficiency of demand. Those problems would have to be tackled by later economists. All three issues were linked to the sector that was driving growth in the 19th century – manufacturing.

# MANUFACTURING:
# WORSHIPPING OUR MAKERS

Drive across the border between Singapore and Malaysia and you are leaving a rich-world country and joining the developing world. But the proximity of Singapore – its port, airport and rich business district – is an enormous opportunity for Malaysia's southern state of Johor. Thousands of Malaysians cross into Singapore to work every day, making the border (a narrow causeway across the Strait of Johor) one of the world's busiest land crossings and a choke point for traffic.

The region also serves as a manufacturing hub, rather like the factories that cluster on the southern side of the Mexican–US border. The Malaysians have set up the Iskandar development area to lure businesses into the region. For all the factories and office blocks, it retains a tropical feel, complete with palm oil plantations and (on the day I visited) the kind of rainstorm that reduces driving visibility to 20 yards.

In the heart of the zone is an industrial estate called i-Park Senai Airport City. The site covers 230 acres and includes accommodation for 3,200 workers, as well as recreation facilities. Companies from the US, Germany, Japan, Switzerland and Australia are based at the site. A Hershey chocolate factory is just outside the gates, and Dyson, a British company famed for its vacuum cleaners and hand driers, has a research and development centre a few kilometres away.

At Resound GN, a Danish company based in the park, Malaysian ladies in headscarves sit in rows and assemble hearing aids. The individual parts are tiny (the entire hearing aid is 2 to 3 centimetres long) and some workers need to peer through microscopes as they manoeuvre the electronics into place. Some use soldering irons to fix the parts; others check to ensure that the aids are working properly. It is a mini-version of the pin factory described by Adam Smith – each worker has a specialised role, allowing more pins (or hearing aids) to be made per day.

In another room, workers engrave a serial number onto the components with a laser; and in a further room, the parts are given a special coating to make them sturdier. Some hearing aids fix onto the outside of the ear; others are made to fit inside the ear and need to be tailored to fit, since people's earholes come in many shapes and sizes. A 3-D printer can make the parts, but they then need to be ground to remove the excess matter, and then polished.

By no means is this unskilled work, but it is not the high-tech part of the business. The electronic components of the hearing aid are made back in Denmark and the Malaysian plant assembles the pieces. Rather than pay European wages (and the associated taxes), it is much cheaper for the Danish company to assemble the aids in Malaysia. And the plant's proximity to the airport means that the aids can be shipped to Australia or Europe within 48 hours.

A hundred yards from the hearing-aid plant is the factory of Bericap, a German company that makes the tops for all sorts of (mostly plastic) bottles – for Coca-Cola, Ribena, bottled water, cooking oil, ketchup and engine oil. Some caps are much more sophisticated than others – those for engine oil, or child-resistant caps made for medicines, for example. In 2017, the plant was on course to make 1.8bn caps that year, out of 60bn made by the company across its 23 factories. That is nearly nine caps for every man, woman and child on the planet

The caps are made with injection machines and passed along a conveyor belt. The only workers observable on the factory floor were sealing the cardboard boxes that contained the caps. It is a truly global operation. The plastic to make the caps is imported from Korea and Indonesia; the injection machines are made by companies in Japan and Switzerland; and the caps are then exported to South-East Asia, Australia and even to Europe.

This is the hub of modern manufacturing, and it is in Asia. Between 2000 and 2015, Asia's share of the value added in global manufacturing rose from 35.1% to 47.5%.[1] China's share jumped from 6.5% to 23.6% over the same period. The US share of value added fell from 25.1% to 17.7%, while Europe's dropped from 12.1% to 9.2%.[2]

This shift has alarmed many Western politicians and is blamed for a loss of manufacturing jobs in Europe and America. And it is true that the proportion of manufacturing jobs in the US economy dropped from 32.5% in 1953 to 8.5% in August 2018.[3] But the decline began long before China rejoined the global trading system after the communist era and has actually flattened out a bit since 2010. Technology is also responsible for many of those job losses. Manufacturing output in the US rose 150% between 1980 and 2015 while the number of jobs in the sector fell by a third.[4] In other words, there were fewer workers, but they were more productive. It is a repeat of the decline of agricultural employment: as a sector gets more efficient, its share of the workforce tends to decline. It seems very unlikely that these jobs will return. In 2014, there were 63m manufacturing jobs in the rich world and 304m in the developing countries. But the rich world's workers added two-thirds of the final value; the low-value jobs are not going to be brought back.[5]

Two historical themes stand out. First, the dominance of Asia in global manufacturing represents a return to the pre-1700 norm, when European consumers desired Indian textiles and Chinese pottery. Second, the post-1700 period led to an understandable economic focus on manufacturing; it was called the "industrial" revolution after all. But factory jobs can be dull and unrewarding, especially if they focus on commodity items like the bottle tops made in Malaysia.

## An ancient business

Manufacturing is best defined as the process of turning raw materials and components into finished goods. In that sense, it has been going on for thousands of years. Iron, bronze and copper have been forged into tools, implements and weapons. Cotton, wool and silk have been spun, woven and stitched to form clothes. And clay has been turned into pottery, for both practical and decorative use.

For thousands of years, most manufacturing was largely done by individuals or small groups in workshops. The modern idea of the "manufactory", a word that was shortened to factory, only emerged in the 18th century, with the textile mill. Even at that stage, most textile production was conducted through the putting-out system; a merchant would deliver fibres to be spun, or spun cloth to be weaved, to families working at home. The finished goods would be picked up a few weeks later, with the workers rewarded on the basis of the number of items completed – the piece-rate system. This system had many advantages for the merchant, who did not have to supply equipment or premises and only paid for work that was satisfactorily completed.

So why move to a big factory, which cost money to rent (or buy)? The answer was the use of new, expensive machinery that no individual worker could afford, and which would not necessarily fit in a home. Employers did not want to take the risk that the machines might be broken or copied. Exploiting economies of scale, and getting the full benefits of specialisation, required the creation of factories.

The new machinery also needed a source of power. In the early stages of factories, this was a waterwheel, and these could only operate in select places. The New Lanark mill in Scotland, owned by the pioneering industrialist Robert Owen in the early 19th century, is now a hotel, but it still has the giant waterwheels that powered the machinery.

For the worker, the shift to factory labour was a dramatic change of lifestyle. Workers were paid, not for each item they produced, but for their time. Josiah Wedgwood, the pottery pioneer, was the first to introduce time cards and a clock. The workday was long, with shifts lasting 12 hours, and Sunday was the one day of rest a week. Many workers could not afford timepieces and had to rely on the foreman to tell them when it was time to leave; this created plenty of scope for unscrupulous employers to extend the working day and shorten the lunch break.[6] Few workers had an alarm clock that would reliably wake them. That created the need for the "knocker-upper", who used a long pole to tap on the upstairs windows, or in some cases, a peashooter to achieve the same effect. The role was referred to in

Dickens's *Great Expectations* and lasted well into the 20th century, with some knocker-uppers still operating in London's East End in the 1970s.[7]

Paying workers for their time, not their output, meant that employers were worried about the scope for slacking. So workers faced the watchful eye of a foreman or overseer, who could discipline them for small transgressions. Many owners held back a sixth of employees' wages, and this portion was paid quarterly as a reward for good behaviour. Bad behaviour included "tying bad knots" as well as absence due to drink.[8] The widespread use of young women and children in early factories was due both to the ease of disciplining them and their cheapness relative to men.

When textile mills were dependent on water power, this often meant that they were built in small towns or rural areas, which required the employer to provide accommodation for their workers. In New England, mills recruited farmers' daughters, and they worked both to help their families and to accumulate sufficient savings so that they could afford to marry. Married women were usually expected to give up work. For the women, it was a disciplined and spartan life, but it may still have been preferable to a life in domestic service, or to remaining within the parental home.

In time, as steam power replaced water, factories became associated with cities, such as Manchester, which was dubbed Cottonopolis in the 19th century. The growth of industrial cities brought its own problems, as the crowding together of people in unsanitary conditions, with polluted air, led to a surge in mortality. Life expectancy in Liverpool and Manchester in the 1850s was just 31–32, about ten years below the figure for England as a whole.[9]

The top-hatted mill owner and his cowed employees is one of the defining images of "capitalism", as it eventually became known. The key difference, as defined by Karl Marx, was that workers ceased to labour for themselves, using their own tools. Instead they laboured for the owners of capital, those who had bought or financed the factories and the textile machinery. And the workers did not receive the full fruits of their labour, since a chunk was skimmed off in the form of profits or dividends by the capitalists.

Why did workers put up with it? From the start, there was plenty of unhappiness. The records of one English mill in 1786 showed that, out of 780 apprentices, 199 ran away, 65 died and 96 were sent back to parents or overseers.[10] Adult workers demanded higher pay and better conditions, and started to organise. The British government passed the Combination Acts of 1799 and 1800 to prohibit trade unions and collective bargaining. Between 1811 and 1816, the Luddite movement burned mills and smashed machinery in protest at the decline in their living standards. The Luddite rebellions were countered with trials and military action, and with laws to prohibit the smashing of machinery.

Despite worker protests, more people were drawn into the industry. Some of this was a lack of choice. A population surge meant that parents were eager to put young children to work; some even lied about their ages to ensure that they got a job. The rise of the factory system also meant less demand for domestically based adult spinners and weavers, and a more efficient agricultural sector meant that fewer people were needed on the farm. Despite the hardness of factory work and the risks of living in crowded, unhealthy cities, enough people must have felt the rewards (in terms of higher wages and independence) sufficient for them to make the leap. The same prospect has lured close to 200m Chinese people to shift from country to city in recent decades.

Even in Britain, it took many decades before the factory became the dominant mode of employment in the textile industry. As of 1820 there were still 240,000 handloom weavers and only 126,000 factory workers.[11] But by 1850 there were only 43,000 handloom weavers left.

The factory dominated in the end because it had many economic advantages. Unlike the putting-out system, the industrialist had much greater control over the speed and the quality of work. The factory could also keep control of its costs, ordering more raw materials when they were needed (and getting a better deal from suppliers when buying in bulk), slowing production when sales were sluggish, transporting goods to customers by canal or railway, and so on. All this was, of course, on top of the productivity advances achieved by the new textile machinery.

By bringing down the cost of yarn, which fell 90% between 1785 and 1795,[12] manufacturers were able to reduce the cost of finished goods. The price of muslin, a finely woven cotton fabric, fell 75% between the early 1780s and the 1830s.[13] In turn this made cotton clothes and sheets available to many more people. Increased demand allowed factories to achieve more economies of scale.

One significant boost to the productivity of manufacturing was the standardisation of parts. This initially arose from a desire of French arms manufacturers to improve the quality and reliability of weapons, and was adapted by American gun makers at Harpers Ferry, Virginia, and Springfield, Massachusetts. The techniques became known as the "American system" as they spread to other goods, including machine tools.[14] The British authorities, revelling in their global economic domination at the Great Exhibition of 1851, were struck by the American skills that were demonstrated at the event, and adopted a similar approach in their own arms industry.

Standardisation of parts reduced the need for businesses to rely on individual craftsmen to make their goods, and increased the push of workers into factories. Perhaps the first standardised commercial product was the Singer sewing machine. A patent for mechanical sewing had been issued by the British authorities in 1755 but the product was not perfected until Isaac Singer (based on a patent by Elias Howe) opened his business in 1851.[15] Singer was one of the first multinationals and its product, which saved women considerable time and effort, was instantly popular; by 1876, it had sold 2m units. This was one of the first brand names to be valued round the world.

Over time, of course, technology developed a wide range of consumer goods, and their associated manufacturing brands, from transport (cars, bicycles, motorbikes and scooters), through household goods (vacuum cleaners, washing machines, radios, TVs, ovens) to machines made for both work and home, such as typewriters and personal computers.

Manufacturers face a multiplicity of challenges. Not only do they need to design a workable product but they must make it stylish enough to appeal to consumers (and of the right size and shape to fit into their homes). They must make consumers aware of the product through advertising and promotion. And they must make it available at a reasonable price. Small wonder that a small number of large firms tend to dominate many markets. The best hope for a smaller manufacturing company is to become a supplier to one of the global groups; to make the widgets or electronics that go into a washing machine or a car.

The requirements of scale meant that there was a tendency towards consolidation from the earliest days of industrialisation. The iron and steel industry required heavy investment to construct the furnaces needed to make the product. This made them large: France's Le Creuset iron and steel works had 12,500 workers in 1870, while the Krupp works in Essen, Germany, employed 12,000 in 1873.[16] High fixed costs created the need for economies of scale. As the investment in plant and equipment was spread over a larger number of items, the marginal cost of each additional item fell. By the same token, however, high fixed costs made the steel companies very vulnerable to a fall in prices. So there was a tendency in America to fix prices, in cartels with the competition, and eventually to merge into one big group, US Steel. The Soviet Union also saw "gigantism" as the aim of steel production; the Magnitogorsk plant was opened in the 1930s under Stalin's five-year plan with the aim of becoming the world's largest steel plant. Even in the late 1980s, it had 63,000 employees.[17]

Iron and steel, along with some types of chemical manufacture, and the production of bulky items such as ships and trains, would generally be classed as "heavy industry". These are the kind of industries that employ lots of people, and they were the industries that many developing countries turned to when they industrialised after the Second World War. They looked at Europe and America, saw their huge steel plants and car factories, and resolved to copy them. Many put up tariffs to keep out Western products and protect their infant industries, a process known as "import substituting industrialisation" (see Chapter 12).

The sheer scale of investment needed often meant that the state took control of these industries. The pursuit of profit took second place behind the urge to protect jobs. In some sectors, this led to chronic overcapacity; between 2005 and 2017, for example, excess capacity in the global steel industry varied between 200m and 750m tons. This led to a squeeze on prices and made steel the subject of geopolitical disputes.[18]

Heavy industries tended to be those that caused the air in large cities to become very polluted. In Pittsburgh in the 1940s, the air pollution was so bad that the street lights could come on at noon.[19] Life was even more dangerous inside the plant. Here is how one worker described his job in 1919:

> You lift a large sack of coal to your shoulders, run towards the white hot steel in a hundred-ton ladle, must get close enough without burning your face off to hurl the sack, using every ounce of strength, into the ladle and run, as flames leap to roof and the heat blasts everything to the roof. Then you rush out to the ladle and madly shovel manganese into it, as hot a job as can be imagined.[20]

Death was common. A biographer of Andrew Carnegie, the American steel magnate, estimated that fatal accidents in steel mills accounted for 20% of all male deaths in Pittsburgh in the 1880s.[21]

Small wonder that these big plants tended to have turbulent industrial relations. Concentrating so many workers in one place also made it easier for trade unions to organise, not just to get better wages but to protect their members from accidents and death. The design of some plants, particularly those using conveyor belts, made it possible to disrupt an entire factory with relative ease. Eventually, workers were able to improve their conditions, but it was a long struggle.

## A feat of management

Operating such enormous plants required a great deal of planning. The power for the machines had to be transmitted via a system of shafts and gears, which could break down and stop production. The raw material had to be brought in at one end (or on one floor) of the factory and the finished product taken out at another. The workers had to be trained and divided according to their specialised tasks.

As industry developed, these tasks became too complex for the original founders (or their families) to oversee. Frederick Winslow Taylor was a consultant who pioneered "scientific" management. He spent 26 years watching people at work, particularly in the steel industry, armed with a stopwatch and a notepad, and observing what they did. That led him to break down tasks into a number of specific actions, train workers to take such actions, and reward them for meeting their targets. Lenin, the Soviet Union leader, was a great fan of Taylor's work.[22] Taylor's aim was to improve efficiency and stop employees from dawdling on the job. But his approach was criticised for turning workers into automatons, and he had a dismissive attitude towards them, arguing that the typical ironworker "is so stupid that the word percentage has no meaning to him and he must consequently be trained by a man more intelligent that himself".[23] Clearly an obsessive, he spent his retirement literally watching grass grow in search of the perfect lawn.[24]

This concern became even greater when Henry Ford developed the moving assembly line in the early 20th century. The workers stayed in one place and the parts were brought to them via the conveyor belt. As Taylor suggested, the worker's day was filled with simple repetitive tasks. In *Modern Times*, a 1936 film, Charlie Chaplin satirises the worker's lot, at one point literally becoming trapped among the cogs of a machine. But these were well-paid jobs; after the Second World War, working on a car production line was one of the most prized careers available. The loss of those jobs in Western nations was the subject of much angst from the 1970s onwards.

Japan was the initial competitive threat to US and European manufacturers. It brought systemic change through the "lean manufacturing" process developed at Toyota. This aimed to combine mass production with craftsmanship. Employees with flexible roles are organised in teams, and each worker is encouraged to stop production when a fault is discovered. The result is that workers are happier, quality is improved, and the management gains from the workers' insights. [25]

But lean manufacturing has not stopped the decline in industrial employment. The worry is that well-paid factory work has been replaced with "McJobs" (after the McDonalds burger chain) in the services sector, with lower pay and poorer conditions. In turn, this may have contributed to the rise of inequality in the developed world. But one study has concluded that "on average, only about one-tenth of the overall increase in inequality between the 1980s and the 2000s can be attributed to the decline in the share of manufacturing jobs".[26]

More than half of all global workers now have a job in services, up from just 33.7% in 1991.[27] People who work in offices or shops have jobs that are just as "real" as those who work in factories. Nor is there a rigid divide between manufacturing and services. A study by the Brookings Institution estimated that 21.4m Americans worked in manufacturing-related services, almost double the 11.5m who worked solely in manufacturing.[28] The number of lines of software code (classed as services) in a high-performance car jumped from 10m in 2010 to 150m in 2016. Software is expected to represent 30% of a car's value by 2030.[29] In contrast, a Boeing 787 aeroplane has just 6.5m lines of code.[30] Apple does not make the components that go into an iPhone, nor does it assemble them. But it still captures most of the value through the design and the operating system.

Part of the decline in manufacturing jobs is down to a statistical distortion arising from the outsourcing trend. Manufacturing plants need cleaning, just like homes and offices. In the past, the manufacturers would have employed their own cleaners; nowadays they outsource the task to a contract-cleaning company. The same is true of the works canteen. These job shifts show up as a transfer from manufacturing to services but, in reality, the effect overstates the decline of the former and the rise of the latter.[31]

Another reason why manufacturing has become less important as a proportion of GDP is, ironically, because it has become more efficient, and the prices of manufactured goods have fallen. Productivity improvements are harder to achieve in services. As the economist William Baumol noted, it takes just as many musicians, and just as much time, to play a Mozart string quartet today as it did when the composer was alive.[32] Healthcare and education are subject to this problem; we do not want doctors and teachers to rush their work. Between 1978 and 2013, the average price increase in the US was 110%. But healthcare costs rose 250% and the cost of a university education rose 440% over the same period.[33] If current trends continue, healthcare costs could comprise 50% of British GDP by 2100, and 60% of US GDP. By definition, that means a smaller share for other sectors, like manufacturing.

A fair portion of manufacturing is simply the assembly of goods that are made elsewhere, like the hearing aids at the start of this chapter. But this is not where the value or the high-paying jobs are created. Putting together an Airbus plane in France is responsible for just 5% of the aircraft's value. Instead, the value can flow from the design of the products, or from those parts that need precision engineering.

This may mean that the highest-value businesses are not what many people would conventionally consider to be industry at all. A Cambridge University report on high-value manufacturing cited Cadbury Schweppes, the confectionery maker, as its first example.[34]

Some companies have found it necessary to switch from manufacturing to services outright. IBM, a name that stood for International Business Machines, was founded as a company that made record-keeping devices that read punched cards, before expanding into electronic typewriters and then computers. But the emergence of cheap personal computers in the 1980s threatened its business model, and in the course of the 1990s and 2000s, the company sold its hardware businesses, which made personal computers, printers and disk drives. Services and software now form the vast bulk of the group's revenues.[35]

The proportion of US personal spending devoted to physical goods dropped from more than 60% in 1950 to around 36% in 2014, with services now comprising nearly two-thirds of the total. There is talk of Western societies reaching "peak stuff".[36] As developed economies have grown richer, a smaller proportion of consumer spending was devoted to food; the same process may now be happening with physical goods. Many of the things that people consume are now in non-physical form. Instead of buying music as LPs, cassettes or compact discs, it is downloaded via streaming services. The same goes for films and TV shows, which used to be bought as DVDs. The revenues of the video-game industry, a virtual industry if ever there was one, were estimated at $138bn in 2018.[37] Rather than owning a car in future, only for it to sit in a parking spot 95% of the time, consumers will rent one when they need it. They will spend their money on "experiences", like holidays or partying with friends.

In contrast, there is little sign of "peak stuff" in the developing world. In China, new car sales rose from 12m in 2010[38] to nearly 25m in 2017[39] and there is a lot more scope for growth. China has

131 vehicles per 1,000 people, compared with America's 850.[40] India has even more room to catch up. As developing economies grow, they seem to follow an S-curve shape; once per capita income passes $1,000, spending on consumer goods takes off. A study by Deloitte, the consultancy, suggests that 510m people will be added to the global middle class between 2015 and 2025.[41] So global manufacturers will still have plenty of customers in the years ahead.

In modern manufacturing, the designs and brands are usually created in the rich nations (which include Japan and South Korea), and the assembly and manufacture occur in the developing countries of Asia, and other places like Mexico. This combination creates high profits for Western manufacturers and low prices for its consumers. But many are not happy with the model. It is not just that workers in the US and Europe worry about the loss of jobs. There has also been controversy about the conditions in Asian factories. In 2005, Nike, the footwear manufacturer, published a report detailing conditions at its 700 worldwide factories, some of which restricted access to toilets and to drinking water during the day, and workers toiled for over 60 hours a week in more than half of the plants.[42] The company has adopted a code to try to improve conditions but still faces regular protests.[43] In 2010 and 2011, Foxconn, the Chinese company that makes parts for Apple's iPhones, saw a wave of suicides at its plants, amid controversy about the sweatshop conditions.[44]

Some Western consumers vowed to boycott products made through unfair labour practices. But many people were only too happy to get the cheap T-shirts, shoes and electronic goods on offer. And Asian workers argued that they should be given the chance to industrialise, as Europe and the US had done. Many Asians were pleased to move from a life on the farm to a job, however tough, in a factory in a city. Developing countries have fought hard to keep the World Trade Organisation, the body that regulates global trade, from enforcing labour standards.

There is also a debate about which standards should be enforced. It is easy to agree that forced labour and slavery should be outlawed. But what about child labour? Many children work on farms. Working in a factory may be more onerous but the extra income could be what keeps the family out of poverty. The proportion of children who work tends to fall rapidly as average income rises.[45] So the best way to reduce child labour may be to allow those countries to enrich themselves. And that is most likely to occur, as it did in China, by joining the global trading system.

## The chain

The car industry is a good example of the interconnectedness of modern business. When General Motors and Chrysler flirted with collapse in 2009, one of the reasons for a government rescue was that jobs were also at risk at the companies that supplied parts (such as tyres or headlights) to the industry.[46] The Motor and Equipment Manufacturers Association (MEMA) estimated that, as of 2018, more than 871,000 American jobs were linked to the creation of cars and trucks.[47]

Furthermore, these supply chains are international. While it is common to talk of the US or German car industries, these manufacturers depend on global supply chains. Parts may cross international borders many times before they are assembled into the finished product.[48] Perhaps 30–50% of the trade in manufactured goods occurs within individual multinational companies.[49] As they became aware of this, many developing countries slashed their tariffs so that they could become part of these global value chains. MEMA estimates that around a third of all the parts that make US cars are imported, while in Germany, the proportion is 45%.[50] Why have car manufacturers done this? To cut costs, of course. That is why imposing tariffs on imports will push up the price of domestically produced cars one way or the other – either the manufacturers will pay the tariffs and pass on the cost to customers, or they will disrupt their supply chains and make cars more expensively at home.

This interconnectedness means that it is not only in the West that manufacturing jobs are under pressure from automation. A paper by the National Bureau of Economic Research estimated that each additional robot replaced around 6.2 workers.[51] Sales of industrial robots have risen from 100,000 a year in the mid-2000s to 250,000 in 2015 and are forecast to hit 400,000 by the end of the decade.[52] The standard joke is that the manufacturing plant of the future will be staffed by a man and a dog; the man's job will be to feed the dog, and the dog's role will be to keep the man away from the machines. And 3-D printing will allow small parts to be made on site, eliminating the need for a part to arrive from a supplier.

This may mean that developing nations may never create manufacturing sectors as large as those seen in Europe and America in the 20th century, or in China today. If the latter is excluded, manufacturing's share of employment in the developing world is lower than it was in the 1980s.[53] Manufacturing's share of the economy peaked in South Korea in 1988 and in Indonesia in 2002.[54] There is an inevitable trade-off between wage levels and employment in some of these sectors. As real wages rise, manufacturers either shift location to a country with lower costs, or automate the tasks done by workers. One day, those ladies in the heart of Malaysia will be replaced by a machine.

The service sector too will be subject to automation, as call-centre workers are replaced by chatbots and analysts are replaced by artificial intelligence programmes that can conduct research both more quickly and more accurately. Over the next 30 years, we will have to invent a whole new set of tasks to keep us employed. But we have done it before: baristas, personal trainers and social media managers were all virtually unknown 30 years ago.

# THE FIRST ERA OF
# GLOBALISATION: 1820–1914

In the 19th century, industrialisation spread well beyond Britain to many parts of Europe, North America and Japan. Globalisation became tangible to ordinary people, rather than being confined to a limited number of luxury goods. By 1914, as John Maynard Keynes wrote, "The inhabitant of London could order by telephone, sipping his morning tea in bed, the various products of the whole earth, in such quantity as he might see fit, and reasonably expect their early delivery upon his doorstep."[1]

The period covered by this chapter also saw big changes in transport systems, in the form of railways and steamships. These allowed people to migrate across the world in much larger numbers than ever before (see Chapter 9). Another important development was the emergence of a new range of industries, based on oil, chemicals and electricity, which have been dubbed the "second industrial revolution".

In parts of the world, it was genuinely possible to talk of a "great enrichment". In 1820, US GDP per capita (in 2011 dollars) was $2,080. By 1914, it was $8,101. The UK was well ahead of the US in 1820, at $3,241 per person; by 1914, it was slightly behind at $7,973 (but this was still an increase of 150%). France almost managed to triple real incomes from a lower base, pushing them up from $1,867 to $5,324.

All this is in sharp contrast to China, where per capita incomes fell from $854 to $786.[2] In 1913, western Europe and North America produced 51% of world output with 20% of the global population.[3]

Importantly, higher living standards were achieved despite a rising population. Global population probably just topped 1 billion by 1820 and was around 1.8 billion on the eve of the First World War.[4] Global life expectancy edged up from 29 in 1820 to 34.1 in 1913, while, in Europe, the gain over the same period was more substantial, from 35.6 to 46.8.[5]

The developed world also urbanised in the 19th century. In 1800, 23% of English citizens lived in towns with more than 5,000 people; by 1910, the proportion was 75%. In Europe as a whole the urban proportion rose from 12% to 41% over the same period, while in the US, the jump was from 5% to 42%.[6] By contrast, in 1900 only 6% of Chinese people lived in towns, a smaller proportion than three centuries earlier.[7]

Finally, the labour force organised itself into trade unions, and started to challenge the owners of capital. It became more common to speak of the "working classes" and to analyse society in class terms, and the words "communism" and "capitalism" were adopted. Businesses developed the joint-stock model of ownership. Private firms grew to immense size and power (Standard Oil and US Steel, for example) and became multinational enterprises. Much of what we think of as modern society emerged.

## A relatively peaceful age

The defeat of Napoleon at Waterloo in 1815 brought to an end a 23-year period of European conflict. The same year also saw the end of an Anglo-American war that had disrupted transatlantic trade. There were many conflicts to come over the next century, including such shameful episodes as the two opium wars. Those were a successful attempt by the British to stop the Chinese authorities from disrupting Britain's lucrative drugs trade.

But most wars were local. Global conflicts like the Seven Years War of 1756–63 (which stretched from North America to India) or the world wars of the 20th century were avoided. The conflicts that allowed Prussia to unite Germany, by first defeating Austria in 1866 and then France in 1871, were mercifully short. The most devastating events of the 19th century were civil wars; China's Taiping rebellion of the 1850s and 1860s, which saw between 20 and 40 million deaths,[8] and the US conflict between the federal government and the confederacy, which cost the lives of around 620,000 soldiers.[9]

In the absence of prolonged international conflict, and with piracy now rare thanks to the British navy, merchants were free to trade across borders. The volume of global trade grew sevenfold between 1840 and 1913; using a different starting point, trade grew from 1% of global GDP in 1820 to 8% just before the First World War.[10] Economists Kevin O'Rourke and Jeffrey Williamson argue that, until the 19th century, global trade was dominated by luxuries. Spice, perfumes and items like tea and coffee were almost two-thirds of the Dutch East India Company's imports in the 1780s, for example.[11] Globalisation only really occurred when commodity markets became integrated, in the sense that prices in different countries were similar, save for the impact of tariffs and transport costs.

Trade grew as transport costs fell. The cost of shipping coal between Nagasaki in Japan and Shanghai in China fell by 76% between 1880 and 1910. In America in 1830, it took the equivalent of $174 in today's dollars to move a ton of goods 100 miles by wagon; by 1901, rail transport had reduced the price by seven-eighths to $22 and the journey time had fallen as well. Thanks to steamships, the cost of sending a bushel of grain from Chicago to Liverpool fell from 35 cents in the late 1850s to around 10 cents in 1912.[12]

This had profound effects. Wheat from the American plains and, after the development of refrigeration, beef from the Argentine pampas was shipped to Europe. The result was cheap food for workers and a rise in their real standard of living. In Britain, the Liberal Party was able to win a landslide victory in the 1906 election in part by arguing that Conservative proposals for tariffs would drive up the price of bread. Back then, free trade could be a "populist" policy.

Indeed, *The Economist* owes its foundation in 1843 to a campaign against tariffs. The Corn Laws were introduced in Britain in 1815 to protect British agriculture from foreign competition; corn could not be imported until the price reached £4 for a quarter (equivalent to 480lb or 217kg). This was popular among the landed aristocrats who supported the Tory Party, which was renamed the Conservatives in 1834. But those who believed in free trade, along the lines of Adam Smith, opposed the tariffs. They received support from industrialists who understood that expensive food required them to pay higher wages.

The abolition of the Corn Laws in 1846 caused a split in the Conservative Party and cemented the hold of free-traders on British policy. British tariffs had already dropped 70% between 1815 and 1827 and another 50% between 1828 and 1841.[13] As cynics have pointed out ever since, free trade suited the British since their early lead in industrialisation made it possible to flood other markets with their textiles and manufactured goods. European countries followed the British lead in the 1850s and 1860s; the Cobden-Chevalier Treaty of 1860 cut British tariffs on wine by 80% and limited French duties on British imports to no more than 30%. Despite this still punitive tax, British exports to France more than doubled in the 1860s. The treaty became a model for others, with Italy arranging 24 trade deals between 1861 and 1870, while Belgium and France agreed 19 each.[14]

The obvious success of the British model led other countries not just to loosen their trade policies, but to adopt the gold standard. This was a system designed to protect the value of creditors' capital by constraining inflation. The amount of money that a country's banks could create was linked to its gold reserves. Customers could exchange their banknotes for an equivalent amount of gold and silver. Germany adopted the gold standard after unification in 1871 and it was followed by France, Italy, Sweden and others in the 1870s. The US adopted the standard in 1873 but faced a long fight with those who argued for bimetallism (using silver as well).

The gold standard lasted much longer outside Britain than did enthusiasm for free trade. By the 1870s, the full impact of transatlantic food imports became evident. British imports of grain rose 90%, and those of meat 300%, between the early 1870s and late 1890s; the last quarter of the 19th century was known in Britain as the great agricultural depression. Other countries were not prepared to suffer the same fate. In 1879, Otto von Bismarck, the German chancellor, imposed tariffs on cereals, which eventually reached 33% on wheat and 47% on rye. The French set tariffs of 10–15% on agricultural commodities and more than 25% on industrial goods.[15] And food was not the only protected category. Duties on European manufactured goods more than doubled between 1875 and 1895.[16] Trade, however, kept growing, in part because economies were expanding and in part because transport costs were falling faster than tariffs could rise.

## Colonial expansion

The late 19th century was the high-water mark of European global power. By 1914, Europe along with its colonies and former colonies like the US (which was mostly populated by European emigrants) controlled 85% of the world's land surface.[17] Trade was certainly a key motive for expansion. In what Paul Bairoch dubbed the "colonial contract",[18] colonies could only trade with the imperial power and transport their wares in the empire's ships, and they were confined to producing raw materials, rather than manufactured goods. The aim was to create a captive market, with each colony in a permanent state of dependency.

Some colonies were highly lucrative. In the 1850s, the island of Java contributed more than a third of the budget of the Dutch state.[19] While profit may have been an aim of imperial policy, it was not the only one. Prestige and FOMO (fear of missing out) were just as important motives. Benjamin Disraeli, the British prime minister from 1874 to 1880, saw imperialism as a way of attracting voter support; that's why he made Queen Victoria Empress of India in 1876. In the 1880s, Bismarck was sniffy about the "scramble for Africa", fearing that colonial disputes would only damage relations with other European powers. He succumbed to the temptation to seize territory at the Congress of Berlin in 1885, in part because he saw empire-building as politically popular at home. But by 1889, he was trying to give away German south-west Africa, arguing that it was "a burden and an expense".

Bismarck's reluctance points to a problem with the standard critique of colonialism, as advanced by Lenin and others. In their view, imperialism was the "final stage" of capitalism. Inequality within the European powers meant that capitalists were unable to sell their goods at home because workers were too poor to afford them. They were thus forced to look abroad for markets.

But the financial benefits were not as clear-cut as Lenin suggested.

A study of British firms found that, from the mid-1880s, the returns from imperial investments fell below those that could be earned at home. The cost of defending these colonies was high and the authors suggest that "in the absence of empire, the burdens on the British taxpayer could have been reduced and resources diverted to more productive activities".[20] Other academics point out, however, that the empire added considerably to British military might, as the First World War was to show, and that the late Victorian empire "does not appear to have been a waste of money".[21]

The two most successful economies of the late 19th century were Germany and the US. The former had a few colonies in Africa, such as Togoland and Namibia; the latter had the Philippines and Hawaii. In neither case did these seem to be hugely profitable. The scramble for Africa was a mistake, and not just for the Africans. Precisely because the African economies were underdeveloped they were unlikely to be a huge source of demand for European goods. France seems to have lost money in its tropical African colonies while making money from Algeria and Indochina.[22]

An alternative argument for colonial expansion is that the Europeans were not interested in exports but in controlling access to raw materials. The most notorious example was in the Belgian Congo, where King Leopold II's regime used forced labour to produce rubber for exports; soldiers cut off the hands and feet of those who failed to meet the quota.[23] South Africa provided Britain with both gold and diamonds, which were extracted from the ground by the long-suffering local population. A diamond rush occurred in Kimberley in the 1870s and the world's largest goldfields were discovered at Witwatersrand in 1886. The land rights of the indigenous population were restricted, turning them into a cheap labour force for white farmers and the mines. Foreign investment per head in South Africa was about 11 times higher than the money ploughed into Britain's other African colonies.[24]

There was a much stronger case for the commodity-driven argument after the First World War, when oil became vital for military purposes – oil that could only be found in a few places on the planet. The British and French vied for control of the Middle East for precisely this reason.

Foreign investment was certainly very popular before 1914, but not always in the colonies. The French were keen buyers of Russian bonds, a decision that proved unfortunate when the communists defaulted after the 1917 revolution. An examination of British overseas investment in 1914 shows that the US was the biggest single destination, followed by Latin America, where British possessions were tiny. Exclude Europe and the fairly independent dominions in Australasia and Canada and colonial investments were less than a third of the total. The returns from the more developed countries in Europe, Australasia and North America were 1% a year higher than those in the developing world.[25]

Rapid growth was not confined to current, or former, parts of the British empire. Mexico managed a growth rate of 8% a year between 1876 and 1910 while the population grew by a half. The country benefited from demand for commodities, particularly metals, and was ruled for 35 years by Porfirio Diaz, a general who seized power in a coup.[26] For a while the British were particular enthusiasts for investing in Argentina, which received almost half of all the country's overseas lending in the 1880s. Argentina enjoyed huge immigration (particularly from Spain and Italy) in the late 19th century, becoming a big agricultural exporter. Between 1880 and 1914, it managed an annual growth rate of 5%.[27] By the start of the First World War, Argentina was the tenth-richest country in the world, in terms of GDP per head.[28] But the country already showed signs of the financial instability that was to dog it in the 20th and 21st centuries. In 1890, Barings Bank of Britain nearly collapsed when it suffered a loss on the sale of the debt of the Buenos Aires Water Supply and Drainage Corporation.[29] European investors were quick to pull their money out in the face of higher risks.

Before this seems too much like a European writer excusing the actions of his ancestors, let us admit that the intentions of the colonial powers may well have been callous and malign. They cared little about the effect of their actions on the peoples of the countries they conquered and made little effort to develop their economies. In the case of India, British rule clearly had an adverse impact. While famines had largely been eliminated from Europe by this period, India suffered five major famines in the second half of the 19th century under British rule, taking around 15 million lives in all. The British tended to justify their failure to intervene on the grounds of cost, an unwillingness to interfere in free markets, or simply a belief that a Malthusian-style culling would reduce the population to more acceptable levels.[30] But for a country that claimed to be both civilised and Christian, these were pathetic excuses. In the 20th century, the famines suffered under Stalin and Mao would be seen as horrendous crimes. Bengal falls into the same category. It endured a terrible famine in 1943–44, in which 3 million died, while the British were still shipping rice out of the country.[31]

Another terrible famine under British rule occurred in Ireland. It was the result of a blight on the potato crop, which had come to dominate Irish agriculture. The British made initial attempts to provide relief but these broke down in 1847. Although Ireland was a net importer of food during the famine, wheat was still being sent from Ireland back to England in the midst of the crisis. The British authorities did spend £10m in relief,[32] but their efforts were severely insufficient; in all one-eighth of the population (one million people) died, while another one million emigrated.

Exploitation took other forms. The British developed a great enthusiasm for Chinese tea but had few goods that the Chinese wanted in exchange. The East India Company allowed poppies to be grown in India, and local people adopted the crop (which is the basis for opium) after the destruction of their textile industry. British traders then smuggled the opium to China where vast profits (2,000% per chest) were available, thanks to the highly addictive nature of the drug.

In 1839, a Chinese commissioner imposed a crackdown and demanded the handover of 20,000 chests or 2.5m pounds of opium; the drug was then destroyed. The furious British, worried about the lost revenue, attacked the Chinese, forcing the emperor to open several ports to foreign trade and to hand over Hong Kong. A few Britons were critical of their government's actions. William Gladstone, a future prime minister, declared that "we, the enlightened and civilised Christians are pursuing objects at variance with justice and with religion". He was not enlightened or civilised enough to give back British gains to China in any of his four stints as prime minister, however.[33]

## Rule by creditor

The Suez canal was one of the engineering wonders of the 19th century. The idea that the Mediterranean could be linked with the Red Sea went back to ancient times, when the Persian emperor Darius first attempted it. The concept was of huge interest to the imperial powers; once opened, the sailing distance from London to Bombay was cut by 41% and to Shanghai by 32%.[34] Construction began in 1859 and the canal opened in 1869. The Egyptian government put up half the capital and around 400,000 Egyptians laboured on the project, working 17-hour days.[35] Some workers were unpaid.

The Egyptian government, which was heavily dependent on cotton exports, struggled to pay its debts, and in 1875 sold its 44% stake in the canal to Britain for the bargain price of £4m. That proved a temporary expedient and the country defaulted on its debts in the following year. This gave an excuse for the Europeans to take control of the country, initially as a joint Anglo-French exercise but then under British rule alone. By 1889, British ships comprised 75% of shipping through the Suez canal and France just 8%. *The Economist* commented at the time that the Suez canal was "cut by French energy and Egyptian money for British advantage". Evelyn Baring was appointed as consul general, and effective power behind the throne, and the British yoke was not completely thrown off until the 1950s. Egypt was not officially a British colony, but it was not independent either.[36]

Something similar happened in the Ottoman empire, which spent most of the 19th century in steady decline. In 1838 a treaty was signed giving Britain and the other European powers the right to trade throughout the Ottoman Empire for a tariff of just 3%. The Sultan's finances did not improve and in 1875 the empire declared effective bankruptcy.[37] In 1881, the Europeans set up the Ottoman Public Debt Administration, which eventually grew to having 9,000 employees, who collected taxes from the empire's citizens in order to pay off European creditors. These two examples of "rule by creditor" were to have many echoes in the 20th century. Nation states had used their military muscle to support their merchants, and they gave the same support to their investors once capital started to flow around the globe.

## Catch-up

Britain's domination of global industry in the first half of the 19th century was immense. In 1851, when it held the Great Exhibition to show off its might, Britain consumed ten times as much coal as France, produced four times as much iron as Germany, and used twice as much steam power as France and Germany combined.[38] Even as late as 1880, Britain produced 23% of the world's manufactured goods while the US made 15%, and France, Germany and Belgium combined made 18%. But the other countries were fast catching up and the US had 33% of the global market (to Britain's 15%) by 1913 (see chart).[39] Germany was producing more than twice as much steel as Britain by the time of the First World War.[40]

In some cases, the technology that had helped Britain industrialise was transferred, or copied, as artisans were lured abroad. Being a late adopter of technology has its advantages. While the British spent decades developing steam engines and inventing spinning and weaving machinery, other countries could simply use the best available versions of those machines.

It was inevitable that a small group of islands off the coast of Europe could not maintain their lead. Other countries were aware of the wealth that trade had brought to Britain and eagerly copied its example. The US vastly expanded its territory in the course of the 19th century, turning into a continent-wide power. Natural growth, along with immigration, meant that the US population rose from 9.6m in 1820 to 31.4m in 1860. This was a massive internal market that American businesses could exploit without worrying too much about foreign trade. Indeed, the US government relied on tariffs for about 90% of its income between 1790 and 1860. By the late 1820s, the average tariff rate was 60%. While tariffs drifted downwards for a few decades, they rebounded to 50% during the Civil War, staying there for much of the rest of the century.[41]

Despite those taxes, the US was still importing manufactured goods in the first half of the century and exporting food and raw materials, cotton in particular. By the middle of the 19th century, the US was supplying 70% of the world's cotton.[42] But manufacturing was also growing in importance and employed about 20% of the labour force in 1860, up from 8% in 1810.[43] A combination of

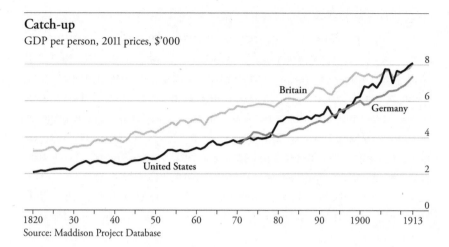

**Catch-up**
GDP per person, 2011 prices, $'000

Source: Maddison Project Database

population growth, the exploitation of raw materials and the development of industry allowed real American GDP to increase nearly fourfold between 1820 and 1910.[44]

Exploiting America's internal market required investment in infrastructure, especially given the vast distances involved. As we saw in the last chapter, there was immense investment in canals and railways. Initially, much of the iron needed to build the latter was imported from overseas. But in the second half of the century, the US began to exploit its own natural resources. Between 1860 and 1910, iron output increased 16-fold and coal production rose 23 times; both were needed to operate a railway network that expanded from 31,000 to 258,000 miles over the same period.[45]

Just as significant was the boom in oil production that followed the strike in Titusville, Pennsylvania in 1859 (see Chapter 5). And by the 1880s, the US was no longer copying European technology but leading the way in innovation, as with Edison's development of the light bulb, and, more significantly, the creation of an electricity generating system.

Here, we might think back to the factors that allowed Britain to be first to industrialise: America had energy resources, a culture that promoted learning, and institutions that did not stand in the way of business. The founding fathers may (mostly) have favoured an economy of small farmers, but they deliberately limited the powers of government, and business had plenty of scope to grow. One could argue that the American institutional structure was too minimalist. America's banking system had a "wild west" quality before the Civil War, and there were regular crises and frauds. Two attempts to create a central bank failed in the face of political opposition and the Federal Reserve was not established until 1913 (see Chapter 13). A shortage of currency meant that foreign coins were still used. The discovery of gold in California in 1848 led to the rapid development of the area and also gave a monetary boost, in the form of extra currency, to the economy. A paper currency, the greenback, emerged during the Civil War and was linked to gold (and at times, silver) in the last decades of the century.

Perhaps the best illustration of the fundamental strength of the American economy was that it overcame the effects of the Civil War. This was helped by government action. The Homestead Act of 1862 gave settlers the chance to occupy 160-acre plots of land if they could improve it; by 1914, 2.5m claims had been registered. Partly as a result, the proportion of US land devoted to farming rose from 16% in 1870 to 39% in 1910.[46] The country became not just a place of freedom (as symbolised by the Statue of Liberty) but a place where young men and women could prosper. An even greater wave of immigration took the population to 92m by 1910, by which stage the economy was more than twice the size of Britain's.[47] It was already clear that, as a continental power, America would have a much greater weight than any of the European nations.

Germany began the period as a splintered state. The Holy Roman Empire had finally been abolished by Napoleon and 38 political units (each with its own tariffs) emerged at the end of the war. The country started to dismantle trade barriers, first in Prussia in 1818, and created a Zollverein, or customs union, in 1834. This area deliberately excluded the Austrian Habsburg territories, part of a long battle for control of Germany between Prussia and Austria that ended with the former's triumph in 1866. The entire country was united under the Prussian Kaiser after a war with France in 1870–71.

Well before unification, parts of Germany were industrialising rapidly. The 1850s was the key decade, marked by a railway boom, the creation of joint-stock companies and banks, and the development of the iron and steel industry.[48] Coal output rose from 2m tons in 1850 to 114m tons in 1913,[49] by which stage the Ruhr region was supplying 60% of the country's coal needs.[50] With the help of fertilisers, the German grain harvest grew 3.7-fold between 1845 and 1914.[51] That allowed the country to feed its growing population, which jumped from 41m in 1871 to 68m in 1913.

As with America, Germany quickly found ways to move ahead of Britain in certain industries. Mauve, the first synthetic dye, was discovered by William Perkin, a Briton, in 1856. But Germany had a large number of trained chemists and expanded its dye industry rapidly after 1870, with a red dye called alizarin the leading product. German firms such as Bayer and BASF became global leaders in the chemical and pharmaceutical industries.

The unification of Germany was followed by a rapid economic boom and bust. In part, this may have been due to an influx of capital from France. Germany demanded 5bn francs of reparations after the 1871 conflict, a figure worth bearing in mind when considering later criticisms of the post-1918 Versailles settlement. In the first three years of the 1870s, as many ironworks, blast furnaces and machine-production factories were founded as had been created in the preceding 70 years.[52] A stock market boom dubbed the Gründer-zeit, with many fraudulent promotions linked to the railways, ended in a crash in 1873, when the US was suffering a similar financial crisis. But this was just a temporary setback. By the time of the First World War, average German incomes were four times higher, in real terms, than they had been in 1850.[53]

Most European countries followed the industrial path. Just before the First World War, Austria was producing almost 12% of Europe's coal and 8% of its iron.[54] The Swiss textile industry, specialising in linen, cotton and embroidery, was the second-largest in Europe, after Britain.[55] Without coal, it relied on water power. Italian industrialisation was confined to the north, but the country had built 19,000km of railways by 1913.[56]

Tsarist Russia, meanwhile, expanded even further in Asia over the same period,[57] although it took much longer to industrialise. The authorities feared that industrial expansion would lead to social change, and thus a threat to their rule, a presentiment that proved correct. However, not industrialising risked the loss of great-power status, so in the last two decades of the century the Russians forged ahead. Between 1880 and 1900, iron and steel output rose tenfold, while overall industrial output grew 5–6% a year between 1885 and 1900, and railway mileage doubled between 1890 and 1904.[58] The country benefited from its natural resources, producing around a third of the world's oil in 1900. Half the country's exports were in the form of grain and only 8% were manufactured goods.[59] Despite its growth, Russia was still well behind the rest of the continent: in 1913, the country's per capita GDP was only 60% of the European average.[60]

## The rise of Japan

The myth is that when Commodore Perry and his "black ships" from the US arrived in Tokyo's harbour in 1853, Japan's society was completely medieval and feudal. In fact, the country had many of the attributes of an early-modern European society. A higher proportion of the Japanese population in the 18th century lived in cities than did those in western Europe.[61] Agricultural productivity had been improving, thanks to irrigation, during the Tokugawa, or Edo, period (1603–1868), allowing the population to rise from 18.5m in 1600 to 32m in 1850. Japan had a greater population density than England in 1801, with 226 people per square mile compared with the latter's 166.[62] Real GDP per head was $1,072 in 1850, or 50% higher than China's at the same stage.[63]

Japanese craftsmen made clothing, furniture and metal items (including weapons) in industries organised in a fashion that resembled the old European guilds. Textiles were produced in a version of the putting-out system (where merchants supplied materials to domestic producers) but also in factories with up to 100 workers: the Mitsui house was reported to have employed over 1,000 people in its Tokyo shops at the end of the 18th century. The Japanese finance system used credit instruments such as bills of exchange and there was futures trading in commodities like grain.[64]

In the 15th and 16th centuries, Japan was a significant trading power, with its merchants travelling to Thailand and India.[65] However, Japan cut itself off from the rest of the world after 1641 for fear of the alien and disruptive influence of Christian missionaries.

For the next two centuries, there were only a couple of enclaves in which foreign trade could take place, and this exclusively with the Chinese and Dutch. Unlike the Chinese, the Japanese had their own supply of silver, so the need to export was less pressing. Their isolation meant that the military superiority of the Americans and the European powers came as a complete shock. On his second visit in 1854, Commander Perry insisted on a trade agreement with Japan and, in 1858, the government opened five ports to foreign traders and signed treaties with the French and the British.

At this point, the Japanese embarked on a rapid series of reforms. The powerful samurai or warrior class was abolished, with members receiving government bonds in compensation (the value of which was then eroded by inflation). The capital moved to Edo (renamed Tokyo), and the power of the emperor was boosted in 1868, events known as the Meiji restoration. A delegation journeyed to the US and Europe to study their societies. On its return, the Japanese adopted the Western calendar, metric weights, a new monetary system and joint-stock companies. Toshimichi Okubo, the finance minister, promoted road and railway building and set up state-run arms manufacturers, shipyards and textile mills.[66] The first Japanese railway opened in 1872 and expansion was so fast that 5,370 miles had been constructed by 1910.[67]

The textile industry was Japan's biggest success. Thanks to a combination of low costs and the rapid adoption of technology, Japan boosted its world share of the cotton textile market from 4% in 1877 to 36% in 1892.[68] Between 1870 and 1913, exports as a share of Japanese GDP went from virtually nothing to 7%.[69] Japan was a very quick adopter of electric power, and, by 1920, 52% of the power used in its manufacturing was electric, a higher proportion than in either the US or the UK.[70]

By the First World War, Japan had emerged as a very modern power, demonstrating its capabilities by defeating Russia in the war of 1904–05. Japan's GDP more than doubled between 1885 and 1914.[71] Some of the big modern conglomerates, such as Mitsubishi, emerged in this period; others, such as Mitsui and Sumitomo, diversified their operations. Already the outline of the country's post-1945 miracle economy could be seen.

## The dawn of the company

Early capitalists often operated on their own, or in small groups, with money borrowed from friends or families. But as the economy developed in the 19th century, this model was no longer sufficient. Joint ventures and partnerships had been used since ancient times. There was also a model for the corporation in the form of state-sponsored companies like the English and Dutch East India companies. But any system that required royal, or government, approval to establish each and every company was both cumbersome and open to abuse.

In the early 18th century there was a flurry of stock market speculation as new companies were set up, mainly to exploit Europe's colonial interests. The rapid inflation and implosion of these bubbles set back the cause of corporate creation for a century. In 1720, the British Parliament passed the Bubble Act, which forbade the creation of joint-stock companies without a royal charter. But the 19th century saw a breakthrough: the idea of a limited liability company. John Micklethwait and Adrian Wooldridge argue that the concept had three important aspects. A company was an "artificial person" that had the same ability to do business as a real person; it could issue shares to a wide range of investors; and those investors could have limited liability.

This last point was crucial. Few people would be willing to back a business venture, controlled by someone else, if their house and all their wealth were at risk of loss. But buy £1,000 of shares in a limited liability company and you can only lose a thousand pounds, while you could gain a lot more. By eliminating the risk of wider losses, the limited liability structure encouraged more people to invest in shares, thereby reducing the cost of capital, allowing more companies to be formed and boosting long-term economic growth. Capitalism, traditionally seen as a very individualist creed, only flourished when investors were able to band together.

The limited liability format was extremely useful for the building of the railways, which required a vast amount of capital and labour. In 1891, the Pennsylvania railway employed three times as many people as the combined US armed forces. Britain had a railway mania in the mid-1840s, when the creation of British companies still required an Act of Parliament; in 1846, 246 railway acts were passed in a single year.[72] Those who invested in railway shares at the peak did not get their money back until the end of the century.[73] That didn't stop investors in other markets from trying their luck. Railways comprised 60% of all issued shares on the New York Stock Exchange in 1898.

Once created, the limited liability company was widely adopted, but it was only in 1937 that an economist named Ronald Coase came up with a theory for why that was so. The key issue, he argued, was the complexity of the tasks involved. Some tasks are simple to organise – ordering a pair of horseshoes from a blacksmith, for example. But an entrepreneur might require the completion and the coordination of a wide range of different tasks in order to create a product. Arranging this via a set of transactions in the market would be too complex and expensive, and any contract to deliver such goods and services would need to cover a variety of contingencies. Hiring people and ordering them to do these various tasks is simpler and cheaper than doing so via the market. That is why firms exist.[74]

The limited liability company was such a good idea that the economist Tim Harford included it as one of the "fifty things that made the modern economy".[75] But it wasn't too long after the spread of the corporate structure before problems started to emerge. As already pointed out, large companies can benefit from economies of scale. By the same token, however, this buying power (and selling power), if sufficiently large, can distort markets.

Shortly after oil was discovered in Pennsylvania in 1859, John Rockefeller moved into the energy business. But rather than take the risk of drilling for oil in promising places, he focused on refining. Oil was shipped on the railways and Rockefeller negotiated lower freight rates, allowing him to undercut his competitors. He even got a cut when competitors transported goods. Many companies sold their businesses to Rockefeller, rather than compete with him, and by 1879, Standard Oil, his company, controlled 90% of the US refining market.[76]

Another industrialist, Andrew Carnegie, worked for the railways before setting up a business to supply iron rails. He opened a steel plant in the 1870s and, with the help of innovations such as overhead cranes and a relentless focus on costs, managed to dominate the industry.[77] In 1901, he sold his business to the banker J. P. Morgan as part of a massive merger that combined ten separate companies into US Steel; this was the first company to be valued at more than $1bn.[78] The group employed 250,000 people and accounted for two-thirds of the country's steel production.[79]

The capital requirements of these giant companies were much larger than a single family could supply, and so the founders had to sell shares to outside investors. This began the long process whereby management and ownership of the largest companies tended to be separated. In the modern economy, share ownership is widely dispersed. Of course, the rich still have a much bigger stake in the stock market than do the poor, but ordinary workers may well own "capital" in the form of an entitlement to a pension, or savings in a collective fund that they use to plan for long-term commitments, such as a child's wedding.

One of the issues with which modern economics grapples is the "principal–agent" problem, in which the interests of owners and intermediaries are imperfectly aligned. This can be true both of executives, who have an incentive to boost their salary and perks at the expense of the shareholders, and of fund managers, who have the incentive to pursue short-term returns to ensure that they retain clients.

In the late 19th century, however, the main worry was monopolies. The risk of monopolies remains that they will abuse their position in order to push up prices. Luckily, the late 19th century was an era when technological improvements were bringing prices rapidly down. The wholesale price of steel fell by 83.5% between 1867 and 1901, while the US domestic price of iron ore fell by half between 1890 and 1905.[80] The harm caused by monopolies was suffered more by rival companies than by consumers.

Many big conglomerates were organised in the form of trusts, which disguised the extent of corporate consolidation. The trusts aroused opposition from those who worried about their monopoly power and their influence over politicians. But efforts to curb them were ineffectual. Congress passed the Sherman Antitrust Act in 1890 but it was little used. When the Ohio Supreme Court ruled that Standard Oil was a monopoly, the company moved to New Jersey, which aimed to attract holding companies. By 1901, two-thirds of all US companies were based in the state.[81] Later on, Delaware succeeded in luring companies away with even more business-friendly rules. Delaware has maintained its appeal to this day, thanks to an approach that minimises taxes and regulations; as of 2016, more than 60% of Fortune 500 businesses were incorporated in the state.[82]

A fierce opponent of the trusts appeared in an unlikely form. Theodore Roosevelt was a member of the business-friendly Republican Party, but he still worried about "the vast individual and corporate fortunes, the vast combinations of capital which have marked the development of our industrial system", and warned that "the state, and if necessary the nation, has got to possess the right of supervision and control as regards the great corporations which are its creatures".[83] Soon after Roosevelt became president in 1901, he filed an anti-trust lawsuit against Northern Securities, a railway holding company, and in 1906, he started a case that eventually led to the break-up of Standard Oil.

Roosevelt also acted to control corporate excesses elsewhere, pushing through the Meat Inspection Act and the Pure Food and Drug Act in 1906 to improve conditions in the food industry.[84] The poor hygiene standards of the meatpacking industry, and the dangerous conditions faced by workers, had been exposed by Upton Sinclair in his novel *The Jungle* in 1904. Sinclair sent a copy of his book to the president, who had the abattoirs investigated and found that the conditions were as bad as the author described. By the time of the First World War, the corporate sector had emerged as a significant economic force. Businesses were becoming multinational, setting up factories and buying mines and plantations in other countries. The US was not the only country to see a trend towards monopoly. In Britain, a series of mergers saw the soap market dominated by Lever Brothers, the forerunner of Unilever. Germany had 275 cartels operating by 1900.[85]

By 1913, around $40bn–45bn, or one-third of global investment, was comprised of foreign direct investment, or FDI.[86] Shares in these companies were traded on stock markets and their rise and fall were beginning to be seen as a sign of economic confidence. The Dow Jones Industrial Average, probably the best-known (although not the best-designed)[87] indicator, was first published in 1896. Many of the original components of the average, such as the Distilling & Cattle

Feeding Company and US Leather, have ceased to exist in independent form, but General Electric survived as a Dow component all the way from 1907 to 2018, when it was replaced by Walgreens Boots Alliance. A mighty engineering firm displaced by a humble chemist.

## The second industrial revolution

Textiles, railways, coal, iron and steel – these are the sectors associated with the earliest stages of industrialisation. What has since been dubbed the "second industrial revolution" emerged in the second half of the 19th century. One element was the chemicals industry, led by Germany. But the two most significant changes were the development of the internal combustion engine and the use of electric power.

The biggest economic impact of these industries did not really emerge until much later. It took a while for manufacturers to understand how best to organise their factories to take advantage of electric power, and for household gadgets to be developed that ran on electricity; most people did not get fridges or TVs until after the Second World War. It also took a while before cars became affordable for most consumers. Mass transport was the first to take advantage of the new technology. In 1890, Britain still used 280,000 horses to pull buses and trams (trolley cars in the US).[88] But electricity started to replace horsepower from the 1880s onwards. By 1917, New York had closed its last horse-drawn line.

But the appearance of cars, electric street lighting and the first aeroplanes all added to the sense of a world in flux. There was a feeling that nations that failed to keep abreast of the latest inventions would become second-rate powers. That was illustrated by the naval arms race between Britain and Germany in the period 1906 to 1914. Britain prided itself on having the most powerful navy in the world; Germany sought to challenge its predominance. The new class of battleship, the dreadnought, equipped with heavy guns and powered by steam turbines, could blow all previous ships out of the water.[89] The destructive side of industrialisation – which helped produce the artillery, machine guns and barbed wire that caused so much death on the Western Front – was about to become apparent.

## Living standards

The year 1848 was marked by a series of revolutions across Europe. It saw Louis-Philippe, the French monarch, overthrown, and the fall of Metternich, the Austrian noble who had promoted the cause of absolute monarchy. These revolutions were driven by liberals who wanted constitutional government, and by independence movements that hoped to escape from the control of imperial monarchies.

The year also saw the publication of *The Communist Manifesto*, by Karl Marx and Frederick Engels. The tract began with the famous declaration "A spectre is haunting Europe – the spectre of communism", and decried the lot of the proletariat, or working classes, "as machinery obliterates all distinctions of labour, and nearly everywhere reduces wages to the same low level". The authors added that the labourer "instead of rising with the process of industry, sinks deeper and deeper below the conditions of existence of his own class. He becomes a pauper, and pauperism develops more rapidly than population and wealth."

At the time of the manifesto's writing, the working classes certainly did not seem to have gained much from industrialisation. It is estimated that output per British worker rose by 46% between 1780 and 1840, while wages (after adjusting for inflation) rose just 12%. Given the harsh working conditions in the early factories and the unsanitary state of the cities, this was a poor bargain indeed. But just as Marx was forming his theories, the situation started to change. In the 60 years from 1840 to 1900, British real wages outpaced output per worker, with the former jumping 123% and the latter 90%.[90]

The economic historian Robert Allen suggests that this pattern emerged because high profits in the first half of the 19th century boosted owners of capital at the expense of labour. Eventually, however, the owners of capital reinvested these profits, generating a jump in productivity that pushed up real wages.[91] Other factors could have been involved. Workers were able to emigrate to America and the British colonies where real wages were higher. Irish workers had acted as seasonal labourers on British farms. They emigrated in such numbers after the famine that real British wages headed upwards. And in the last three decades of the 19th century, cheap grain from the New World reduced food prices and boosted spending power.

Workers also benefited from the wider range of goods that were on offer, particularly in the form of cheap clothing. They could travel by cheap rail on their days off, and when they visited the big cities, walk on gas-lit streets. These were improvements in living standards that may not have shown up in the conventional statistics. What's more, many people who benefited from new technologies did not have to put up with factory work. The 1851 British census showed, for example, that while there were around 500,000 cotton workers, one million people worked in domestic service and 2 million on farms.[92] Half of all French workers were on the farm at the end of the 19th century.

Inequality did increase in the 19th century. The main reason seems to have been that a higher GDP meant that a small portion of the population could enjoy a higher standard of living without driving everyone else below the starvation point. The peak of inequality was reached in about 1867 in Britain and in the early 20th century in America; after those points, real wages grew more rapidly, allowing workers to catch up.[93] Eventually, most people benefited from economic growth.

### Trade unions

As industrialisation spread across the world, workers organised to fight for better pay and conditions. In Britain, trade union membership went from 674,000 members in 1887 to nearly 2 million in 1905; in France, membership rose from 139,000 in 1890 to 614,000 in 1902; and in Germany, figures increased from 95,000 members in 1887 to 887,000 by 1903.[94]

Clashes between labour and business could turn very violent. In 1892, Andrew Carnegie cut the wages of workers at his steel plant in Homestead, Pennsylvania. When the workers went on strike, they were locked out and replacements brought in. This led to a battle between the strikers and members of the Pinkerton detective agency, in which nine of the former and seven of the latter were killed. The governor sent in 8,000 members of the state militia and the strike collapsed.

Industrial unrest was common in Europe too. Some 400,000 French workers went on strike in 1906 to demand an 8-hour day;

and miners in Germany's Ruhr district took action regularly between 1905 and 1912. Britain saw the first national railway workers' stoppage in 1911 and the first national miners' strike in 1912.[95] Strikes in these industries could be particularly effective because the economy had become dependent upon them. Without coal to power the factories, or railways to transport their goods, other sectors would quickly grind to a halt. During the 1911 railway strike, Winston Churchill sent troops into Llanelli and six men died – an incident that many in the labour movement held against him for decades.

Female workers were treated even worse. The match girls at Britain's Bryant and May factory worked from 8am in winter and 6.30am in summer and continued until 6pm, with breaks of 30 minutes for breakfast and an hour for lunch. The work was done standing up and paid 4 shillings a week, but girls could be fined 3d for talking or going to the toilet without permission.[96] In 1911, 146 workers died (123 of them women) when the Triangle Shirtwaist factory in New York caught fire. The owners had locked the doors to the stairwells to prevent theft and unauthorised breaks.[97]

The growing militancy of unions across Europe worried governments, who feared that they might form the basis for a broader revolutionary movement. This may have encouraged some governments to take a more aggressive approach to foreign policy and to use patriotism as a way of distracting workers from their economic concerns. If that was the aim, then the irony was that the turmoil of the First World War led to a genuine revolution in Russia and the fall of monarchies elsewhere. But the broader question is why Marx's predictions of inevitable revolution did not come true.

The answer is that the benefits of industrialisation, for the majority of people, were sufficiently apparent by the late 19th century. Crucially, agricultural output kept pace with the rise in population so the factory workers did not starve. A survey of agricultural output across 25 countries shows that it doubled between 1870 and 1913.[98] Both Germany and France increased their use of machinery such as threshers and reapers in the late 19th century, while Russia managed to grow its grain production almost sixfold between the 1860s and 1914.[99]

Governments also offered welfare benefits to head off the threat of socialism and communism. Bismarck introduced health insurance, accident insurance and pensions to Germany in the 1880s; France brought in health insurance and childcare help in the 1890s and 1900s; and Britain offered pensions and unemployment insurance in the first decade of the 20th century.

In the second half of the 19th century, life expectancy also started to make significant gains. One reason was that scientists developed the germ theory of disease, and realised the terrible effects of insanitary conditions. It took time for these theories to be accepted. In 1847, Ignaz Semmelweis, a Hungarian obstetrician, correctly identified that puerperal fever was spread by doctors, and insisted that his colleagues wash their hands. But although the death rate of new mothers fell dramatically, his theory was not widely acknowledged. Semmelweis had a nervous breakdown and was beaten to death by guards in an insane asylum, never knowing that his ideas would become widely approved.[100]

In 1854, John Snow, a doctor who had written about cholera transmission, successfully traced an outbreak of the disease to a water pump in London: when the pump was taken out of service, cholera cases declined.[101] Between 1859 and 1870, a team led by Joseph Bazalgette created a network of sewers under London that stretched for 550 miles (885km) and connected to a network that was 13,000 miles (21,000km) in all. The scheme was rejected five times by Parliament and was only approved after the Great Stink of 1858, in which the curtains of the House of Commons were coated in lime to reduce the smell.[102] Sewerage systems began to be built in US cities in the late 1850s, and in Germany and France in the 1860s. The Frankfurt sewer system managed to cut the death rate from typhoid from 80 per 10,000 inhabitants in 1868 to ten in 1883.[103]

As well as getting healthier, workers were becoming more educated. In the first half of the 19th century, governments were beginning to introduce education for younger children. A few of America's north-eastern states had achieved universal enrolment by 1840, and by 1850, 61% of all white American children aged 5 to 14 attended school. The only place with a higher enrolment rate was Prussia, which had introduced schooling in response to early defeats in the Napoleonic Wars. It managed a 73% enrolment rate in 1850. France and England were around the 50% mark.[104]

Another significant social change was the emergence of the middle classes. In Norway, the proportion of the labour force working in professional occupations rose from 6% in 1815 to 22% in 1914. The number of clerks in England and Wales grew from 129,000 in 1871 to 461,000 in 1901.[105] As well as clerks, the new, more sophisticated, economy needed more lawyers and engineers.

These middle-class workers demanded the right to vote, and in Britain they got it via the Reform Acts of 1832 and 1867. From 1870, all adult males in Germany aged over 25 had the right to vote in Prussia, although the parliamentary system was rigged in favour of the aristocracy and the monarchy exercised effective control. Universal male suffrage was introduced in France in 1849, but restricted again under Napoleon III, before becoming properly established under the Third Republic after 1871. These voting extensions may well have been an attempt by elites to head off revolution, particularly given the events of 1848.[106]

The middle classes moved out of the inner cities and into the suburbs; they could afford the cost of commuting. And they were important customers of the retail empires that emerged in the second half of the 19th century. Department stores created display windows to lure customers into the shop. They had regular sales to boost business, and they offered conveniences such as escalators and elevators. The new stores were vast. In 1889, Bon Marché in Paris attracted 70,000 customers a day, during its sales, attracted by a perfume department with a silver fountain and a lace department, where Emile Zola observed that "mad desires were driving all the women crazy". [107]

In the US, in 1888, Richard Sears first decided to sell his watches and jewellery with the help of printed flyers. By 1894, he extended his range, offering goods such as clothing, musical instruments and bicycles, with slogans such as the "Cheapest Supply House on Earth".[108] The catalogue, sent through the mail at a cheap rate, reached households in the vast areas of the continent away from the coastal cities. Many people lived on farms a long way from any store that sold more than basic food or tools; the Sears catalogue offered them a glimpse of the wider world. In later years, Edgar Rice Burroughs, the creator of Tarzan, would write for the catalogue, while the artist Norman Rockwell designed the covers.[109]

This enthusiasm for material goods was widely noticed. Adam Smith had argued that consumption was the "sole end and purpose of all production" and, as noted before, the idea that people were motivated to work longer in order to afford new goods like tea or crockery was a perceived driver of the "industrious revolution" in the 17th and 18th centuries. But not everyone approved of this material-ism. In 1899 Thorstein Veblen published *The Theory of the Leisure Class*, in which he coined the term "conspicuous consumption".[110] Consumers bought goods to demonstrate their wealth and status, rather as a bower bird decorates its nest to attract a mate. The result is that some products are only worth having because of their exclu-siveness. So-called Veblen goods are those where an increase in price will push up demand.

There was always something snooty about the attitude of some commentators towards mass consumption. How dare the common people take pleasure from buying stuff? Indeed, it brings to mind the medieval sumptuary laws against buying clothes, which tried to prevent poorer people from wearing fabrics and colours that were favoured by the aristocracy.

One of the great benefits of industrialisation is that it enabled citizens to buy useful things at affordable prices. Frank Woolworth opened what he called "Woolworth's Great Five Cent Store" in Utica, New York, and, when that failed, tried again the following year in Lancaster, Pennsylvania. The key to success turned out to be offer-ing goods for five or ten cents (in stores nicknamed five-and-dimes), rather like the dollar and pound stores that operate today. The chain's success was such that, in 1912, it floated on the stock market with 596 stores in total, and in the following year, the Woolworth Building, the tallest in the world at the time, was opened in New York.[111] Wool-worth's formula, which a later storeowner would dub "Pile 'em high and sell 'em cheap", would have many imitators in the 20th century and, in the form of Amazon, the 21st.

Some of the world's great brands first emerged in this era. The leaves of the coca plant had long been chewed by South American people for the stimulatory effect of their key ingredient, cocaine. John Pemberton, an American pharmacist, was one of many people to try to create a drink linked to the coca leaf. He had the bright idea of combining coca with an extract from the kola nut, a stimulant used in Africa. The first version of Coca-Cola in 1886 contained traces of cocaine. After Pemberton's death, a man named Asa Candler masterminded the drink's success. By 1895, it was selling in every US state.[112]

The creation of a sugary drink was not a great leap forward for mankind. But people freely chose to drink and enjoy it. Coca-Cola is said to be the second-most understood word in the world after OK.

## The cycle

An agricultural economy was driven by the harvest, and the success and failure of crops could be explained as the result of "acts of God". But as the global economy became more commercial and industrial, a more distinct form of cycle, in the shape of boom and bust, began to emerge. There was pretty much one every decade from the 1830s onwards, with some being centred primarily in America and others in Europe. There are a number of potential explanations for these patterns. The first relates to business investment.[113] Building a factory and buying machinery requires a heavy initial outlay. It is a different calculation from hiring workers or buying raw materials; the workers can be laid off and the raw materials sold. Entrepreneurs will only tend to take the risk of fixed investment if they are sure there is a market for their goods. Naturally, then, entrepreneurs will tend to invest when the economy is booming and profits are high. In aggregate, this investment will give the boom more momentum, as more machines are ordered and workers hired.

Eventually, however, the market will become so crowded that profits start to fall as businesses compete on price to sell their goods. Costs will rise as businesses pay more to hire workers and buy raw materials. Faced with this deteriorating outlook, some businesses will postpone their investment plans, or lay off workers; some companies will go bust. In aggregate, this will reduce demand for goods and the cycle will go into reverse.

All this was dimly understood by most people at the time. But the price was paid by workers who were thrown out of work during the regular downturns, at a time when welfare assistance was minimal. To them, the workings of the cycle seemed arbitrary and cruel. It is little wonder that, in the aftermath of the First World War, workers began to demand more social protection.

But in the late 19th century, European workers had another way of avoiding economic hardship: to head to the New World.

# IMMIGRATION

## The island of lost souls

Take the tourist boat to Ellis Island, from the southern tip of Manhattan, and one of the highlights of the trip is a close view of the Statue of Liberty, with its inscription: "Give me, your tired, your poor, your huddled masses yearning to breathe free. The wretched refuse of your teeming shore. Send these, the homeless, the tempest-tossed to me, I lift my lamp beside the golden door."[1]

The same glorious sight greeted immigrants who arrived on the east coast of the US between 1892 and 1954, when Ellis Island was the first point of embarkation. Over 12 million immigrants passed through the site. After the first processing centre burned to the ground in 1897, the immigrants entered a vast castle-like Victorian building that is still there today. Once off the boat, their first port of call was the baggage hall, now filled with display cases about the global history of immigration. They could bring as much as they were able to carry; children often had a roly-poly walk as they were wearing all the clothes they possessed.

But the bags had to be abandoned in the hall as the new arrivals walked up an imposing staircase. Doug Treem, my guide for the day, explained that this was the first test. Doctors were watching them as they made the climb, looking for any sign of infirmity that might prevent them from supporting themselves. Around one in ten immigrants were pulled aside and marked PPC, for "potential public charge". The doctors were equipped with buttonhooks so they could lift up the immigrants' eyelids and look for trachoma, a bacterial infection that could lead to blindness. Some were sent to hospital, although nine in ten of those were accepted eventually.

Those who survived the medical test faced a legal inspector. Officials had a list of 31 questions, but the most important was "Who are you?" The individual's name was then checked against the ship's register; a sample register on display shows a lot of Mulligans, Kellys and Steins. My guide denied it but there are many stories of names being changed in the process. My wife's grandfather, Sally at birth, became Sol when he reached America. Immigrants were supposed to have $15 with them so that they could make a start in life; not an easy thing in the days before foreign exchange bureaux. The story is that some inspectors kept $15 with them so that they could hand it over to immigrants in order for them to pass the test, whereupon the money was handed back. All told, the rejection rate at Ellis Island was just 2%, half for medical and half for legal reasons.

If you passed the inspectors, you headed back down the stairs to collect your baggage. You could buy a ticket to anywhere in America. Around a third of those who passed through Ellis Island stayed in New York in one of the many enclaves for immigrants, like Germantown or Little Odessa. One arrival with a poor command of English mistakenly bought a ticket for Houston, Texas, rather than Houston Street in Manhattan. But he made it all the way south and became a successful tailor.

Another immigrant had an unusual tale. He had travelled in third class to hide from the authorities but claimed to have $40,000 in cash. In Russia, he had been the personal wigmaker and cosmetician of Tsar Nicholas II. Having been accepted into the country, he initially settled in Philadelphia before hitting on the bright idea of using his cosmetic skills in the movie industry. His name was Max Factor.

Since humans left Africa, they have been on the move. They moved to escape flood, or drought; they moved to find new lands to farm, or seas to fish; they moved to find new opportunities away from their clans or tribes; they moved to escape conquering armies and oppressive states; they moved unwillingly, in the case of the 10 to 12 million Africans subjected to the Atlantic slave trade; they moved as invaders, like the European colonial powers or the Mongol empire; and they moved, as was the case with most immigrants at Ellis Island, in search of a fresh start in a new world.

All humans are immigrants, or are descended from them, differing only in the date when we, or our ancestors, arrived at our current home. Over history, these flows have had enormous political and economic significance.

The terms "immigration" and "emigration" are tied up with the notion of the nation state, as are the paraphernalia of passports, visas, customs duties and border posts. In earlier history, it was both easier and more difficult to move. It was easier, in the sense that there was no bureaucracy to overcome or border checks to pass. But it was also more difficult. Travel by land and your speed was slow. Your resources in the form of wealth or food were limited to what you could carry. You faced the danger that others might steal what you had. Travel by boat and you were at risk from storms or the vagaries of wind and current.

So to the extent that people did move, they would often travel in groups. As mentioned in Chapter 1, this phenomenon played a part in the fall of the Roman empire. The problem began with the Huns, a group of people whose origins are not well established but which may have been in modern Kazakhstan.[2] As they moved west, the Huns seemed to have caused political turmoil among the tribes who lived between them and the Roman empire. This prompted a request for asylum in 376CE by two Gothic groups, the Tervingi and the Greuthungi, who arrived on the banks of the Danube. This was the start of a whole series of population movements over the next 35 years that seem to have destabilised and overwhelmed the western Roman empire, and led to the sack of Rome in 410CE. While the Romans tried their usual tactic of co-opting these tribes, the effort proved too much. Local landowners, who had previously owed their allegiance to the imperial centre, were forced to deal with the tribal hierarchy. The edifice of the empire, including its important economic links, gradually collapsed.[3]

The fall of the Roman empire is an example of the double-edged nature of imperial rule. It is tempting to see the Romans solely as colonial oppressors – the arrogant overlords portrayed in the French comic strip *Asterix the Gaul*. Ruthlessness and brutality are required to build an empire, but, as the historian Ian Morris points out, the disintegration of empires can be ruinous.[4] When a government fails to keep order, trade declines because banditry becomes more profitable than industry. Ronald Reagan famously said that the nine scariest words are "I'm from the government and I'm here to help"; on the contrary, Ian Morris says, the ten scariest words are "There is no government, and I'm here to kill you."

Migration in the form of invasion is such a common historical development that the descendants of the invaders can easily forget that it happened. English people talk proudly of their Anglo-Saxon roots, without dwelling too much on the fact that the Angles came from Schleswig-Holstein and the Saxons from Germany. The English language and English place names are a confusing mix of German, Viking and Norse words (and much else besides). The Rus people who created the Russian state came originally from Sweden.

As people spread, they bring with them their own cultures, and their own institutional structures. The British took political control of North America, and the Spanish and Portuguese conquered Central and South America. In the north of the continent, small farmers developed a property-owning democracy; in the Spanish and Portuguese areas, property was parcelled out to a few wealthy land-owners and democracy was slow to appear.[5] And in Europe, German peasants and miners moved eastwards in the 12th and 13th centuries, creating cities like Berlin and bringing their agricultural techniques with them.[6]

Smart imperialists realise the importance of encouraging trade within their borders, if only for the extra tax revenues it can create. Just as Roman invasions created a single trading area in western Europe, so the Islamic expansion of the seventh and eighth centuries created a trading area in the Middle East, North Africa and parts of Asia, and the Mongol attacks did the same for central Asia in the 13th and 14th centuries. Within the boundaries of these empires, trade could increase and people could prosper: why would a peasant care who sat on the throne hundreds, or thousands, of miles away as long as they were left alone to harvest their crop?

European colonisation of the Americas and parts of Asia and Africa created an enormous world market. Of course, this process involved terrible costs to the indigenous people of the countries they invaded, although this was true of most imperial expansions, including those of the Mongols.

## Forced migration

Migrants can arrive as conquerors but also as the conquered and dispossessed. Asians expelled from Uganda in 1972 by Idi Amin brought their business skills and work ethic to Britain.[7] Another highly successful group in economic terms were the Huguenots, a Protestant group expelled from France in 1685. About 200,000 fled the country, of whom 50,000 settled in England, and their expertise in silk-weaving boosted the British textile industry.[8] Sir John Houblon, the child of Huguenot refugees, was the first governor of the Bank of England.

There are of course less happy examples, including the expulsion of Jews from Spain in 1492 and of Moriscos (Muslims who had converted) in 1609; Stalin's forced deportations of a wide variety of ethnic groups to Siberia; the shift of Muslims from Greece and Christians from Turkey after the First World War; and the mass population movement that accompanied the partition of India and Pakistan. Quite apart from the human misery caused, such disruption had a significant economic impact, as businesses were abandoned and people were forced to leave behind their possessions as they fled to safety.

The worst case of forced migration was, of course, the slave trade. As has been noted elsewhere in this book, slavery in various forms existed from ancient times. Forced labour helped to build the pyramids of Egypt and the canals, and other irrigation systems, of China. The Romans and Greeks had large numbers of slaves, and owning slaves was a mark of wealth in China in the early 12th century.[9] The Muslim conquerors of Spain took slaves from the local population, and between 850 and 1000CE perhaps as many as 2.5 million Africans were shipped from south of the Horn of Africa, which was dubbed the "Cape of Slaves".[10] And Viking raiders made slaves from the peoples of eastern Europe. (This was so common that "Slav" became the basis of the word slave.)

The Atlantic slave trade was different in terms of its sheer scale; it was the industrialisation of brutality. From the start of the trade in the 1440s to its final abolition in the mid-19th century, around 12 million Africans may have been transported to the Americas. Such was their inhumane treatment on the ships that transported them that perhaps 1.5 million died en route. Each slave was given a space around 63 inches (1.6m) high and 52 inches (1.32m) wide. In these crowded conditions, sickness was inevitable. Around a third of the deaths on board were from dysentery, with smallpox the second-biggest killer.[11] In one notorious case, 132 sick slaves were thrown overboard to drown so that the owner could claim on the insurance.[12]

The Atlantic slave trade was driven by economics, not conquest. The European Christians who invaded Palestine in the course of the Crusades came across sugar cane (sugar beets were not cultivated until the 18th century),[13] and they took a taste for the crop back with them. The Islamic empire had spread sugar cultivation around the Mediterranean, including North Africa and Spain, and Europeans took over sugar planting as they reconquered some of these territories, initially using forced peasant labour. But a shortage of labour in the wake of the Black Death resulted in the growing use of slave labour, particularly on the islands of Crete and Cyprus.[14]

As the Portuguese started to explore the west coast of Africa in the first half of the 15th century, they discovered the islands of Madeira and the Azores. They also started to buy slaves from Africa, trading them for European goods such as textiles, glass from Venice, wine and sherry, and metal implements like knives and swords.[15] And they established sugar plantations on the island of Madeira, worked by slaves from the Canary Islands and Africa. Madeira experienced a phenomenal boom and bust, with sugar production rising from 280 tons in 1472 to 2,500 tons in 1506, before falling 90% by 1530. In the process, Madeira, whose name means island of wood, was almost completely deforested, since sugar production required massive amounts of energy.[16]

After the discovery of the Americas, the Portuguese first planted sugar cane in Brazil in 1516, and started to produce a commercial crop after 1550. At first they relied on indigenous workers, but there was a huge death rate from disease. So they focused instead on slaves from West Africa, where there was a rivalry between the kings of Congo and Ndongo (modern Angola) over who should be their main supplier.[17] For African leaders who handed over prisoners of war, or other unfortunates captured during raids, it was a highly lucrative business.

In the late 17th century, sugar production shifted to the Caribbean where Barbados, Guadeloupe, Jamaica and Haiti all became major centres. The crop was brought over by the Dutch (who had occupied part of Brazil) but the British and French quickly dominated the market. Sugar was known as "white gold" to the British colonists, such were the profits from the business, and slaves were used since the local population had been almost wiped out by disease and ill-treatment.

Work in the hot, humid conditions of the fields was bad enough; Europeans did not want to do it. Life was even worse in the sugar mills, where the cane had to be fed into the machinery so that it could be burned. A slave with a machete stood beside the machine-worker, ready to hack off a limb if it became trapped . One contemporary report stated: "If a Mill-feeder be catch'd by the finger, his whole body is drawn in, and is squees'd to pieces. If a Boyler gets any part into the scalding Sugar, it sticks like Glew, or Birdlime, and 'tis hard to save either Limb or Life."[18]

Although slavery had existed in many areas and in many cultures before this point, it was the combination of scale, brutality and harsh working conditions that marked out the Atlantic trade. The plantation owners generally wanted males for hard labour. By contrast, two-thirds of the Arabian slave trade (which also took people from Africa) comprised women and children.[19] Many of them were destined for domestic service, rather than the brutal conditions of a plantation or sugar mill. Islamic law said that slaves should be treated with justice and kindness, and liberating slaves was seen as a praiseworthy act. The Mamluk rulers of Egypt were soldier-slaves who had converted to Islam and been freed.[20] While some owners in America did free slaves from time to time, such freemen had little prospect of social advance.

The profitability of the Atlantic trade meant that, by the end of the 17th century, the Dutch, English, French and Portuguese all had forts and trading stations in West Africa, and were transporting 24,000 slaves a year.[21] In 1713, the British took over the *asiento*, or right to carry slaves to the Spanish colonies, under the Treaty of Utrecht. (The British got Gibraltar under the same deal.) The right was promptly sold to the South Sea company, the subject of the famous bubble of 1720.

By the 18th century, the classic pattern of the Atlantic triangle had developed. Europeans sailed to Africa and exchanged manufactured goods (usually textiles) for slaves. The slaves were then taken to America and swapped for raw materials like sugar and cotton. Those goods were then taken back to Europe. Most slaves were bought from local traders in Africa rather than captured by Europeans themselves.

Slavery was also practised by the colonists of what became the United States: in 1703, 42% of households in New York had slaves. But the biggest demand was in the southern states, in places where sugar, tobacco and cotton were farmed. Charles Mann suggests that malaria (brought over by infected Europeans) played a key role.[22] The dividing line between areas where malaria was endemic and where it was not roughly coincides with the Mason–Dixon line that divided slave from non-slave states. Europeans sickened quickly from malaria when working on the farms. So too did the local population, when the colonists enslaved them. But around 97% of the population of West and central Africa were immune to vivax malaria (the most frequent form of the disease). Alas, this genetic advantage proved a terrible curse.

All the same, slavery might have declined naturally in the US were it not for Eli Whitney's invention of the cotton gin, which removed the seeds from the raw fibre. This allowed American cotton exports to leap from 138,000 pounds in 1792 to 35m pounds by 1820 and significantly increased the demand for slave labour. The number of US slaves increased by a third between 1800 and 1810, and by another third in the following decade.[23]

The Europeans started to develop some moral qualms about the trade in the late 18th century. Two influences were at work: the Enlightenment, which emphasised the rights of men, and evangelical Christianity. After the French Revolution, the national assembly granted citizenship to black people in the colonies, although Napoleon restored slavery in 1802. The British, and the cities of Bristol and Liverpool in particular, profited heavily from the trade; in 1790, around a quarter of the ships visiting Liverpool were involved in the business.[24] But evangelical Christians became increasingly vocal in their opposition. One example was John Newton, who captained three slave ships and was an investor in the trade. It was during this period that he wrote the hymns "How Sweet the Name of Jesus Sounds" and "Amazing Grace".[25] But late in life he denounced the business in a pamphlet, *Thoughts Upon the Slave Trade*, and joined the abolitionist campaign led by William Wilberforce.

The campaign was successful in abolishing the international trade in 1807, whereupon the British navy started to intercept the trading ships of other nations. Nevertheless, around 500,000 slaves may have been shipped from Africa to the Americas in the 1820s; the British action may just have pushed up prices and profits for the remaining traders.

Not everyone in Africa was happy about the shift. In many areas of West Africa, such as Ghana and Nigeria, land was owned collectively, so slaves were a widespread form of personal wealth.[26] As well as being captured in battle, people could be enslaved for criminal offences or for failing to repay debts. Rather than being forced to take part in the slave trade, African rulers were willing participants. In the 17th century, Europeans actually sold 40,000 to 80,000 slaves to African traders in modern Ghana.[27] When the British cracked down in the 19th century, King Gezo of Dahomey complained that "The slave trade has been the ruling principle of my people. It is the source of their glory and wealth."[28]

Whether you view the British conversion to abolitionism as deeply cynical or morally commendable may depend on your nationality. It is worth noting that the institution of slavery was not abolished in the British empire until 1833. Compensation was paid to the owners and not to the slaves themselves. By 1840, as the trade was winding down, more than three times as many Africans had arrived in the Americas as had Europeans.[29] Slavery continued in the Americas, with Brazil the last to abolish the practice in 1888.

The effects of this abominable trade have been long-lasting. Even after abolition in the US, the rights of African Americans were officially restricted for the next 100 years. African countries were scarred by a business that involved violent raids on other tribes and the abduction of millions of young people. One study found a negative relationship between the number of slaves taken from a given country and its subsequent economic performance: "The African countries that are the poorest today are the ones from which the most slaves were taken."[30]

## Indentured labour

Slaves were not the only "unfree" labour to move to the New World, although they were the worst treated. In the 17th and 18th centuries, the cost of a passage to America was simply too high for poor people; in 1650, the price would have been the equivalent of five months' wages.[31] The alternative was to sign a contract, and, in return for free passage on the ship, emigrants would be required to work for a number of years, usually four to seven. At the end of this period, if they survived, they could become property owners; after all, the colonists had a limited population and lots of land. (The rights of the indigenous population to that land were ignored.) Around a third to a half of all European arrivals in the first century of colonisation arrived as indentured servants.[32]

In the 19th century a new version of the practice emerged, in the form of indentured labour from Asia, and in particular from India and China. More than 50 million Indians and Chinese emigrated to South-East Asia, Africa, Australia and the Americas.[33] Even at the time, this approach was seen as a substitute for slavery. As with the slave trade, the best interests of the workers were often neglected by those who carried or employed them. The boats that transported Chinese workers were known as "coffin ships", because of the number of those who died during the voyage – the mortality rate on ships carrying indentured workers was much higher than for other passengers travelling on the same routes.[34] When the workers arrived, conditions were poor; Indian labourers in Trinidad, for example, were confined to crowded barracks in insanitary surroundings. Many suffered from dysentery and cholera, as well as from malaria.[35] Half of imported workers in Cuba did not survive their term of indenture.[36]

These workers built the railways, shifted cargo in the docks, and worked in the mines. Like the slaves, they did the dirty and dangerous work that locals were reluctant to do. They also suffered some of the same punishments as slaves. Those who tried to run away before the end of their contracts, or were simply disrespectful towards their overseers, were beaten or placed in shackles.[37] It is true that the workers were paid a wage and that eventually (after eight or ten years) their contracts came to an end. Indian workers returning from Mauritius in the 1870s brought back cash equal to, on average, about four years of income.[38] However, not all were so lucky. In some cases, indentured labourers were obliged to sign a new contract with the same master or face deportation. The system may have been better than slavery, but in some cases that was not saying much.

Indentured labour changed the demographic pattern of many countries. People of Indian origin comprise more than half the population of Mauritius, almost half that of Fiji, and around a third of some Caribbean islands.[39] Mohandas Gandhi, the Indian civil rights campaigner, made a start fighting for the rights of his fellow citizens in South Africa. A Chinese diaspora settled in many South-East Asian nations, such as Singapore, becoming a very important part of the trading community, and providing links with other countries.

## The huddled masses

If you combine slaves with indentured servants and convicts, more than four-fifths of all immigrants to the New World by 1820 were not free. But from that point onwards, everything changed. In the following 60 years to 1880, more than four-fifths of the arrivals were free labour.[40] This was one of the great migrations in history. From an average of just under 13,000 a year in the 1820s, immigration to the US multiplied to an average of 275,000 in the 1850s. In the course of the 19th century, 60 million Europeans emigrated to other continents.[41]

Three factors seem to have driven the change. The first was that it became a lot cheaper to travel across the ocean thanks to the arrival of steamships. Passenger fares between Britain and New York fell by 71% between the early 1840s and the late 1850s.[42] This brought emigration within reach of low-paid workers, just as package holidays allowed European workers to holiday abroad from the 1970s onwards. The introduction of the railways also made it cheaper for potential migrants to make it from the European hinterland to the Atlantic or Mediterranean ports.

The second factor concerned wages. As these rose in the middle of the 19th century, workers found it easier to afford the transatlantic fare (or the fare to Australia). But even those higher wages were far below the income that workers could make in the New World; in 1846, American real wages were 89% higher than those in England.[43]

Pure economics was not the only factor that drove workers to make the trip. Desperation in the aftermath of the Great Famine of the 1840s sent many Irish people across the Atlantic; and persecution and prejudice caused Jews to flee the Russian empire in the late 19th century.

Another driver was more benign. A sudden improvement in life expectancy (down to better sanitation, food supply, etc.) meant that Europe had lots of young adults and, relatively speaking, little land. In contrast, the US, Canada, Argentina, Australia and other "new world" countries had lots of land and relatively few people. It made sense for people to move. The result was that the gap started to narrow. In the late 19th century, wages in Europe started to catch up with those in the US, while land prices in the New World soared.[44]

Over time, the origin of the immigrants shifted. At the start of the 19th century, Britain and Germany dominated. Later, there were flows from Scandinavia, Italy, the Austro-Hungarian empire, and then Russia, Spain and Portugal. The scale of the population shifts was amazing. In the first decade of the 20th century, 3% of the entire populations of Britain, Italy and Sweden emigrated; in Spain, it was 5% and in Portugal a remarkable 7%. The extent of immigration into Argentina that decade amounted to 43% of the existing population.[45]

Inevitably, there was a political reaction. In the 1850s, the US saw the sudden rise of the American Party, based on a secret society with an initiation rite and a password. Members swore to answer all questions with the phrase "I know nothing" and the group then became known as the Know Nothing party. It wanted a 21-year naturalisation period for immigrants and the banning of all Catholics from public office. At its peak, the party had more than 100 congressmen and eight governors, but it was split apart by the issue of slavery.[46]

Racism was even more prevalent than anti-Catholicism (which may, in any case, have been motivated by dislike of the Irish and Italian immigrants who were arriving in large numbers after 1850). The use of Chinese workers to build the transcontinental railroad caused unrest among workers who feared that their wages were being undercut, and inspired much Sinophobia; a riot in Los Angeles in 1871 killed 17 to 20 Chinese residents. In the face of trade union pressure, the US passed the Chinese Exclusion Act in 1882, preventing immigration of Chinese labourers. It was extended in 1892 and made permanent in 1902.[47] Other states settled by European colonists passed similar measures, such as the "White Australia" Act of 1901.

None of this did much to slow the flow of huddled masses from Europe that arrived at Ellis Island and elsewhere in the late 19th and early 20th centuries. The proportion of foreign-born people in the US reached 14.8% in 1890, and 14.7% in 1910. In that first decade of the 20th century, the foreign-born total rose by a then record 3.2m.[48]

All told, this was one of the greatest population movements in history. The peopling of North America created the world's largest economy, while the opening up of the plains and the South American pampas, combined with the development of steamships and refrigeration, transformed the global food supply.

## A sudden stop

Migration was sharply curtailed, for understandable reasons, during the First World War. European governments were eager to recruit young men into their armies rather than to see them head abroad. Travel across the Atlantic became a lot more dangerous as the British and German navies battled each other.

When the war ended, there was an immediate rush of refugees, as the new borders were redrawn; one of the biggest shifts came in 1923 as 1.6 million people were exchanged by Greece and Turkey. But the pre-war pattern of economic migration did not resume. US industry had been forced to manage without European migrants during the war years and had instead employed more women, as well as African Americans from the rural south. Between 1916 and 1970, around 6 million African Americans moved north to cities like Chicago and Detroit.[49]

By the 1920s, global migration was well below pre-war levels. The decline probably had many causes. The gap between wages in the US and Europe was not as large as it was before 1900, and after the Great Depression hit, the US was not such an attractive home for a job-seeker. It was an era of greater nationalism, in which suspicion of foreigners increased. Just as the trading links between nations were shut down in the 1930s, so was the movement of people.

Migration started to resume again after the Second World War. A labour shortage in West Germany meant that the country adopted a *Gastarbeiter* (guest worker) programme in the 1950s, with people from Turkey being the largest group. And the colonial powers, like France and Britain, had drafted soldiers and workers from their empires during the two world wars – the future Vietnamese leader Ho Chi Minh, for example, had worked in both Paris and London. As the empires were wound down after 1945, European settlers returned home and governments sometimes invited colonial citizens to join them, including the group that sailed to Britain on the *Windrush* from Jamaica. They were outnumbered by those moving from south Asia, particularly Punjab and Bengal. French migrants largely came from the North African states of Algeria, Morocco and Tunisia.[50]

US immigration policy remained fairly restrictive for nearly 50 years after the First World War. An act of 1921 limited the total number of migrants and established a quota system, designed to favour existing (ethnically European) immigrant groups. That was changed in 1965 when the Immigration and Nationality Act, part of the civil rights legislation that aimed to end discrimination between races,[51] agreed to accept immigrants from all nationalities on a roughly equal basis.

The Act had enormous long-term consequences. It led to "chain migration", as a worker, once established, sent for his relatives. The proportion of foreign-born citizens in the US, which reached a low of 4.7% in 1970, rose to 12.9% by 2010.[52] In 1960, seven of every eight migrants were from Europe;[53] by 2010, that proportion was down to just one in eight. More than half came from Mexico and the rest of Latin America, while 28% came from Asia.[54]

More generally, there was a big surge in international migration, although not on the scale of the late 19th century. In 1960, there were around 79 million people living outside their country of birth;[55] by

2017, the figure had risen to 258m.[56] The US was the most popular single destination, attracting around one million migrants a year in the first 15 years of the current millennium. But the big change from the Victorian era was that Europe had become a net importer rather than an exporter of people, with Spain, Germany, Italy and the UK attracting significant inflows.

In part, migrants were drawn by economic opportunities. Real wages have consistently been higher in the rich world than in Africa, for example. But economics was not the only factor; around 111 million people relocated within the developing world, with many driven abroad by conflicts in the Middle East and in Africa.

Almost 6 million people fled from Syria in the course of its civil war, with over half going to Turkey and more than a quarter ending up in the small, neighbouring countries of Lebanon and Jordan (which have a combined population of around 14.5 million).[57] But the media focused on the arrival of Syrian refugees in Europe and on the tragic flow of migrants in unseaworthy boats across the Mediter-ranean, where thousands drowned. The UN High Commissioner for Refugees estimated that the global total of displaced people in 2016 was 60 million, a post-1945 record.[58] In another repeat of the 19th and early 20th centuries, there was a political reaction: anti-immigrant parties did well in Europe and Donald Trump was elected president of the USA, in part because of his anti-immigration stance.

## The economic impact of migration

It might seem obvious that an influx of immigrants will be bad for the wages of indigenous workers. After all, an increase in supply will lead, other things being equal, to a fall in price. But other things *aren't* equal. If more workers mean lower wages, then how come the rise in the global population from 1 billion to 7 billion hasn't led to mass poverty? The obvious answer is that each worker is also a source of demand. Each immigrant spends the money they earn on local goods and services.

Economists talk about the "lump of labour" fallacy; a belief that there is only a certain amount of work to do. The fallacy has been used to argue that women should stay out of the workforce to leave more jobs for men, and that older workers should retire early to create jobs for the young.

Immigration may have an impact on the real wages of unskilled labour. A study by Claudia Goldin, an economics professor at Harvard, on the effect of US immigration in the late 19th and early 20th centuries found that a one percentage point increase in the foreign-born share of the population may have reduced wages by 1–1.5%.[59] The influx may also have persuaded workers in the eastern US to move to the Midwest and the West Coast.

However, in Britain, which experienced a surge in immigration after 2004 because of the entry of new countries into the EU, studies have failed to find any significant link between migration and changes in employment for natives, either in general or for specific groups, such as the young. There may have been a small downward impact on the wages of unskilled workers in services; this impact was around 1% in total over the course of a decade. Higher immigration levels were not associated, at the local level, with an increase in health service waiting times, nor did the achievement levels of native English-speaking schoolchildren suffer.[60] Furthermore, people who travel across the world to relocate often have unusual drive and initiative. A survey of the so-called "unicorns" – American businesses that were valued at more than $1bn but were not yet quoted on the stock market – found that more than half were founded by one or more immigrants.[61]

For the global economy as a whole, there is little doubt that migration is a great benefit. Workers in a poor country can be far more productive when they move to a rich one: they have better tools and benefit from better institutions, which ensure that they are rewarded for their labour. It is also much easier to move labour from one nation to another than it is to create better institutions in a struggling country. A world with completely free movement of labour would, one study estimated, be $78trn richer, an average gain of $10,000 per head.[62] Politics makes this impossible; indeed, even the politicians who argue most vigorously for free markets in capital and goods are rarely willing to advocate the same liberty for people.

# WORLD WARS AND
# DEPRESSION: 1914–1945

It is hard to think of a bleaker period of modern history than the three decades from 1914 to 1945. Perhaps as many as 19 million people died in the course of the First World War, and around 60 million in the second, including those who suffered from war-related disease and famine. In between the two conflicts occurred the worst economic setback in history – the Great Depression.

This was an era that rejected globalisation in favour of national-ism. Exports were 14% of global GDP in 1913, just under 12% in 1929, but dropped to 5% in 1935. They did not recover to pre-Depression levels till 1974.[1] In real terms, world trade was stagnant between 1914 and 1944.[2] As well as goods, capital and people moved less freely. Foreign direct investment as a proportion of world output dropped from 9% in 1913 to 4.4% in 1960.[3] America turned its back on immi-gration, with strict quotas that excluded Asians.

There are many competing theories about the outbreak of the First World War, with blame for the conflict being attributed to Britain, Germany, France and Russia, or to more general causes such as imperialism. The most convincing explanations revolve around the idea of cock-up, rather than conspiracy. Each of the powers took a strong diplomatic position in the hope that it would prompt the others to back down. A combination of overconfidence and pride meant that the powers were "sleepwalkers" heading to war.[4]

Europe's leaders may have been deceived by the speedy outcomes to mid-19th century wars between Prussia and Austria, and Prussia and France. The appropriate precedent, however, was the US Civil War, which dragged on for four years despite the economic and military advantages enjoyed by the northern side.

Stock markets are supposed to be guided by the "wisdom of crowds", as investors use their judgement to assess the outlook. But as the historian Niall Ferguson has pointed out, the markets barely reacted to the assassination of the Austrian Archduke Franz Ferdinand on June 28th 1914 – the event that sparked the drive to war. It was not until July 21st that investors began to respond, as the Austrians made threatening noises towards Serbia, whose agents were deemed to be behind the assassination. By July 27th, the Austrian markets had to close; they were quickly followed by others, with London and New York shutting on August 1st.[5]

If the war was a capitalist plot, it was a very odd one. Trade and financial markets were immediately disrupted. In 1909, Norman Angell had published *The Great Illusion*, a book that argued that the cost of war would be too great for European countries to undertake. He was right about the cost but they did it anyway. The Rothschild family had banking interests across Europe and strived hard to prevent war; they received a dose of anti-Semitic abuse for their pains. Most German businessmen and bankers advised against war,[6] while more than half of Russian overseas debt was in the hands of German creditors.[7] Had the term "globalist" been around in 1914, it would have been thrown in their faces. Arms manufacturers, no doubt, were happy about the prospect of war, but they were only a small part of industry in 1914.

The politicians who were in charge of the major powers tended to be those drawn from the aristocracy, or upper middle classes. They were motivated more by issues of prestige and power projection than they were by economics. Indeed, had they realised the extent to which taxes would have to rise to finance their war they would have been horrified. The state became much larger in the course of the 1914–18 war and never retreated to its previous level.

The conflict led to much more government intervention in the private sector than before. British government spending increased from 10% of GDP to 70% at its peak, and even the US, which entered the war late, pushed up spending from less than 2% of GDP in 1916 to 25%.[8] The US abandoned its free-market approach, setting up, in 1917, the War Industries Board, which had the power to set production quotas and allocate raw materials.

Stricter planning was forced on the Central Powers of Austria-Hungary and Germany, which faced a war on two fronts. In 1916, under the Hindenburg programme, Germany's generals set munition targets, offering to pay for the costs of production and guaranteeing industrialists a fixed rate of profit. Germany faced a severe problem over food supplies. A naval blockade by Britain cut Germany's dairy imports by 80% and meat imports by around 90% between 1916 and 1918. But nitrogen, needed for fertiliser, was diverted to making munitions, while draught horses were sent to the front. In 1915, free trade in grain and flour was prohibited and bread rationing was introduced. In 1916, rationing was extended to a wide range of other foods.[9] By the end of the war, Germans were being forced to eat a kind of bread called K-Brot, containing potatoes, oats, barley and even straw.[10]

Economics may have decided the conflict. The Western Allies (France, Britain and Russia) began the war with greater economic resources than their opponents in Germany and Austria-Hungary, and had the enormous bonus of US help. They easily out-produced the Central Powers in terms of machine guns and ammunition.[11]

For three great royal houses, the war brought not glory but the end of their rule. A Habsburg had been Holy Roman Emperor as far back as 1273, and the dynasty had held the office continuously from the 15th century onwards. As rulers of Austria-Hungary, the Habsburgs oversaw the second-largest state in Europe. Austria-Hungary dissolved in 1918. The house of Romanov had ruled Russia, the largest country in Europe, ever since 1613. The last tsar was overthrown in 1917 and then executed, along with his family. The Hohenzollern dynasty had been kings of Prussia since 1701, and then emperors of Germany from 1871. In 1918, Kaiser Wilhelm II abdicated and fled to the Netherlands.

The scale of the conflict was massive. Around 65 million people served on the two sides of the war,[12] while 1.5bn artillery shells were fired during the conflict,[13] and the British alone possessed 5,000 merchant ships carrying more than 13m tons of supplies.[14] The great manufacturing ingenuity that had been displayed in the 19th century was now turned to the creation of instruments of death – cannons, rifles, bombs, bullets and poison gas. It proved hideously effective.

The financial as well as the human costs were enormous. Germany, Britain and France spent more than $100bn in the course of the conflict, with their collective national debts rising by $70bn. The British national debt, held down during the Victorian era by a rigorous approach to fiscal rectitude, rose 11-fold.[15]

Britain ran up these debts despite a big increase in the tax burden. The country was heavily dependent on supplies from over-seas, particularly the US. To help pay the bills, Britain liquidated around a quarter of its pre-war holdings of foreign assets. France and Germany financed near all their wartime expenditure via borrowing, confident that, in the case of victory, they could recoup the cost from the defeated powers.

The gold standard was suspended for the duration of the war. The ability to exchange your banknotes for gold coins at the Bank of England disappeared, never to return. That allowed govern-ments to resort to the printing press. Notes and coins in circulation almost doubled in Britain, rose nearly fivefold in France, and 12-fold in Russia. Inevitably, this led to rapid inflation: prices doubled in France and Britain, trebled in Germany, and rose more than 11-fold in Austria-Hungary.[16]

Some of the economic damage was limited by government action. The US economy was the biggest beneficiary of the conflict, as it was able to supply its European allies. It was in recession at the start of the war but started a boom that pushed unemployment down from 7.9% in 1914 to 1.4% in 1918. With many able-bodied men in uniform, there was huge demand for labour. The German unemploy-ment rate was down to 0.8% by early 1918, for example.

Many women joined the workforce for the first time. In Germany, female employment rose 45%.[17] In Britain, the labour force partici-pation rate among women rose from 24% in 1914 to 37% in 1918, meaning that 2 million joined the workforce. In 1917, around 80% of the country's munitions were made by women, who also worked as conductors on buses and trams, while another 260,000 joined the "land army" to work on farms.[18] Their efforts were rewarded in 1918 when those over 30 were granted the vote.[19]

As if the population of Europe had not suffered enough, an outbreak of influenza, dubbed "Spanish flu", swept the continent in 1918. (The Spanish, a neutral country with fewer press restrictions, were just the first to report it.). At least 50 million and possibly as many as 100 million people died, many times the military casualty rate. The disease spread quickly among troops, packed together as they were in the trenches, and when they went home on leave, they took it with them. Food shortages probably made people more susceptible.[20]

When the war finally ended, the global economy had been transformed. The European powers were devastated by the loss of manpower and, in France and Belgium, the destruction of capital. Russia was involved in a civil war and had effectively withdrawn from the global economy. American economic dominance was effectively unopposed.[21]

## A squandered peace

Woodrow Wilson, the wartime president of America, had set out a 14-point programme for peace. This included such concepts as freedom of the seas and the removal of the economic barriers to trade. When he arrived in France for the Versailles peace conference in 1919, he was hailed as a hero by adoring crowds. But Wilson's idealism came up against two obstacles. First, there was the determination of the victorious powers, France and Britain, to get compensation for their losses and to ensure that Germany could not threaten them again. Second, lasting peace required a commitment by America to stay involved in European affairs. But while Wilson may have desired that, the American public did not. Wilson's attempts to get Congress to ratify US membership of the League of Nations (the precursor to the United Nations) ended in failure. The effort destroyed his health and he was replaced by a Republican, Warren Harding, who campaigned on a policy of isolationism.

The Versailles conference was a failure. A sense that the treaty was unjust, because it took away German territory and landed the country with the blame for starting the war, fuelled the rise of Adolf

Hitler. Europe was back at war by 1939. In his book *The Economic Consequences of the Peace*, John Maynard Keynes attacked the idea of reparations. The economies of the Allied powers, he argued, would be best served by a strong Germany, not a weak one. His warning was ignored, because feelings were too high. Germany had, after all, insisted on reparations from France after 1871 (see Chapter 8) and would have demanded reparations again from France had it been victorious in 1918.

Shortly after the war, much of the developed world suffered a sharp deflationary recession. In America, this lasted from January 1920 to July 1921, according to the National Bureau for Economic Research.[22] Output fell by around 9% and unemployment reached 19%.[23] This was in response to tight monetary policy, as central banks, led by the Federal Reserve, tried to bring an end to wartime inflation. In this they were far too successful: consumer prices fell by 13–18% and wholesale prices by as much as 36%. Fiscal policy was tightened as well, as governments tried to bring down deficits that had soared due to wartime spending. In Britain, government spending fell from £2.7bn in 1917–18 to around £1bn in 1920–21.[24]

Eventually, the Fed lowered rates and the US economy bounced back quickly. But while the US may have experienced the "roaring Twenties", things were not so great elsewhere. In June 1921, British unemployment passed 2 million and did not drop below one million before the Second World War.[25] Industrial relations were poor. The mines, under public ownership during the war, were handed back to the private sector. In 1926, the owners demanded lower wages and longer hours. When the miners refused, they were locked out of the pits. A general strike was called. Around 1.7 million workers took part but the mood was scarcely revolutionary; police and strikers even organised games of football. After nine days, the strike was called off by all bar the miners, who held out for another six months. In the end, they were forced to accept the owners' terms.

The inter-war performance of the British economy has been given a revisionist polish by recent historians.[26] Growth in output per worker between 1913 and 1950 (a period chosen to avoid wartime distortions) may have been worse than it was in the US or Canada, but it was better than that of France, Germany, Italy and the Netherlands.[27]

A poor performance in the 1920s was offset by a better one, in relative terms, during the 1930s. But the British faced much more competition in export markets, particularly from America, than they did before 1914. The industries that had driven Britain's 19th-century rise – textiles, iron and steel, shipbuilding – were also under threat from overseas producers. In productivity terms, Britain was a long way behind the US.

Germany's immediate post-war history was marred not just by the humiliation of Versailles but by attempted revolution on the left and paramilitary thuggery on the right. The Social Democrats who signed the Versailles Treaty were never forgiven by the conservative forces, which included many former soldiers. And the new Weimar Republic faced a seemingly impossible task. The German economy had been weakened by war and by loss of territory. In 1919, both industrial production and grain output were less than half pre-war levels.[28] With these reduced resources, the government simultaneously tried to provide welfare measures to demobbed soldiers and to pay its reparations bill. The temptation was to use the printing press to pay the bills. Bad move: inflation soared and the currency declined. Before the war, the US dollar was worth 4 marks; by the end of 1919, it was worth 47, and by November 1921, 363.[29]

Thus began the famous hyperinflation, an event that still affects German economic attitudes today. At its height, workers needed wheelbarrows and shopping baskets to carry their wages; prices rose so fast that the bill at the end of a meal could be far greater than that advertised at the start. On a single day in November 1923, the price of a loaf of bread rose from 20 billion marks to 140 billion.[30] By that stage, it took 233 billion marks to equal a dollar. The economic impact was to wipe out the savings of the middle classes and, by and large, to erode the wage premium earned by skilled workers. These two embittered groups were to prove important sources of support for Hitler. Poland, Hungary and Austria suffered similar inflationary problems.

Hyperinflation had occurred before – in the Confederacy during the Civil War, for example. And it would occur again in the immediate aftermath of the Second World War, and in modern developing countries such as Zimbabwe and Venezuela. Eventually the debased currency becomes literally not worth the paper it is written on. People turn to alternative currencies, such as the dollar.

In Germany, stabilisation was achieved with the help of a new currency, the Reichsmark, and through an international agreement known as the Dawes Plan. This cut back Germany's debt service obligations, while a foreign loan was organised, with the US providing half the money.[31] This set the pattern for the rest of the decade: Germany was kept afloat with the help of American loans, which, in turn, helped to keep reparation payments flowing. For a while, the German situation looked hopeful, and in the 1928 elections, Hitler's Nazi party received just 2.6% of the vote.

France emerged from the war with substantial losses of both manpower and money. In the early 1920s, the costs of reconstruction were funded by government borrowing and the French franc steadily depreciated. In 1925 and 1926, it fell as far as 41 to the dollar, making it worth just over 2 US cents.[32] It had been worth 5 to the dollar, or 20 US cents, in 1913.[33] There was an inevitable flight of capital overseas, as French investors anticipated the imposition of higher taxes to reduce the deficit.

In 1926, the crisis was resolved as Raymond Poincaré, the prime minister, cut the deficit without resorting to a wealth tax. The franc stabilised at 25/$ and France started to attract large quantities of gold. The success of these "orthodox" policies made France very committed to the gold standard, which it rejoined in 1928.

In contrast, America seemed to have a trouble-free 1920s. Between 1921 and 1929, it managed an average real growth rate of 5% a year. This was a period when many households started to get electricity and acquire household goods like irons, vacuum cleaners, radios and, of course, cars. Real wages for industrial workers rose by nearly 25% in the 1920s.[34]

All this was achieved without any inflationary pressures. Thanks to a burst of deflation at the start of the decade, the US price level at the end of 1928 was well below its level at the start of 1920, and on a par with the level at the end of 1921.[35] There was thus little need for the Federal Reserve, the central bank established in 1913, to increase interest rates or otherwise tighten credit conditions. A combination of easy credit and a roaring economy led to a stock market boom:

trading volumes on the New York Stock Exchange rose from 1.7m shares a day in 1925 to 4.1m in 1929. Some investors could acquire shares by paying just 10% of the purchase price, with the remaining 90% being borrowed. The amount of money lent by stockbrokers rose from $1bn at the start of the decade to $8.5bn at the 1929 peak.[36]

Borrowing money to buy shares seemed like a no-brainer when the market was going up. The Dow Jones Industrial Average was 97.8 at the start of 1924, and it began 1929 at 307.95: share prices had trebled in five years.[37] The peak of 381 was reached on September 3rd 1929. The corporate sector was doing well in the 1920s, but not that well. The best long-term valuation measure for shares is the cyclically adjusted price-earnings ratio, which compares the share price with the profits earned by companies, averaging them over ten years to allow for the effect of the economic cycle. From a ratio of 6 at the start of 1920, this measure climbed to 32.6 in September 1929. In other words, if you bought a portfolio of shares, and each company paid out all of its profits to investors, it would take nearly 33 years to get your money back. Such a ratio assumed a lot of optimism about profits growth; it would not be surpassed until the dotcom boom in the 1990s.[38]

The stock market was not the only source of speculation in 1920s America. There was a land boom in Florida, again financed on margin; investors could make a non-refundable down payment with the rest due in 30 days.[39] Many speculators had no intention of paying the rest of the money. They hoped to sell their stake to someone else before the 30 days were up – the so-called "greater fool" theory. The bubble burst by 1926 and the fallout was largely local. But the lesson that easy credit often served to inflate asset prices would need to be learned again and again.

### The Soviet alternative

Russia had entered the First World War to protect its Slavic ally, Serbia. Its potential power had so worried the Germans that they devised a plan to outflank the French forces and achieve a quick victory in the west, before turning back to the east. They needn't have worried so much. As it turned out, the Russian government under Tsar Nicholas II was hopelessly inefficient at prosecuting the war, despite its vast manpower. Worse still, the tsar failed to ensure that enough bread was delivered to the towns. As the war dragged on, with little hope of it ending, strikes became widespread. After the army garrison in Petrograd joined the strike,[40] the tsar abdicated in March 1917.

A provisional government was formed, but it made the fateful mistake of continuing the war. Soldiers were deserting in their droves, many of them returning to their farms, where land was being seized from the old aristocracy. The economic crisis deteriorated, with urban prices more than doubling between March and October 1917.[41] The provisional government proved to be a leadership without followers and the Bolsheviks were able to seize power with relative ease in November.[42]

In his eagerness to consolidate power, Lenin, the leader of the Bolsheviks, accepted a harsh peace at the hands of the Germans. Under the Treaty of Brest-Litovsk in March 1918, Russia lost territory that supplied half its grain, coal and iron. A civil war with anti-communist forces followed, in which diseases and malnutrition killed 8 million people. By 1921, even after some of the territory lost to the Germans had been restored, Russian factory output was an eighth of its pre-war level.

The Bolsheviks implemented their programme by nationalising industry, banking and transport.[43] But in 1921, in the face of a naval mutiny, Lenin retreated from communist purity and agreed to a "new economic plan". Peasants were allowed to keep some of their produce and sell it in the market. They could also hire their own labour. Private shops could operate and some light industry was left in private hands. A revival in agricultural production and in the overall economy duly followed.

But Lenin died in 1924 and the new economic policy was eventually abandoned by his successor, Josef Stalin, who favoured rapid industrialisation and the collectivisation of agriculture. The paranoid Stalin was convinced that rich peasants, termed kulaks, were holding back grain supplies. In 1930, he drew up a plan to send 60,000 kulaks to labour camps and move another 150,000 into exile in places like Siberia and Kazakhstan.[44] Anyone who refused to take part in farm collectivisation could be denounced by their neighbours. In the early

1930s, the seizure of grain from Ukraine, and a policy that stopped farmers from moving in search of food, resulted in some 4 million to 5 million deaths, or 13% of Ukraine's population, in an episode known as the "Holodomor".[45] Farm output dropped by a quarter between 1929 and 1932 and many peasants slaughtered their livestock rather than surrender the animals to the government.[46] Not until the mid-1950s did agricultural output consistently regain its pre-1914 levels.[47]

The Soviet Union's industrialisation plan was much more successful. The first five-year plan set unrealistic goals, which were, in some cases, not reached until 1960. But industrial output rose 170% between 1928 and 1940. People were forced off the farms and into manufacturing: the non-agricultural workforce rose 190% over the same period.[48] The Soviet focus was on heavy industry, iron, steel, concrete and tractors. Investment rose from 8% of GDP in 1928 to 19% in 1939. One of the reasons that the country triumphed over Germany in the Second World War was that its industry was able to produce vast quantities of tanks and ammunition, despite the loss of territory.

Many left-wing observers were impressed by Russia's industrial growth and contrasted the Soviet Union favourably with the depression-hit west. But Russia might well have grown fast if the revolution had never occurred. One study compared Stalin's record with a counterfactual, which assumed that the pre-1913 trends in tsarist Russia had continued. It found that the loss of welfare (as measured by aggregate consumption) between 1928 and 1940 was around 24%.[49] And that figure does not account for the human cost of the gulags.

## The gold standard revived

The war had brought a lot of economic and financial, as well as physical, destruction. So policymakers had a hankering to return to pre-war conditions. In particular, after the surge in wartime inflation, they wished to see a return to the gold standard. The rapid rise and fall of prices in the immediate aftermath of the war was unsettling, and suggested that floating exchange rates were a cause of instability. Furthermore, a fixed exchange rate was perceived to be a good form of discipline, stopping governments from cheating creditors by repaying them in depreciated currency. In Britain, many believed that the decision to return to the gold standard after the Napoleonic Wars had been the key to the country's 19th-century success.

But a return to the gold standard was deeply problematic. The pre-war standard worked because there was rough parity between the big economies of America, Britain and Germany (with France a bit behind) and a willingness to cooperate to keep the system running. But the spirit of cooperation was damaged by the disputes over reparations and wartime debts. Gold bullion was now unequally distributed. The three big European economies, Britain, France and Germany, had half their pre-war level of reserves while, by 1923, the US had three times as much gold reserves as the three of them put together.[50]

Since the European central banks lacked gold, they held the currency of other countries instead (some dubbed the system the "gold exchange standard"). By the end of 1928, foreign exchange was 24.5% of total reserves, compared with 15.9% before the war.[51] This created a potential source of instability. If one country left the gold standard, their currency would fall, and that would cut the value of other countries' reserves. Faced with this threat, the temptation was to sell the currency of any country that looked in trouble, increasing the risk of damaging speculation.

The second problem was that war had massively pushed up the debts and price levels of many countries. Returning to the pre-war exchange rate was like binge eating for six months and then trying to squeeze back into your sports kit. Britain, in particular, was obsessed with returning to the pre-war exchange rate against the dollar. But its competitive position vis-à-vis the US economy had deteriorated significantly since 1913. Keynes, in another of his polemics, wrote that Britain's decision to rejoin the gold standard in 1925 at a rate that was 10% too high was the equivalent of a 10% cut in wages.[52]

The pre-war gold system had also operated with a fair degree of bluff. Britain's gold reserves were quite thin considering its prominent position in international trade. At times of crisis, such as the Barings collapse of 1890 (see Chapter 8), the Bank of England depended on help from others. International cooperation was needed to keep the system going.

After the war, that was harder to achieve. The Federal Reserve was now the world's most important central bank, given the strength of the US economy. But American politics was isolationist and the Fed had to be careful about appearing to put the interests of other nations ahead of those of the US. In 1927, the Fed cut interest rates by half a point in order to ease pressure on the pound. That gave an extra fillip to the stock market, and marked the start of its steepest climb. It would double in the next two years.

Cooperation became more difficult after that, especially as Ben Strong, the head of the New York Fed and a close ally of the Bank of England, became ill and died in 1928. The seeds of the Depression may well have been sown that year. Worried about stock market speculation, the Fed pushed up interest rates four times from 3.5% to 6% and drained liquidity from the system. The French acquired $300m of gold, or 3% of global reserves, as they came back on the standard.[53]

At the time, Keynes warned in a letter that "I cannot help feeling that the risk just now is all on the side of a business depression. If too prolonged an attempt is made to check the speculative position by dear money, it may very well be that the dear money, by checking new investments, will bring about a general business depression."[54] (He can't be given too much credit for successful forecasting, as he lost a lot of money in the 1929 crash.)

The initial impact of restrictive US policy was felt overseas. Germany had been dependent on American lending, but that dried up as the money stayed at home, attracted by higher rates and booming share prices. German unemployment rose from 1.3 million in January 1928 to 1.9 million by the start of the following year and was 2.5 million in the spring.[55] With British gold reserves dwindling, the Bank of England raised rates to 5.5% in February 1929, even though unemployment was 1.5 million. Faced with a similar problem, the German central bank pushed rates up to 7.5%. This was the logic of the gold standard. Maintaining the exchange rate took priority over the health of the economy.

Under the Dawes Plan, Germany was set to step up its reparations payments in 1929, which would reach the equivalent of 5% of GDP. A conference early that year almost broke down before Germany agreed to make payments of $500m a year, or around 4%

of GDP, for 36 years, with a further set of payments that would only come to an end in 1987.[56] The concept of such an extended commitment was absurd. It was only a few months before creditors agreed to a temporary cut in payments and even then a loan was needed to allow Germany to pay its reparations in 1930.

## The crash and after

Tighter credit put the brakes on the global economy. American goods exports declined after March 1929 and US industrial production peaked in July.[57] The US recession actually started in August 1929, according to the National Bureau of Economic Research.[58] The stock market's high for the cycle occurred shortly after, on September 3rd. In that same month, the business empire of the British financier Clarence Hatry collapsed (he was sentenced to 14 years for fraud), and, in the resulting panic, some British investors may have cut their holdings in the US market in order to cover their losses.[59]

The big sell-off on Wall Street came in late October. The US market fell 4.6% on Wednesday, October 23rd, and the next day, "Black Thursday" as it was dubbed, there was record trading, with the market falling 11% at one stage. Even bigger declines occurred on the following Monday and Tuesday, pushing the Dow to 230, or 40% below its early September high.[60] Those people who had bought stocks on margin were desperately selling stocks to cut their losses.

The contribution of the Wall Street crash to the Great Depression is still debatable. The event was so dramatic that it may have been a case of the *post hoc ergo propter hoc* fallacy; just because the crash came first, does not mean that it caused the Depression.[61] There did seem to be an immediate economic impact, with industrial production falling in both October and November. But the Fed did its best to help, cutting rates and injecting liquidity into the banking system. By April 1930, no leading company or bank had failed, and share prices were trading around their level at the beginning of 1929.[62]

The biggest problem may not have been the stock market but a resurgence of nationalism. Even before Wall Street's collapse the US Congress was debating whether to increase tariffs. The Smoot–Hawley Tariff worked its way through Congress in the first half of 1930, despite a letter from 1,028 economists opposing the idea in *The*

*New York Times.* The bill increased tariff rates from an effective level of 35.65% to 41.14%, not that huge a rise. But because the tariffs were set at a flat rate, their impact increased as prices fell in the subsequent deflation. The effective tariff rate reached 59%.[63]

It is not clear how big a role the Smoot–Hawley act played in the Depression but it was a needless measure. As the 1,028 economists pointed out, US factories already produced 96% of the manufactured goods that their citizens consumed. If America wanted its wartime allies to repay their debts, those countries needed the ability to sell goods abroad and tariffs made this more difficult. Canada, Italy, Spain, Portugal and Switzerland all retaliated with tariffs of their own. Trade went into a downward spiral.

With the developed world turning protectionist, independent countries in Asia and Latin America naturally turned in a more nationalist and insular direction. These countries started to seize foreign-owned assets; and in 1938, Mexico nationalised American and British oil companies. Even India, still subject to British rule, was making 70% of its own steel in 1938, up from 14% in 1919.[64] This process would continue, with a vengeance, after the Second World War. Latin American countries were badly hit by the Depression. Ten countries in the region suffered an export drop of more than half. Chile's exports fell by 83% and its income per capita dropped by a third.[65]

The crisis accelerated over the course of 1930, when industrial production fell 20% in Britain, 25% in Germany and 30% in America.[66] Banks started to fold, with 600 US institutions failing in the last two months of 1930. The most serious demise was that of the Bank of the United States in New York's Bronx district. The collapse was partly due to a seeming reluctance to bail out the bank's 400,000, mainly Jewish, depositors.

The American government had yet to introduce deposit insurance. So the rational response of bank creditors was to withdraw their money from a troubled bank in case the rumours were true. A run could thus become self-fulfilling. And a bank that was losing deposits would be forced to demand that businesses repay their loans, causing a wave of corporate failures in the area.

Things were going wrong in Europe too. In March 1930, the

German coalition fell when the Social Democrats refused to cut unemployment benefits. President Hindenburg, the wartime general, took the chance to install a "cabinet of experts", which would rule with the help of presidential powers. This government was led by Heinrich Brüning, a former army officer who hoped to see the monarchy restored. Brüning imposed deflationary measures, cutting government spending, including unemployment benefit.[67] This only exacerbated the anger among those who were out of work. In the September 1930 election, the Nazi Party received 6.4m votes, becoming the second-largest in the Reichstag. Together with the Communists, anti-democratic parties received almost a third of the vote.

Financial chaos then played its part. In May 1931, Credit Anstalt, Austria's leading bank, failed. The French blocked an international rescue of the bank because they were concerned about plans for a customs union between Germany and Austria. In July, Danatbank, Germany's second-biggest, also failed. As with US bank failures, the result was a hit to confidence.

Also in July 1931, a committee recommended that the British government react to its budget deficit by cutting public spending, including a 20% cut in unemployment benefit. That put enormous pressure on the minority Labour administration, which had not been elected to inflict poverty on the working classes. A cabinet meeting agreed to around half the proposed cuts, including a 10% reduction in benefits. This was a classic British compromise, although the cabinet only passed the vote by 11 to 9.

The Bank of England insisted that further cuts were needed in order to restore investors' confidence and maintain the link to gold. But the bank refused to tell the government the actual level of reserves, and Montagu Norman, its eccentric governor, left work on July 29th "feeling queer", and may have suffered a nervous breakdown. He did not return for months. Under pressure, Ramsay MacDonald, the Labour leader, agreed in August to take part in a coalition government that was dominated by the Conservatives. Spending cuts were imposed, but reserves kept dwindling, and a naval mutiny at Invergordon in Scotland caused alarm. On September 19th, Britain abandoned the gold standard. "Nobody told us we could do that", Sidney Webb, a former Labour minister, lamented.

It was a deeply symbolic moment. Britain's embrace of the gold standard had been seen by many countries as a crucial part of its success. If it gave up the fight, why should others continue? At one stage, 47 countries were on the post-war gold standard; by the end of 1932, only seven major nations stuck to it.[68] In a democracy, asking the voting public to endure financial hardship in order to protect the wealth of a minority creditor group was too difficult a task.

Freed from the need to protect their currencies, nations that abandoned gold could, and did, cut interest rates. By itself this gave a shot to economic recovery. Currency depreciation also gave them an advantage in export markets, if only for as long as their competitors did not devalue. In aggregate, the effect was to loosen global monetary policy, and thus to help global recovery.

The crisis also brought a burst of common sense to the issue of sovereign debt. Since 1919, America had stubbornly resisted any link between the reparations owed by Germany to the Allies, and the money owed by the Allies to Washington. But in June 1931, Herbert Hoover, a more interventionist president than he has been portrayed, proposed a general moratorium on debt payments. The French delayed their agreement long enough to force Germany off the gold standard. Hoover's moratorium expired after a year, but at the Lausanne conference in 1932, Britain and France suspended repayments. Germany never paid another pfennig. France defaulted on its payments to the US as well.

Overall, inter-war politicians were caught on the hop by the crisis of the 1930s. The scale of the collapse was beyond their comprehension, and they were at a complete loss for answers. New leadership was required.

## Roosevelt and the New Deal

Between August 1929 and March 1933, US industrial production fell by 55% and wholesale prices dropped 37%. The unemployment rate in the US rose from 4.6% in 1929 to 24.9% in 1932.[69] Car production fell by two-thirds, as did business investment, while GDP dropped by a quarter (see chart). More than 1,000 US banks closed in every year from 1930 to 1933,[70] and as deposits vanished into thin air, the money supply fell by a third.[71] Commodity prices were particularly hard hit, with wheat prices falling by two-thirds in two years.[72]

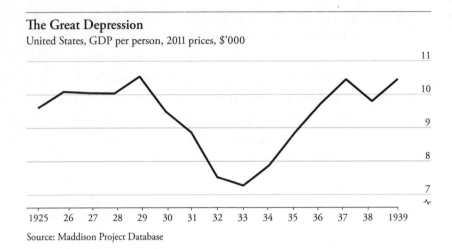

**The Great Depression**
United States, GDP per person, 2011 prices, $'000

Source: Maddison Project Database

This created a problem, defined by the economist Irving Fisher as "debt deflation". The income of farmers depended on the level of crop prices and thus dropped by around 65%.[73] But the value of their debts was fixed in nominal terms. The same problem was true of property owners; their rental income fell but their debt payments were unchanged. The natural inclination was to sell assets to try to pay off the debts. But a fire sale of assets only reduced prices, making the deflationary problem worse.

Germany, which suffered an economic catastrophe on a similar scale, turned to the Nazis. In July 1932, the Nazi Party became the largest party in parliament, with 37% of the vote. At the end of January 1933, Hitler was installed as chancellor, although conservative politicians believed they could control him.

By contrast, in November 1932, the Americans voted for a completely different figure, Franklin Roosevelt. He was an American drawn from the upper classes, who had been stricken by polio in the 1920s, but still served as governor of New York from 1929 to 1932. Blithely confident in his own judgement, Roosevelt had no clear policy positions. During the 1932 campaign, an aide presented the candidate with two speech drafts – one in favour of high tariffs, one against them – and was told by FDR to "weave the two together".[74] The best summary of his approach was this quote: "The country needs and, unless I mistake its temper, the country demands bold, persistent experimentation. It is common sense to take a method and try it. If it fails, admit it and try another. But above all, try something."[75]

Not everything worked and some of Roosevelt's measures were overturned by the Supreme Court. But he had the ability to communicate his confidence to the general public. His famous declaration in his inauguration speech that "the only thing we have to fear is fear itself" was followed by his "fireside chats" over the radio to explain his policies. At a time when democracy seemed to be faltering, Roosevelt's administration was a shining example of a government that was at least trying to do its best for ordinary citizens.

His first task was to deal with the banks. The governor of Michigan had declared a statewide bank holiday on February 14th, before Roosevelt was inaugurated. This was an era without credit cards, debit cards or any form of electronic payment – consumers and retailers depended on cash or cheques, which usually needed a bank to cash them. Depositors in other states did not wait for their own banks to falter and took out their cash as quickly as possible, which only led to more financial difficulties. By inauguration day on March 4th, 28 of the then 48 states had enforced bank holidays, while another ten had partial closures.[76]

Roosevelt promptly closed down all the banks and for a while, the economy had to get by with IOUs; some cities even issued their own local currencies. After nine days, the first banks were allowed to reopen in a three-stage approach. The soundest banks were reopened first, then a second tier of banks, to which the government had provided financial support, while the weakest banks were closed for good. Roosevelt explained the process in one of his fireside chats on March 12th. He was clearly convincing. The next day, as the banks reopened, people queued to deposit money rather than take it out.[77]

There followed a blizzard of activity in the first 100 days of office, a record that subsequent presidents have struggled to match. Emergency relief, in the form of soup kitchens and blankets, was provided to the poor; a work programme was set up to generate employment; the Tennessee Valley Authority was set up to provide power and jobs in a depressed area; and the Agricultural Adjustment Administration was established to boost crop prices. Activity revived, with industrial production rising 28% between FDR's inauguration and the end of the year.[78]

The most momentous step was to abandon the gold standard. Gold exports were suspended on Roosevelt taking office, and in April 1933 he announced that he was dropping the link to gold. One of his aides pronounced that "this is the end of western civilisation", but the stock market climbed 15% in the next few days and the deflationary spiral was broken. Inflation averaged 3.2% a year between FDR's announcement and October 1937.[79] Eventually, Roosevelt settled on a gold price of $35 an ounce, a big leap from the $20.67 level that prevailed before 1933. In practice, this was a massive devaluation of the dollar.

But if Roosevelt had the aim of injecting demand into the economy, as Keynes would have suggested, he was far from consistent. Another of his early measures cut $1bn from public spending, including a 15% reduction in the salaries of federal employees. In contrast, the National Industrial Recovery Act aimed at getting private sector companies to increase the minimum wage, gave unions more rights to bargain for higher pay, and encouraged companies to band together in cartels so that they could increase prices.

The latter act signified the great break in Roosevelt's policies from the past. Whereas many presidents, such as Calvin Coolidge (in office from 1923 to 1929), believed that the federal government should do as little as possible, FDR was an instinctive activist. He built the foundations of a US welfare state through the Social Security Act of 1935, which offered pensions for those aged over 65, although not for the self-employed or for farm workers. The act also introduced unemployment benefit. In theory, the pensions were financed by deductions from workers' wages. In reality, what people paid in was not entirely related to what they got out of the scheme, and the Social Security Trust fund has always invested in government bonds – a claim on future taxpayers. But Roosevelt proclaimed that "We put those payroll contributions there so as to give contributors a legal, moral and political right to collect their pensions and their unemployment benefits. With those taxes in there, no damn politician can ever scrap my social security program."[80] History has proved him right.

Among Roosevelt's other important reforms were the introduction of deposit insurance, which reduced the temptation for bank runs, the Glass–Steagall Act, which separated commercial from investment banking, and the creation of the Securities Exchange Commission to regulate the finance sector. The idea was to make sure that the riskiest parts of banking, linked to asset trading, did not pull down the conventional business of taking deposits and making loans.

Things went wrong in Roosevelt's second term. Frustrated by its rejection of some of his legislation, he unveiled a plan to pack the Supreme Court with friendly justices, and managed to unite Congress against him. Taxes went up, in part to fund Social Security, while the Fed tightened monetary policy.[81] In 1937, the economy fell back into recession, with industrial production dropping 30% between August 1937 and January 1938.[82] This was the third-worst recession of the 20th century, with GDP falling 10% and unemployment rebounding to 20%. Recovery began in 1938 when policy was loosened again: the dangers of tightening policy too early in a recovery had been made clear.

## The Nazi alternative

The Depression may have brought Hitler to power but this was not because the Nazis had a fully fledged economic programme. They did not adopt work creation as a core policy until the spring of 1932.[83] A public works programme was announced in June 1933, although the plan was merely an extension of a programme suggested by the previous administration. The initial efforts focused on land clearance in rural areas but a good deal of the stimulus money was diverted to finance military infrastructure such as airfields and barracks.

The autobahns, oft cited as Hitler's great economic achievement, had a military aim as well – getting troops quickly to Germany's borders. Very few Germans owned cars in the 1930s. Hitler may have championed a people's car but the regime did not manage to deliver a single Volkswagen to a civilian customer.[84] Nor were the roads that great at creating jobs. After a year, only 38,000 workers were involved in their construction.[85]

Almost half of German output growth between 1935 and 1938 was directly due to rearmament. But this was still effective in terms of generating work. By the end of 1936, unemployment had fallen by three-quarters to 1.5 million. The German aeroplane industry went from employing 3,200 people in 1932 to 54,000 in 1935 and 250,000 in 1942, for example. Growth was very much focused on heavy industry rather than consumer goods; private consumption in 1935 was still below its pre-crisis level.[86]

Still, together with his foreign policy successes (Germany reoccupied the Rhineland in 1936), the decline in unemployment probably strengthened Hitler's appeal among the German people. Opposition was very difficult, as the trade unions had been smashed and many left-wing supporters were sent to labour camps. German businessmen enthusiastically funded the Nazis as a way of reducing the power of the workers. They paid a price for this in terms of taxes and heavy regulation, with industries herded into compulsory cartels. Exports were subsidised and imports restricted. A bureaucracy was created in which importers needed licences to obtain goods. In effect, a wartime regime was already in place. But profits rose, as the economy recovered and foreign competition was restricted. German imports in 1938 were 59% below their pre-Depression level. [87]

While the Germans had jobs, their real wages in 1938 were lower than they were when the Nazis took power, and they were consuming less milk, eggs and meat than they did before the Depression.[88] This was guns not butter, as both Goebbels and Göring accepted. Furthermore, the thuggishness of the regime was very quickly apparent. A boycott of Jewish businesses was announced on April 1st 1933; Jews who tried to flee the country in response to Hitler's threats were subject to a heavy tax. In 1934, the left-wing elements of the Nazi party were purged in the "Night of the Long Knives", when hundreds were murdered. Much worse was to follow. The concentration camp at Dachau had opened by March 1933. Just a month later, four Jewish inmates were shot "trying to escape"; and in May, four trade union officials were beaten to death by storm troopers. The nightmare had begun.

## War again

World war in 1939 was not as surprising as it had been in 1914. Hitler's territorial ambitions had been very clear from the start and other powers were rearming in consequence. In Asia, Japan had been locked in a struggle to control China since 1931 when it invaded Manchuria; full-scale invasion followed in 1937. Economic factors were important drivers of conflict. Japan perceived itself as being short of raw materials, particularly oil. South-East Asia was a tempting target thanks to oil in Indonesia and agricultural commodities elsewhere.

In July 1941, after the Japanese moved into French Indochina, the US froze Japanese assets and imposed an embargo that blocked most of Japan's oil imports. This tempted the Japanese into attacking Pearl Harbor as a way of eliminating the American threat. The initial Japanese successes brought a lot of territory under Japanese control, and Kaya Okinori, the finance minister, said the country would "pursue a so-called policy of exploitation". In the peak years, Japan managed to extract around a quarter of Indochina's GDP.[89]

One of the German war aims was *Lebensraum*, or "living space", a policy of territorial expansion in which Germans could settle in annexed lands (while the native population was deported or exterminated); such territories could in addition supply food for the conquering country. Germany was also dependent on imports for 60% of its pre-war oil supply. The decision to invade the Soviet Union was driven, in part, by the desire to capture the oil supplies in the Caucasus. More conventional loot was another goal; when Germany annexed Austria in 1938, it doubled its foreign exchange reserves.[90]

The Nazis were ruthless in exploiting the countries they occupied. One study found that, in the peak year of 1943, Germany extracted 55.5% of French GDP. The total bill for the occupation period was around 111% of a single year's GDP for France, a figure far higher than the German wartime reparations that dogged the interwar period.[91] Other estimates suggest that, from all occupied countries, Germany managed to extract a sum equivalent to 40% of its domestic tax revenue. Poland had the misfortune to be occupied by both Germany and the Soviet Union; during the war, it lost 65% of its industrial plants, a third of its railway lines, and more than half its livestock.[92]

There were periods of intense hunger in occupied Europe, including famines in Greece in 1941 and 1942, in the Netherlands in 1944 and 1945, and in Germany at the end of the war and beyond. In occupied Poland in 1941, the average daily energy intake was around 900 calories (a healthy diet is around 2,500 for a man and 2,000 for a woman).[93] As noted in Chapter 6, Bengal suffered a terrible famine under British (mis)rule.

Economic resources played a large part in the Allied victory. Britain and France alone (if their empires are excluded) had only 70% of the GDP of the Axis powers of Germany, Italy and Japan. But by 1942, both the US and the Soviet Union had joined the war on the Allied side. So even though Germany had occupied much of Europe, the Allies now had a GDP that was 30% higher than that of the Axis. In terms of munitions the advantage was much greater, with the Allies producing 150% more than the Axis powers.[94]

In those countries that were directly affected by the fighting, the economic impact of the Second World War was devastating. German GDP rose in the early stages of the conflict, but by 1945 it was nearly 20% below its 1939 level. A similar pattern was seen in Japan, where 1945 GDP was 22% below its 1939 level. In France, the decline was almost half; in Italy a third.[95]

Conversely, in America, the war provided an enormous economic stimulus, which turned out to be far more effective than any of the New Deal programmes. Production of war-related goods – aircraft, ships, tanks, guns, and so on – grew from 2% of GDP to 40%. Real GDP grew by more than half between 1939 and 1945. Unemployment fell from 14.6% in 1940 to 1.9% in 1945. And the government's role expanded enormously from 9% of GDP in 1939 to almost 47% at the peak in 1943.[96]

As with the First World War, the 1939–45 conflict brought more women into the workforce, largely to cover for males who had been drafted into the military. The emblematic American figure was "Rosie the Riveter", a cartoon character used in government campaigns. At the end of the war, many women lost their jobs again. Still, by 1950, the proportion of American women who were in paid employment was around 10 percentage points higher than it had been in 1939.[97] Women would enter the workforce in much greater numbers in subsequent decades.

## The good news

While the geopolitical environment may have been toxic, the 1914–45 era saw both new technological innovations and the diffusion of previous advances. This was the period when American factories reconfigured themselves to take advantage of electric power. By the mid-1930s, passenger airlines were operating in planes that were 130 times more powerful than the machine developed by the Wright brothers.[98] The first synthetic nitrogen fertilisers were sold in the 1920s, a development that would massively boost crop yields. Another boost to agricultural productivity came with the adoption of tractors; hardly any farmers owned one before 1914, but by 1945 there were more than 2 million in use in the US. In total, the tractor saved 1.7 billion man-hours of labour by 1944.[99]

From this period, consumers began to benefit from a much wider range of products, particularly in the US. The first self-service supermarket was opened in 1916 by Clarence Saunders, founder of the Piggly-Wiggly chain. Clarence Birdseye developed frozen food in 1926 and it was on sale in the 1930s.[100] The first refrigerator was sold for $900 in 1916, more than the cost of a Model T Ford, and by 1937, nearly 6 million fridges were being made each year in the US.[101] Air conditioning, which had been invented before 1914, spread round the country; by the late 1930s, most cinemas possessed it. After the Second World War, air conditioning would make it possible for the US population to shift south and west. In another boost for human comfort, the proportion of Americans with indoor flush toilets rose from 20% in 1920 to 60% in 1940.[102] The first televisions were developed in the 1920s and some broadcasting occurred in the 1930s, albeit to tiny audiences.

New materials were created. DuPont first produced nylon stockings in 1939, and the first 4 million pairs were snapped up within 48 hours. But the supply of nylon was interrupted by the war effort. When sales resumed in 1945, the queue to buy them in Pittsburgh numbered 40,000 people and was a mile long.[103]

The Second World War also saw the large-scale production of penicillin, the introduction of synthetic rubber (in response to wartime shortages), and the development of new technologies like radar and the microwave. Enormous advances in productivity were achieved in wartime conditions. The time taken to produce a ship at the Richmond, California yard fell from 355 days to 12 days. After the war, these techniques were applied to consumer goods.

Finally, workers were also able to achieve better conditions in the inter-war period. In Europe, the working week fell from 56 hours before the First World War to 48 by 1929, while two-week annual holidays became common.[104] For workers who managed to keep their jobs, deflation also meant that their real wages generally rose during the Great Depression.[105]

## Economics rethought
The Great Depression was a challenge to the traditional understanding of economics. Short-term economic disruptions had occurred before, but the system had shown that it could adjust to a shock. The "rottenness" would be purged from the system, as Andrew Mellon, Hoover's Treasury secretary, put it. Inefficient businesses would fail, but new companies would emerge and hire the laid-off workers. If prices were too high, they would fall until buyers were found. If wages were too high, they would fall until workers found jobs.

The Depression showed that this did not happen automatically. In his *General Theory of Employment, Interest and Money*, published in 1936, Keynes outlined why this might be. When firms laid off workers, or cut their wages, those workers had less money to spend. If this happened across the economy, there might be a general shortfall of demand.

So why didn't new businesses spring up and hire all those unemployed workers? The problem was uncertainty about the future prospects for the economy, and thus the profitability of investment. This uncertainty is all the greater when the economy is struggling. Businesses will be reluctant to invest, whatever the level of interest rates. They may prefer to pay down debts, or hold cash. Keynes described this as a "liquidity trap".

Instead, Keynes said that the government should step in and boost demand. In the short run, governments face no practical limits on their borrowing capabilities since investors tend to regard government bonds as a safe asset. The government could then employ people in, say, construction projects. These workers will then spend their wages elsewhere, boosting demand for private sector goods. In a sense, it doesn't really matter how the workers are employed; the government could bury five-pound notes and wait for the private sector to dig them up, he quipped. The result of this government spending will be a "multiplier effect" in which demand created is greater than the size of the stimulus. In practice this did happen although, unhappily, spending on rearmament was the most effective tool for ending the Depression.

Orthodox economists were far from happy with Keynes's theory, not least because it prescribed a much bigger role for the state than had been seen in the past. The critics argued that government spending would be inefficient, and that it would "crowd out" the private sector. Later theorists argued that the policy mistake in the 1930s was not the lack of fiscal stimulus, but the failure of central banks to prevent the collapse of the banks and the shrinking of the money supply. Some said that consumers would react to news of a tax cut, or a public spending increase, by anticipating that future taxes would have to rise to pay for it. This was known as "rational expectations" theory. But it seems doubtful that anyone who is not an economist would ever think along those lines.

Keynes's book was published well after the launch of the New Deal. But his ideas very much set the tone for the post-war era. Politicians had no desire to see a repeat of the 1930s and Keynesianism offered an alternative. Two world wars had also made them much more receptive to the idea of government involvement in the economy.

The tone had already been set in Scandinavia. In the course of the 1930s, Sweden instituted work-creation programmes, unemployment and health insurance, maternity and childcare, subsidised school lunches and higher pensions.[106] And in the post-war era the Swedish model would prove even more alluring to Europeans than the American one.

# TRANSPORT: THE VITAL NETWORK

Ｈigh above the magnificent marble hall of New York's Grand Central terminus, there is a glass walkway from which you can gaze down at the 750,000 passengers who pass through the station every day. As each traveller scurries off in a different direction, it is hard not to be reminded of the frantic activity within an ants' nest. Just as each ant has a purpose to its apparently random path, regular passengers know their best route through the maze of walkways and tunnels on the 49-acre site. In the morning rush hour, a train arrives every 47 seconds, allowing commuters to arrive at their place of work in Manhattan.

The cathedral-like hall of Grand Central might not still be with us if past owners had had their way. In 1961, they petitioned to lower the ceiling to 15 feet and install three tiers of bowling alleys in the space.[1] Luckily for commuters (and a few film directors) they were turned down.

New York would be unable to function without Grand Central (which brings passengers from the north), or its sister, Penn Station (which ferries commuters from New Jersey and Long Island); nor indeed could it manage without its extensive subway system. Manhattan's streets are clogged enough with trucks and delivery vans, without adding millions more car drivers to the mix.

Few commuters probably pause to think about the effort of coordination that was required for them to make their daily journey. Above their heads on the sixth floor of Grand Central, a room full of controllers monitors the arrival and departure of trains on the station's 42 tracks. When I visited, a train was being taken round the "loop" track that surrounds the station so that it could change direction – an extremely rare event.

But in economic terms, the steps taken to make the commuter's journey possible are almost beyond counting. The trains are made by two companies: Kawasaki, a Japanese firm, and Bombardier, a Canadian company. The signalling system comes from Alstom, a French multinational; and trackside power is through ABB, a Swedish-Swiss multinational group. But that is only the start of it. The LED lights that illuminate the magnificent zodiac ceiling on the main concourse were made by Toshiba, a Japanese company, and the marble surrounds came from Italy, as did the expert restorers when the station was revamped in the 1990s. (Until then, the ceiling was black from cigarette smoke, while the station itself was a notorious hangout for the homeless; few commuters wished to linger.) Now Grand Central is a tourist destination in its own right; 10,000 people come every day just to have lunch, not to catch a train.

Those lights, those trains, those power companies depend on raw materials that have been dug from the ground – steel, aluminium and copper wire. Someone had to design and build the train seats, including the textiles needed for the seat covers. The generators needed to power the station (housed deep within the basement) had to be built, and of course the electricity generated from fossil fuels (which had to be extracted from the ground). The food served in the station is grown all round the world. And all the raw materials had to be brought to the station by ship or by truck, taking us to another degree of separation; the ships and trucks had to be built, as did the containers in which the goods were transported. Furthermore, someone had to build the ports at which the goods were offloaded and the roads on which the trucks travelled. All told, many millions of workers were probably involved at some stage or another in the process of bringing each and every commuter to work.

Our global transport system takes people to work, but also sends them on holiday, allows them to visit relatives, and brings them goods from all over the world. As wealth is spread round the globe, more people are able to travel. Around 4 billion passenger journeys were made by plane in 2017, almost double the level of 2005.[2] In terms of trains, around 3 trillion passenger-kilometres are travelled each year, with over 1 trillion each in China and India. And both figures will be dwarfed by car use; the average American travels around 18,000km a year in their automobile.[3]

Changes in transport have been incredibly influential in the development of the world, and of its economy. The first boats allowed humans to reach the Pacific Islands from Asia more than 60,000 years ago.[4] For thousands of years, transport by boat was by far the cheapest way of transporting bulky goods. Steadily, the design of boats was improved, with the addition of lateen sails, the rudder for steering, the compass for navigation and so on, as we saw in Chapter 4. Chinese shipbuilding was well advanced by the 12th century, using iron nails, double hulls with watertight bulkheads, and even lifeboats.[5] Better boats and navigation techniques brought the Europeans to Asia and the Americas in the late 15th and 16th centuries, and allowed the Europeans to dominate the Indian Ocean trade.

The railway and the steamboat brought American agricultural goods to Europe, and took European immigrants back to the Americas. The advent of the railways also allowed people to travel for their holidays for the first time. The train encouraged workers to move to the suburbs; the very concept of a "commuter", someone who travelled a long distance to work, was unknown until the Victorian age.

The first commuter railway line started operation in 1836 from Greenwich in south-east London to London Bridge. The term "commute" comes from American railways, which offered a commutation, or reduction, in fares for regular travellers. But many early London commuters travelled by a horse-driven public carriage, or omnibus, rather than a train.[6]

The car gave a new impetus to the expansion of cities. The proportion of Americans living in suburbs rose from 20% in 1940 to 33% in 1960 – 11 million of the 13 million houses built between 1948 and 1958 were suburban. The giant container ship allowed goods to be shipped cheaply, boosting world trade volumes and globalisation.

The aeroplane took tourists and businesspeople all over the world, encouraging the development of multinational corporations. And all these forms of transport required large amounts of energy, ushering in further economic changes (see Chapter 5).

For much of human history, there were only two ways of transporting goods and people. The first was by land, either on foot or with the help of a pack animal – a camel, a horse or a mule. With the exception of specialised horse-based messenger services (such as the Mongols possessed), this was a slow process; it was also expensive and risky. The other way to move goods was via river, sea and canal. This too was slow and risky (pirates, shipwrecks) but it was cheaper, and boats could carry more bulky items.

The development of powered transport – the railway, the internal combustion engine and the aeroplane – was genuinely revolutionary. As Grand Central does every day, a big city must move millions of people from their homes to their workplaces and back again, with a minimum of disruption. A lucky few may live close enough to walk to work (and some will brave the traffic on a cycle). But the vast majority must come by car, bus, train (underground and overground) or ferry. A disruption to the transport system is the economic equivalent of a heart attack. When researching this book, I was in Boston during a snowstorm. The offices and many shops were closed. Almost the only vehicles on the streets were snowploughs, which struggled with their Sisyphean task from dawn to dusk.

The development of the railway and the economic shift dubbed the Industrial Revolution were intertwined. Coal was needed to power the engines, and the trains ran on iron (later steel) rails, so the growth of the railway boosted both the mining and iron industries. Indeed, the coal industry sparked the idea for the railway.

Men or horses had been used to haul goods on wooden rails since around 1350; moving a cart on rails required only a sixth of the energy needed to transport it on a bumpy track.[7] The steam engine was originally developed to pump water out of the coal mines. Richard Trevithick, a Cornish engineer, then had the bright idea of putting a steam engine on rails; he managed to haul a load of 9 tons at 5mph.[8] Coal production creates a powerful incentive to improve transport, as coal needs to be shifted from a single spot (a mine) to the cities.[9] George Stephenson, the man usually credited with inventing the railway, built his engines for hauling coal on the Stockton to Darlington line; and the first French railway (pulled by horses) was in a coal-producing region.

Coal was not the only emerging industry of the time. The creation of the Liverpool–Manchester line was driven by the need to get cotton from the former city's port to the latter's mills. And the railway was also associated with the development of another revolutionary technology: the telegraph. In 1848, around a half of Britain's railway tracks had a telegraph running alongside.[10]

It was one thing to haul coal or cotton, but another to carry people. Some feared that passengers would have their eyes damaged, or be driven insane, by travelling at high speed. The first railway accident did not take long. At the opening of the Liverpool and Manchester railway in 1830, William Huskisson, the home secretary, crossed the line to speak to the Duke of Wellington and was struck and killed by Stephenson's engine, the *Rocket*.

But people quickly overcame their fear of the "iron horse". Half a million passengers travelled in the first full year of the Liverpool–Manchester railway's operation, with some taking special trips to horse-race meetings. The technology spread remarkably quickly: the first section of the Baltimore & Ohio railway also opened in 1830, while Belgium and Germany began operations in 1835, the Austrian empire in 1838, and Italy and the Netherlands in 1839.[11] It became much cheaper to transport goods as a result. In Germany, the price for carrying a ton of goods on the railways in 1850 was a quarter of the cost of road transport in 1800. This was an enormous boost to economic efficiency, and trade across the country became much more attractive.[12]

Such was the enthusiasm for the new technology that many countries saw periods of "railway mania" as investors poured capital into new lines. At one point in the 1830s, planned railway investment in Britain equalled 8% of GDP. There were too many lines, on too many competing routes, for them all to succeed. After 1845, railway shares lost two-thirds of their value, dropping to pre-1835 levels; among those who lost money were Charles Darwin and the Brontë sisters.[13]

The building of the American railways involved an extraordinary combination of outright chicanery and government support. Congress believed that the railroads would bring progress but did not want to tax their constituents to pay for them. So they subsidised the companies by granting them land. For every mile of track they built, they would get 12,800 acres and any iron or coal underneath it. Union Pacific received land grants equal to the size of New Hampshire and New Jersey combined.[14] It cost the government nothing since the land was effectively confiscated from Native Americans.

There was an enormous railroad boom after the end of the Civil War (the South's relative lack of a network had weakened its campaign). The national system doubled in miles from 35,000 in 1865 to nearly 71,000 in 1873, and, during that period, the two coasts were symbolically linked when the Transcontinental Railroad met at Promontory Point in Utah. But as in Britain, the sponsors had overestimated demand. A financial panic in 1873 saw widespread bond defaults and by 1878, railroad share prices had fallen 60%.[15]

### Synchronise your watches

The railways affected more than just the way we travelled. They changed our measurement of time itself. When the railways began, time was set at the local rather than the national level, based on astronomical observation. East Anglian clocks were a few minutes ahead of those in London; Plymouth, in the south-west of England was 20 minutes behind. In that era, this created no practical difficulties. Anyone who owned a watch would adjust it on arrival in a new place, by observing the town clock. But passenger railways required a timetable so that journeys could be planned, and the companies shifted to the national standard (as derived from the Royal Observatory at Greenwich). For a while, many places still distinguished between local time and "railway time" until Parliament imposed uniformity, in the wonderfully named Time Act of 1880.[16]

The US had a similarly chaotic time system, with Illinois and Michigan each having 27 different time zones. The country's trains, travelling vast distances, had to cope with all this, as well as with the inherent uncertainty caused by rudimentary technology and a variable geography and climate. That made the trains very unreliable;

the phrase "to lie like a timetable" entered into common parlance.[17] Standard time, with four zones for the US (and an extra zone for Canada), was agreed by the railways in 1883. Congress did not catch up until 1918.[18]

Railway journeys were initially too expensive for ordinary workers. To ease the burden, Britain ruled that railway lines should provide certain journeys for only a penny a mile. Later on, light railways or trams were built in many city centres. These were cheaper than trains and could carry more people than buses. By making it easier and cheaper to travel to work, trams and trains made it possible for workers to escape the cramped and unsanitary conditions that blighted Victorian cities.

London opened the world's first underground railway in January 1863; in its first year of service, the Metropolitan line carried 9.5 million passengers for a fare of a penny each way. Initially it was a very unpleasant experience, as the trains were powered by steam and ventilation was poor. It was more than 30 years before Hungary became the second country to build an underground railway. The Budapest metro opened in 1896.[19]

The railway was not the first transport revolution in America. As with Britain, it was preceded by a frenzy of canal building. Canals are an ancient technology, and were a major part of China's transport system from the fifth century CE. In 1681, the French opened the 150-mile-long Languedoc canal linking the Bay of Biscay with the Mediterranean. The aim was to avoid the long trip around Spain.[20] But the Industrial Revolution gave canal-building a new impetus; bulky goods needed to be transported over long distances. The Bridgwater canal took coal from the Duke of Bridgwater's mine to Manchester and was estimated to have cut the cost of coal in the city by 50%.[21] Until the railway, transport by water was much cheaper than transport by land (although roads were being improved in the late 18th century, cutting the journey time between London and Edinburgh by around a half).[22]

The first great American infrastructure project was the Erie canal, which was designed to link the Great Lakes with the Hudson river and thus New York. This was very much a government-driven idea, with New York governor Dewitt Clinton raising the money from the legislature. Construction of the 363-mile canal on a route that went through a mountainous area, and involved a 600-foot cumulative height difference, was so complicated that the project was known as "Clinton's folly". But it worked. Before the canal was completed in 1825, a ton of flour worth $40 could be shipped overland from Buffalo to New York in about three weeks, costing $120; on the canal it could be transported in eight days for $6.[23] The port of New York, and thus the city, was given an enormous boost by the resulting canal traffic.

Canals were a cheap way of transporting bulky goods. Britain has more than 3,000km of canals, and the networks of Amsterdam, Bruges and Venice are popular tourist attractions. But they could not compete with the speed of rail travel and their golden age was over by 1850.

## The car

If the railway created a transport revolution in the 19th century, the car was an even more transformative technology in the 20th, creating a huge manufacturing sector, transforming the layout of cities, and building its own subculture of drive-in movies and drive-through restaurants. The first petrol-powered motor vehicle was built by Karl Benz in Mannheim in Germany in 1885. At around the same time, Gottlieb Daimler, another German, created a motorcycle by attaching a petrol engine to a purpose-built frame.[24] The early vehicles were rudimentary but the idea was quickly developed by other pioneers such as Armand Peugeot and Emile Levassor of France. Initially, cars were the playthings of aristocrats and rich businessmen. They only became a mass market when Henry Ford of Michigan launched the Model T.

Ford was, like many other early auto leaders, both a visionary businessman and a thoroughly nasty person. In 1920 he published a series of pamphlets with the title *The International Jew: The World's Foremost Problem*, which earned him a citation in Adolf Hitler's *Mein Kampf*. As late as 1939 Ford sent Hitler a cheque for $50,000 on his birthday and, in the following year, claimed that "international Jewish bankers" had caused the outbreak of war. Louis Renault was another anti-Semite and Nazi collaborator; the British carmaker William Morris funded Sir Oswald Mosley, Britain's wannabe Führer; and Giovanni Agnelli of Fiat backed Mussolini.[25]

Perhaps there is something about being a pioneer in a fast-expanding industry that creates delusions of grandeur. However, luck as much as skill played its part in the pioneers' success. Henry Ford's first car business failed and he was sacked from his second (which became the Cadillac motor company). His third business focused on the Model T, a car that was pretty crude. But it was cheap and it became even cheaper when Ford introduced the automated production line, an idea that may have occurred to him when he inspected the distribution system of Sears, the giant retailer, the previous year, where they used conveyor belts to speed the flow of merchandise.[26] The assembly line increased efficiency significantly, a process helped by the fact that Ford was producing a single, simple car; the time taken to put together a chassis fell from 748 minutes to 93.[27]

Ford had discovered a virtuous circle. Greater production speed meant lower costs, and lower costs meant higher sales, which reduced costs even further, and so on. The real price of a Model T fell by 80% and sales rose from 10,000 a year to more than 2 million by 1925.[28] In total, 16.5 million Model Ts were sold, and it was not until 1972 that its sales record was overtaken by the Volkswagen Beetle.[29]

In his early years, Ford was famous for treating his workers well, paying them Christmas bonuses and increasing pay to $5 a day in 1913. But this was something of a Faustian bargain. Workers were not allowed to sit or talk on the factory floor, and officials even visited their homes to check on their behaviour. In the 1930s Ford's hired goons beat up, and even shot, labour activists.[30]

By that stage, Ford had lost his dominant position in the industry. Consumers' tastes gradually became more sophisticated – they wanted more than the plain, monochrome Model T.[31] A rival group consolidated many of the early brands under the banner of General Motors. Alfred P. Sloan, GM's boss, was a new kind of corporate leader; not a pioneer but a general manager. He developed a tier of brands, from the Chevrolet to the Cadillac, catering for all kinds of customers, spent money to advertise them, and instituted annual model updates, to encourage customers to upgrade.[32]

As the world's most prosperous economy, with a huge domestic market, America came to dominate the car industry; in 1950, the US produced three-quarters of all the vehicles in the world. But other countries developed their own mass-market models, from the Volks-wagen Beetle to the Citroën 2CV to the Mini, a symbol of Britain's "swinging Sixties".

The car quickly became an integral part of modern culture. Passing the driving test was a rite of passage for American teenagers, giving them the freedom to escape from their parents' control. Iconic brands were celebrated in popular music. The Beach Boys, in a refer-ence to Ford's Thunderbird, promised "fun, fun, fun till her Daddy takes her T-bird away", Prince hymned the "little red Corvette", and Chuck Berry sang of the joys of driving even when there was "no par-ticular place to go". A car was seen by many as a personal statement; a sports car symbolised carefree hedonism, a Rolls-Royce or Cadillac was a sign of having made it in society.

These cars required a lot of infrastructure to support them. Filling stations appeared in the US in 1905 and the first drive-in service station was opened in Pittsburgh, Pennsylvania in 1913.[33] The first motel was built in California in 1925, but the term only came into common use after 1945. In 1951, Kemmons Wilson, a housebuilder, became frustrated while on vacation with the poor choice of places to stay; he founded a chain named Holiday Inn, after the movie starring Fred Astaire and Bing Crosby. He gave each room air conditioning and a TV, and the first hotel had both a restaurant and a swimming pool. Franchising the idea allowed it to spread across the country and, by the early 1970s, the chain had more than 200,000 rooms.[34]

As well as needing somewhere to stay, drivers needed something to eat. The first drive-through restaurant opened in 1947 in Missouri, and Jack-in-the-Box, a drive-through burger chain, began in 1951. (McDonald's didn't open a drive-through until 1975.)[35] Shopping centres with their own parking lots emerged as early as 1907, but the first enclosed shopping mall was built in Minneapolis (where the winter weather can be brutal) in 1956. By 1987, shopping malls accounted for more than half of all US retail spending.[36] To cater for entertainment, the first drive-in movie theatre was opened in 1933, although the phenomenon really took off in the 1950s; one site had space for 2,500 cars.[37]

All this created the familiar layout of the outskirts of Ameri-can cities – a long strip of highway dotted with gas (petrol) stations, car dealerships, fast-food restaurants, and mini- or strip-malls. These outlets catered for the many millions of people who lived in the suburbs. The number of suburban shopping centres rose from eight in 1946 to more than 4,000 by the late 1950s.[38] But they also hollowed out the centres of towns, since motorists were put off by the prospect of congestion and a lack of parking space. Anyone who could not afford a car, or was too infirm to drive, was out of luck: many American cities have made limited provision for public transport.

Most importantly, the age of the car required lots of roads. Back in 1919, a young Lieutenant Colonel Eisenhower took part in a cross-country convoy of US Army vehicles that took 62 days to get from coast to coast; many parts of the trips involved dirt roads and mountain trails. As supreme commander of the Allies in the Second World War, Eisenhower admired the German autobahns. So, when he became president in 1953, improving the nation's roads was a major priority, not least for national defence. In 1956, he managed to push through a programme to fund the interstate system of motorways, funded by a fuel tax. Eventually, 46,000 miles of motorway were built, allowing goods and people to move all across the continent.[39]

These early road-building schemes were a classic example of how government-funded infrastructure can boost economic growth. But at a certain point diminishing returns start to set in. Many modern cities like Los Angeles are built around the car but are beset by traffic jams. The rapid rise in car use in the developing world has led to similar problems. Thailand, Indonesia, Colombia and Venezuela are all deemed to be more clogged up than the US, while Moscow, São Paulo and Bogota are among the ten most congested cities.[40]

Building more roads might seem to be the answer, but studies show that this simply encourages more traffic; if a city increased its road space by 10% between 1980 and 1990, the amount of traffic rose by the same amount.[41] This is an example of the "tragedy of the commons": in trying to exercise their own freedom, the decisions of individual drivers lead to congestion. Drivers in the world's big cities lose almost $1,000 a year through being stuck in traffic jams.[42]

Indeed, our love affair with the car has soured a bit since the 1950s, which many motor enthusiasts regard as a golden age. Back then, fuel was cheap and American car designers indulged their imaginations, creating monster vehicles with grilles that looked like shark's teeth and tailfins that resembled rockets. In the subsequent decades, the drawbacks of our enthusiasm for cars began to be revealed. In 1965, Ralph Nader published *Unsafe at any Speed*, a book that detailed the poor safety records of many cars, which at the time lacked seat belts, airbags and other features later regarded as standard. In 1967, the British introduced a legal limit for drivers' alcohol consumption; US states followed suit in the late 1970s. These safety measures did reduce road fatalities, which peaked in absolute terms in the US at 55,000 per year in the late 1960s; in terms of fatalities per mile travelled, the rate has halved since that period.[43]

Big changes also came in the 1970s when the surge in oil prices that followed the Yom Kippur War (between Arab nations and Israel) encouraged fuel-efficient cars. The giant "gas guzzlers" produced by Ford and General Motors lost market share to smaller Japanese imports. Governments also encouraged manufacturers to improve fuel consumption. The small-car phase did not last that long. When oil prices were low again in the 1990s, consumers bought larger cars in the form of sports utility vehicles (SUVs) and minivans. But these were fairly "boxy" vehicles with nothing like the fripperies of the 1950s models.

The big development in recent decades has been the rapid adoption of cars in the developing world, particularly in China. Global car sales in 2017 were 79m, more than double the 1990s average.[44] But the trend may head in the opposite direction in the rich world. Young people struggle to afford car ownership and can rely on taxi services like Uber, short-term car hire, or shared ownership, for the journeys they need. In the future, autonomous vehicles may provide another option.

Of course, cars are not the only motorised vehicle on the roads. Trucks or lorries play a vital part in taking goods direct to retailers and to our doorstep. According to the American Trucking Association, the US alone has 3.6m heavy-duty trucks, which, between them, transport 10.5bn tons of freight a year, 71% of all the goods moved within the country. [45] Other countries are equally dependent on these giants of the road. As this book was being written, the Brazilian economy was hit by a blockade of truck drivers protesting against higher fuel prices.[46] In 2015, when heavy rains swept away part of a road in Mombasa, Kenya, the result was a 30-mile tailback of trucks that lasted three days.[47]

## The box that contains multitudes

A trucking magnate also helped change the nature of international trade after the Second World War with a simple innovation: a standard metal container. Without it, the ports of Felixstowe and Singapore, featured at the start of this book, could not operate anything like as efficiently. The old docks operated in a rough-and-ready fashion. Goods were placed in the hold in a higgledy-piggledy fashion and unloaded again in the same way. It might take a week or more for the ship to be offloaded.

A job as a docker (or stevedore) was highly prized. But the work was dangerous and insecure; the men lined up at the gates each day looking for employment. In addition, labour relations were poor and strikes were common: dockers' wages could eat up half the costs of an ocean voyage.[48] Indeed, an academic study found that "the handling of cargo was almost as labour-intensive after World War II as it was during the beginning of the Victorian Age".[49]

In the 1950s, a businessman called Malcom McLean tried to tackle the inefficiencies of the industry. He wanted the containers carried on his company's trucks to be loaded straight on to ships. But this required wholesale changes in the design of ships, the operation of docks, and the working conditions of dockers; something that was bound to be opposed by the unions. So he established a new port in Newark, New Jersey, on the other side of the river from Manhattan. On April 26th 1956, the first container ship, SS *Ideal-X*, set off for Houston, Texas. Cranes that could lift the boxes on and off the redesigned ships had to be installed. And agreement was needed on a standard for container size. Initially, this was based on a 20-foot-long box called a TEU (twenty-foot equivalent unit) although modern boxes tend to be 40 foot long (or 2 TEUs).

It was not until the mid-1960s that containerisation really took off. The Vietnam War gave the process a boost since the US military found that using the metal boxes cut their transport costs in half. The long-term savings in shipping costs were even greater, from

$5.86 a ton to 16 cents. In addition, ships were unloaded in less than a day, reducing idle time. Petty theft fell sharply, cutting insurance costs, and container ships required fewer crew to operate them. In the decade after 1966, international trade in manufactured goods grew at more than double the pace of either manufacturing output or global GDP.[50] Some people estimate that the container was more influential than international agreements on tariff reduction in increasing global trade in the second half of the 20th century. Indeed, analysis suggests that trade between developed-world countries that adopted containers rose almost ninefold over a 20-year period.[51]

Unions fought a rearguard action against the shift but they were bypassed. The port of Felixstowe owed its rapid rise to a union ban on containers in London ports. In turn, this meant that manufacturing companies moved, since they no longer needed to rent expensive space in big cities in order to be near the docks. The result was a huge decline in blue-collar jobs in areas like Manhattan and east London.

Without containerisation, it would be impossible to run the kind of global supply chains that multinationals operate. Indeed, it would also be impossible for companies to have low inventory levels; they can have minimal supplies of stocks because they know they can resupply themselves quickly. All this from the adoption of a humble metal box.

## Jet-setters

If we could transport our great-great grandparents forward in time, what might surprise and alarm them most? It could, of course, be the sheer volume and speed of traffic on the roads. But surely the most astonishing sight would be the huge metal objects travelling overhead, without any apparent means of propulsion.

The first powered flight by Orville and Wilbur Wright in North Carolina in 1903 lasted for only 37 metres. Almost five years elapsed before a plane managed to fly for a kilometre. But after that, progress was rapid, with Louis Blériot crossing the Channel between France and England, a journey of around 31 miles, in July 1909. During the First World War, military men saw the potential for aeroplanes for reconnaissance, and the first fighter and bomber planes emerged.

A commercial use for airlines wasn't immediately obvious in

the aftermath of the war. Early planes were not robust enough to carry passengers. But an airmail service was created after 1925, and Charles Lindbergh, having been the first man to fly across the Atlantic, piloted PanAm's first service to South America in 1929. By the late 1930s, the DC-3 was large enough to seat 21 passengers. Shirley Temple, the Hollywood child star, was the first passenger to buy a sleeping ticket on a flight.[52] Early airlines realised what Thomas Petzinger dubbed the "first rule of airline economics": if a plane is going to take off anyway, any extra payload in the form of passengers or goods is almost pure profit.[53]

In the early years of commercial aviation, flying was seen as a glamorous business. People would dress up to go on a flight. But only the well-off could afford it. All this changed significantly in the 1970s. Jimmy Carter signed the Airline Deregulation Act in 1978, bringing to an end a four-decade period in which routes and fares had been tightly controlled by the US government. In 1960, US airlines carried 62 million passengers; by 2017, they carried almost a billion.[54]

The first British package holiday was created in 1950 by a Russian émigré called Vladimir Raitz, who offered tourists a six-hour journey (including a refuelling stop) to a campsite in Corsica.[55] In the 1960s, Clarksons introduced cheap flights to Spain, spurring the huge development of the Costa Blanca. Exchange controls, which stopped Britons from taking more than £50 out of the country, initially limited the market. But the trend was clear. The introduction of bigger jets such as the Boeing 747 allowed both airlines and travel companies to increase the economics of scale.

The airline industry may have grown hugely but it has not been enormously profitable. Warren Buffett, probably the world's most successful investor, once quipped that "if a farsighted capitalist had been present at Kitty Hawk, he would have done his successors a huge favour by shooting Orville down".[56] There are huge costs involved: planes that must be bought (or leased) and maintained; landing slots at airports; and large numbers of staff. Fuel costs can be highly volatile, as can passenger numbers in the face of economic downturns and terrorist incidents. The companies promise a regular timetable, so the planes must be flown whether or not they are full.

Many of the pioneering names of the industry are no longer

around; companies such as Pan Am, TWA, or BOAC, which merged into British Airways. (Their frailties earned them ironic nicknames such as Pick Another Airline Mate, Try Walking Across and Better On A Camel.) Low-cost airlines such as EasyJet, Ryanair, and JetBlue have eaten into the business of the traditional carriers. Non-Western carriers have emerged, such as Emirates, based in Dubai, and China Southern. Today, flying is a far less glamorous business for most passengers; a combination of cramped seats and extra charges for taking your own luggage.

But the economic impact of the industry has been enormous. Aeroplanes don't just carry people. Federal Express, UPS and other logistics companies carry large numbers of parcels round the world. At UPS's Louisville site in Kentucky, 2,000 packages arrive every 17 seconds and rattle round 155 miles of conveyor belts. Around 250 flights depart very day and they can be loaded and unloaded within 20 minutes with the help of some fancy automated equipment.[57] Thanks to these hubs, we can order goods from all round the globe and expect them to arrive within a few days. Internet shopping is thus boosted, and traditional retailers are threatened.

The ability to travel the Atlantic in one hop destroyed the business of the old ocean liners, which took at least four days to make the trip. But the arrival of jet transport gave people with quite modest means the chance to visit countries all over the world. Under Chairman Mao, only a few privileged Chinese people were able to leave the country. Even in 2000, the number of overseas trips made by Chinese citizens was just 10.5 million; by 2017, it was 145 million.

Not everyone sees the growth of global tourism as a boon. Airline travel contributes to global warming through the burning of fuel and the vapour trails in the atmosphere; hordes of tourists marching over the most popular sites can ruin the landscape and drive away wildlife; and beautiful stretches of coastline have been turned into long strips of concrete and neon. Diseases like SARS can spread more easily in the airline age. But the sector has a big economic impact. In 2016, the World Travel and Tourism Council estimated that the industry was responsible for 109 million jobs and made a direct contribution to global GDP of $2.3trn.[58] And hundreds of millions of people look forward to their annual holidays as a chance to escape from the stresses of work, get some sun, and enjoy the cultures and cuisine of another country. This was simply not possible for most workers even 50 years ago.

Indeed, the combination of the car, truck, train, plane and container ship means that the ordinary person can live further from work, travel further for their holiday, and buy goods from further away than ever before. Globalisation is literally dynamic. More change is on its way. Driverless cars and trucks will reduce the death toll from road transport. Electric cars will make our streets less polluted. Drones and pavement-travelling robots will deliver our goods. And a greater emphasis on home working will reduce the need for the daily commute. Our grandchildren may not understand the concept of a "rush hour" at all.

*Right:* Economic activity was already sophisticated by the time of Hammurabi, the ruler of Babylon in 1754BCE, seen here standing at the left, receiving his royal insignia from Shamash, god of justice. Hammurabi's legal code covered issues such as minimum wages, debt cancellation and financial derivatives.

*Below:* The Romans encouraged trade, and in 42CE the Emperor Claudius began building this deep-water port at Ostia, near Rome, to accommodate seagoing cargo vessels.

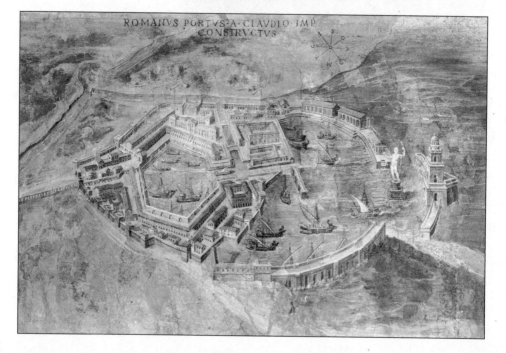

ROMANVS PORTVS A CLAVDIO IMP CONSTRVCTVS

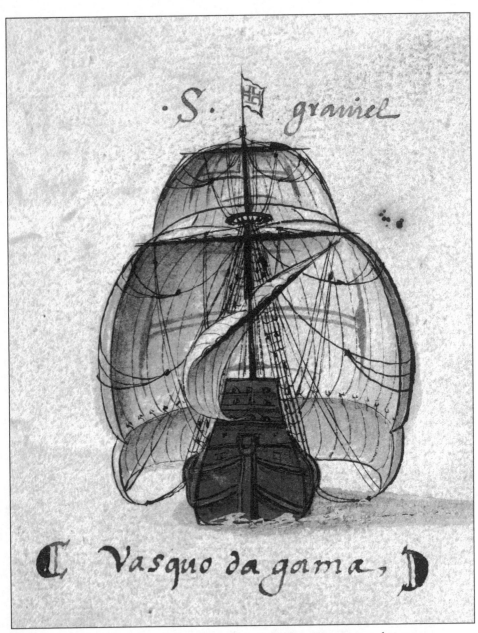

·S· grauiel

℃ Vasquo da gama, ⅅ

Improvements in shipbuilding allowed the Europeans to muscle into
Asian trade. Vasco da Gama of Portugal led the way in his carrack, the
*São Gabriel* (seen here in a 16th-century illustration) in 1497.

Chinese pottery was much prized around the world and led to a flourishing trade. This hoard was recovered in the 21st century from an ancient shipwreck off Indonesia.

Britain was at the forefront of the Industrial Revolution in the early 19th century, helped by new developments in the textile industry such as the spinning jenny, invented in 1767.

*Left:* Silk was an important Chinese export until well into the 19th century: Europeans are seen here trading with a Chinese silk merchant.

*Below:* Modern economic activity would not be possible without the discovery of new energy sources. The US oil boom started in Titusville, Pennsylvania, in 1859.

The slave trade transported millions of Africans in brutal conditions to work on sugar and cotton plantations in the Americas: it continued well into the 19th century.

In the late 19th and early 20th centuries, Europeans flocked to the New World to take advantage of higher wages. Many, such as those seen here in 1912, disembarked at Ellis Island in New York harbour.

The assembly line introduced by Henry Ford in the 1920s brought down the cost of cars and revolutionised manufacturing.

The Great Depression of the 1930s was an unprecedented economic disaster, caused in part by a loss of confidence in the banking system. In this picture, customers queue to withdraw their money from a small bank on the East Side of New York.

In recent decades, manufacturing has shifted to Asia. Here workers in Malaysia assemble hearing aids for export.

A new form of farming: growing vegetables in metal containers,
as a way of producing food in remote areas.

The modern economy is truly global, with goods transported on giant
container ships to be offloaded in ports such as Felixstowe in the UK.

# FROM THE WONDER YEARS
# TO THE MALAISE: 1945–1979

The three decades after the Second World War were a period of increasing prosperity in the Western world. In France, they were known as *Les trentes glorieuses*; in West Germany, as the *Wirtschaftswunder*. Unemployment stayed low and there was barely a recession. The consumer goods that had been invented in the previous 50 years finally came within the reach of most families.

All this happened because the developed world avoided many of the mistakes that followed the First World War. After 1943, it became fairly clear that the Germans would be defeated and the Allies started to plan a post-war settlement. Among the first issues to be settled was the monetary system. A return to the full gold standard seemed out of the question, not least because the US economy was even more dominant than before. But politicians worried about adopting floating exchange rates, which seemed a recipe for chaos.

A conference was duly organised at the Bretton Woods hotel in the mountains of New Hampshire. Harry Morgenthau, the US Treasury secretary, said at the opening ceremony that "We came here to work out methods which would do away with the economic evils – the competitive currency devaluations and destructive impediments to trade – which preceded the present war."[1] The British were represented by their top economist, John Maynard Keynes, and the Americans by Harry Dexter White, a Treasury official who was passing secrets to the Soviet Union, according to KGB archives. (White was not a communist and may have naively believed he was helping world peace.)

Keynes favoured an ambitious scheme in which countries with both trade deficits and surpluses would face constraints, rather than all the pressure falling on the deficit countries as happened under the gold standard. Trade balances would flow through a clearing union, a bit like the banker in Monopoly, which would oversee the system. The accounts of this union would be maintained in an artificial currency called *bancor*, a way of avoiding dollar dominance. A country with a large deficit would be forced to devalue its currency and a country with a surplus would be required to revalue.

But the Americans were suspicious. It was clear that the US would be a surplus nation and that many other countries (including Britain) would run trade deficits. Keynes's scheme sounded like a way for other countries to buy goods from the US while paying funny money in return.

What emerged instead was the International Monetary Fund (IMF). Its role was to act as a lender of last resort for countries in balance of payments difficulties. White made sure that the size of the fund was much smaller than Keynes desired; again, the Americans feared that a large fund would leave them financing the rest of the world.

The second element of the system was the World Bank, which was initially set up to provide loans for post-war reconstruction. That role was superseded by the Marshall Plan (see below) and the bank eventually specialised in making loans to the developing world, particularly to finance infrastructure projects. A tradition quickly developed that the World Bank would be chaired by an American and the IMF by a European.

The exchange rate system that emerged was a more flexible version of the gold standard. Most currencies were pegged against the dollar, which was linked to gold at $35 an ounce. Other central banks could exchange their dollars for gold at that price. Crucially, countries had the flexibility to devalue (or revalue) their currencies in a way that did not require leaving the system altogether. This avoided the need to impose harsh deflationary measures in order to defend the currency, the dilemma that had tormented policymakers in the 1920s and early 1930s. European countries, which naturally struggled to create goods for export in the midst of post-war chaos, duly devalued en masse in 1949.

All currency systems are subject to a trilemma, in which countries can choose two options but not all three. The three options are a fixed exchange rate, an independent monetary policy, and free capital movement. Under the gold standard, the currency was fixed and capital could flow freely. But monetary policy had to be adjusted in order to maintain the currency peg, with interest rates rising or falling regardless of domestic economic conditions.

The Bretton Woods system chose a different pairing. Exchange rates were fixed but countries had freedom (with some limits) to adjust their own monetary policy. The only way such a system could work was by restricting capital flows. If they had not been, investors would have been free to move their capital to whichever country had the highest interest rates, confident that they could not face a currency loss by devaluation. Exchange controls blocked this kind of speculation.

Rather than return to the protectionist policies of the inter-war period, the Allies aimed for free trade. In 1947, representatives of 23 countries signed a General Agreement on Tariffs and Trade (GATT), which operated on the most-favoured-nation principle. That meant that any reduction in trade barriers between two signatories was extended to all members. Further GATT rounds followed in 1949 and 1951, and by the following year, import tariffs in most European and North American countries were around half their pre-war levels.[2]

After the war, Germany was divided into four zones, run by the Americans, British, French and Soviets respectively. No monetary reparations were imposed on the western zones, which eventually became West Germany. (Some patents and trademarks were confiscated, and the US recruited top German scientists like Wernher von Braun.)[3] The Soviet Union, which had suffered disproportionately from German occupation, took much material out of East Germany, as well as its own crop of scientists.

Another important development was that the Americans took

up a global role, in contrast to the retreat into isolationism of the 1920s and 1930s. They were smart enough to realise that a more prosperous Europe would be a lucrative market for US exports. And they also feared that economic collapse in western Europe would lead to further gains for communism. George G. Marshall, a former general who was secretary of state under President Harry Truman, proposed a programme of European aid. Western European nations eagerly accepted it but Eastern European governments, under instructions from the Soviet Union, rejected it. The Marshall Plan eventually provided $13bn of aid between 1948 and 1952, or around 5% of US GDP.[4] In effect, the Americans lent the Europeans the money to finance their trade deficits, and the Europeans used that money to buy American goods.

In Japan, the Americans also refused to impose a Carthaginian peace. Wartime destruction had been immense, including the terrible atomic bomb blasts that devastated Hiroshima and Nagasaki. Japan had lost 80% of its ships, a third of its industrial machinery, and almost a quarter of its land-based transport.[5] The Americans allowed the emperor to stay on the throne but purged the military and introduced a pacifist constitution. Land reforms were introduced to boost small tenants, at the expense of big landowners, and greater rights were given to women.[6] Proposals to break up the conglomerates (zaibatsu) were watered down, while plans to dismantle the nation's factories were also ditched. The economy struggled for a while, with prices rising 13-fold in the three years after the war.[7] But the economy was given a boost by the Korean War of 1950–53, when its factories supplied the American forces with equipment. The US ended its occupation in 1952, although it retained military bases, largely on Okinawa.

## The European recovery

Conditions in the immediate aftermath of the war were terrible. In Hungary, a hyperinflation emerged that outranked even that achieved by the Weimar Republic. At one stage, the inflation rate in Hungary reached 41.9 quadrillion per cent (419 followed by 15 zeros), and the central bank issued a 100 quintillion pengő note (1 followed by 20 zeroes).

In many German cities, including Berlin, Hamburg and Dortmund, more than half the homes had been destroyed. Between 18 million and 20 million people had been made homeless. Chaos meant that hunger was widespread; in the spring of 1947, people living in German cities were consuming only 800 calories a day.[8] In the Soviet Union, 32,000 factories had been destroyed, while Yugoslavia had lost a third of its industrial wealth.[9] In 1945, as many as 17 million people in Germany were displaced, with more than a third being foreign labourers who had been forced to work for the Nazis. After the war, around 11.7 million Germans were expelled from their homes in Poland and Czechoslovakia.[10]

The sheer scale of destruction brought some advantages. Far-right politicians had been discredited for a generation, as had any appetite for military adventure (on the European continent at least). Millions of people could leave the military and take more productive jobs. They could also move away from the farms. In 1950, half of the working population of Spain, Portugal and Greece was employed in agriculture; the same was true of a third of Austrians, almost 30% of French workers, and nearly a quarter of West Germans.[11] As they shifted into industry and services, these workers became much more productive. West Germany also received an influx of around 8 million workers in the immediate aftermath of the war, and another 3.8 million people before East Germany built the Berlin wall in 1961.

Europe also enjoyed catch-up growth that reflected the lost investment of the war years. By 1949, industrial production in all the countries participating in the Marshall Plan (bar West Germany and Greece) was higher than it had been in 1938. There was an investment boom as industry replaced destroyed and outdated equipment. In West Germany, gross fixed investment reached 18% of GDP, compared with 11% before the war; the shift in France over the same period was from 12% to 17%.[12]

West Germany had to sort out the monetary chaos that had followed the war. This required, for the second time in a quarter of a century, a new currency, with the Deutschmark replacing the Reichsmark in 1948. The reform came with a relaxation of rationing on key items of consumption. The effect was dramatic, with industrial production rising 50% in the second half of the year. As the

European economies gathered speed in the 1950s, they were able to make enormous productivity gains as they caught up with American technology and methods; West Germany averaged 6.4% per year in the decade, Italy 5.9%, and France 4.3%.[13]

So many resources had been devoted to defence spending that European consumers had not been able to buy the goods, such as cars, that a great many Americans enjoyed; indeed, in 1950, a large number of European homes lacked even indoor plumbing. So there was plenty of pent-up demand waiting to be satisfied. West Germans owned just 200,000 cars in 1948 but 9 million by 1965.[14]

The West German economy became an export machine, driven by the production of capital goods. An enduring aspect of the German system was that the big manufacturers had a strong relationship with a group of smaller suppliers, known as the *Mittelstand*. The French economy laid a greater emphasis on planning than did the German, and had particular success in car manufacturing, thanks to Citroën, Peugeot and Renault. Italy had its strengths in Fiat, the car manufacturer, chemicals companies like Edison, and the fashion industry. The Netherlands had Philips, the electronics group, a successful chemicals industry, and, from the late 1950s onwards, enjoyed a gas boom. Western European prosperity was thus widespread.

## Common market

At the start of the 20th century, Europeans felt that they dominated the world. The only challenge to their power was the US, which was largely a home for European migrants. Things looked very different after 1945. Eastern Europe was now dominated by the Soviet Union. Russia had always been a relative outsider among the European powers but at least under the tsars its royal family was related to the other monarchs. Stalin was a much more alien, and threatening, leader, with an army strong enough to defeat western Europeans, if they did not have the shelter of the American nuclear umbrella. The Russians also operated a spy network across the continent, including such high-profile figures as Günter Guillaume, the personal secretary of Willy Brandt, the West German chancellor.

So if Europe was to recover, the countries needed to cooperate. In 1949, the first step, encouraged by the Americans, was the creation of a European Payments Union that would help with the financing of temporary trade deficits. A more momentous development occurred in the following year with the European Coal and Steel Community, the forerunner of the European Union. The aim was to create a "common market" for these two vital materials. Six nations joined the club – Belgium, France, Italy, Luxembourg, the Netherlands and West Germany. They would go on to be the founder members of the European Economic Community (EEC) in 1957, under the Treaty of Rome.

The treaty aimed to get the six countries to eliminate all internal tariffs and to have a common external trade policy – a customs union. It took its time to succeed, as internal tariffs were not quite eliminated until 1968.[15] From the start, the EEC had a complex political structure, with a commission (in effect, a civil service) based in Brussels; a parliament that alternated between Strasbourg and Luxembourg (the duplication was a needless expense); the European Court of Justice to enforce the rules;[16] and a Council of Ministers, to thrash out agreement between governments.

The EEC had a political as well as an economic aim. By linking the European economies more closely together, it was hoped that war between the countries would be unthinkable. There was also something of a bargain between Germany and France; the former wanted tariff-free access for its manufacturers and the latter wanted financial support for its farmers. This led, in 1962, to the Common Agricultural Policy (CAP), which offered subsidies to food producers and protection against imports from outside the area. The CAP has been one of the most controversial elements of the European project, being expensive for consumers and taxpayers, and on occasion leading to overproduction, as in the cases of the "butter mountain" and "wine lake" in the 1970s.

Britain opted out of the EEC at the start, partly because it felt closer affinity with the Commonwealth (a club of states that had been part of the empire), and with the US. In addition, Britain was not invaded in either world war so did not feel the same need for common security. In 1960, Britain was a founder member of the European Free Trade Area (EFTA), along with Austria, Denmark, Norway, Portugal, Sweden and Switzerland.[17] Like the EEC, EFTA aimed to eliminate tariff barriers, but it lacked the EEC's political aims. It was solely a trade arrangement.

But EFTA was never likely to rival the EEC as an economic area. All of the member countries bar Portugal traded more with EEC countries than with each other. Britain's trade with the EEC grew faster in the first half of the 1960s than with other EFTA members.[18] So in 1962, the British government applied to join the EEC, only to be rebuffed by the French president, Charles de Gaulle.[19] Britain continued to worry that it was falling behind European living standards and, in 1967, it applied again, and faced a second veto by De Gaulle. The UK only managed to join the EU in 1973 (along with Denmark and Ireland) after De Gaulle left office. The move was designed to stop the rot in Britain's economic performance: in 1950, the UK's per capita GDP was almost a third larger than the average of the six original EEC members, but by 1973, it was 10% below it.[20]

In the immediate post-war period, Britain made an enormous effort to repair its position, restricting domestic consumption through rationing and focusing on overseas trade; by 1950, the country produced 22% of global manufacturing exports.[21] Yet it was dogged by balance of payments issues and sterling crises, and by its poor industrial relations record. By the end of this period it was known as "the sick man of Europe" and was forced to turn to the IMF for a rescue package in 1976.

### The social market economy

Post-war politicians were determined to avoid another period of hardship like the Great Depression. First, economic policy aimed to keep unemployment low. Second, governments set up a system of benefits to protect the poorest in society. This policy shift towards much greater government intervention was driven by a bipartisan consensus. When the Republicans regained the presidency of the US in 1953, Dwight Eisenhower did not seek to roll back any of the welfare programmes introduced by Franklin Roosevelt.

In Europe, many of the leading parties after the war described themselves as Christian Democrat. While happy to ally with the US, Christian Democrats worried that the free market could be both intensely disruptive and a potential recruiting sergeant for the communist parties. The French and Italian communist parties were particularly strong in the four decades after the war.

The European approach had emerged in some smaller countries like the Netherlands and Sweden before the war. One feature was that the leading employers and trade unions bargained for wages at the national level, and avoided costly and bitter industrial disputes. The leading banks and companies were closely linked, with representatives on each other's boards. Private business was allowed to operate but taxes were high, both to limit the scope for inequality and to fund the welfare state. The model protected the right to own private property, albeit subject to some restrictions. Tenants were safe from arbitrary eviction by a landlord while rent rises were capped. One German historian described the approach thus: "The market as an allocation mechanism is altered in order to attain results that are seen as socially acceptable."[22]

European governments also owned significant chunks of industry. In Britain the mines and railways were nationalised after the war, along with the power generators and the steel sector (which subsequently bounced between the private and public sectors a couple of times). The post office and the main airline were already in public hands. France nationalised the utilities and the carmaker Renault, in retaliation for the owner's alleged collaboration with the Nazis. In the 1960s there was an effort in many countries to build up "national champions" in sectors such as aerospace and electronics, in a belief that this would enable Europe to close the gap with the US; in part, this motivated the creation of the Anglo-French supersonic airliner, Concorde. Mergers were encouraged in the hope that large companies could benefit from economies of scale. [23]

Alfred Muller-Armack coined the term "social market economy" for a structure that was a middle way between socialism and a laissez-faire economy. This structure also attempted to balance the aims of economic efficiency and income redistribution.[24] Welfare programmes were a key part of this balance.

Varieties of the social market economy appeared in the British settler colonies of Australia, Canada and New Zealand. In colonial times the Australian economy had prospered by exporting wool to Britain, before a series of discoveries in the second half of the

19th century led to the development of gold, lead, zinc and copper exports. Pensions were introduced there before the First World War, and more welfare programmes, including unemployment insurance, were introduced during the Second World War.

The Canadian economy had been built on raw materials, initially fish, fur and timber and, later, wheat. The economy suffered during the Depression but rebounded in the Second World War, thanks to military spending (including US bases). The boom continued after the war, helped by the discovery of new oil fields in Alberta. The Canadian government introduced welfare measures such as free childcare and old-age pensions and, in measures passed in 1957 and 1966, brought in a publicly funded healthcare system that is a marked contrast with the private system of its southern neighbour.

New Zealand was a prosperous economy in the aftermath of the war, with the fifth-highest per capita GDP in the OECD, a club of developed economies.[25] The country had introduced a range of welfare benefits in 1938, including pensions, unemployment pay and sickness benefit. All three dominions attracted lots of emigrants from the UK, and all benefited from being able to sell raw materials to the developed world during the post-war boom.

## The great compression

The post-war era was marked by a sharp reduction in inequality within the Western economies. Inequality has been a part of society ever since mankind shifted its economic focus from hunter-gathering to farming. Walter Scheidel's bleak assessment was that a reduction in inequality normally required one of four shocks: mass mobilisation warfare, revolution, state failure, and lethal pandemics.[26] In other words, the cures for inequality are worse than the disease.

In its early stages, industrialisation seemed to increase inequality. When the overall economy grew, most of the gains were made by the owners of capital, the factories that churned out textiles, and the mines that dug out coal. Thomas Piketty, the French economist, has argued that the key equation that drives inequality is when the return on capital is higher than the economic growth rate ($r>g$, in his formulation). Capital in this sense means wealth; if the return from owning land, or equipment, or financial assets is greater than the growth of GDP, then the rich (who own most of the capital) will keep getting richer.[27]

But the trend did seem to change as industrialisation developed. British inequality peaked in around 1867 and US inequality in the early 20th century.[28] Simon Kuznets, the economist who devised GDP measures (see Appendix), suggested that inequality would decline as societies became richer. More people would be educated, and would be able to take high-skilled jobs; they would also demand policies that redistributed income in their favour.

The very high taxes required to finance the two world wars clearly made a dent in inequality. Britain had already imposed inheritance taxes before 1914, and some of its great country houses were requisitioned as schools or convalescent homes during the conflict. In France, the value of the top 0.01% of the country's estates fell by 90% between 1914 and 1945. When the US occupied Japan after 1945, it levied a property tax with a top rate of 90% and transferred 70% of the property of the richest 5,000 households to the state.[29]

Taxes remained high after the war. The highest marginal rate of US income tax was 91% as late as 1962,[30] while the top tax rate in Britain in the late 1970s was 83%, with an extra 15% rate on investment income on top, taking the total to 98%. This was the era when many wealthy people made great efforts to avoid tax, with the Rolling Stones fleeing to France to record *Exile on Main Street*, while the Swiss banking secrecy laws provided a home for hidden fortunes.

Tax was not the only factor that reduced inequality. In the labour market, wage differentials narrowed after 1945, whether measured in terms of education, job experience, region or occupation. The main driver seems to have been that there was a rise in demand for unskilled labour (as the economy expanded and unemployment fell) while the supply of skilled labour (thanks to greater education) increased.[31]

All told, the income share of the top 1% of the US population peaked at nearly 50% in 1929 and then dropped to between 30% and 35% for much of the period between 1942 and the late 1970s. Inequality started to widen again at the very end of our period.[32]

## Superpower status

Some Americans look back to the post-war period as a golden age (although not African Americans, who were still denied their civil rights). America's economic dominance was overwhelming; in the immediate post-war period, it accounted for half of the world's manufacturing output, producing 62% of its oil and 80% of its cars.[33] Growth was spectacular by pre-war standards. The US economy grew 3.8% a year between 1946 and 1973.[34]

There was still scope for plenty of productivity gains, as techniques learned in wartime production were applied in the private sector. As well as its enlightened policies on free trade and overseas aid, the US developed a better-trained workforce via measures like the GI Bill (which helped military veterans to retrain) and the expansion of universities. Almost twice as many people took undergraduate degrees in 1970 as in 1950.

This was the era when Americans got TVs, freezers and record players; when they moved to the suburbs and drove to shopping malls and fast-food restaurants; and when they bought ever more elaborate cars. They took paid holidays and drove to resorts in Florida or on the New Jersey shore. Blue-collar workers in the car and steel industries could earn a high enough wage to support their families and buy their own homes. (In 1950, only 29% of women worked but, by 1970, that proportion rose to 42%.) And retiring workers could count on a state pension, as the Social Security system kicked in, while many received a company pension as well. The US lifestyle, as exemplified in its movies and pop music, set the standard for consumers all over the world.

### The Japanese miracle

Japan's defeat had a silver lining. As in West Germany, militarism was discredited. The country's pacifist constitution meant that Japan could leave defence to the Americans and concentrate on building up its economy. The government had no intention of simply leaving growth to the market, setting up the Ministry of International Trade and Industry (MITI) in 1949 to coordinate activity. In the 1950s, MITI prioritised the expansion of traditional heavy industries like coal, iron and steel, while in the 1960s it favoured other industries like electronics and cars. Favoured companies were given tax breaks, offered the best locations, and given permission to expand faster than other groups.[35]

Economists debate whether MITI played a vital role in boosting growth. The bureaucrats were often unpopular with the businesses they regulated, particularly in later decades. Honda, now one of the world's most successful carmakers, was discouraged by MITI from moving into the sector.[36] But Japan's tradition of consensus meant that these rows rarely came out into the open. Policy was fairly stable, since, while the average tenure of a Japanese prime minister since the war has only been about two years, the Liberal Democratic party has been in office for the vast majority of the post-war period.

Success came on many fronts. Between 1950 and 1965, Japanese steel production increased more than eightfold. In the 1950s, Sony developed the transistor radio, the first in what would be a long series of popular electronic innovations. In the course of 1967 and 1968, Japan overtook France, Britain and West Germany to become the second-largest economy in the free world.[37]

For a while, "made in Japan" was a synonym for cheaply made, shoddy goods in Western markets. But the Japanese were influenced by a management guru called W. Edwards Deming, who emphasised that manufacturing was vulnerable to a loss of quality through statistical variation. Managements that focused on reducing that variation could improve the overall quality of their goods. Responsibility for improving the quality of goods could be passed to groups or circles of workers (see Chapter 7).[38] By the 1970s the quality of Japanese goods had improved by so much that American rivals were completely surprised by the competitive threat. In 1950, American car workers were three times more productive than their Japanese rivals; by 1980, the Japanese were ahead.[39]

## Mao and China

The 19th and early 20th centuries were dismal ones for China. Its economy was overtaken by the West, and it suffered the indignities of the opium wars and the forced opening of treaty ports. In 1911, the infant emperor was dethroned and a republic declared. Sadly, the result was not a democracy but a long period of "warlordism" where there was no central authority. The dominant figure who emerged was Chiang Kai Shek and his Kuomintang party. Although Chiang was a brutal leader, he struggled to impose his authority in the face of

Japanese invasion and Communist rebellion. The economy suffered accordingly. During the Second World War, inflation also surged. The cost of living in Shanghai in 1946 was 900 times its level at the start of the war with Japan.[40]

After the war, Chiang Kai Shek steadily lost control of the country, and the Communist Party under Mao Zedong seized power in 1949. Mao inherited a much weakened country. In 1820, Chinese incomes were on a par with those in Europe, but by 1950, Angus Maddison estimated that Chinese incomes were only a tenth of European levels.[41]

Mao turned out to be a brutal ideologue. An early sign of his approach came when 99% of businessmen in Shanghai were held to be guilty of at least one crime and 500 were executed. Deaths in the aftermath of the revolution have been estimated as being anywhere from 800,000 to 5 million.[42] "The more people you kill, the more revolutionary you are", Mao said. Like Stalin before him, he favoured a policy of rapid industrialisation and the collectivisation of agriculture. Between 1955 and 1956, the proportion of peasant households that were collectivised rose from 14% to 92%.[43]

Among the most deadly follies of Mao's rule was the Great Leap Forward, a plan launched in 1958 to increase industrial output rapidly and overtake Western economies. This involved the setting up of backyard furnaces in the countryside, in which farmers made iron and steel from pots, pans and door knobs. As peasants were taken off the farm for forced-labour projects, famine spread. Rice and wheat output fell by around 40% between 1957 and 1961.[44] A crazy sidebar to this scheme was a campaign to eliminate sparrows (because they ate grain) by making so such noise that the birds could get no rest; the sparrows duly died and so were not around to eat the pests that devoured the crop. Historian Frank Dikötter, who combed through Chinese records, estimated that 45 million people died. People resorted to cannibalism and eating mud. Mao's callous response was to say that "When there is not enough to eat, people starve to death. It is better to let half of the people die so that the other half can eat their fill."[45]

The follow-up came in 1966 when Mao launched the Cultural Revolution, designed to drive "bourgeois and revisionist" elements out of the party. Young people joined the Red Guard and humiliated local leaders, imprisoning them or pushing them out of the cities into the country. The Red Guards proclaimed fanatical devotion to the thoughts of Chairman Mao (as detailed in his Little Red Book) and his picture was everywhere. In effect, he was the most powerful and terrible emperor in China's history.

Some revisionists offer praise for Mao, pointing out that economic growth was a little under 3% a year during his rule. But much of this was a catch-up after the dismal performance in the first half of the 20th century. Between 1950 and 1973, per capita GDP in China rose 87%; in Taiwan, ruled by the exiled Chiang, it rose fourfold over the same period, and in Japan, sixfold.[46] China was only able to enjoy a similar rate of growth under Mao's successors.

## The Soviet Union and Eastern Europe

The Soviet Union had suffered most in the battle with the Nazis, with perhaps 26 million dead, 11 million of whom lived in occupied territory where they were often worked, or starved, to death. But the regime contributed its own brutalities, with 600,000 sent to the labour camps during the war, some for offences as trivial as admiring an American jeep.[47]

If Soviet citizens were hoping that victory would bring a relaxation of Stalin's grip, they were disappointed. The focus remained on industry, rather than agriculture; on investment goods, not consumption. Peasants were taxed heavily, and in 1952, the average urban wage was no higher than it had been in 1928. In 1953, the year of Stalin's death, 5.5 million Soviet citizens were still in labour camps.[48]

In the aftermath of the war, the Russians held on to those parts of eastern Europe they had already occupied, and installed communist governments in countries, like Czechoslovakia, that showed signs of edging towards independence. The Soviets brought the same emphasis on industrialisation to their occupied territories, with each country required to produce a five-year plan. To combat the appeal of the Marshall Plan, Stalin created the Council for Mutual Economic Assistance, or Comecon, in 1949 to tie together Eastern Europe. For much of the next four decades, countries in the communist bloc traded largely with each other.

As in the West, there was a post-war recovery, with most countries surpassing pre-war industrial production levels by 1949.[49] Unemployment fell sharply as workers were mobilised into what was, effectively, still a wartime economy, with coal, iron and steel the favoured industries. In the long run, however, the problem was that every country in the Soviet bloc was trying to produce the same kinds of goods. Who were they supposed to sell them to? The lack of price signals also meant that there was no incentive to produce goods that consumers wanted. The Hungarian footwear industry in the 1950s produced 16 kinds of shoes, not as a result of demand, but on the basis of which were easiest to make.[50]

Attempts at reform occurred, including giving local managers more power and allowing a free market for prices in some areas. But there was little encouragement for private markets to develop. Indeed, managers had an incentive to produce more goods, regardless of the quality. Whenever reform went too far, and looked like challenging communist power or doctrine, it was crushed, as in East Germany in 1953, Hungary in 1956 or Czechoslovakia in 1968.

Many observers were seduced by the military might of the eastern bloc, and its success in heavy industry and the space race, into thinking that it was stronger than it was. Paul Samuelson was one of the most esteemed American economists of the era, but he consistently overestimated the potential of the Soviet economy. In the 1961 edition of his textbook for undergraduates, he predicted that Soviet national income would overtake the US in 1984 or 1997; in the 1980 edition, he went for 2002 or 2012.[51] The resource riches of the Soviet Union did prove a boon, particularly when oil prices rose sharply in the 1970s. Even so, the contrast between the lifestyles of consumers in the eastern bloc and those in the West was very apparent.

## The developing world

Neither South Korea nor Taiwan would have been an obvious pick to be a fast-growth economy in the immediate post-war period. In 1950, per capita GDP in the former was $854 (in 1990 dollars) and in the latter $924.[52] Korea was about to suffer invasion and a three-year war with the North; Taiwan was adjusting to its new exiled Chinese rulers. Even in the early 1960s, the average income of South Koreans was 30% lower than that of either Haiti or Ethiopia. In the 1950s, it followed a policy of import substitution that delivered little growth but allowed domestic industry to develop. The key policy shift was an export drive from 1962 onwards. Between 1962 and 1979, Korean exports grew at an annual rate of almost 34% while GNP increased by an average rate of 9.3%. Manufacturing and mining grew from 12% of the economy in the mid-1950s to 30% in the late 1970s, while agriculture's share more than halved. There was a rapid expansion in South Korea's steel, shipbuilding and car-making industries.

This was not a free-market story; the government invested heavily in infrastructure, and provided subsidies, tax breaks, cheap loans and import protection for favoured industries. Industries tended to organise in big conglomerates called *chaebol*, which had close links with government. It is also worth noting that this economic expansion was achieved before South Korea's shift to democracy. Perhaps the key elements of the country's success were the outward-looking focus, the partnership between government and industry, and the well-educated workforce.[53] As Acemoglu and Robinson point out,[54] one could not have a better contrast in the effect of economic policies than the two Koreas. Before the Korean War, the peninsula had a long period of shared culture and language with most of the industry in the north. South Korea became one of the richest countries on the planet and, eventually, a democracy; North Korea is a hereditary dictatorship, marked by repression, famine and poverty.

As with South Korea, Taiwan's growth surge was driven by an export boom after 1960. In the early years, this was dominated by relatively simple products such as clothing and footwear. It was not until much later that the country moved into more sophisticated products like semiconductors and electronics.[55] The export boom was encouraged by a 19-point government plan. It was, in part, focused on emulating the Japanese example and also driven by the need to find new sources of revenue to replace US aid. The result was an economic growth rate of around 10% a year in the 1960s and 1970s.[56]

Singapore, a city state that gained independence from Britain (and then Malaysia), and Hong Kong, a city that stayed under British rule until 1997, were if anything even more successful than South Korea or Taiwan. Their success owed much to governments that were determined to let business prosper and that had an outward focus. Perhaps this was natural since both cities had huge harbours that made them centres of trade. But together with Japan, these countries formed an appealing model for other countries looking to become prosperous. In 1950, Asian GDP per person was less than a third of that of Latin America and Eastern Europe, and even below that of Africa. By 1973, Asian GDP had grown fourfold in real terms.[57]

India's post-war economic history was decidedly mixed. The region gained independence from Britain in 1947 in a chaotic process that divided the subcontinent into three: India itself and the largely Muslim Pakistan and East Pakistan. The eastern region eventually split off to become Bangladesh. In all three countries, population rose sharply after independence; the Indian population was 345 million in 1947 and reached 1 billion by 1999.[58] As noted in Chapter 2, from the late 1960s, the region benefited from the "green revolution", as seeds developed by Norman Borlaug were combined with increased fertiliser use. In India, life expectancy at birth rose sharply from 32 to 51 between 1950 and 1968, as death from diseases like cholera declined.

Jawaharlal Nehru, India's post-war leader, was a great believer in state planning and unleashed the first of a series of five-year plans in 1951. His aim was to build up heavy industry and for the state to control the "commanding heights" of the economy. But the key difference with South Korea and Taiwan was that Nehru had little interest in foreign trade and relied on foreign aid to fund vital imports. New businesses also faced excessive regulation (dubbed the licence raj).[59] All this left Indian growth lagging well behind that of China, let alone the South-East Asian tigers. In the late 1950s and late 1960s, India managed respectable per capita growth rates of more than 2% a year. But in the early 1960s, and throughout the 1970s, annual income growth was less than 1%.[60] Jagdish Bhagwati, an economist, argued that India's socialist planning system did not give more people access to goods and services but merely allowed the well-connected to jump the queue.[61]

The post-war history of Latin America was dogged by military coups and populist politics. As mentioned in Chapter 7, the favoured policy was import substituting industrialisation (ISI). The idea was to develop the manufacturing sectors that had brought the West prosperity and to reduce the dependence on raw materials that were so volatile in price. Industry was supported with subsidies while the state's role was expanded, creating jobs for the middle classes.[62] To the extent that this strategy had any success, it was by shifting resources out of agriculture and into manufacturing. There was growth of more than 5% a year in both the 1950s and 1960s.[63] However, populations were rising rapidly, particularly in the cities, and in per capita terms, growth was a less impressive 2.6%. And ISI produced inefficient companies making inferior products. By 1973, Latin America was exporting just 3–4% of the manufactured goods it produced, compared with 50% in Taiwan.[64]

Post-war Latin America also suffered from an inequality problem; the top quintile (20%) of the population received 60% of income, compared with 45% in the developed world.[65] Some attempts were made to reform the distribution of land but, with the exception of Cuba, which fell to Fidel Castro's communists in 1959, little was achieved. In Cuba, the top decile's (10%) share of income dropped from nearly 40% to 23% in the 1960s.[66]

It was in the 1970s that Latin America's problems really started to become clear. Salvador Allende was elected as president of Chile in 1970 with 36% of the vote. He embarked on a rapid programme of nationalisation, including the banking system, and accelerated the seizure of property from large landowners. Big wage increases were granted and public sector employment rose 40% in three years; by 1971, the public sector deficit was 15% of GDP. This was financed with printed money, and, by 1973, the deficit was 30% of GDP and inflation reached 600%.[67] There then followed a coup in which the air force bombed the presidential palace. Allende committed suicide and General Augusto Pinochet took over.

Argentina had a similar experience. Juan Peron, an army colonel, was the best-known populist in the region and ruled the country from 1945 to 1955 before being pushed out in a coup. He regained power in an election in 1973, ushering in a wave of violence that eventually led to a coup against his widow (and successor in office), Isabel, in 1976. By this stage, inflation had reached 750%.[68] As in Chile, the new regime took a brutal approach towards opponents, torturing and executing many, leaving families desperately searching for news of the "disappeared".

The peculiar tragedy of Argentina was that it was one of the ten richest countries in the world in 1914. But the war and the Depression were devastating for its main focus – exporting meat and grain – and after 1945, just as the world was opening up trade again, Peron shifted the country towards protectionism. Over the last century, the country has suffered several episodes of high inflation and has defaulted several times on its debts.

By the end of the 1970s, the defects of the Latin American model were fairly clear; too much debt, inefficient industries, and too much state control (in 1979, the Brazilian government owned 28 of the country's 30 largest firms).[69] Those defects would prove catastrophic in the 1980s.

Africa, alas, also had limited economic success in this era. The continent largely managed to throw off its European colonial masters, with the obvious exceptions of South Africa and Zimbabwe (then Rhodesia). But the newly independent countries were dependent on commodity exports, and were often run by kleptocratic dictators. The per capita growth rate from 1950 to 1973 was 2%, below the world average, and half the growth rate of western Europe.

### The collapse of Bretton Woods

In 1960, an economist named Robert Triffin predicted to the US Congress that the Bretton Woods system would eventually collapse. His argument related to the conflict between the dollar's domestic and international roles. The dollar was the centrepiece of the Bretton Woods system since it was the currency to which others were pegged. That meant that central bankers in the rest of the world wanted to accumulate dollars as part of their foreign exchange reserves. (In a crisis, they could sell their dollars and buy their domestic currency to support their exchange rate.)

But how could central banks accumulate dollar reserves? The answer was for their nation to run a current account surplus. By selling more goods than they bought, they would acquire dollars from abroad. If all countries managed to do this, America would be required to run a current account deficit. But a series of trade deficits would sap foreign confidence in the stability of the dollar, causing the system to break down.[70]

Roughly speaking, this is indeed how the crisis unfolded. The

Bretton Woods conference gave other central banks the right to exchange their dollars for gold. But by 1966, foreign central banks and governments had $14bn of dollar reserves. The US had $13.2bn of gold reserves, but only $3bn of that was available to pay foreigners; the rest was needed to back the domestic money supply.[71]

At the time, the US was pursuing an expansionary fiscal policy (with spending outstripping tax revenues), as President Lyndon Johnson tried to finance both the Vietnam War and his "war on poverty", including the Medicare and Medicaid health insurance pro-grammes. The American authorities tried various expedients to stop the dollar outflow. In 1963 and 1964, they passed the Interest Equali-sation Tax, making it less attractive for Americans to buy overseas assets. But that change merely encouraged the development of a new financial market, whereby foreigners lent and borrowed dollars from each other. This Eurodollar market, as it became known, quickly became a home for global capital, and a crucial factor in the develop-ment of London as an international financial centre.

After 1966, however, the problems started to multiply. Private investors demanded to exchange their dollars for gold. In 1967, in the face of its repeated trade deficits, Britain devalued the pound for the second time under the system. In the following year, the US stopped redeeming privately held dollars for gold. The IMF created a new composite currency, the Special Drawing Right, as an alternative to the dollar. But the pressure continued, with foreign investors swap-ping their dollars for German marks and Japanese yen, since gold was not available.[72]

In a sense, this was inevitable. The Bretton Woods system had been set up at the end of the war, when European and Japanese econo-mies were shattered and the US was dominant. Eventually, Germany and Japan (in particular) recovered, and their exchange rates should have appreciated to reflect this shift. The German mark and Dutch guilder revalued in 1961 but this was not sufficient, nor was another mark revaluation in 1969. As the anchor of the system, the US was the only country that was effectively subject to the traditional gold stand-ard constraints. But American politicians had no desire to tighten domestic policy, and thereby threaten their re-election prospects, in order to maintain an international agreement.

In 1971, President Richard Nixon suspended the convertibility of gold, and imposed a 10% surcharge on imports, as a way of forcing other countries to revalue their currencies. Later that year, the Smithsonian Agreement devalued the dollar (pushing the gold price up to $38 an ounce) and allowed other countries to fluctuate within bands against the American currency. But Nixon was unwilling to adjust US policy to make the Smithsonian Agreement work, memorably telling an aide "I don't give a shit about the lira".[73] By 1973 the dollar was floating against other currencies.

The Europeans did not like the idea of floating currencies at all. The motivation behind the common market was to integrate European economies, making it easier for them to trade with each other. But exporters and importers found it more difficult to trade if currencies were floating. A French manufacturer importing parts from Germany might find that the price had risen sharply because the franc had dropped against the German mark. Alternatively, a German manufacturer who agreed to be paid in francs might find that the receipts were worth much less in terms of the mark.

In 1972, the six members of the EEC duly established the "snake", a system whereby their currencies could move against each other within limited bands (the name came from the expectation of wriggling currency movement). Britain joined and then withdrew after two months. The underlying problem with the snake was that the West German economy was stronger than many of the others in the group and there was a natural tendency for the mark to rise. Despite two revaluations of the mark, the French withdrew from the system in 1974 and again in 1976.[74] The first attempt to align European exchange rates thus proved a failure.

Milton Friedman, the US economist, argued that floating exchange rates could be an improvement on a fixed rate system, provided that flexible rates were accompanied by a policy regime that could control inflation. First of all, he was a great believer in free markets, which would be more likely to establish the most appropriate exchange rate than central bankers or politicians. Second, fixed rate systems required a lot of adjustment in wages and prices. "It is far simpler to allow one price to change, namely, the price of foreign exchange, than to rely upon changes in the multitude of prices that together constitute the internal price structure", he wrote.[75] By and large, since the 1970s, the big global currencies, the dollar, yen and mark (later euro) have floated against each other.

The collapse of Bretton Woods was a watershed for the global economy. Gold and silver had played a monetary role for thousands of years. Paper currency was, in theory, just a claim on those metals. Now the last remaining link was gone. Each nation had "fiat money", where money was what the government declared it to be. Creditors no longer had the certainty that they would be paid back in a coin of the same value.

In truth, the change had been a long time coming. The Federal Reserve did not have enough gold to back every single dollar in issue. So if the public were happy to use a currency that had only a tiny gold backing, it was not a big leap to use currencies that were not backed by gold at all.

Nor was it obvious why the amount of global currency should be linked to the gold and silver that miners could find. Lord Addison, a British peer, said that he was not convinced that "to dig gold out of the ground in South Africa and to bury it, refined, in a cellar in the United States, in fact adds to the wealth of the world".[76]

But the worry was that, freed from the constraints of an exchange rate peg, government would simply debase their currencies and let inflation rip. Looked at from the perspective of the gold price, that has indeed happened. In 1970, with the gold price at $35, a dollar bought a thirty-fifth of an ounce. At the time of writing, the gold price was $1,232, so a dollar was worth less than a thousandth of an ounce.

## Opec and inflation

The collapse of the Bretton Woods system was followed almost immediately by the inflation that many had feared. In the US, the inflation rate rose from 5.8% in 1970 to 11.1% in 1974 and 13.5% in 1980.[77] In Britain the annual inflation rate rose from 6.5% in 1970 to 22.7% in 1975, and did not fall below 5% until 1983.[78] In Japan, inflation reached 23% in 1974.[79]

What caused these price rises? This was an era before central banks had independence, and Arthur Burns, the chairman of the

Federal Reserve, found it difficult to tighten monetary policy in the face of opposition from President Nixon. US money supply growth was above 12% in 1971 and 1972, while real short-term rates were negative (inflation was higher than the interest rate) from 1973 to 1979. In Britain, controls on bank lending and credit creation were relaxed and there was an explosion of lending, particularly to the property sector; money supply growth was 23.6% in 1973 and 25.5% in 1974. Real British short-term rates were negative from 1970 to 1979 and were minus 13% in 1975.[80]

Rather than tighten fiscal or monetary policy, many governments opted for statutory, or voluntary, restraints on wages and prices. In 1971, President Nixon imposed a 90-day freeze. Britain, meanwhile, had a series of incomes policies, sometimes compulsory and some-times hammered out after negotiations with the trade unions. The aim was to imitate the West German example of industry-wide agree-ments between management and unions. But the approach had lots of problems. No government could control the prices charged by over-seas suppliers. So any retailer or manufacturer that relied on imported goods would have to swallow the increase in costs. If they could not afford to do so, they would simply fail to offer the product; the result would be widespread shortages. In response, governments could and would offer exemptions to some businesses. But that only angered workers, who saw prices rise but were barred from getting wage rises in compensation. Strikes multiplied. Furthermore, incomes policies may have restrained inflation in the short term but as soon as the regime was relaxed, prices and wages took off again.

Inflation was also driven by what economists love to call an "exogenous event". On October 6th 1973, during the Jewish holiday of Yom Kippur (a day of fasting and atonement), Egypt and Syria launched a simultaneous attack on Israel. The war came after Israel's rapid success in the previous 1967 conflict, which resulted in the occupation of the Gaza Strip, Sinai, the west bank of Jordan and the Golan Heights in Syria. That led to the long series of Palestinian protests against the occupation that continue to this day.

The Israeli forces were caught by surprise in 1973 and turned to the US for help. That caused outrage among the Arab nations of the Middle East, many of which were members of the Organization of

Oil Petroleum Exporting Countries (Opec). Their first step was to declare an embargo on oil exports to the US and the Netherlands, key Israeli allies. They also demanded a higher price for the oil they did export. Within three months, the price had quadrupled.[81]

This was an enormous shock to the oil-consuming countries in the West. In the US, gasoline (petrol) had been cheap for so long that the public had become used to driving huge, gas-guzzling cars. Lines formed at gas stations, with some offering fuel only to regular customers. (The crisis proved great news for Japanese carmakers, whose smaller, fuel-efficient vehicles started to gain market share.) The national speed limit was lowered to 55mph, Nixon asked homes to turn down their thermostats to 68 degrees Fahrenheit (20 degrees Celsius) in winter, and some towns turned off their Christmas lights. In Britain, where the miners compounded the problem by going on strike, the country was placed on a three-day week.

For policymakers, Opec's actions posed a difficult problem. Clearly, higher oil prices pushed up the headline rate of inflation. The classic policy response would be to increase interest rates to try to bring inflation back down again. But higher oil prices were also a tax on Western consumers. Money was taken out of European and American wallets and sent to the coffers of the oil producers in the Middle East. As a result, businesses and consumers had less money to spend at home. The effect was to weaken the Western economies. The US suffered five quarters of falling GDP in the period between the middle of 1973 and the spring of 1975, at a time when inflation was rising sharply.[82]

This combination of a weak economy and higher prices led to the creation of a portmanteau word, stagflation. It caused economists to rethink their ideas. Previously, they had thought in terms of a trade-off between unemployment and inflation, known as the Phillips curve after the economist who described it. The aim of policymakers in the three decades after the Second World War had been to keep unemployment as low as possible, without letting inflation rip.

As we shall see in Chapter 16, the crisis eventually led to a redirection of economic policy, in part driven by the monetarist and small government ideas of Milton Friedman. It also led to a retreat from the Keynesian agenda. At the 1976 Labour Party conference, Jim Callaghan, the British prime minister, proclaimed (in words written by his son-in-law, the economist Peter Jay):

> We used to think that you could spend your way out of a recession and increase employment by cutting taxes and boosting government spending. I tell you in all candour that that option no longer exists, and in so far as it ever did exist, it only worked on each occasion since the war by injecting a bigger dose of inflation into the economy, followed by a higher level of unemployment as the next step.

## The malaise

The three decades after the war may have been a period of rapid economic growth but that did not automatically translate into voter happiness. The young people who came to maturity in the 1960s were particularly fond of protest. A series of student demonstrations and wildcat strikes in France in 1968 were so alarming that, for a time, President de Gaulle fled to a military base in Germany.

In America, there were two big causes. Civil rights protests by African Americans had begun in the 1950s, after nearly a century in which they had been denied the right to vote in the former slave states, and had been forced to use inferior eating, travel and education facilities. Those injustices were redressed in the 1960s but many African Americans still felt that they suffered from racism and discrimination. The second cause was the Vietnam War, in which many young Americans were drafted to fight in Asia for a cause in which they did not believe. (Better-off whites were able to avoid service, so the burden fell disproportionately on African Americans.) At the Democratic national convention in 1968, protesters were beaten and gassed by Chicago police; in 1970, four unarmed students at Kent State University were shot dead by the National Guard, while protesting against the bombing of Cambodia.

The era was marked by three big assassinations in the US – of President John F. Kennedy in 1963, his brother Bobby in 1968, and Martin Luther King, the civil rights leader, in 1968. And terrorism flared up in several places. In Northern Ireland, Catholics who had been treated as second-class citizens by the Protestant majority, began a long period of protests that quickly deteriorated into shootings and bombings by the provisional IRA and rival Protestant groups. Palestinians hijacked a number of commercial flights and murdered Israeli athletes at the Munich Olympics. In Italy, terrorists carried out a number of attacks, including the kidnapping and murder of Aldo Moro, a former prime minister; West Germany had the Baader–Meinhof gang; and the US had the Weathermen and the Symbionese Liberation Army.

Politicians struggled to cope with these developments. After all, by creating the welfare state, they had hoped to protect workers from the vagaries of the economic cycle and to head off popular discontent. As has already been noted, this was a moment when economic inequality was lower than at any other point in modern history. But this was an era of "rights" politics, marked not just by the US civil rights campaign but by the rise of feminism and what was then known as "gay liberation". There was a sense that materialism was not enough, since many people sought to improve their social status and to pursue their lifestyle choices.

The environmentalist movement got going in this period, sparked by the publication in 1962 of *Silent Spring*, a book by Rachel Carson about the adverse effects of pesticides on wildlife. The pollution caused by modern industry was an increasing concern too. In 1956, after a series of deadly smogs, Britain passed the Clean Air Act, which limited the burning of dirty fuels, like coal, in cities. (The idea that London is perpetually shrouded in fog has been harder to eliminate.) The US passed similar acts in 1963, 1967 and 1970. Water pollution was another issue. In 1967, the SS *Torrey Canyon* hit rocks off Cornwall, spilling 100,000 metric tonnes of oil into the English Channel and covering local beaches with sludge.[83] Two years later, the Cuyahoga river in Cleveland was so polluted that it caught fire.[84] President Nixon responded by setting up the Environmental Protection Agency.

As well as pollution, many worried about scarce resources. In 1972, a think tank called The Club of Rome published a book called *The Limits to Growth*, which predicted that mankind would start to run out of resources in the 21st century and that this would lead to "sudden and uncontrollable decline in both population and industrial capacity". (The book was much ridiculed in later years but, since the crunch point was not due to occur until around 2070, the authors have yet to be proved wrong.)[85] A much more pessimistic forecast appeared in *The Population Bomb*, a book published in 1968, which wrongly forecast mass starvation in the 1970s and 1980s. The clear lesson to all pundits is to set your forecast so far in the future that if your prediction proves false, you will no longer be around to find out.

Trade unions were at their most powerful in the post-war years, thanks to a low level of unemployment and governments that supported their right to organise. In the 1960s, there were strikes at General Motors and Chrysler plants in the US, and teachers' strikes in New York and Florida. Britain was beset by strikes, including those by postal workers, building workers and the miners; the last of these brought down the Conservative government in 1974. There were mutterings at the time that the country was ungovernable.

In 1979, Jimmy Carter, a decent man who turned out to be an unsuccessful president, gave a speech to the American public that was a long way from the upbeat message that politicians like to deliver. He spoke of "a crisis of confidence. It is a crisis that strikes at the very heart and soul and spirit of our national will. We can see this crisis in the growing doubt about the meaning of our own lives and in the loss of a unity of purpose for our nation."[86] It became known as the "malaise" speech and it did nothing for Carter's popularity. The ideological tide was turning and the Western economies were about to head in a new direction. Power shifted away from politicians and towards the technocrats who ran the central banks.

# CENTRAL BANKS: MONEY AND TECHNOCRATS

Every day we are involved in acts of faith, whether we are religious or not. When we go to work, we trust that we will be paid at the end of the week or the month. When that pay comes, it will be in the form of pieces of paper or, more usually, an entry in a computer that we call our bank account. And when we spend that money by cash, card or bank transfer, the store owner trusts that those pieces of paper, plastic cards and computer entries have value.[1]

Our collective faith in the value of money seems to be justified because the system works. Everybody is happy to accept paper and plastic because they know that everybody else is happy to accept it. The high priests of this faith are the world's central banks. Like Goldilocks, they have to ensure that there is not too much money, so as to cause inflation; or too little, so as to cause recession; but an amount that is "just right".

In the decade since the 2008 financial crisis the power of central banks has increased. They have bought trillions of dollars of assets in an attempt to revive economic activity. Every utterance of the chair of the Federal Reserve, or the European Central Bank (ECB), or the governor of the Bank of England, is pored over by investors as if it were holy writ. Their forecasts move financial markets and their policy changes affect the cost of lending for homeowners and businesses, and the returns for savers. In deciding how the global economy performs, the big central bank governors have more influence than most prime ministers and presidents.

It is not an easy task. Central banks can be attacked for keeping monetary conditions too tight, leading to economic misery; for bailing out banks when they go astray; or for pumping up asset prices and boosting the wealth of the rich. In a sense this criticism reflects an underlying problem: governments have asked central banks to pursue several goals at once. They have been required to stabilise currencies, fight off inflation, safeguard the financial system, and revive economies. Often it has proved impossible to achieve all these goals simultaneously.

The very first central bank was Sveriges Riksbank in Sweden, set up back in 1668 (the celebrations over its tercentenary in 1968 saw the creation of the Nobel prize in economics). But the template for central banking as we know it was the Bank of England. Its creation was an expedient to deal with a financial crisis. William of Orange had become ruler of both Britain and the Netherlands in the "Glorious Revolution" of 1689. The British had invited him to overthrow James II, a Stuart king who seemed determined to reintroduce Catholicism. James II had allied with Louis XIV of France, the enemy of the Dutch, and William III was happy to take advantage of British economic and military power. But he needed money.

A group of bankers, led by William Paterson, agreed to lend William III £1.2m in return for the right to set up the Bank of England and issue banknotes. The link to the crown helped to make the notes acceptable as payment and that remains the "magic" of central banking to this day. It is the association with the state that makes the currency acceptable. This can be traced all the way back to the sixth century BCE when rulers started to put their faces on coins. Personalising coins was a way of asserting authority, but it worked in part because traders and consumers reckoned that the monarch had the power to enforce the acceptability of the coins; they could be used for paying taxes, for example. Coins issued by the great powers of the day – the Athenian owl, the Roman denarius, the Byzantine bezant – were used outside their territory of origin.

The association between state and currency can be double-edged.

Early coins tended to be made from precious metal; stamping the face of the monarch on the coin was a way of asserting its quality. But cash-strapped monarchs also realised that this could be a money-making operation. Suppose a coin with a face value of ten units only had eight units of gold or silver within it. The extra two units could be kept as profit.

Gold and silver are clunky, and risky, to carry around. The original function of banknotes was as a substitute for the hassle of carrying coins. They represented a claim on the gold and silver within the bank's vaults. Since notes (and other forms of paper money like letters of credit) were so convenient, banks quickly found that most of the gold and silver they held stayed in the vaults. Only a small proportion was withdrawn each day. They could lend out this "spare" money and earn a profit. This is the essence of "fractional reserve" banking and thus the modern banking system.

Central banks could operate with a similar leeway. For much of the period from the early 18th century to 1914, Britain operated under the gold standard. Customers could exchange their notes for gold coins if they wished. Other countries joined the standard in the course of the 19th century. While customers conducted these exchanges at commercial banks, central banks stood behind the system, keeping gold in reserve in their vaults. When commercial banks ran short, they would turn to the central bank for help. But central banks did not back every paper note in issue with the exact amount of gold it was worth; they did not need to.

In a sense, this flexibility undermined the system in the long run. After 1913, 40% of US banknotes in issue had to be backed by gold, held by the Federal Reserve. That means 60% were not backed by gold, and this system worked fine until the Great Depression. But if you can get by on 40% gold backing, why not 20%? Or 5%? When gold backing was dropped, people continued to use the notes. In the end it was the faith in the central bank (and the state behind it) that mattered for the acceptability of the currency.

A group of economists called "Chartalists" argue that the state has immense power thanks to its ability to demand that citizens pay taxes in the currency of the government's choice. The state can also decree that the currency is the only legal tender of the realm. This forces citizens to hold the currency and, in practice, they are likely to use it for most transactions. This means that there is no need for a currency to have any intrinsic value (such as a link to gold) at all.[2]

## Guardians of sound money

For the first two centuries of their history, central bankers would have regarded such thoughts as heretical. One of their main jobs was to ensure the soundness of money; and money was only sound when backed by a precious metal such as silver or gold. Without such backing, governments and banks would simply issue paper money at will. In the end, such money would become worthless. As was explained in Chapter 4, that is what happened in China, the first country to experiment with paper money under the Mongol emperors.

One of the earliest experiments in central banking seemed to prove the point. Early in the reign of Louis XV (1715–74), an adventurer called John Law persuaded the French regent to allow him to establish a national bank, and to decree that all taxes and revenues would be paid in its notes. The idea was to relieve the pressure on the indebted French monarchy. The bank then assumed the national debt, and investors were persuaded to swap their government debt for shares in the Mississippi Company, which would exploit France's American possessions.

This was an early example of financial engineering. Shares in the Mississippi Company soared; the word "millionaire" was coined in the process. John Law was the toast of French society. A key element of his plan was that the shares could be bought in instalments, so a large sum could initially be bought with a small stake. But every time an instalment became due, the bubble was tested; people had to be confident enough to pay over more of their own money. Everything depended on a rising price. Once it stopped rising, investors had no incentive to pay for the next instalment, and every incentive to sell.

The whole edifice was built on sand, or rather swampland. The French Mississippi territories of the time had no gold or vital commodities, but lots of mosquitoes. Law resorted to desperate measures, such as parading tramps with tools through the streets, supposedly on their way to the colonies. But once the share price fell, the system collapsed. John Law fled the country and the French developed a long-lasting suspicion of high finance and a preference for gold.

In Britain, a similar scheme had the long-term impact of strengthening the Bank of England. A rival bank, the South Sea Company, agreed to buy government debt in exchange for its shares. The company did have one profitable asset – the right to sell slaves to the Spanish colonies in the Americas. But the share price of the South Sea Company followed a similar trajectory to that of its French counterpart: up like a rocket, down like a stick. Even Sir Isaac Newton was caught up in the mania, leading to one of his most famous quotes: "I can calculate the motion of heavenly bodies but not the madness of people."

The demise of the South Sea Bubble left the Bank of England unchallenged as Britain's premier financial institution. And the bank played an important role in the rise of Britain as a global power in the 18th century. The sound finances of Britain and the Netherlands meant that they could borrow at low interest rates, and not only did this make it easier for them to finance military spending, but industry also benefited from access to cheap capital.

So sound were the Bank of England's finances that George Washington remained a shareholder throughout the War of Independence. Another revolutionary leader, Alexander Hamilton, wrote of Britain's "vast fabric of credit … 'Tis by this alone she now menaces our independence."[3] American finances were chaotic in the aftermath of independence. Its first currency, the Continental, was subject to hyperinflation. Hamilton believed that a reformed financial structure, including a central bank, would create a stable currency and a lower cost of debt, making it easier for the economy (and the emerging manufacturing sector) to flourish.

But his opponents argued that the bank would be too powerful, and would act on behalf of northern creditors. Only three congressmen from southern states voted in favour of the bank's charter; only one from the northern states voted against.

The central-bank issue was one of the most controversial in the new republic's first half-century. The first bank's charter was not renewed in 1811 and, while a Second Bank of the United States was set up in 1816, it too was resented by many. The populist Andrew Jackson vetoed its charter renewal in 1836. That left the US without a central bank until 1913.

Back in Britain, the role of the Bank of England changed in the course of the 19th century. The first step occurred in the wake of the Napoleonic Wars: given the financial demands of the conflict, the government had suspended the convertibility of banknotes into gold. After much debate, convertibility at the old rate was restored in 1819.

Domestic bank depositors were reassured by the existence of the gold standard, but so were foreigners: they knew that a pound would be worth a set amount of gold. By maintaining the gold standard, the Bank of England was committed to the stability of sterling as a currency. This made sterling assets attractive to hold, particularly for wealthy people living in countries that were not committed to the standard. In the long run, it seemed likely that other currencies would weaken relative to the pound. Buying sterling was thus a way of preserving their wealth.

Indeed, one of the main motivations for the gold standard was to protect the interests of creditors. It ensured that the real value of creditors' assets, such as bonds and loans, was maintained. Lend someone £1,000 for ten years and, a decade later when the loan was repaid, it could still be used to buy the same amount of gold. In 19th-century Britain, with the country governed by the creditor classes, it was hardly surprising that the economic system was designed with their interests in mind. The voting franchise was limited to men of property; it was a good time to be a rentier, someone who lives off investment income.

The result was that long-run inflation was absent in the 19th century; the cost of a taxi ride was the same at the end of the century as it had been when the Bank of England was founded.[4] But the gold standard raised tricky questions when the economy suffered a shock. One obvious example of a shock was the failure of a commercial bank.

Fractional reserve banking is prone to crises. Banks have a natural mismatch. They owe money to depositors who can withdraw it at any time, while on the other side of their balance sheets they lend money to individuals and businesses for long periods. If enough depositors want to withdraw their money at once, even a well-run bank will get into trouble. Once a bank run starts, it is hard to stop. If depositors fear a bank will go bust, it makes sense for them to withdraw their money immediately. But this loss of confidence only makes the crisis worse.

At this point, the central bank can step in and lend money to the ailing bank to tide it over. It took time for the Bank of England to accept this responsibility. The bank was privately owned until 1947 and its directors were naturally interested, in its early years, in preserving their profits. In theory, that should have made them as reluctant to lend in a crisis as any other banker.

Many financial panics occurred in the 19th century. In 1825, the British economy was described by William Huskisson, a cabinet minister, as being "within twenty-four hours of a state of barter".[5] That is because a bank panic has widespread effects. Normal business gets disrupted as banks are reluctant to lend money for fear that their depositors will demand to withdraw their savings in cash. But many parts of the economy – shops, factories, building firms – depend on loans. If they can't get credit, they go bust. And if businesses go bust, they can't repay their loans to the bank. That causes depositors to panic further and the cycle continues.

The 1825 panic saw a dispute between the Bank of England and the Treasury over who should be responsible for calming the system. The government won the argument and, after this point, the convention was established that the bank was the "lender of last resort". Following another financial crisis in 1866, Walter Bagehot, then editor of *The Economist*, defined this doctrine in his book *Lombard Street*: the central bank should lend freely to solvent banks, which could provide good collateral at high rates. The idea was not universally accepted and a former governor dubbed it "the most mischievous doctrine ever breathed in the monetary or banking world".[6] But the role of backstop gave a central bank a measure of control over interest rates.

Every day, banks lend and borrow from each other (and from other institutions) in what are called the "money markets". Sometimes a bank will find its books slightly out of balance, and the central bank can fill the gap, charging for the privilege of lending money. This rate sets the benchmark for other lending rates in the market, since commercial banks will not want to lose money by paying more to borrow than they receive from their debtors. So when a central bank increases or cuts the official rate, this ripples through the market.

Playing the role of "lender of last resort" opens central banks up to criticism from both sides. If they act too slowly, they can be accused of sending the economy into an unnecessary crisis. On the other hand, when they do bail out the banking sector, they are accused of helping the undeserving. Critics said that the bailouts of 2008 risked taxpayer money in order to protect bankers who had pocketed billions in salaries and bonuses in earlier years. It was a case of privatising the profits and nationalising the losses. The long-term risk was of "moral hazard"; privately owned banks will feel free to take more risks if they believe that the central banks will always bail them out.

Ideally, central banks would be able to distinguish between banks that have a liquidity problem and those with a solvency problem. All banks can run into liquidity problems, but, given enough time, they would be able to pay their depositors in full. But some banks may be genuinely insolvent; they have lent money to people who are unable to pay them back. Such banks should not be rescued. This distinction is easy to make in theory, but in a widespread crisis, when the economy is in recession, the risk of general insolvency shoots up; indeed, central bank inaction would make insolvency more likely.

Banking crises also created a further problem for a central bank in the era of the gold standard. Foreign creditors would be just as alarmed as domestic ones, and would withdraw their money and convert it into gold, diminishing the central bank's gold reserves. The central bank's usual response to falling reserves would be to push up interest rates to attract depositors. But in the midst of a banking crisis, higher interest rates would only make matters worse for borrowers, making it harder for them to repay their loans. The role of "lender of last resort" and "protector of the currency" would come into conflict.

Those were two of the Bank of England's roles. The third was to manage the nation's debts and help the government raise money as cheaply as possible. Despite the occasional crisis, other countries considered Britain's economic model to be a success.

## The creation of the Fed

What eventually tipped the Americans into approving a central bank was the financial panic of 1907, which was only resolved by the financial acumen of J. P. Morgan. Congress disliked the idea that crisis resolution was dependent on a single individual, but getting a central bank through Congress was tricky given the long-standing resentment of financial power. A group led by Senator Nelson Aldrich had a secret meeting on Jekyll Island to hammer out a plan. The resulting compromise gave the new Federal Reserve an unwieldy structure, with regional, privately owned banks and a central, politically appointed board.

The Fed was created in 1913. Just one year later, the start of the First World War shattered the international financial structure. Before the war, central banks had cooperated with each other to keep exchange rates stable; both the French and Russian central banks helped out the Bank of England during the Barings crisis of 1890, for example.

War placed the needs of domestic economies well ahead of any international commitments. No central bank was willing to see gold leave the country and end up in the vaults of the enemy. The Bank of England suspended the right of individuals to convert their notes into gold and silver, a right that has never been reinstated.

The huge financial demands of the war caused central banks to focus on their original task of drumming up investor demand for debt. Their role of safeguarding the value of the nation's currency had to go by the wayside; the war led to massive expansion of the money supply and rapid inflation.

By the end of the First World War, European powers were exhausted politically and financially, and economic power shifted decisively to America, which would have to be the centrepiece of any post-war financial system. This placed an enormous burden on the newly created Federal Reserve, and required a difficult balancing act on the part of Benjamin Strong, who emerged as its de facto head by virtue of his post at the New York branch. As was noted in Chapter 10, central banks struggled to fulfil their mandate as guardians of sound money with the need to revive economies in the face of the Great Depression.

The Great Depression was a failure that has haunted central banks ever since it happened. They failed both to preserve currency parities and to safeguard the financial system, particularly in America where thousands of banks went under. In retirement, Montagu Norman reflected on his career and that of Ben Strong: "Nothing that I did, and very little that old Ben did, internationally produced any good effect – or indeed any effect at all except that we collected money from a lot of poor devils and gave it over to the four winds."[7] A later Fed chairman, Ben Bernanke, said in a speech to mark the 90th birthday of the economist Milton Friedman, who blamed the bank for the Depression: "You're right, we did it. We're very sorry. But thanks to you, we won't do it again."[8]

## Under the thumb

During the Second World War, central banks were once more reduced to the role of debt managers to the government. After 1945, interest rates around the world were kept deliberately low to try to revive the economy. When Fed chairmen tried to reassert some independence, they faced resistance from the White House. William McChesney Martin, who was Fed chairman from 1951 to 1970, was pressured by Harry Truman to keep rates low despite the inflationary consequences of the Korean War. He refused. After he left office, Truman passed Martin in the street and uttered just one word: "Traitor".[9]

Lyndon Johnson was more direct. Upset with the Fed's policy, he summoned Martin to his Texas ranch and bellowed: "Boys are dying in Vietnam and Bill Martin doesn't care." Typically, Richard Nixon took the bullying furthest, leaking a false story that Fed Chairman Arthur Burns was demanding a 50% pay rise. In the face of press attacks, Burns retreated and kept interest rates low, which helped Nixon's re-election efforts in 1972.[10]

The Fed had more independence than most. In many countries, finance ministries set interest rates. Central banks only had the responsibility for financial stability and exchange rates, which were fixed under the Bretton Woods regime. When that system collapsed in the early 1970s, inflation took off. Worse still, many countries suffered high unemployment at the same time. It was this crisis that gave central banks their chance to develop the powers they hold today. Clearly a change of approach was needed. The first superstar of modern central banking was Paul Volcker, who was appointed to head the Federal Reserve in 1979. He tightened monetary policy aggressively in a bid to slow money supply growth. The policy was unpopular. Farmers protested outside the Fed headquarters in Washington, and car dealers sent in coffins containing the keys of unsold cars.

After the failed experiment of monetarism (see Chapter 14), economists argued that the key to fighting inflation was "credibility". Consumers and business had to believe that the central bank could deliver low inflation. As a result, they would ask for limited wage rises and would only push the prices of products up slowly. The result would be that the target was delivered.

## State of independence

Credibility required making central banks more independent, a trend that started with New Zealand in 1989 and saw Britain, Japan and the euro zone all following suit. These banks were given an inflation target and left to get on with the job of meeting it. Central banks hired vast hordes of economists, sought out new data, interviewed businesses and consumers for evidence of their outlook, and published detailed forecasts for growth, unemployment and inflation.

For a long while, this approach seemed to work perfectly. The 1990s and early 2000s were dubbed the era of the "great moderation", with inflation low and the economy stable. Alan Greenspan, Mr Volcker's successor, was dubbed the "maestro", and, rather than being bullied by presidents, Greenspan's approbation was sought by them for their policies.

In Europe, the biggest development was the creation of the European Central Bank (ECB) in 1998, which was formed to take charge of the new single currency, the euro. Previously, EU members had been responsible for maintaining their own currencies and financial systems through national central banks. The ECB was a compromise between the French, who wanted a single currency to tie a reunited Germany into the EU, and the Germans, who worried that the single currency would require them to bail out other profligate governments. To reassure the Germans, the bank's headquarters were in

Frankfurt and its main target was price stability. It was specifically prohibited from bailing out member governments.

The first signs that central banks might not have all the answers came in Japan. More than four decades of rapid economic growth came to an abrupt end as the 1980s drew to a close. When the bubble started to pop in 1990, the Bank of Japan (BoJ) was relatively slow to react.

Western critics berated the BoJ for not cutting interest rates fast enough or reorganising the banks. But a similar crisis was building in the US and Europe. After 1982, financial markets began a long bull run as yields fell from the high levels of the inflationary era. When markets wobbled, as they did on "Black Monday" in October 1987, central banks were quick to slash rates. They were trying to avoid the mistakes of the 1930s, when they were too slow to respond to financial distress. Over time, however, the markets seemed to rely on the Fed stepping in to rescue them. Faith in the Fed's backing was known as the "Greenspan put", after the then Fed chairman and an option strategy that protects investors from losses. Critics argued that the central banks were encouraging speculation.

The problem was that raising interest rates to deter stock market speculation might inflict damage on the wider economy. And while central banks were supposed to ensure financial stability at the macro level, supervision of individual banks was not always in their hands; the Fed shared responsibility with an alphabet soup of other agencies. There was similar confusion in Britain, where the Financial Services Authority replaced the Bank of England as financial supervisor in 1997.

Nevertheless, central banks can be criticised for failing to worry about the huge rise in debt levels in the early years of the millennium. Their excuse was threefold. First, there was no sign of an increase in consumer prices, their primary responsibility. Second, to some extent greater debt is a sign of a more sophisticated economy; it allows consumers and businesses to adjust their expenditure over time. Third, every debt is also an asset on a creditor's balance sheet; the world's net debt is zero. Besides, a lot of the debt was owned by institutions such as pension funds and insurance companies who were well placed to deal with the risk of default.

When the credit bubble finally burst in 2007 and 2008, central banks faced the same dilemmas that have occurred down the centuries. Worries about moral hazard quickly evaporated in the face of the implosion of the banking system. Central banks lent money freely and also pushed interest rates down to historic lows, and even to negative levels. They unveiled a programme of quantitative easing (QE), in which they created money and used it to buy bonds and other assets (see Chapter 18).

But these actions aroused criticism. QE pushed up the value of financial assets, which are disproportionately owned by the better-off. A paper from the Bank for International Settlements, the central bankers' club, concluded that QE had increased inequality by boosting share prices.[11] Many elderly savers complained that low rates had cut their retirement income.

In the US, these actions revived the old critique that central banks inevitably favour the moneyed classes rather than the heartland economy; Wall Street rather than Main Street. Others feared that QE was a repeat of the money-printing policies that created German hyperinflation in the 1920s (although inflation has not yet resulted).

In Europe, the European Central Bank was attacked from a different direction. It was berated for favouring the creditor nations, particularly Germany, and punishing the indebted ones, like Greece. The overarching problem is that, in the aftermath of the 2008 crisis, central banks have been drawn into the political debate. In part this is because they have carried a lot of the burden of reviving the global economy. The effect is that unelected central bankers are taking the big economic decisions, the ones that redistribute money from one group of people to another.

Central banks were given these powers because they were experts, technocrats who were better at making decisions than politicians. This presupposes that their expertise makes them wiser than elected politicians. But the crisis made central banks look rather fallible. They came under attack.

The billions spent on rescue operations for the banks prompted American right-wingers to campaign to "Audit the Fed" to examine how the bank had invested its money. In his election campaign, Donald Trump said that Janet Yellen, the Fed chair, should be "ashamed" for keeping interest rates so low. After he replaced Ms Yellen, Trump criticised her successor, Jerome Powell, for pushing rates up too quickly. In Britain, Brexiteers criticised the Bank of England for being too gloomy in its forecasts of the economic impact of leaving the EU.

On the left, some economists have criticised central banks for being too timid, and for failing to revive the economy. Some favour Modern Monetary Theory, which argues that a government that prints its own money cannot go bankrupt, and that there is thus no need to worry about budget deficits and plenty of scope for governments to spend money on infrastructure and social benefits.[12] MMT advocates admit that inflation is a constraint on this process.

Nevertheless, to a prudent central banker, this sounds like the "monetisation" of budget deficits and is the sort of thing that leads to the hyperinflation seen in Weimar Germany, and, more recently, in Zimbabwe and Venezuela. If ever a government in a developed nation decides to pursue this theory, expect to see either a conflict with the central bank or (more likely) the end of central-banking independence.

There is a fundamental problem about turning over policy decisions to central banks on the grounds of their expertise. Economics is a social science. Making precise forecasts is not possible in the way that it is in chemistry. There are too many variables to analyse, not least that the mere act of publicising economic forecasts can alter people's behaviour. In the last ten years, politicians have had little real cause for complaint. Central banks have been cutting interest rates and buying government bonds, making it easier for them to fund their promises. They may be less happy when rates rise and central banks try to sell the bonds they bought. That may provoke a deeper clash.

# THE SECOND ERA OF GLOBALISATION: THE DEVELOPED WORLD, 1979–2007

Four of the most decisive turning points in modern history occurred within 12 months at the end of the 1970s. In December 1978, Deng Xiaoping, who was in the process of becoming China's leader, made a speech pushing the country in the direction of economic reform. Without that shift, China would not be the second-largest economy in the world today.

In January 1979, the shah of Iran fled into exile. The subsequent revolution saw the rise to power of an Islamist regime. Not only did this start a long clash between the Islamic world and the West, but it also, along with the hostage crisis that followed, doomed the presidency of Jimmy Carter and helped ensure the election of Ronald Reagan, a strong advocate of free markets and a fierce anti-communist. In May 1979, Margaret Thatcher, a politician with similar convictions, became British prime minister.

Ronald Reagan's electoral prospects were given another boost by the anti-inflationary policies of Paul Volcker. As mentioned in the last chapter, he became chairman of the Federal Reserve in August 1979 and swiftly pushed up interest rates to eye-watering levels. Mr Volcker was the first modern example of the powerful central banker. Finally, in December 1979, the Soviet Union invaded Afghanistan, a disastrous decision that weakened the Russian regime, and eventually created a recruiting ground for Islamist militants.

**The two eras of globalisation**
World exports as % of GDP

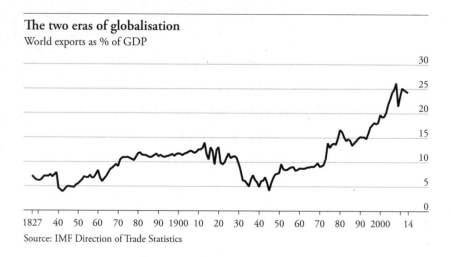

Source: IMF Direction of Trade Statistics

In short, in the space of 12 months, the world saw the start of China's economic growth, modern Islamic militancy, the rise of independent central banks and the free-market right,[1] and the beginning of the end for the Soviet Union. In turn, the Soviet Union's collapse and China's move towards a more market-focused economy drove the second great wave of globalisation in history, after that of the late 19th century. Capital, as well as goods, flowed around the world; as globalisation accelerated, foreign direct investment grew at 40% a year between 1996 and 2000.[2]

Globalisation tends to be painted as a project that benefits a rich elite. But the four decades since the late 1970s have seen significant reductions in poverty and gains in life expectancy round the globe. African life expectancy was 47 in 1973 but had risen to 60 by 2015, despite the AIDS epidemic. That means that Africans live more than twice as long as they did in 1925. In global terms, life expectancy rose more than 11 years between 1973 and 2015.[3] From the point of view of the average human, the second era of globalisation has been good news (see chart).

So much happened in this period that the subject needs to be divided into two. This chapter will deal with developments in the rich world before picking up the story of the developing world in Chapter 16.

### Another oil crisis and recession

These developments were not predictable in the immediate context of 1979. The immediate problem the world economy had to deal with was another oil shock. In the turmoil surrounding its revolution in early 1979, Iranian oil production fell by 4.8 million barrels a day, or 7% of global output. Many oil users reacted by building up their inventories, thus creating extra demand; and Opec added further pressure by announcing a price increase in December 1979. The combined weight of all these factors caused the oil price to more than double between April 1979 and April 1980.[4]

The headline rate of US inflation was duly pushed up to 9% by the end of 1979. US interest rates were already 11% before Paul Volcker took charge of the Fed, but he drove rates even higher, with the peak being 19% in 1981.[5] Other central banks followed a similar path. In Canada, rates reached 21%; in Britain, 17%. In the face of this monetary tightening, the US suffered two recessions (defined as two successive quarters of falling output) in short order; in the first half of 1980 and then from July 1981 to November 1982.[6]

As inflation fell from 13.5% in 1980 to 3.25% in 1983, Volcker was able to cut interest rates, and a recovery started in late 1982. But there was a significant difference in its shape in the US and in Europe. In America, unemployment rose from 7.1% in 1980 to 9.7% in 1982 and fell to 7.2% in 1985; in the EEC (precursor to the EU), unemployment kept rising, from 5.8% in 1980 to 11.2% in 1985. And that average was dragged down by a fairly low rate in West Germany. In Britain, Italy and the Netherlands, unemployment rates in 1985 were still at or above 12%.[7]

What explains this divergence? In the 1960s, European unemployment rates were below US levels; in the 1980s, they were persistently higher. Between 1975 and 1985, the US created 25 million jobs while European employment fell over the same period. There was talk of "Eurosclerosis", a slowing of the continent's growth caused by over-regulation. In 1986, Olivier Blanchard and Larry Summers produced a paper that talked of "hysteresis", a scientific term describing a system that is dependent upon its history.[8] In this case, they postulated that there was a sharp division between those who were unemployed and those in work. The former group found it harder and harder to get jobs once they were out of the labour market since employers were reluctant to hire people who had not worked in more than a year. The result was that the available pool of workers was smaller, allowing those still in the labour force to bargain for higher wages. Inflation and unemployment could both be high.

This analysis led some economists to argue that the problem in Europe was inflexible labour markets, which made it too expensive to hire workers (because of additional costs and taxes) and too difficult to fire them.[9] That led to calls for "structural reform" – policies that allowed employers to hire workers on more flexible contracts (the conservative view) or diluted workers' rights (the left-wing attitude). Britain moved fastest in the US direction during this period, and eventually had some success; in 2000, the British unemployment rate was 5% while the German rate was 10%.[10] This gap prompted Gerhard Schröder, the German Social Democrat chancellor, to push through a series of measures known as the Hartz reforms, which increased the incentives for the unemployed to find work. Since then, German unemployment has been well below the European average, although that may be down to the country's success in exporting capital goods to China and the emerging markets, rather than the reforms themselves.[11]

Attempts to make the labour market flexible led to a long argument about whether it was better to reduce unemployment, even if the only jobs available had lower wages and reduced rights. In the US, such jobs were found in the fast-food sector or in call centres. The problem was tied up with the general decline in manufacturing employment (see Chapter 7), which meant that most new jobs were created in the service sector.

One significant component of economic growth in this period was the addition of women to the workforce. In 1948, just over 30% of American adult women worked, but by 2000, the proportion was 60%. (It has dropped back a little, along with male participation, since then.) There was an upward trend in other developed countries as well. In developing economies, female participation tends to be high in any case, as women are heavily involved in agriculture. Participation falls as economies grow, and as subsistence farming becomes less important. But it rises again as women become more educated, leading to the postponement of childrearing and a decline in the size of families.

A report by the International Labour Organization in 2017 estimated that, if the gap between female and male participation rates could be reduced by a quarter by 2025, global GDP would rise by $5.8trn, or 3.9%.[12]

### The conservative renaissance

The drive for labour market flexibility was part of a reaction against the policy consensus that had been in place since the end of the Second World War. Until 1970, conservative forces had been largely in retreat, faced with the success of economic policy in maintaining rapid growth. Right-wing parties accepted the existence of the welfare state, and the policy aim of low unemployment. But the stagflation suffered in the mid-1970s suggested that post-war policies were no longer working. And the high level of taxation was starting to cause voter discontent. The clearest example of that was the passage in 1978 (via referendum) of Proposition 13, which aimed at capping property taxes in California, traditionally a left-leaning state.

This conservative renaissance took its inspiration from a variety of sources. Back in 1944, Friedrich Hayek had argued, in *The Road to Serfdom*, that the amount of planning required by socialism, and indeed by social democracy, would lead eventually to tyranny. No central planning authority could possibly assess all the needs and wants of millions of individuals. Instead, it would force people to work in government-approved industries and to accept government-approved goods. Not only would this be coercive, it would be inefficient. Resource allocation is best achieved, he argued, through the price system, which gives clear signals to producers as to which goods are popular and which are not.[13]

As a critique of communism, Hayek's arguments were spot on. But he was clearly wrong about social democracy; no one would describe Sweden as a tyranny. As Keynes pointed out, Hayek accepted that an extreme position of laissez-faire was impossible. In a letter to Hayek he wrote that, as soon as you accept this, "you are done for … since you are trying to persuade us that so soon as one moves one inch in the planned direction you are necessarily launched on the slippery path which will lead you in due course over the precipice".[14]

As well as Hayek, conservative campaigners took their cue from Milton Friedman, who argued that the rise in inflation in the 1970s resulted from the failure of government policies. In their determination to manage the economic cycle, governments had repeatedly stimulated the economy via fiscal and monetary policy. But there was a "natural rate" of unemployment that it was futile to ignore. Attempting to push unemployment below that rate would simply drive up inflation.

Friedman also put forward the "permanent income hypothesis", which said that rational individuals smoothed their consumption over their lifetimes. In a downturn, people would cut their spending less than their incomes, since they would expect the downturn to end. There was thus less need for the government to intervene by boosting its own spending as Keynes had suggested.

Friedman argued, too, that employment can be increased through the use of monetary policy only if increased inflation was unanticipated. But workers would learn that their real incomes were being eroded and demand higher wages. The effect would not be increased output or employment but higher inflation. If the equilibrium rate of unemployment is not socially acceptable, Friedman argued that the remedy was not to boost the money supply, but to make the labour market more flexible.[15] Rather than focusing on demand, this was "supply side" economics.

When it came to controlling inflation Friedman argued that this "is always and everywhere a monetary phenomenon".[16] The answer was for the government, or central bank, to limit the annual growth of the money supply, an approach that became known as monetarism. This got rid of the need for income and price controls of the type introduced by President Nixon.

Clearly, in the case of hyperinflation such as in Weimar Germany, there was a link between money printing and high inflation. However, when central bankers and governments tried to put Milton Friedman's theories into practice, they ran into problems. The underlying theory behind monetarism was an equation, MV=PT, in which M was the amount of money in circulation, V was the velocity with which it changed hands, P was the price level, and T the number of transactions. On the basis of this equation, a rise in the money supply (M) would cause an equal rise in prices (P), provided that V and T were unchanged.

But that turned out to be an erroneous assumption. As it turned out, monetary velocity (V), the speed at which money moved, was not particularly predictable. In the US, it rose 14% between 1977 and 1981, before falling again. Later there would be a big increase, between 1987 and 1997, and a collapse after 2006.[17] This latter decline was an example of a phenomenon that Keynes worried about in the 1930s; people tend to hoard cash when they are concerned about the economic outlook.

A further problem with monetarism was that it was hard to define exactly what "money" was. Notes and coins were only a small part of the money in circulation. Consumers also have money in deposit accounts and short-term savings accounts, and have unused balances on their credit cards. Monetarist policies were being attempted just as there was a lot of financial innovation, so the nature of money was changing. Economists first debated which monetary measure was most important, and then, when the link between money supply growth and inflation seemed to break down, the policy was abandoned altogether.

In retrospect, monetarism seems a classic example of an economic policy proposal that looks convincing in theory, and has some mathematical backing, but which crumbles in the face of the complexities of the real world. It is rather like the sports fan who can describe in detail how the professionals got it wrong, but who would fall flat on his face if he ever made it on to the pitch.

### The new wave of politicians

Margaret Thatcher and Ronald Reagan were both elected, in part, because of the mess left by their predecessors. Among the first acts of both politicians was to cut taxes, particularly for the highest earners. In America, these were 70%, and in Britain 83% at the end of the 1970s. By the time Thatcher and Reagan had left office, the highest US income tax rate was 28% and the British rate 40%.[18]

Reagan was a former Hollywood actor whose sunny personality proved electorally popular, after Carter's troubled presidency. His reign coincided with a boom that arose from the easing of monetary policy in the mid-1980s (by Volcker) and a programme of tax cuts. Reagan was untroubled by budget deficits or rising government debt. In his first year in office, 1981, he persuaded Congress to allow the national debt ceiling to rise above the $1trn level, a figure that seemed incredibly high at the time. By the time he left office in 1989, the national debt was $2.6trn.[19]

Thatcher's first term was marked by high unemployment, the collapse of manufacturing industry, strikes, and urban riots. Had it not been for the Falklands War, in which Britain repelled an Argentine invasion of islands in the south Atlantic, she might never have been re-elected in 1983. She was also lucky in that the opposition Labour Party was split into rival factions.

Thatcher's second term was marked by a year-long miners' strike, the failure of which symbolised the decline of trade union power. And it also saw the speeding up of the transfer of businesses from the public to the private sector, a process that was known as privatisation. The telecom and gas industries were privatised with the help of marketing campaigns aimed at the general public. The goal of this "popular capitalism" was to create a class of share- and property-owners who would be resistant to the appeal of socialism.

All told, 50 companies were privatised or sold under Thatcher, including the national airline, the airport operator, the main steel company and the water utilities. The electricity and railway companies would follow under Thatcher's successor, John Major. It was a massive shift: when Thatcher took office, nationalised industries generated 12% of Britain's GDP; by the time the Conservatives fell from power in 1997, their share was just 2%.[20] Eventually, the idea spread to Europe, with both France and Germany selling off their holdings in telecom companies and Spain privatising its national airline. The amount raised in European privatisations rose from around $10bn in 1990 to $104bn in 1998.[21]

Privatisations certainly raised a lot of money for governments, allowing them to please their electorates by cutting taxes or spending more on services. But the broader rationale for privatisation was that it would make companies more efficient. Nationalised industries, it was argued, became more focused on the interests of insiders (managers and workers) than on consumers; they lacked the market discipline needed to keep them competitive. At times, too, they could be starved of investment, given the many competing demands on government coffers.

Few would argue now that telecoms services have not been improved in private sector hands, or that competition has not brought down airfares. The debate is over whether sectors that seem to be natural monopolies, such as power utilities or water or railways, are improved by being in the private sector. There is a clear public interest in allowing citizens to have affordable access to power, water and transport. Privatised industries thus often face regulation of their prices, a way of governments reasserting partial control. The result pleases few: the public complains both about the lack of competition in the sector, and the way in which profits that might have been used for investment are diverted to investors.

## Corporate power

The push for smaller government, lower taxation and less regulation was encouraged by business lobbying. Along with the banks, the corporate sector asserted its political power in this period. In a 1971 memo, Lewis Powell (a lawyer who would become a Supreme Court Justice later that year) wrote that "the American economic system is under broad attack", adding that businesses "have responded, if at all, by appeasement, ineptitude and ignoring the problem". He argued that "Few elements of American society today have as little influence in government as the American businessman, the corporation, or even the millions of corporate stockholders", and he called on spokesmen for the enterprise system to "be far more aggressive than in the past".[22]

This fight was carried forward by the US Chamber of Commerce and by right-wing think tanks such as the Heritage Foundation and the American Enterprise Institute. In Britain, a similar role was played by the Institute of Economic Affairs, the Adam Smith Institute, and the Centre for Policy Studies. The underlying argument of these groups was that government intervention was stifling economic growth, and that by cutting taxes and reducing regulation, businesses would be liberated to create jobs.

This intellectual movement helped spark an enormous increase in US election spending as companies and their lobbyists tried to win politicians around to their view. Spending in the 2018 mid-term election was around \$5bn compared with \$1.6bn in the equivalent polls in 1998.[23] Much of that money came from corporate lobbyists. In 1983, corporations spent just \$200m on lobbying; by 2000, that spend had reached \$1.6bn and by 2017 \$3.3bn. Even after adjusting for inflation, that is a huge increase.[24] From 1998 to 2012, between 90% and 95% of the organisations that spent most on lobbying were from business, not unions or environmental groups. In 2018, the highest-spending individual companies were Alphabet (the parent company of Google), AT&T, a telecoms group, and Northrop Grumman, a defence and aerospace company.[25]

The temptation to be nice to corporate lobbyists is only enhanced by the so-called "revolving door" between politics and lobbying. A study in 2016 found that about half of retiring US senators and a third of retiring house members registered as lobbyists; that was up from less than 5% in the 1970s. Many could increase their income fivefold by switching.[26]

The result of all this is that rich constituents get listened to far more than do poor ones. Research by Larry Bartels, a political scientist, found that the views of the richest third of constituents were given 50% more weight than those of the middle third by US senators, while those of the poorest third were given no weight at all.[27] And it is not just that the rich contribute to campaigns; they vote more often. In the US, 80% of the richest tenth of people (by income) vote, while just 40% of the bottom tenth do so.[28]

Globalisation also works in the favour of the rich and of the corporate sector. In a world where the most talented employees are mobile, and where companies can shift production to other countries with ease, it is hard for politicians to push up tax rates very far.

### Finance reigns supreme

Under the Bretton Woods system, capital movements were restricted because of the need to protect currency pegs. But once currencies were free to float, there was no need to retain these restrictions. The US, Canada, Germany and Switzerland all abolished controls quite quickly; Britain followed suit under the Thatcher government.

This shift fitted into the philosophy espoused by Milton Friedman. If capital was free to move, it could be invested in the most profitable opportunities around the world, and this would improve economic growth in the long term. Investors would also act as a source of discipline on spendthrift governments, demanding higher yields before lending them money. Politicians began to fear the "bond market vigilantes".

The asset management industry matured in this era. Fund managers look after the money of individuals and institutions, and offer the benefits of diversification. By pooling assets, they can spread their portfolios across a wide variety of securities and reduce the risk that any one investment goes wrong. Many fund managers also claim to have the skill to outperform the overall market, by beating the index, but very few have consistently been able to do so. (By definition, the average manager cannot outperform the average return.) Worse still, when fees are deducted, client returns will be below that of the market benchmark.

These managers do not own the assets they look after, but they still have power. They can vote with their feet, by selling the shares of companies they dislike, and they can vote more directly in annual general meetings to get rid of executives they think are performing poorly (although this rarely happens). This is a system where power is diffused, unlike that of the 19th century, when powerful men like John Rockefeller controlled their own companies. It could be called "agency capitalism" or "financial capitalism".

In 1982, the best-known US stock-market indicator, the Dow Jones Industrial Average, was trading at around 1,000, a level it had first touched back in 1965. Given the amount of inflation that had occurred in the meantime, this was a very poor performance in real terms. But in 1982 a long bull run began that brought fortunes to many of those who worked in the financial sector. The "best and the brightest" of America's graduates queued up to join investment banks like Morgan Stanley and Goldman Sachs.

The boom was driven by a combination of falling interest rates and rising corporate profits. In 1982, the Treasury sold 30-year bonds yielding almost 14.6%, a return that was very appealing at the time (and proved very profitable in retrospect). But as bond yields fell, equities looked more competitive. The bull market was not without its hiccups. On October 19th 1987, the Dow dropped almost 23% in a day, the largest-ever percentage fall. At the time, there were echoes of the 1929 crash, and worries that this would herald another economic disaster.

The reasons for the decline were fairly mysterious; the US economy had grown 3.5% that year. But the crash seems to have been exacerbated by a practice known as "portfolio insurance". Investors tried to protect themselves against market falls by selling contracts in the futures market. But this led to a self-feeding cycle in which falls in the futures price caused the main stock market to fall, prompting more selling of futures. It was an early indication of the way in which derivatives contracts could be "weapons of financial destruction", as the investor Warren Buffett later called them.

Central banks cut interest rates in response to this market sell-off. There were more reasons for the Federal Reserve to keep rates low: a crisis in the savings and loan industry. These institutions, which took money from savers and lent it to homeowners, were deregulated in 1980. They then went on a lending spree that ended in disaster when interest rates rose and borrowers failed to repay; all told, institutions with a net worth of $519bn collapsed.[29] Lower rates seemed to do the trick for a while; the US economy grew in 1988 and 1989 and the stock market rebounded from its temporary slump.

Corporate takeovers, often using borrowed money, were widespread in the 1980s and 1990s. A series of predators, like T. Boone Pickens, Carl Icahn and Ivan Boesky, made headlines by taking significant stakes in businesses in a practice known as "greenmail"; either the existing management would buy them out at a profit, or another predator would use their stake as the basis of a deal. The process was dramatised in the film *Wall Street*, in which Michael Douglas's character, Gordon Gekko, proclaims that "Greed is good."

The main function of the takeover wave was to break up conglomerates and force companies to focus on a single industry. (The argument was that conglomerates were inefficient; shareholders could get the benefits of diversification by investing in a wide range of companies.)[30] The value of takeover deals in the US in the 1980s was $1.3trn and 28% of the country's largest 500 companies in 1980 had been bought by the end of the decade.

Another driver of the takeover phenomenon was a new class of investment vehicle called private equity funds. These funds raised money from traditional institutions like pension schemes and insurance companies. They then borrowed money to take over struggling companies, sold off activities deemed to be "non-core" to pay off the debt, and incentivised the company's managers with shares. To their defenders, the private equity managers were a way of making industry more efficient; to the critics, they were asset strippers who laid off workers, and focused too much on the short term. By the late 1980s, private equity funds were responsible for more than 20% of all US takeovers. The best-known example was the takeover of RJR Nabisco, the tobacco and food group, which saw rival private equity groups battling for control, and was laid bare in the book *Barbarians At the Gate* (by Bryan Burrough and John Helyar).

The private equity funds benefited from the structure of the US tax system, which made interest payments on debt tax-deductible. They also thrived when interest rates were falling since this made it cheaper to do deals. When rates moved higher in the 1990s, many deals went wrong and the enthusiasm for private equity cooled for a few years.

Private equity managers set their fees on a generous basis (for themselves); an annual fee of 2%, plus a fifth of the outperformance of an agreed benchmark (so if the benchmark is 4% and the fund earns 9%, the managers get an extra 1%). The same approach was adopted by the hedge funds that also came to prominence in this area. The concept of a hedge fund was dreamed up by a journalist called Alfred Winslow Jones who wanted to find a way in which fund managers could offer a return, regardless of the overall direction of the stock market. As well as buying stocks he favoured, he "went short" (bet on a falling price) on the shares he disliked. Provided he picked the right securities, he could thus make money whether the market was rising or falling. In the 1980s and 1990s, however, the most prominent funds had a "macro" approach, moving in and out of currency, bond and commodity markets.

The result was that looking after "other people's money" was one of the quickest ways of getting rich. In 2017, the top 25 hedge-fund managers earned an average of $615m each, while *Forbes* magazine calculated that there were 310 finance sector billionaires in 2018, or 14% of the total. There were more billionaires in 2018 from the field of finance than from any other sector. An old joke went "Why don't fund managers look out of the window in the morning? Because then they would have nothing to do in the afternoon." From the 1980s onwards, those days were over.

## Japanese omens

The first signs that financial excess could store up long-term problems were in Japan. In the 1980s, Japan's manufacturing success was so marked that America started to fear the competition. By the mid-1980s, foreign manufacturers had 30% of the US car market and President Reagan secured a commitment from Japan to limit its exports.[31] Partly in response, Japan started to establish factories within the US. Honda, Nissan and Toyota all have several plants there, mostly in the southern states where trade unions are less strong.

There was resentment in the US that their companies did not have easy access to the Japanese market. Only 9% of manufactured goods in Japan were imported, compared with 32% in the US.[32] Japan's consistent trade surpluses meant that it built up large holdings of US Treasury bonds and also privately held assets such as the Rockefeller Center in New York and Columbia Pictures in Hollywood. This led to some paranoid thrillers about a Japanese takeover of the global economy, such as *Rising Sun* by Michael Crichton and *Debt of Honor* by Tom Clancy.[33] These fantasises were a sign that many people see trade as a "zero-sum game" in which if one side wins, the other might lose. The fact that, thanks to the Japanese, Americans got cheaper cars and electronic goods, as well as lower borrowing costs, tended to be overlooked.

Another focus for trade talk was the strength of the dollar in the early 1980s, which flowed from Volcker's high interest rate policy. This made US exports less competitive and Japan's exports more so. In 1985, under the Plaza Accord (named after the New York hotel where it was agreed), Japan and Germany agreed to boost domestic demand, while the US cut interest rates to reduce the attractiveness of the dollar. The agreement worked as far as currencies were concerned; the yen climbed 46% against the dollar by the end of 1986.

That slowed Japanese export and economic growth and the Japanese authorities responded by cutting rates and taxes.[34]

But Japan started to resemble the late 1920s boom in the US as both property and share prices soared. The speculative excess included a spending spree by Japanese tycoons, who paid record prices for Van Goghs and Renoirs. Property was so expensive in Japan itself that in theory the country's land was valued at around 100 times the average of land in the US.[35]

When the bubble burst in 1990, the BoJ was initially relaxed. But by the second half of 1991, the Japanese economy had dropped into recession, in part because of a downturn across the Western world. This made it more difficult for borrowers to service their loans. A 1930s-like cycle developed: when borrowers sold assets to repay loans, prices fell, putting more borrowers in difficulty. Japanese banks preferred to let failing companies survive rather than force them into bankruptcy, but this meant that "zombie" companies clogged up the economy; resources were not released so that they could not be transferred into more efficient businesses. Furthermore, everyone knew that the balance sheets of banks were full of bad debts. Confidence in the sector fell. Japan has never really recovered from this setback.

### Mastered by the universe

In 1997 and 1998, there was a crisis in emerging markets, which involved South-East Asia and a Russian debt default. Caught in the middle of all this was a hedge fund called Long-Term Capital Management (LTCM), run by some of Wall Street's best-known bond traders and advised by two Nobel prize-winners in economics, Robert Merton and Myron Scholes. The fund followed a policy of risk arbitrage, buying less liquid assets with borrowed money. At one point, it borrowed 30 times its capital.[36] This proved disastrous when markets fell, so banks refused to keep lending the fund money. A private sector bailout was organised and the Fed cut interest rates again.

However, the Fed's repeated reactions to market wobbles created a problem of "moral hazard"; traders were encouraged to think that central banks would ride to the rescue in a market crisis, with a flurry of rate cuts. Thus the Fed may have increased the incentive to speculate.

As LTCM was collapsing, another bubble was emerging. This was linked to the internet, which encouraged a flood of start-up companies that promised to transform their industries. Every twenty-something seemed to have an idea for a website. Many of these companies were then floated on the stock market and investors snapped them up, although the businesses were not making any profits. Share prices soared and then crashed again over the period 1999 to 2002. This bubble proved less damaging than many since it was built on equity, rather than debt, and thus did not involve the banking system.

Indeed, the internet bubble did not dent the advance of Wall Street. The big investment banks like Goldman Sachs and Morgan Stanley advised on corporate takeovers. They helped companies issue bonds or equities, and they traded the same bonds and equities. Some of them managed investment funds. They earned fees or commissions, or made trading profits along the way, and the best performers received annual bonuses in the millions of dollars.

Whether all this activity was socially useful is another matter. Paul Volcker once claimed that the only useful modern financial innovation was the automated teller machine or ATM. High-frequency trading was another development with dubious benefits. This involved some firms using computer programmes to buy and sell shares within a matter of milliseconds in order to take advantage of minor price discrepancies. It is a long way from the idea that finance's role is to provide long-term capital to the most promising businesses. Many in the financial sector point to the fall in the cost of trading as a sign of the greater efficiency brought by this approach. But while the cost of individual transactions has dropped, money is changing hands more often. A study by Thomas Philippon of New York University found that the overall costs of financial intermediation (the cut taken by the finance industry) have hovered at around 1.5% to 2% since the 19th century.[37]

Taking a small percentage out of trillions of dollars of trading volume generates a lot of wealth, and wealth brings influence. In their book 13 Bankers, Simon Johnson and James Kwak recount how Brooksley Born, the chairwoman of the Commodity Futures Trading Commission, wanted to regulate financial derivatives in 1998. She was told by Larry Summers, then the Treasury secretary, that "I have thirteen bankers in my office and they say if you go forward with this you will cause the worst financial crisis since World War II." Ms Born didn't get her way. Lax regulation of the financial sector, which allowed banks to operate with risky balance sheets, was to bring economic disaster in 2007.

## The euro

In the 1970s, the Europeans attempted to replace the Bretton Woods exchange rate system with their own version, dubbed the snake (see Chapter 12). Although that collapsed, European governments were determined to try again. In 1979, they launched the European Monetary System (EMS), under which member currencies had to stay within a 2.25% band, either side of their central rate (at times, a wider 6% band was allowed for some currencies). In practice, the key relationship was with the Deutschmark, which was naturally the strongest currency in the bloc. West Germany had established a post-war reputation for low inflation, and other countries hoped to "import" this approach by linking to the mark. In a sense, this was a "mark standard" rather than a gold standard.

But the system, which was also known as the Exchange Rate Mechanism, faced the same kind of problems as the snake. The economies of Europe had not converged sufficiently for their currencies to stabilise naturally against each other. In the early 1980s, inflation differentials between EMS member countries were wider than across European countries that were not part of the system. So there were 11 currency realignments in the period between 1979 and 1987.[38]

In 1990, three things happened. First, Germany reunified and West Germany allowed conversion of the East German mark on a 1:1 basis. The Bundesbank worried about the inflationary implications of this, and pushed up interest rates in response. Second, remaining capital controls within the EU were eased as part of the single market process, aimed at integrating economies more closely, and the lack of controls made it easier to mount speculative attacks against a weak currency. Third, Britain joined the system in the hope that ERM membership would deliver the discipline needed to control inflation.

The tighter monetary policy that followed German reunification exacerbated an early 1990s recession. The US had a mild downturn from July 1990 to March 1991 that was associated with higher rates and another oil shock after Iraq invaded Kuwait and was subse-. quently expelled by a Western-led coalition.[39] British interest rates were in double digits for much of its ERM membership, inflicting considerable pain on the domestic economy. Speculators, of whom the most prominent was George Soros, a hedge-fund manager, bet on a falling pound and the Bank of England's reserves started to dwindle.

On September 16th 1992, the British government first pushed up rates to 12% and then to 15% in a desperate attempt to support the currency. But the tactic failed and the pound continued to fall. Britain pulled out of the ERM that evening, an event that damaged the reputation of the Conservative Party for a long while afterwards.[40] The Italian lira, which had also been under pressure, followed suit. Over the next 12 months, other countries were forced to devalue or drop their pegs. Finally, in June 1993, the ERM bands were widened to 15%, a range so wide that the system barely imposed any constraints on currency movements. It seemed that Mrs Thatcher's saying "You can't buck the market" had been proved right.

The EU's next attempt at currency stabilisation was much more ambitious. If European exchange rates could not be stabilised, then the answer was to get rid of them altogether. A single currency – the euro – would eliminate the need to exchange Belgian francs for Italian lira or Austrian schillings for Spanish pesetas. That would make trade easier between the member countries.

But it was a big gamble. The US has a single currency in the form of the dollar, but it is one nation, with a single language, and a single legal and taxation system, in which it is easy for workers to move from one state to another. Europe is a complex mix of nation states, with many different languages, a long history of diverging inflation rates and employment practices, and separate central banks. The Germans worried that a single currency would require them to bail out profligate nations in the rest of the EU. So the eventual deal placed the European Central Bank, which would be the cornerstone of the new system, in Frankfurt, with the hope that it would be as disciplined as the Bundesbank. And countries could only qualify for the euro if they passed financial tests, limiting their budget deficits to 3% of GDP.

In technical terms, the creation of the euro was a success. Exchange rates were tied together from 1999 and the new notes and coins were introduced in 2002, without real problems. But the seeds of future crises had already been sown. Several countries indulged in creative accounting to pass the budget test, and another criterion – a 60% cap on government debt to GDP – was effectively ignored. And the decline in interest rates across the region fuelled speculative bubbles, as we shall see.

## The build-up to the crisis

The crisis that ended this era had its roots in an unexpected place – the American housing market. What happened to US house prices in the late 1990s and early 2000s was most unusual. Robert Shiller of Yale University had looked at the long-term history of house prices in the US and found that the real price increase between 1890 and 1997 was about 12%. Then, in the eight years between 1998 and 2006, they rose 85%. Nothing like it had been seen before. This was not caused by population growth, which was only rising steadily, nor by building costs. Nor could it plausibly be ascribed to a shortage of housing. If that had been the case, rents would have risen just as fast. But the cost of buying a house, relative to renting one, doubled between 1997 and 2006.[41]

There were similar housing booms elsewhere. In Australia, real house prices rose 6% a year between 1995 and 2005, compared with 2.5% growth in the previous 50 years.[42] In Ireland, the average price of a new house rose 250% between 1996 and 2006. The country was building too many houses in the boom. A similar speculation-fuelled construction boom occurred in Spain. In 2007, the country started more houses than did Britain, France, Germany and Italy combined, and 13% of the workforce was in the construction sector.[43]

In the case of both Ireland and Spain, the fundamental problem may have been the "one size fits all" monetary policy that was part of being in the single currency. Both countries had much higher interest rates than Germany before they began the process of joining the euro. As rates fell, borrowing money began to look very cheap. And borrowing money to buy a property that was rapidly rising in price seemed like a no-brainer.

Another factor behind the bubble was the very low level of bond yields. This seems to have been driven by the reaction of Asian countries to the late 1990s crisis. They ran trade surpluses, accumulated foreign exchange reserves, and then invested them in US government bonds. In the view of Ben Bernanke, who became Fed chairman in 2006, this led to a "savings glut" that kept yields low.[44]

All seemed to be going well for the world economy in 2006. The liberal market economy – a combination of the welfare state, free markets and a buoyant financial sector – had been adopted across the developed world and was accepted by centre-left politicians like Bill Clinton and Tony Blair as well as by conservatives. Tony Blair retired as British prime minister in June 2007. His reputation had been tarnished by the Iraq War of 2003, but, in economic terms, he was seen as a success. He did not say, like Louis XV of France, "Après moi, le déluge". All the same, the skies were about to open.

When they did, politicians' lives became much trickier. As public finances deteriorated, they faced some awkward choices about the relationship between the state and the banking sector, and about the level of public spending.

# GOVERNMENT: AN EVER-PRESENT FORCE

The Advanced Manufacturing Research Centre in England's South Yorkshire is a gleaming temple of modern industry. The visitor is surrounded by low-rise, spacious buildings in glass and metal. Some of the biggest names in high-tech manufacturing have facilities in the area, including Boeing, Airbus, Rolls-Royce and McLaren, the racing car manufacturer.[1]

The site might seem like a prime example of the virtues of the private sector. But its history is a lot more complex. in 1984, the same location staged one of the worst battles between police and organised labour in British history, the so-called "Battle of Orgreave", when picketing miners tried to stop lorries from collecting supplies from a coking plant. The miners lost and by the late 1990s the site was derelict. Two local men, Adrian Allen, a businessman, and Professor Keith Ridgway of Sheffield University, had the brainwave of reviving the area by creating a manufacturing centre of excellence.[2]

That took a lot of help from Boeing, which became the founding tenant of the new centre. But it also required assistance from the UK government's Department of Trade, the local Rotherham council, Yorkshire Forward (a regional development agency), and the university, all of which are public bodies. In addition, the centre has received £70m in funds from the UK government since its foundation and another £70m from the EU. It is an important centre for apprentice-ship training for the engineering industry, a UK government priority.

So is the centre a private or public sector initiative? Clearly, it is a bit of both. Without the government, it might never have started; without the private sector, it would not be a training ground for apprentices, keen to qualify for high-skilled jobs in manufacturing. And that reflects much of economic history. Sometimes governments have penalised or hindered the growth of the private sector. Some-times, the private sector has got into such a mess that governments have been forced to come to its rescue. Sometimes, private sector for-tunes have been made on the back of innovations first developed by the government. The fortunes of the two are frequently intertwined.

At the most basic level, business needs a reasonable level of law and order if it is going to operate. If its products are stolen on the way to the factory, or customers refuse to pay without suffering a penalty, there is no point in operating. Commerce needs an independent judiciary that can make unbiased decisions in contract disputes. Businesses depend on public infrastructure – the roads, bridges and tunnels – that bring in supplies and take out the final goods. Even where some parts of the infrastructure are privately owned, they may still depend on public support; privately operated airports and air-lines depend on public air-traffic control systems, for example.

In most countries, businesses rely on workers who have been educated by the public sector, and whose health will be maintained by public health systems. In the case of an emergency, such as fire and flood, the public sector will be the first to respond. Many technolo-gies, including the internet, have been developed by public sector research.

All these public services – defence, law, justice, transport, edu-cation, health, etc. – need resources, and in much of the world, the funds come from taxes paid by the private sector. Of course, there were many 20th-century societies where the state attempted to fund all services by taking direct control of the private sector. But the record clearly suggests that an economy will grow fastest, and thus more money will be released for the public sector, in a mixed economy. Contrast living standards in North and South Korea, or in China, before and after the post-Mao reforms.

For the past 100 years, one of the most heated economic debates has been the role of the state within the economy. One common myth is that there once was an "Eden", when the government limited its action to enforcing the law and defending the nation's borders. This book has already cited many examples of ancient projects – pyramid building in Egypt, the Grand Canal in China – built by forced state labour; and under the European feudal system, peasants were made to perform duties for local nobles who derived their authority from the state. The English and Dutch merchants who went out and conquered large parts of the world in search of spices in the 17th and 18th centuries were working for state-chartered organisations. An absolute monarch like Louis XIV of France regarded the nation's assets and revenues as his own, to dispose with as he saw fit.

To the extent that early modern governments thought about the economy at all, they saw its function as being to generate the revenues that could pay for the nation's defence (and court luxuries). For a while, this manifested itself in a philosophy crudely known as mercantilism – trade was a zero-sum game in which the aim was to ensure that your own nation's coffers had more gold and silver and other countries had less. This led governments to favour their merchants at the expense of those of other nations.

Under the influence of evangelical Christianity, governments started to intervene in the economy, not simply to increase wealth, in the form of precious metals, but to increase welfare, in the sense of the greater good. There was recognition that markets might not always boost the latter. In particular, there was the issue of what economists call "externalities". A chemical factory could dump toxic waste into a river or pollute the air without any market penalty; only the government could act to stop such abuses.

Even in the Victorian era, Britain was never a completely "laissez-faire" economy in which the private sector could do what it liked. The governments of other countries were involved to an even greater extent than that. As already noted, the American railway system was built with the help of generous land grants from the federal government, while Napoleon III of France promoted both the banking system and the railways.

As the economy has become more sophisticated, governments

have vastly expanded the role that they play. In 1880, the German and British government spent around 10% of GDP, while American government spending was even less than that at around 2%. The two world wars saw big leaps in outlays, and while governments retreated in peacetime, the trend was strongly upwards. By the 1970s, many European governments were spending 50% of GDP. There was some retrenchment in the 1980s and 1990s but the most notable shift was at the extremes. Public spending as a share of Swedish GDP rose from 25% in 1955 to 58% between 1965 and 1985, and peaked, in the midst of a financial crisis, at 77% in 1993.[3] By 2017, it had dropped to 47%.[4]

## The role of democracy

In a sense, the opening up of national economies to global trade also required social spending in order to cushion the blow of the inevitable downturns. The private sector may deliver growth in the long run, but at the expense of short-term volatility. The Great Depression made it very apparent that democracy and capitalism imperilled themselves when they failed to prevent a general economic downturn. The generation of politicians that emerged after 1945 learned that lesson and offered much greater social protection.

The rise of government spending is clearly related to the shift towards democracy. When countries were governed by aristocrats and large merchants, they naturally steered governments towards protecting their own financial interests; keeping the size of the state small so that taxes were low and maintaining the value of the currency via the gold standard. Taxes were largely in the form of customs duties, which had a bigger proportionate impact on the incomes of workers than on those of the rich. As more workers got the vote, and demanded more services, taxes on income gradually became more important as revenue raisers. When these taxes were at the highest levels, during the world wars and the 1960s and 1970s, they had a significant impact in reducing inequality.

Taxes on the highest incomes were cut back in the 1980s. In part, this was because of the perception that very high rates created disincentives to work or create new businesses, and thus were bad for growth. But another problem was that, from the 1980s onwards, it became much easier for capital and people to move round the world.

A high-tax jurisdiction thus risked losing businesses and highly skilled people to low-tax areas. Ireland, for example, cut its tax rate on corporate profits to 12.5% at the turn of the millennium and succeeded in attracting many US multinationals.

An economic boom in the 1990s meant that government finances generally looked healthy, so this was not initially perceived as a risk. But the long-term problem was that competition eroded the tax base while the demands on government coffers continued to rise.

The biggest components of spending tend to be welfare (benefits paid to the elderly, unemployed and so on), education, health, defence, law and order, and housing. In contrast, foreign aid, a regular target for attack by some on the right, comprises only around 1% of the budget in the US and less than 2% in Britain. But let us focus on the three main categories, where the growth has been greatest.

## Welfare

An economy based on manufacturing and services is a lot more complex than one based on agriculture. In a farming-based economy, the main fear was food shortages. As noted in Chapter 1, grain was a crop that could be stored, and power accrued to those who supervised the storage process. The Romans distributed grain to all citizens, and the Venetians stored food to help the city through a siege. There may not have been elections but monarchs who failed to keep their populations fed put themselves at risk; a shortage of bread was one factor behind the French Revolution.

In a sense, a poor harvest represented the "recession" stage of the economic cycle. Most governments acknowledged, albeit grudgingly, a need to help the disadvantaged in some way. The Abbasid caliphate, which ruled much of the Middle East and North Africa from the mid-eighth century CE to the mid-13th century, levied taxes to help the needy, while charitable giving is one of the five pillars of Islam.

In a peasant economy, unemployment tended to be seasonal in nature; there were jobs at harvest time but not in the winter. Families tended to look after their own members and had their own food supplies (a garden, chickens, etc.) that they could share round. As people moved away from the land, this safety net was no longer available. The English Poor Laws were passed in the late 16th century and provided relief to the old and the sick. By the 19th century, these laws were amended in favour of a system that distinguished the "deserving" from the "undeserving" poor. It was assumed that any able-bodied person could find work if they were willing, so poor relief was made as unpleasant as possible, with recipients confined to the workhouse.

As the industrial sector grew, so did the power of factory workers to paralyse the economy via strikes. Governments welcomed the extra wealth and the boost to military strength brought by the factories, but feared that workers would be seduced by the appeal of socialism and communism. So they sought ways to buy them off. Otto von Bismarck, the German chancellor, was worried about the rise of the Social Democratic Party and thus pursued a two-pronged strategy, banning left-wing parties while offering old-age pensions and health and accident insurance to undercut the socialists' appeal. The reforming British Liberal government, first elected in 1906, introduced a similar series of reforms, including labour exchanges to help the unemployed find work. Liberal politicians had a more sincere belief in social reform than did Bismarck; nevertheless, they were clearly hoping to head off an emerging electoral challenge from the Labour Party.

The First World War required the mobilisation of large sections of the male population. In the circumstances, it was hard to deny those men a vote on their return in 1918, and politicians competed to offer servicemen the prospect of a better life. Women had entered the workforce to replace the absent soldiers and they too were given the vote in many (but not all) countries. The Russian Revolution of 1917 also frightened the political elite into offering policies that favoured the working classes.

But the Great Depression was the turning point, in terms of government involvement in the economy. The collapse in GDP and the accompanying surge in unemployment seemed to demand action. The argument that the market would correct itself sounded hollow. According to traditional theory, wages would fall far enough to make it attractive to employ more workers, but the Great Depression showed that this did not always happen. In the 1930s, the totalitarian states of Germany and the Soviet Union were taking action to provide jobs for their people. Their apparent economic success made some inclined to overlook, or dismiss as propaganda, the brutality of those regimes – the concentration camps and the gulags, or the famine in 1932–33 that killed millions of Ukrainians. The democracies were much slower to bring down unemployment, even under Roosevelt's New Deal. Ironically, they eventually did stimulate their economies when they rearmed in the face of the threat from Hitler's Germany.

The widespread suffering caused by the Second World War created the demand that societies should make a new start after 1945. The famous report of William Beveridge, a British Liberal politician, argued that governments should tackle the five "giant evils" – want, ignorance, disease, squalor and idleness. In much of western Europe, power alternated between social democratic parties and right-wing parties of the "Christian Democrat" variety, which were happy to offer welfare benefits.

Welfare spending creates a number of potential trade-offs. The first is whether benefits are universal (such as state pensions for all those who reach retirement age) or means-tested and thus aimed at those in greatest need. Universal benefits are obviously more expensive. But means-tested benefits can be politically unpopular. A lot of bureaucracy is required to establish which people are the most deserving, a process that can be very intrusive and causes resentment. Inevitably, there will be hard cases in which the rules are misapplied and people suffer needlessly. Furthermore, benefit spending can be perceived as taking money from those in work and giving it to those without. Means-testing implied that many of the taxpayers who funded the benefits would never receive them; universal benefits, however, avoided that problem. Hence many benefit plans were sold as insurance schemes in which workers paid in now, so they would receive payouts later.

Another trade-off relates to incentives. If benefit levels are high relative to paid work, then people will choose to stay at home. But if benefits are too low, families will suffer. One way round the problem is to make benefits payable to those in work as well. But it is a tricky line to walk. As benefits are withdrawn, it is theoretically possible for workers to face a marginal tax rate of over 100%; for every extra $1 they earn, they lose $1.10 of income. The more complex the range of benefits, the more likely it is that disincentives will occur.

Complexity also creates another set of trade-offs. Not all people on benefits will need the same level of support. Some will live in expensive cities; some in cheaper rural areas. Some will have children, or elderly parents, to look after; some will not. Governments may also be concerned that making a large payment to one adult (usually the father) may result in the wife and children being short of cash while the man spends all the money down the pub. So benefits come in a variety of forms. Food stamps, for example, are designed to insure that families get enough nutrition; another approach is free school meals. But such an obviously targeted benefit may result in stigma being attached to the recipients. Another problem is when the government decides to subsidise rent via housing benefits. The result may simply be that those on benefits can afford higher rents, so the landlords, not the tenants, are those who make the biggest gains.

In political terms, the left has tended to worry that stringent benefit rules, designed to eliminate fraud, will leave genuine claimants in need. The right has worried that generous benefit rules, designed to help those in need, will create too much scope for fraud and idleness. European states have been at the more generous end of the benefit scale. A few years ago, Angela Merkel, the long-running German chancellor, voiced concern about the fact that Europe had 7% of the world's population, 25% of its GDP, and 50% of its social costs.[5] Many attempts have been made to cut welfare spending, but this has proved hard as the population ages and more money needs to be spent on pensions and healthcare.

### Education

Roughly 12% of the global population was literate in 1800.[6] Many peasants had little need to read. Books were expensive and newspapers were rare, while the focus of people's work was practical and learned by copying the actions of others. By 1900, this literacy rate had edged up to 21%. Further acceleration took the rate to 35% by 1950 and around 85% today.

In part, this is down to the changing nature of work, which requires employees to follow written instructions or to interact with colleagues and customers via a computer. Illiterate citizens will find it difficult to perform many jobs. Child labour has reduced substantially and parents are required, in many countries, to send their children to school.

Educated officials have always been necessary for the operation of a centralised state; China, for example, operated an examination system to seek out the best-qualified individuals from 605CE onwards. The time and resources needed to pass the exams meant that such jobs tended to be occupied by the children of higher social ranks. The medieval church needed priests who could understand the Bible and the liturgy (in Latin, of course). Merchants who traded using bills of exchange, or on the basis of legal partnerships, needed to be literate to read such documents.

Prussia introduced compulsory state education in 1763, but elsewhere the drive for a more general education only emerged in the 19th century. In part this reflected the need for a more educated workforce. In theory, landed elites might have resisted the spread of education through a fear that the literate population might be more politically active. In practice, however, the economic argument held sway. In Sweden, for example, a study found that districts governed by local elites spent substantially more on primary schooling than those where power was more equally distributed.[7]

Many parents preferred their children to work in the fields, where they could be of use, or in the factories, where they could earn their households extra income. But Victorian reformers tried to end child labour. In Britain, a series of acts from 1870 to 1880 set up school boards to manage the system in England and Scotland, and made education compulsory for children between the ages of five and ten. In America, compulsory education was gradually introduced at the state level, starting with Massachusetts in 1852 and ending with Mississippi in 1918.

Over time, the age range for education has been extended, with most countries requiring children to attend school until at least 15, and in some cases 18.[8] The 20th century also saw a massive expansion of university education; the proportion attending college rose from less than 1% in 1900 to around 20% by 2000, or 100 million students.[9]

In some countries, the proportion is significantly higher. In 2015, 40% of American employed individuals aged 25 to 64 had a college degree, and around 14% possessed postgraduate qualifications. There is plenty of incentive for young people to take further education. Those workers who only completed high school earned just three-fifths of the hourly wages of those who graduated from college and less than half the rate earned by postgraduates.[10]

Some of this education is supplied privately. But governments have seen it as in the country's interests to expand education, especially as low-skilled jobs are being automated or shifted to low-wage centres in Asia.

## Health

As late as 1820, life expectancy at birth was only around 29 worldwide, and 36 in Europe. By 1913, it had edged up to 34 worldwide but was in the mid-40s in Europe and America. By 1970, the global average was 60, and Europeans could expect to live into their seventies.[11] By 2015, the global average was 71.4 years, more than double that of a century earlier.[12]

This is an immense, and oft-overlooked, achievement. In part it is down to a big fall in the child mortality rate; the global rate for infant mortality has dropped from 18% in the 1960s to 4% today (see chart).[13] Governments have played a huge role in this decline. It is not just about building hospitals and training doctors. Governments have also delivered clean water and sanitation to households, and have sponsored medical research and public health campaigns, such as vaccination (around 88% of the world's children now receive some kind of vaccination).[14]

However, healthcare costs seem to be on an inexorably rising trend, increasing from 5.5% of EU GDP in 1970 to more than 9.4% by 2012.[15] In America, the rise has been even faster, from 5% of GDP in 1960 to 17.9% in 2016.[16] As people live longer, they are more inclined to get chronic illnesses like diabetes and heart disease, which involve prolonged and recurring treatment; those who suffer from cancer or strokes can survive for many years. All this costs money. And as the population of the developed world ages, the costs seem set to rise. More than half of total American health spending in 2015 was devoted to people aged 55 and over.[17]

Different countries have different ways of paying for these costs, with government provision supplemented by private insurance

**Save the children**

Child mortality, share of world population, %

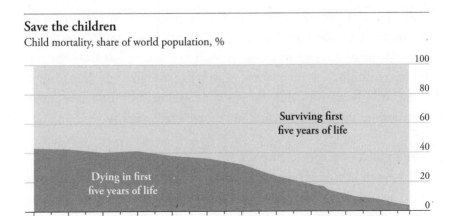

Sources: Gapminder; World Bank

schemes for those who can afford them. Some argue that treatment at no cost to the patient, as provided by systems like Britain's, means that there is no way of capping demand for health services. But the most expensive healthcare system in the world is America's, which has a large private sector element, and it delivers a lower life expectancy and a higher infant mortality rate than many European nations.[18]

Healthcare spending is an example of a policy trilemma, in which all three goals cannot be simultaneously achieved. There are three "C"s – costs, choice and coverage. You can control costs, offer people a choice of treatment, or cover everyone, but not all three. The British system covers everyone, but restricts choice; the American system offers lots of choice, but the costs are high, and some people cannot afford treatment. A 2015 Gallup survey found that almost a third of Americans delayed medical treatment in the previous year owing to the cost.[19]

Again, there are trade-offs here. The laudable aim of public provision is to ensure that no person is denied medical treatment because of a lack of resources. Public healthcare also aligns the interests of patients and medical staff; no one wants to feel that their doctor might put profit before the best course of treatment. And there is an economic interest in ensuring that the population is healthy and able to work. But the public sector can struggle to meet the demand for healthcare, and the result is that services are rationed, meaning that patients can face a long wait for treatment. An insurance-based approach has problems too. Unless insurance is compulsory, there is a danger of adverse selection. Young healthy people will not buy policies but old, sick people will. This will drive up costs. In addition, there will always be a need to cover people who do not have insurance; no doctor wants to turn away a car-crash victim.

## The macro-economic impact

The growth in government spending and taxation in the 20th century was about more than simply providing welfare, health and education. Governments were attempting to manage the economy by preventing deep recessions. The lesson they had learned from the 1930s and from the teachings of John Maynard Keynes was that depressions could be caused by a contraction in demand. The last thing that a government should do in the circumstances would be to try to balance its budget by raising taxes or cutting spending. Indeed, welfare spending acted as an "automatic stabiliser" for the economy; by paying benefits to the unemployed, those citizens would be able to keep spending, maintaining demand for the goods and services produced by those in work.

In the 1950s and 1960s, European governments attempted to manage the economic cycle through fiscal policy (tax and spending decisions) or, where central banks were not independent, through monetary policy (changing the level of interest rates and widening, or tightening, the availability of credit). Following the 1970s, the use of fiscal policy for this purpose declined somewhat, and monetary policy took the strain. That said, from 1945 onwards, voters did seem to regard economic management as one of their government's primary responsibilities; as Bill Clinton's presidential campaign in 1992 put it: "It's the economy, stupid."

What has varied over the decades has been the primary target of economic policy. In the immediate post-war years, while memories of the Depression were still strong, the main aim was to keep unemployment low. By the 1970s, the concern started to switch from unemployment to inflation.

From the 1980s onwards, governments moved away from stimulating demand to trying to boost supply, and thus long-term growth.

This became even more the case when responsibility for fighting inflation was given to central banks. These supply-side reforms, as mentioned in the last chapter, often focused on making the labour market more flexible. The theory is that businesses will be reluctant to employ workers if they feel that tax and other social costs are high, and they will be unable to shed labour if conditions deteriorate. In an inflexible labour market, the risk is of a division developing between insiders who have lifetime jobs and outsiders who spend long periods in unemployment; that has been the pattern in Spain and France.

Even before they tried to manage the whole economy, governments intervened in industry to promote certain sectors and to block others. Britain pushed through the Navigation Acts in the 17th century to promote domestic shipping, and banned foreign calicoes (cotton textiles) in the 18th century in order to protect the wool sector.

There are many options for governments that want to promote particular businesses: tariffs (or outright bans) on foreign goods; subsidies, or tax breaks, to encourage domestic production; and the granting of monopolies to certain groups, like the East India Company. Such policies were favoured by many developing countries after the Second World War. Politicians argued that "infant" industries needed protection from foreign competition until they could build up the necessary scale (this is the import-substituting industrialisation referred to in earlier chapters). Another argument was that some industries were strategic; a country needed its own steel supplies so that it could not be cut off by foreign producers.

But the dangers of this approach are pretty clear. First, companies that are protected have less incentive to be efficient, or to respond to consumer demand. The result is that they produce goods that are more expensive, or are of poor quality; think of the Trabant cars that East Germans were forced to buy under communism. Second, such arrangements are easily corrupted. Producers have a big incentive to reward politicians who keep the subsidies in place. Even when the arrangements are legal and transparent, they tend to be very hard to shift; US sugar subsidies were first introduced in 1934 and are still in place, although they cost consumers hundreds of millions a year.[20] But the programme is supported by sugar producers in Florida, who are keen contributors to political coffers in a large, electorally significant state. A subsidy is worth a lot to a small number of producers and the cost is spread among millions of consumers, who do not have sufficient incentive to campaign against it.

## Governments and technological change

A much more positive case can be made for the way that governments boost industry by funding research and innovation, like the Sheffield centre featured at the start of the chapter. Many innovations have been based on government research, particularly those developed for the defence industry. Both the internet and global positioning satellites (the ones that enable satnav systems in cars) were developed by the military. The Second World War provided an enormous boost to the development of the computer, while the microwave oven was a side effect of the development of radar. Google's search algorithm was funded with the help of a grant from the National Science Foundation, while touchscreen technology was developed by publicly funded academics.[21]

Marianna Mazzucato, an economist at University College, London, argues that a myth has been created in which the state is always lumbering and bureaucratic, whereas in reality it has been vital in funding high-risk investments in areas like pharmaceuticals and technology.[22] In 2013 countries in the OECD spent about $40bn on publicly funded research and development, and another $30bn on tax breaks for R&D.[23]

It is tough to assess the long-term record of government investment. For all the successes noted by Ms Mazzucato, there have been plenty of examples of governments backing "white elephant" projects; Concorde, the supersonic airliner, for example, or costly nuclear power stations. The private sector makes mistakes as well, of course. But once governments commit themselves to these projects, it can be very hard for politicians to admit their mistakes and cut their losses.

But it is pretty clear that there is a public interest in funding long-term research. Private companies may be unwilling or unable to commit funds to projects that may require decades for a pay-off to be seen. Or they may not fund drug research to treat diseases that are rare, or are confined to poor countries. Governments can step in and fill the gap.

Indeed, this points to one of the most powerful arguments for government intervention. The private sector, left to its own devices, will not solve all problems and can create its own. There may be a tendency towards monopoly, as with Standard Oil in the late 19th century, that results in consumers being overcharged (or other producers being unfairly kept out of the market). There may be "negative externalities", as with a chemical company that dumps pollutants into the river or the air. There may be asymmetries of information or of power, with consumers or workers being in no position to negotiate on equal or fair terms with big companies. In such cases, regulation will be needed.

## Autarky and authoritarian capitalism

What has been described so far is the mixed economy of a Western democracy. But this is far from a universally accepted model. Authoritarian regimes of the left and right have traditionally believed that the private sector's interests should be subordinated to those of the government. The rationale for such an approach is sometimes ideological and sometimes practical.

Under communism, governments controlled the "means of production, distribution and exchange". The rationale was twofold. First, the aim was to ensure that workers received the full fruits of their labours, instead of a sizeable portion being siphoned off to owners of capital in the forms of profits, dividends and interest payments. Second, communists argued that the private sector was inefficient, and that only in a planned economy could it be ensured that the right quantity of goods was produced.

Some absolute monarchs were suspicious of industrialisation, fearing that it would bring disruptive change to the economy, which might threaten their rule. Given the role played by workers in the Russian Revolution, this perception was not entirely wrong. In the 20th century, authoritarian regimes were suspicious of the private sector as a rival source of power and of trade as a potential source of foreign influence. Both Hitler's Germany and imperial Japan believed that it was vital for a country to control its own resources, and thus sought either to develop home-grown substitutes or to annex those resources via conquest.

In strict terms, autarky is the idea of national self-sufficiency. It is hardly surprising that it is the aim of warlike regimes, since in wartime, countries often find themselves cut off from foreign supplies. The British and the French both tried to cut the other's supply lines during the Napoleonic Wars. Even today, countries impose economic sanctions on rivals they dislike.

Few states aim for autarky today. The modern model is what might be called "authoritarian capitalism". In Russia, the end of communism was followed by a wave of privatisation, with the result that industries were controlled by a set of oligarchs. Those titans may have made themselves rich but they serve at the pleasure of the government, something that was made abundantly clear when Mikhail Khodorkovsky, the head of the oil company Yukos, was stripped of his wealth and sent to prison after he opposed President Vladimir Putin.

China has followed a different variant of this model. It has introduced private markets, and allowed various entrepreneurs to get rich. But the state still has big stakes in leading companies, businessmen rely on credit from state-owned banks, and a link to a senior party official is wise if the company wants to operate over the long term. Foreign companies are allowed to operate in the country, but they need a domestic partner, and many complain that their intellectual property has been stolen by Chinese groups.

It is hard to argue with the Chinese model when it has delivered such rapid growth. But plenty of other countries have shown that state capitalism is prone to great corruption. Energy-rich countries are subject to the "resource curse" in which so much money is available from the oil and gas industries that the elite simply focuses on taking the "rents" from that business; other sectors are neglected.

In many countries, it is simply too hard to open a business. In the 1980s, the economist Hernando de Soto tried to open a small garment workshop in Lima, Peru. To get legal authorisation took 289 days of work, at an average of six hours a day. The cost was 31 times the monthly minimum wage. In many countries, it is very time-consuming and expensive for someone to get legal ownership to their land; in Haiti, it took 19 years, de Soto found. But without legal title, it has historically been difficult in developing countries for people to get credit, since banks often insist on collateral, in the form of property.[24] This is a real barrier to economic growth.

The World Bank publishes an "ease of doing business" index, which reflects the amount of regulation and the strength of property rights. Unsurprisingly, some of the poorest countries in the world, such as Eritrea and Somalia, were at the bottom of the index in late 2018, along with Venezuela, an oil-rich country ruined by bad policies.[25] While some worry that corporations can have too much influence over governments, in some cases they can have too little.

In short, governments will always be subject to competing pressures – from consumers and from workers, who will want more regulation of the private sector, and from corporations, who want less; from consumers of public services, who want higher spending and more benefits, and from taxpayers who resent paying for them. For all the apparent ideological differences between political parties, the governments of most developed countries spend something between 30% and 50% of GDP.[26] That is much higher than a 19th-century politician would have considered possible. But it seems to be the natural range for a modern democracy.

In the last couple of decades of the 20th century, the most interesting developments in the relationship between government and the private sector occurred in the developing world. Many countries pursued policies that sought to encourage private business, particularly when they sold their goods in the global market. As we shall see, some had great success.

# A TRULY GLOBAL ECONOMY:
# THE DEVELOPING WORLD,
# 1979–2007

Napoleon famously said: "Let China sleep. When she wakes, she will shake the world." The world's most populous country emerged from the nightmare of Mao's rule in 1976, or, as Stephen Radelet, an economist, wrote: "In 1976, Mao single-handedly and dramatically changed the direction of global poverty with one simple act: he died."[1]

The speed of China's economic advance since that date is surely unprecedented. In 1980, China's GDP per capita was lower than that of Chad or Bangladesh. By 2012, its real GDP had increased 30-fold over the 1980 level.[2] By that stage, it had become the second-largest economy in the world. It reshaped global trade in the process (see chart).

The first step of Deng Xiaoping, Mao's successor, was to reform agriculture. Farmers still had to hand over a proportion of their output to the state but they were allowed to sell the rest and limits on prices were lifted. There was some inflation but the effect on food output was spectacular. Yields rose by 40% per acre and rural incomes rose by 18% a year between 1978 and 1984.[3] Farmers also started to plant different crops, like rapeseed and sugar cane, which party commissars had frowned upon. With a greater incentive to produce more, farmers also bought more equipment; the number of agricultural

**A growth miracle**

China, GDP per person, annual growth, %

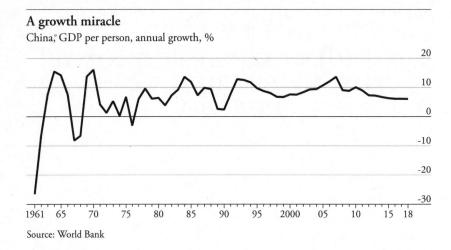

Source: World Bank

trucks rose from 74,000 in 1978 to more than 600,000 by the end of the 1980s.[4]

There followed a wave of reforms that were, in part, an experiment to see what worked and, in part, an attempt to reward local initiative. Deng's philosophy was that "It doesn't matter whether a cat is black or white as long as it catches mice." Yuen Yuen Ang, a political science professor, argues that one important reason for his success was that the Chinese government created the markets first, and let the institutions develop afterwards. Another was that the incentives were right. Local leaders who achieved economic growth were promoted, and local governments were allowed to keep a sizeable chunk of any extra revenues generated.[5]

One of the biggest growth areas was the creation of town and village enterprises or TVEs, which were owned by local governments. Like the farmers, they had to hand over part of the revenue to the central government but could keep any excess for themselves. By 2000, there were 20 million TVEs employing 100 million people, producing a quarter of national output.[6] Another approach was to create special enterprise zones (SEZ), which were given tax breaks and subsidies that were designed to attract foreign investment. The first SEZ was Shenzhen, just across from Hong Kong, which was still under British rule at this stage (and an example of what might be achieved with pro-growth policies). The coastal areas quickly prospered and set up factories that attracted workers from the inland rural areas.

After a decade of the economic reform programme, a sudden surge in food prices caused a wave of protests in 1989 that eventually included calls for more democracy. There were hopes that this would lead to political liberalisation but the protests were crushed by tanks in Tiananmen Square in Beijing. Ironically, this happened just before communist governments started to fall in Eastern Europe. The Chinese party has not relaxed its grip since, a sign that prosperity need not always lead to democracy.

But the protests did persuade Deng to undertake a tour in order to promote economic development. In 1993, his successor, Jiang Zemin, declared that the country was establishing a "socialist market economy" with five pillars: modern enterprises, market mechanisms, macroeconomic controls, income redistribution, and a social safety net.[7]

This was quite a different model from the Western system. It was authoritarian capitalism, in which most companies were either owned by the government or had links to a powerful official. Even in 2019, by which stage the private sector generated 60% of GDP, China had around 150,000 state companies, which accounted for 70% of all corporate debt.[8] The party has the most significant voice in the appointment of chief executives and the setting of their pay. In 2009, it reshuffled the bosses of China's three largest airlines, and, in 2010, did the same for the oil companies.[9] Purely private companies have succeeded in China but they have to tread carefully. Several executives were arrested in a corruption crackdown in 2015–17.[10]

In its earliest growth phase, China concentrated on the low-value goods where its low wages gave it a clear competitive advantage. By 1990, it had become the world's largest textile exporter.[11] Later on, the country moved into electronics and became a key part of the global supply chain. By 2018, China was home to more than half of the world's manufacturing capacity for electronics. Foxconn, which is Apple's largest supplier, employs 250,000 people in Shenzhen alone.[12] When Lenovo, the Chinese technology group, bought IBM's personal computer business in 2004, it seemed a symbolic power shift from west to east.

As South Korea and Taiwan had done in the post-war period, China launched an export drive, with its share of global exports rising from 1% in 1980 to 14% in 2015.[13] This was accompanied by an astonishingly high savings rate, which rose from 35% of GDP in the 1980s to 41% in the 1990s and 53% in 2007.[14] These savings translated into high rates of investment, as China built massive cities, factories, roads and power stations – in some cases virtually from scratch. One statistic stands out. In the years 2011 to 2013, China used 6.6 gigatons of concrete; that was more than the US deployed in the whole of the 20th century.[15] (A gigaton is 1bn metric tonnes.)

China's rapid growth at such a sustained rate has had profound effects on the global economy. It was China, more than anywhere else, that drove the second great phase of globalisation. Between 1980 and 2007, world trade growth averaged nearly 5.9% a year.[16]

In 1994, the Uruguay round of trade negotiations led to further cuts in tariffs and the establishment of the World Trade Organisation (WTO) to set the rules of global trade. China was accepted into the WTO in 2001 in the belief that this would lead to a liberalising of its economy. The country did cut tariffs, from 25% to 9%, but China did not open up as much as the outside world had hoped.[17] China's massive trade surpluses, and the sense that it was not playing by the same rules as the developed world, led to resentment in other countries, particularly in the US.

## Asian tigers

China was not the only Asian economy to record spectacular growth. Between 1970 and 1996, a range of nations managed average annual growth between 6.8% and 8.4%, including Hong Kong, Indonesia, Malaysia, Singapore, Thailand and (as mentioned in Chapter 12) South Korea and Taiwan. This was much more rapid growth than western Europe or North America had ever achieved in their industrialising phase. Success was built on a high level of investment, a focus on manufacturing for export markets, and government support for business.[18]

All this came to a spectacular halt in 1997 and 1998 in what became known as the Asian crisis. The problems first emerged in Thailand, where the government had pegged its currency (the baht) to the US dollar. The peg encouraged overseas capital to flow into the country (13% of GDP poured in during 1995),[19] and it also prompted Thai companies and banks to borrow in dollars, since they could get lower interest rates in the US currency. A lot of this money was short-term, or linked to property speculation.

The problem came when the money wanted to flow out again. The Thai authorities tried to defend their currency by using their reserves (selling dollars, and buying bahts) and pushing up interest rates to attract capital. But the reserves ran low and high interest rates damaged the economy. The only alternative was to devalue the currency, but when the Thais did that, there was a financial crisis. All those companies and banks that had borrowed in dollars now faced a much bigger bill for repayment. And once investors saw the Thais devalue, they worried about the prospect of other countries follow-ing suit. There was a sell-off across the region, and at one point, the Indonesian currency dropped 80% against the dollar.[20]

This brought many criticisms of the Asian model, as it was dubbed. The most significant was that the economies were marked by "crony capitalism", in which governments handed out favours such as monopoly rights or subsidies to friendly businessmen. The clearest example was President Suharto of Indonesia, who had ruled for 30 years and whose family had amassed assets of around $30bn in the process.[21] One study found that the family had significant stakes in 1,246 companies.[22] Suharto was forced to call in the IMF, which insisted on its standard package of spending cuts and the dismantling of monopolies. In the midst of the chaos, Suharto fell from power, in May 1998.[23]

Paul Krugman, the economist, had argued, even before the crisis, that the Asian "miracle" was down to a surge in capital investment and a rise in labour participation that could not be sustained. In Singapore, for example, the proportion of the population in employ-ment rose from 27% in 1966 to 51% in 1990; over the same period, investment as a share of output had risen from 11% to 40%.[24] In some countries, this investment was incredibly inefficient. Thai Airways was run by the air force, and the fleet was a mix of different aircrafts and engine types because individual officers had negotiated their own deals.[25]

The crisis dragged on through 1998 and led to some sharp recessions in several Asian countries. But recovery came eventually, and the main long-term impact of the crisis was a change in attitude among Asian governments. They realised that depending on foreign capital made them vulnerable and decided instead to focus on generating trade surpluses so that they could build up foreign exchange reserves. This would have significant global effects in the next decade.

### India reforms

The transformation of India was not quite as dramatic as that of China but it was still hugely significant. In 1991, the Indian economy faced another crisis. It asked for a loan from the IMF and had to airlift 47 tonnes of gold to the Bank of England as collateral.[26] In response to the crisis, Manmohan Singh, the finance minister, unveiled a package of reforms that cut regulations, invited foreign investment, and devalued the rupee. This was not a completely free-market approach, but it was a repudiation of the planned economy favoured by Nehru.

The results were highly positive. Over the following 20 years, growth averaged 7% a year, allowing the economy to increase almost fourfold in size. The roots of the Indian recovery had emerged in the 1980s when Infosys and Wipro, two technology companies, moved to Bangalore. The Bengal province proved attractive to international companies, thanks to a well-educated, English-speaking workforce. A swathe of operations were outsourced to Bangalore, including call centres, insurance processing, tax and audit preparation and IT maintenance.[27]

The Tata group was another symbol of India's revival. It had been founded back in 1868 under British rule and opened a steel plant in Jamshedpur in 1912, becoming the largest steel plant in the empire by the Second World War. Since then it has become a very diversified conglomerate, turning the tables on the former colonial overlord by buying some of its biggest brands, including Tetley tea, Jaguar Land Rover, and, most symbolically, the largest part of the British steel industry (Corus).

Most importantly, this economic growth reduced the high poverty rate. Between 2004 and 2011, the proportion of the Indian population living in extreme poverty (on less than $1.90 a day) fell from 39% to 21%. By 2018, India was no longer the country with the most people living in poverty (Nigeria took its place).[28]

## Russia and Eastern Europe

China was not the only communist country that tried to reform in the 1980s. Russians were aware that their standard of living was below that of the West and there was much cynicism about economic management; the running joke was "we pretend to work and they pretend to pay us". A new leader, Mikhail Gorbachev, emerged in 1985 with ideas to change the system. The key words were *perestroika*, for economic reform, and *glasnost*, for transparency in government. Gorbachev was a committed communist who believed the system could be saved.

As it turned out, reform seemed only to undermine the regime's legitimacy, and a fall in oil prices weakened the economy's main source of strength. Protests occurred in the eastern European nations that had been occupied since the war. Gorbachev, to his eternal credit, refused to follow the example of his predecessors by sending in the tanks. Eastern Europeans started to cross borders and the guards did not stop them; more than four decades of oppression had ended. Most symbolically, the Berlin Wall fell in November 1989. In a remarkably short period, Germany was reunited, Eastern European nations seized their independence, and the Soviet Union dissolved.

Russia was by far the largest of the 15 independent countries that emerged from the Soviet Union. Under Boris Yeltsin, the country adopted a process of shock therapy, which involved the elimination of price controls and subsidies, and the privatisation of many industries. But this reform programme was far less successful than that pursued in either China or India. Russia suffered a burst of hyperinflation that reached 1,500%, and its industry was quickly controlled by a bunch of oligarchs with good connections. Between 1991 and 1998, the Russian economy shrunk by around 30% and life expectancy fell sharply. Russia's first experience of capitalism was dismal and it was hardly surprising that a strongman in the form of Vladimir Putin was able to take control in the 2000s. The modern Russian economy remains highly dependent on its oil and gas resources.

The rest of the Soviet bloc also had problems in making the shift away from communism. The underlying problem was that many state enterprises were inefficient, producing substandard goods. Many of these goods had been sold to the Soviet Union, but Russia was going through its own problems, and was no longer an automatic buyer. In the free market, Eastern Europe's businesses would be crushed by competition. Under communism, many prices had been kept artificially low by subsidies; the result may have been low prices, but there were frequent shortages. In the 1980s, the waiting list for cars in East Germany was 15 years; in Bulgaria, it could take 20 years to get an apartment; while Romanians were limited to one 40-watt bulb per room.[29] Liberalising the price regime led to rapid inflation, at a time when workers were losing their jobs.

As a result, the 1990s were pretty dismal, in economic terms, for most eastern European citizens. In the five years after 1989, the average decline in GDP across eastern European and Baltic nations was 32.6%.[30] But by 1998, two countries in the bloc, Poland and the Czech Republic, had regained their 1989 levels of GDP. This recovery was driven by the decision of many western European manufacturers to shift production to the region because the wages were cheaper: Volkswagen moved into Bratislava (now the capital of Slovakia) in 1992, for example.[31] In the early 2000s, many countries in the former communist bloc enjoyed a boom. Then, in 2004, eight countries (the Czech Republic, Estonia, Hungary, Latvia, Lithuania, Poland, Slovakia and Slovenia) joined the EU. Many workers took advantage of freedom of movement laws to take jobs elsewhere and send part of their wages home.

By 2012, most eastern European economies had been integrated into western Europe, with around 70% of their exports going to the EU. And their post-communist growth records were respectable; GDP per capita grew 47% between 1990 and 2011 while consumption per capita grew 53%, faster than the global average. By 2012, eastern Europeans were more likely to own an apartment, or a car, ate more fruit and vegetables, had greater freedom to travel, and lived four years longer than they had under communist rule.[32]

## The Latin American crisis
The oil price surge of 1979, and the US tightening of monetary policy,

had a huge impact in an unexpected place – Latin America. In 1972, the average oil price was $2 a barrel; in 1980, it was $35.50.[33] This brought immense riches to oil-producing states, many of which were Middle Eastern states with relatively small populations. The money came in faster than the governments could spend it, and the surpluses tended to be deposited with the US banks. And once banks receive a deposit, they must lend out the money at a higher rate if they are to make a profit. In the 1970s, the lucky recipients of much of that money were Latin American governments, at a time when they were struggling to balance their budgets. In 1970, total Latin American debt was $29bn; by 1982, it was $327bn.[34]

This debt was largely denominated in dollars, and thus subject to shifts in US interest rates and changes in exchange rates. As the Fed tightened policy and economies fell into recession, the debt clearly became unsustainable. In 1982, Mexico declared that it could not service its $80bn of debts. Fifteen other Latin American countries followed suit, along with 11 other developing nations.

This was not just a problem for the countries concerned. In 1982, the nine largest US banks had outstanding loans to developing countries that were almost three times the value of their capital.[35] Outright default would bring down the banking system. So regulators allowed the American banks to put their potential losses to one side when calculating their capital ratios. Rather than negotiate separately with the Latin American nations, the creditors formed a coordinated group, with the IMF in the lead role.

But IMF money came with conditions, and usually required economic reform. The reforms, dubbed the "Washington consensus", included budget discipline, a reduction in subsidies, financial liberalisation, and privatisation. The overall aim was to reduce the role of the state and to give markets a bigger role in the economy. These policies proved immensely controversial, especially since balancing the budget often involved cuts to social safety nets, while the abolition of subsidies pushed up food and petrol prices.

New lenders were reluctant to commit money to the region, given its history of defaults. The result was that Latin America was actually transferring capital back to the West, rather than attracting funds that could build up the region's industry and infrastructure.

The 1980s was dubbed "the lost decade" because per capita income in the region was no higher at the end of the period than it was at the start.[36] Faced with these failures, Nicholas Brady, the US Treasury secretary, came up with a plan in 1989 that allowed for partial debt forgiveness, in which creditors swapped their claims for new debt, backed by American government bonds.

Perhaps the best way of focusing on the complex economic history of the region is to concentrate on two countries: Argentina and Mexico. At the start of the period, Argentina suffered persistent hyperinflation, which required several currency reforms, with the peso argentino replacing the previous version in 1983, at a rate of 1 new peso for every 10,000 of the old currency. That currency lasted only until 1985, when the austral replaced the peso at a rate of 1 to 1,000. And the austral was itself replaced by another peso in 1992 at a rate of 1 for every 10,000 australs. In effect this peso was worth 10bn of the old version that was in circulation less than a decade previously. This turmoil was accompanied by a dismal growth performance, with income per head falling by 1% a year between 1976 and 1989. The state telephone system was so inefficient that the waiting list for a landline was more than six years and people were employed with the sole task of holding a phone for hours until a dialling tone could be heard.[37]

The underlying problem was that the government repeatedly expanded the money supply to fund its budget deficits. In the 1990s, Domingo Cavallo, the economy minister, introduced an ambitious reform programme based around a currency board, in which the peso was pegged at one-to-one versus the dollar. The board had to be backed by dollar reserves, with the aim of preventing the government from taking the money-printing route. Inflation duly fell from 3,000% in 1989 to 3.4% in 1994 and the economy's growth rate in the early 1990s was 8%.

But the pressures on the currency board steadily rose. The government failed to maintain fiscal discipline, and its exporting competitiveness was hit when Brazil, its biggest market, devalued its currency by 30% in 1999. Argentina went back to the IMF for a further loan but it was not enough. Deposits started to flee the banks and, in the second half of 2001, the economy shrank at an annualised rate of 11%. In December, the government restricted bank withdrawals, sparking a wave of public protests.[38] As a succession of presidents came and went, Argentina defaulted on its debts, and it abandoned the currency board in 2002.

Sadly, in 2018, Argentina suffered another currency crisis, and turned to the IMF again. Under the rule of the Kirchners (husband and wife), the old problems of wide fiscal deficits and soaring inflation re-emerged. A successor, Mauricio Macri, tried to clear up the mess but this involved sky-high interest rates of 60%.[39]

Mexico set off the Latin American debt crisis in 1982 and suffered another bout of turmoil in 1994, when it had to be rescued with an emergency loan from the US. In that same year, however, Mexico became a member of the North American Free Trade Agreement (NAFTA), along with the US and Canada. NAFTA largely abolished tariffs between the three countries, although the process was a slow one. The whole thing was set up on a bipartisan basis; the deal was negotiated by President George H.W. Bush (a Republican) and implemented under his Democrat successor, Bill Clinton.

Regional trade duly surged, rising from $290bn in 1993 to more than $1.1trn in 2016, while US direct investment in Mexico jumped from $15bn to more than $100bn.[40] To American critics, the deal was responsible for the transfer of jobs from the US to Mexico. Certainly, a lot of factories appeared just over the border, taking advantage of lower Mexican wages. However, US companies were able to make their products more cheaply and became more globally competitive as a result. In many cases, they just used Mexican factories as part of the assembly process. The effect on Mexico's economy has been rather disappointing, with growth between 1993 and 2013 averaging just 1.3% (or 1.2% per capita). The manufacturing sector did well, but the agricultural sector lagged behind and the country has been dogged by corruption and a high crime rate.

Latin America's sorry economic experience, relative to South-East Asia, has many potential explanations. One has been the region's consistent reliance on producing commodities, rather than manufactured goods. The nationalist and protectionist policies of the 1960s and 1970s left a long legacy.

All through the period, the region was also hamstrung by its tendency to borrow heavily in dollars. While not as harsh as the gold standard, that imposed similar constraints. Any country that ran persistent trade deficits, or high inflation, would face the prospect of pressure on its currency. At that point, as also occurred in Asia in the late 1990s, the nation would have a stark choice: hiking up interest rates to defend the currency (and provoking a recession) or devaluing and driving up the cost of repaying its dollar debts. Borrowing in their domestic currencies was occasionally an option, but creditors were often suspicious because of Latin America's record of devaluations. To date, the region has been unable to replicate Asia's post-1998 strategy of running persistent trade surpluses.

The international community also has responsibility for the mess. When bailing out the region, it placed too much emphasis on fiscal tightening, regardless of the economic conditions. The effect was to worsen recessions, and place a heavy burden on the poor – an approach which, as well as being unfair, weakened the political support for reform measures. The IMF also took a fairly naive approach to the free movement of capital. Countries found themselves the recipients of short-term capital flows that often led to short-term bubbles and caused crises when, inevitably, the money flowed out again.

### Inequality rises (and falls)

The problems of Latin America and the economic setbacks suffered by Russia in this era were significant. But overall, the developing world made good progress. That makes a big difference when one looks at figures for global inequality. Between 1988 and 2008, the real income gains were highest for people in the median of the global income distribution. (The median is the middle of a range of numbers. If 100 people were ranked from richest to poorest, the median would be the 50th.) Nearly nine out of ten of the people in the median group lived in the emerging Asian economies, notably China, India and Indonesia. The global Gini coefficient (the standard measure of inequality) declined from 0.72 in 1988 to 0.67 in 2011.[41]

The picture looks very different in the Western world. Between 1945 and 1979, inequality was declining. But things then changed. In 2015, the average income of the richest 10% of the population in

OECD countries was about nine times that of the poorest 10%, up from seven times in 1990.[42] In the US, the Gini coefficient rose from just under 0.35 in 1980 to 0.41 in 2013.[43] Between 1979 and 2011, the top 1% of Americans saw their income rise by 4.9% a year, while the bottom 20% gained only 1.2%. And that figure is after taxes and transfers; without the help of benefits, the bottom 90% of Americans would have seen a decline in real income.[44]

There are a number of potential explanations for this shift, one of which relates to globalisation and, especially, the entry of China into the world economy. Adding so many workers to the global labour supply may have driven down the wages of unskilled workers in particular.

However, many economists point to the influence of new technology, which they dub skill-biased technological change (SBTC). Workers who can handle new technology are more valuable than those who cannot, while low-skilled workers may be replaced by robots or computer programmes. But a problem with this theory is that the widespread use of computers really occurred in the 1990s, while the sudden jump in inequality occurred in the 1980s. Similarly, the gap between the earnings of college graduates and others did not widen significantly in the 1990s, but did in the 1980s.[45]

A related argument is that there has been a war for talent. Just as football teams compete for the services of Ronaldo and Messi, companies compete for the best executives, lawyers and the like. In 1980, the ratio between the pay of US chief executives and workers was 32; by 2000, when the dotcom bubble was making many executives rich, it was 344, and in 2017, it was still 312. The average pay of those executives was nearly $19m.[46] Shareholders seem not to care. Since the market value of these companies is measured in the billions of dollars, $19m or so barely registers. However, the main reason why chief executive pay has risen so far is that their packages have been linked to share options. The rising stock market has done the rest. In Japan, where share prices have struggled, chief executive pay is much lower. But presumably you need to be as talented to run Sony or Toyota as you do to run General Electric or Ford.

Another factor is "assortative mating" – well-educated people are increasingly likely to marry each other. In 1960, 25% of men with university degrees married women with the same level of education; in 2005, 48% did.[47] And another element has been the decline in trade union membership and the loss of collective bargaining power. On average, only 17% of workers in OECD countries were unionised in 2013.[48] The decline of the big factories clearly had an impact. Workers in the service sector are more dispersed and harder to organise.

One shift from 100 years ago is that wealth tends to be earned rather than inherited. Again, the financial sector plays a big part; these workers tend not only to earn high salaries but to own financial assets. The likelihood that someone in the top 1% of earned income is also in the top 10% of investment income went from 50% in 1980 to 63% in 2010.[49]

The impact of inequality also depends on the tax and benefits system. Welfare states reduce after-tax inequality by redistributing income. But the top rate tax cuts pushed through by Reagan and Thatcher gave a huge boost to the disposable incomes of the better-off.

So in global terms, income has become more equal, while, within individual countries, it has become less so. China has become much less equal, for example. But because the developing world has been catching up with Europe and North America, the global trend is more positive.

In 1993, almost 2 billion people around the world lived in extreme poverty, defined as an income of less than $1.25 a day; by 2011, the figure was down to 1 billion (see chart). That was still too many, but it was a remarkable achievement in such a short time. The proportion of the population in developing countries living in extreme poverty fell from 42% in 1993 to 17% in 2011. Improved economies also lead to better living conditions. Since 1960, the proportion of children in developing countries who die before their fifth birthday has fallen by three-quarters.[50]

So how can the world lift that last billion out of extreme poverty and, indeed, bring greater prosperity to those who are merely getting by? Paul Collier, an economist, says that the countries in the bottom billion are concentrated in Africa and central Asia.[51] These countries were poorer in 2000 than they were in 1970. Their life expectancy is ten years lower than that of other developing countries and their infant mortality rate is three times higher. In some cases, these

### The wealth spreads

Global population living on less than $1.90 a day, at 2011 purchasing-power parity, %

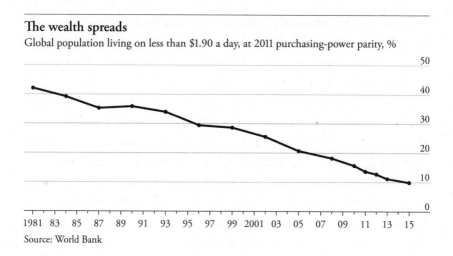

Source: World Bank

countries are going backwards. In 1980, Americans were 30 times better off than citizens of the Central African Republic; by 2015, the ratio was 90.[52]

Paul Collier says that these countries tend to fall into one of four traps: they are mired in conflict; have too great a reliance on natural resources; are landlocked, with bad neighbours; or are cursed with bad governments. Helping these countries can be very difficult. When the government is corrupt, either at the national or the local level, aid money is wasted or diverted. In Chad, less than 1% of the money released by the Ministry of Finance actually reached the rural health clinics to which it was intended. Lending money with conditions does not always work: the government of Kenya promised the same reform to the World Bank five times over a 15-year period.[53]

Africa suffers from a number of long-term problems. Much of the continent is tropical and this makes it home to diseases like malaria and yellow fever, and energy-sapping parasites like the guinea worm. Sub-Saharan Africa has the lowest agricultural yields in the world: farmers produce 1.2 tonnes of grain per hectare, compared with an average of 3 tonnes in the developing world and 8 tonnes in North America and Europe.[54] The continent has also been handicapped by terrible government. Independence from the European colonial powers did not bring democracy but rather one-party rule, whether in the form of a kleptocrat like Mobutu of Zaire (now the

Democratic Republic of Congo) or a socialist state like Tanzania. In the latter, President Julius Nyerere nationalised industry, seized foreign-owned businesses, and forced peasants to sell grain to the government for as little as a fifth of its value.[55]

The 21st century has seen an improvement in Africa's fortunes. Technology has helped. In Kenya, the M-Pesa service has brought banking services to millions who had previously been denied them. One study found that a doubling in mobile-data usage increased annual growth in GDP per person by half a percentage point.[56] In the ten years to 2012, real income per head in Africa grew more than 30%. In the previous two decades, it had fallen by almost 10%. Foreign direct investment rose from $15bn in 2002 to $46bn in 2012.[57] Much of this success was linked to a commodity boom driven by Chinese demand; Africa's raw material exports grew fivefold between 2002 and 2011.

Over the longer term, commodity resources have been a mixed blessing for African nations. Oil wells, copper mines and diamond mines are a tempting prize for any government, or local warlord, to seize; and, unlike other sectors, a commodity producer cannot move elsewhere. Governments have a tendency to focus exclusively on getting their hands on the booty from commodities, and pay much less attention to the needs of business in other sectors. But there has been some improvement in governance. At the end of the cold war, Africa had only three democracies. By 2017, it had eight "flawed democracies" and another 15 countries classed by the EIU as "hybrid regimes".

There is little that outsiders can do to improve governing standards (other than stopping their own companies from bribing officials). Foreign intervention with the aim of unseating a corrupt government is costly in terms of money and lives, and it rarely works. The best hope is that countries manage to unseat their unsatisfactory governments and that wiser minds take over. The Chinese managed to do it, after all.

But the growth rates achieved by many developing economies in the late 20th and early 21st centuries were extremely significant. They showed that improved living standards need not be confined to Europe, North America and Japan. They showed that prosperity could be achieved with more than one model, including the Chinese approach of a heavy state presence. But they also demonstrated that openness to the world economy, a willingness to trade with other countries, and to allow some private sector involvement, could deliver enormous gains. In that sense, economists were proved right.

# TECHNOLOGY AND INNOVATION

The ExCel centre is a vast, hangar-like, building in east London. While it is big enough to have hosted events like boxing and judo in the 2012 Olympics, its usual role is as a venue for exhibitions and trade fairs.

For the stallholder, every stand is a chance to display their ingenuity, make some sales, and keep their business growing. They are trying to entice customers, make connections and get that one step closer to the worldwide success on which they have built their hopes. Sadly, many casual visitors will only give each stall a brief glance. But entrepreneurial hope springs eternal.

In November 2018, the centre was occupied by the Battery Technology Show. At one stand, a company called ZapGo promised "nanocarbon" technology that would "reduce the charging time on electric vehicles from hours to minutes". Their invention, which is an improvement on the supercapacitor, charges a battery more quickly than current devices but then allows it to discharge more slowly. The group is based in Oxford, but the devices are being made in Zhuzhou in China's Hunan province.

Each stall offered its own feast of technological jargon. A company called Acota supplied "dielectric coolant fluids for vehicle electrification", while Ansys offered a "unique platform to generate physics-based solutions for battery systems management", and Nubaru Blue Laser was involved in "battery foil and tab welding".

Eighteen months earlier, the same site was home to the rather more consumer-friendly Wearable Technology conference. One of the products on display was Hushme, a mask worn over the mouth for keeping your mobile phone conversations secret; it came complete with voice-masking mode (with options such as monkey, squirrel and Darth Vader) in order to distract eavesdroppers.

Another offering was the Kerv ring, a contactless payment device in a ring – for those who don't want to use a card or a phone to settle their bills. Then there was Dreem, a headset designed both to help you sleep and to monitor the quality of that sleep – it sensed when you were in "deep sleep" mode and sent sounds designed to lengthen your rest; Tapdo, a device that allowed the owner to use his or her fingerprints to control different devices; and Petcube, which allows owners to monitor (and speak to) their pets from anywhere in the world.

Elsewhere, the hall was crammed with any number of gadgets designed (like a Fitbit) to allow wearers to monitor their health; virtual reality devices designed to train surgeons and nurses; and headsets to help firefighters or allow bosses to supervise workers.

Such is the speed with which modern technology is adopted that one of these gadgets may be a hit by the time you are reading this book, although most will have failed to find a market. But it is a foolish person who tries to predict the winners in advance. Ultimately, millions of consumers will decide whether these devices meet their needs and whether the stallholders' dreams are realised.

## From the iron age to the information age

Humans are a remarkably ingenious species. By using fire, they have been altering their environment, and improving their food hygiene, for tens of thousands of years. We will never know the name of the person who realised that wheat could be turned into bread or who realised that iron and copper could be fashioned into tools. Think of the imagination that must have been required.

The modern human thinks of technology in terms of computers, robots and electronic gadgets. But technology can be a lot simpler than that. The stirrup made it easier for men to ride horses in battle. The collar made it easier for horses to pull heavy objects, like iron ploughs. The compass made it possible to navigate.

And innovation does not depend purely on physical objects. The limited liability company was a legal development that allowed companies to expand, and grow the economy. As we have seen, moving from a two-field crop rotation system to a three-field approach was an idea that lifted output by up to 50%.

In the remote past, innovations spread fairly slowly as humans passed on their knowledge while migrating, or when trading with each other. In some cases, such as farming, the same idea seems to have occurred to people in different places at roughly similar times.

What has changed in the last five centuries is that technology and innovation has spread much more quickly. The printing press allowed knowledge to be passed between people who would never meet. The same is true for 20th-century innovations such as radio, television and the internet. Modern transport systems mean that it is possible to gather people from all over the world to trade fairs like the ones at ExCel. People come to those events not just to make sales and contacts, but to exchange ideas.

The greater the number of people who are connected to a network, the greater the chances that they will cross-fertilise each other's ideas. Our local pub has a weekly quiz night, with a jackpot prize. Teams are limited to six people because larger teams have an advantage; someone will be able to recognise all the Kardashians, another person will be an expert on sport, and so on.

Of course, the larger the team, the harder it is to organise, and the greater the chance that the team captain will pick the wrong answer. But that is where a market economy comes to the rescue. The innovator does not have to convince a monarch or a bureaucrat of the merits of their idea. The product or service can be launched on the market, and consumers can make their choice.

Innovation turns out to be the key factor in long-term economic growth by making each worker more productive. The economist Paul Krugman said that "Productivity isn't everything, but, in the long run, it is almost everything. A country's ability to improve its standard of living over time depends almost entirely on its ability to raise its output per worker."[1] Of course, as an economy adds more people, its potential output becomes larger. More workers can produce more stuff. If those workers save and invest, they can also add more capital, which will help them to produce more. Eventually, however, this capital will produce diminishing returns and in the premodern world, a growing population would eventually be faced with food constraints, as Malthus argued.

But instead of relying on more people or stuff, economies can advance by using the existing people and stuff more efficiently. In an article published in 1957, Robert Solow examined the history of the US economy between 1909 and 1949 and found that just one-eighth of the increase in output per worker was down to the availability of more capital, with the rest being the result of increased productivity.[2]

A crucial insight, attributed to both Kenneth Arrow and Paul Romer, is that knowledge can be subject to increasing returns. As the latter wrote, an innovation by one company "cannot be perfectly patented or kept secret".[3] Eli Whitney failed to make a fortune out of his cotton gin because other people grasped his idea and found it easy to replicate. Tinkering means that even ancient technologies can be improved; the horse shoe was not perfected until 1900 even though the Romans first developed it in the second century CE. Knowledge is also a "non-rival" good. Two or three people may be able to share an ice-cream cone. But if one person eats it, no one else can. In contrast, an idea can be used by anyone on the planet.[4]

Software is a good example of increasing returns. It takes a lot of time and effort to devise a software programme. But once it is created, additional copies of the programme are virtually costless to produce. The same is true of video games or music files on streaming services.

Many technologies benefit from "network effects". The greater the number of people who use them, the more valuable they become. Had Alexander Graham Bell created a single telephone, it would have been a useless novelty. Once one family member got a phone, others had an incentive to get one too; and then shops and businesses needed phones to speak to their customers. Facebook is a more modern example. People join the network in order to keep in touch with their friends; and the greater the number of people on the network, the more want to join. Apple allowed other companies to create applications to use on the iPhone. The more apps that were created, the more appealing an iPhone became for consumers. And as the number of iPhone users grew, the greater the incentive to create new apps.

## Chips with everything

Some innovations are "general purpose technologies" that can be adapted to a wide range of uses: steam engines, the internal combustion exchange and electric power are three examples. In the modern era, the most striking example has been the computer. The computer's origins can be traced back to Charles Babbage, one of a great tradition of Victorian gentleman inventors. In the early 19th century, Babbage discovered that astronomical tables were riddled with errors. These errors tended to persist as scholars copied the work of their predecessors. So Babbage envisaged a machine, called the difference engine, which could perform the calculations without errors. The government gave him a grant, worth around $1m in today's money, to pursue the project. After many failures, he was helped by Ada Lovelace, an accomplished mathematician. He went on to devise a more sophisticated machine called the analytical engine, which included many of the elements of modern computers, including the memory, central processing units and Lovelace's algorithms (or programmes) needed to make the calculations.[5]

But Babbage was too early. What was needed was a practical reason to develop a calculating machine. This came, in the first instance, in the form of the cash registers that spread in the late 19th and early 20th centuries. But governments also played a role, because of the vast administrative task of undertaking the national census. The 1890 US census was conducted with the use of a punched card system for recording the results. This led to the creation of the Computer-Tabulating-Recoding company, the forerunner of IBM.[6]

The Second World War accelerated the process of computer development. Navies needed help with calculating the trajectory of shells fired over a range of several miles, while at sea.[7] The code-breaking team at Bletchley Park, led by Alan Turing, developed a computer to crack the Enigma code used by Germany. At the time, however, computers weighed about 30 tons and still had less processing power than most modern, compact devices. The Cray supercomputer, launched in the early 1970s, cost $37m in today's money and had a memory of eight megabytes: a modern laptop costing just a few hundred dollars offers six gigabytes of memory, or 750 times more than the Cray.[8]

The reason that those early computers were so heavy was that they depended on vacuum tubes for the switches, which, by being on or off, represented the required information in binary form. The first breakthrough in shrinking the computer came in 1947 with the invention, at Bell Laboratories, of the transistor, which was smaller, faster and generated less heat than the vacuum tube. William Shockley, one of the developers of the transistor, left to form his own company. In turn, after personality clashes, eight employees of Shockley's company departed to found Fairchild Semiconductor. In 1959, Jack Kilby and Bob Noyce of Fairchild developed the microchip, which could be made with silicon or another material that acted as a semiconductor. On the chip was an integrated circuit, consisting of tiny transistors, resistors and capacitors.[9]

In 1965, Gordon Moore, another Fairchild employee, wrote a famous paper, stating that, by shrinking transistors, engineers would be able to double the number that fit on a chip every year. While he later amended this to a doubling every two years, he correctly forecast the exponential growth of computing power.[10] Along with Bob Noyce, Gordon Moore founded Intel in 1968. Fifty years later, Intel is one of the largest technology companies in the word, responsible for designing semiconductors and microprocessors.

Shockley, Fairchild and Intel were all based in the Santa Clara Valley, an area just south of San Francisco that has since become known as Silicon Valley. Its origins can be traced to when Bill Hewlett and David Packard founded the Hewlett-Packard business in a Palo Alto garage in 1938. The area became a cluster for technology groups, in part because of its proximity to Stanford University and in part because many investment groups based themselves there. These financiers back early-stage companies in a process known as "venture capital". While most of the companies they back will fail, the venture capitalists hope to fund the big successes, like Facebook and Google, that will multiply their stake manyfold.

Initially, the biggest use for microchips was in the handheld calculator market. But the chips also made it possible to create computers that were much smaller than the giant machines familiar from 1960s science fiction movies. The first personal computer (PC) was the Altair, which had to be assembled by the purchaser and lacked a keyboard and a screen. The best it could do was flash some lights. Two young programmers named Paul Allen and Bill Gates developed software for the Altair, which allowed them to establish Microsoft.[11]

## PCs gone mad

Expansion of the PC market occurred in the 1980s when IBM launched its own range, choosing Intel to provide the microprocessor and Microsoft to develop the operating system. Crucially, Bill Gates persuaded IBM to allow Microsoft to sell the operating system, known as MS-DOS, to other providers. This allowed Microsoft to dominate the software business, which turned out to be the most valuable area; in hardware, IBM faced competition from "clones" produced by the likes of Compaq.[12]

The personal computer revolutionised clerical jobs. When this author started work in 1980, the office still had a large room set aside as a "typing pool" in which (usually) women typed up the letters and memos written by the rest of the staff. As late as 1986, when I joined the *Financial Times*, articles were still written by typewriter on small sheets, each with carbon copies. Rewriting a long piece was a very fiddly business, usually involving the use of Tippex to white out mistakes. These articles were turned into print by the use of "hot metal" that was pressed into the page, a technology that was a century old.[13]

However, computers would not have had a huge impact on society if they had merely replaced the electric typewriter. Here again, the government played a vital role. The US defence department's Advanced Research Projects Agency (ARPA) was created in 1958 and succeeded in connecting remote computers in 1969. By 1985, 2,000 computers were connected to the network, dubbed the ARPANET.[14] Tim Berners-Lee, a software engineer at CERN, the particle physics laboratory in Geneva, developed a protocol and a language, the Hypertext Transfer Protocol, or HTTP, which allowed computers to talk to each other and enabled users to send links to individual documents. Others adopted the system, which was known as the World Wide Web.

Further steps were still needed before the web, or internet, could be commercially useful. A browser called Mosaic was developed in the early 1990s by Marc Andreessen and Eric Bina at the University of Illinois; and, along with Jim Clark, Andreessen then founded Netscape, the company that started the boom in internet shares. Eventually, Andreessen became one of the best-known venture capitalists in Silicon Valley. Internet service providers like AOL, meanwhile, brought access to the general public. With so much material available online, a variety of search engines were developed, with Google eventually dominating.

So what are the economic benefits of the internet? First, of course, there are the jobs created in making computers and smartphones, devising applications for them and building the associated infrastructure, such as routers and the fibre-optic cable that links computers round the world. Second, there is instant access to information. Retailers can keep track of which goods are selling well, and order more when supplies start to run low. This saves them tying up capital in excess stock. Fishermen and farmers can find out the current market prices for their produce, and sell them where they are most profitable. And consumers can easily compare prices to stop themselves from being ripped off. Third, transaction costs have fallen. The internet can eliminate the role of middlemen. Booking a holiday, for example, used to involve a visit to a travel agent and a trawl through brochures, but now everything can be purchased online. Part of this cost saving is in the form of time, as doing an internet search means that consumers can find the goods they desire much more quickly. In the UK, British Telecom used to run an advert that showed a kindly old gent looking for the book *Fly Fishing* by J.R. Hartley (the punchline being that he is the author). After an exhaustive tour of second-hand bookshops, he finds the tome via a phone call. Nowadays, he could have searched the internet and never left his armchair.

Fourth, the internet makes more transactions possible by linking buyers and sellers who would otherwise not have been able to contact each other. This can be true for rare books, or old toys. But it is also true for services like Airbnb, where people who want to rent out their property can make contact with those looking for an alternative to hotel accommodation. And the internet allows companies to alert customers to their latest offers, whether they are cheap pizzas or luxury flats. Indeed, the company can target its marketing to customers who are more likely to be interested in their product.

These potential benefits have been amplified by the adoption of the smartphone. The first device to have the characteristics of a smartphone was produced by IBM in 1994. It had the ability to receive e-mail and included a calendar and an address book.[15] In 1999 the Japanese telecoms group NTT DoCoMo launched a series of handsets linked to the internet, and in 2000 Ericsson unveiled the first device to be called a smartphone.[16] But the breakthrough came with the BlackBerry, which had great success in the business market (being dubbed the "crackberry" for its addictive powers), and then with the iPhone, which was launched by Apple in 2007. The latter's touchscreen technology proved a great hit, removing the need for a fiddly keyboard.

The size and convenience of the smartphone made it both popular and habit-forming, and forced companies to adapt to survive. Facebook, the social media network, was designed for the personal computer but switched its focus to smartphones in 2012; by 2016, income from mobiles was 84% of the business.[17] And the evolution of the phone industry was so quick that the handset manufacturers were caught out. In 2008, Nokia, the Finnish group, had half of the global phone market. By 2012, its market share was in free fall and its share price had dropped 90%; the following year, it sold its handset business to Microsoft.

## Where's the beef?

The appearance of all these technological marvels raises a tricky question. Why, given such advances, is overall economic productivity growing so slowly? Between 1891 and 1972, US productivity (measured as output per hour) improved at an average annual rate of 2.36%. That helps explain why America became so wealthy. After 1972, the improvement slowed to 1.38%. For a brief period between 1996 and 2004, there was another surge to 2.54%. This was the time of the dotcom boom. But after 2004, the rate slowed right back again.[18]

Robert Gordon, an economist, argues that the latest wave of innovation is more limited than the first, steam-based, industrial revolution, or the second, based on electric power and cars. The new wave has been based on entertainment, information and communications.[19] Other changes have been much more limited. Cars may have many more gadgets and comforts than they did in the 1970s, but congestion means that people do not travel any faster; the average speed of traffic in central London in 2015 was 7.4mph, on a par with a horse-drawn carriage in the 18th century.[20] Aeroplane travel is cheaper than it used to be, but less comfortable (legroom is restricted), and the experiment with supersonic flight was abandoned. And there have been no new household gadgets in the last 40 years to rival the fridge, the vacuum or the microwave for convenience, not to mention the boost to human comfort and hygiene brought by indoor plumbing.

A more optimistic view, taken by Andrew McAfee and Erik Brynjolfsson of MIT, is that the full benefits of the internet and other technologies such as machine learning, have yet to come through.[21] Such is the speed of modern communication that 90% of all digital data was created in the last 24 months. Technology is reducing coordination costs through search engines, cheap communication networks and free information. That allows companies to outsource tasks to the cheapest and most efficient providers. Artificial intelligence can be used to create designs that humans would not devise on their own; when a neural network called DeepMind was asked to come up with a system for cooling a data centre, energy use fell 40%.[22]

The debate on the economic impact of the internet is not easily settled. It is true that past technologies were slow to have an effect; it was 60 years after the Wright brothers flew before people commonly took commercial flights. The camera was invented in the middle of the 19th century but most people did not own one until after the Second World War.[23] On the other hand, the nature of modern technologies is that they are adopted very quickly. Facebook was only launched in 2004 but passed 100 million users in 2008 and 1 billion in 2012.[24] By 2018, it had 2.2 billion users.[25] Apple had sold 1 billion iPhones by 2017, ten years after the device's introduction.[26]

The optimists can argue that the full benefits of new technology do not show up in the statistics. Google Maps, for example, must have saved people a lot of time (and avoided a lot of arguments) by preventing them from getting lost. But the same was true of past improvements. The full benefits of central heating and antibiotics – bringing greater comfort and avoiding disease – are not captured in GDP.

The blessings of the internet are also a temptation. The ability to listen to music, or watch films, or shop, provides a lot of pleasure. The downside is that 89% of employees in a 2014 survey admitted to wasting some time online at work every day, with almost a third frittering away an hour and another 26% wasting more than that.[27] Conversely, the availability of electronic communication means that work eats into our leisure and family time, as we answer e-mails from managers and customers. How all this washes out in the productivity numbers is very hard to calculate.

## To HAL and back

Technological change has not always been welcome. Monarchs have occasionally been suspicious of the social changes wrought by technology, while workers have worried about the loss of jobs. Joel Mokyr argues that the modern era is marked by the acceptance that the ancient world did not have all the answers, and that progress is not just possible but beneficial.[28] But there have always been worries that science and technology will get out of control. Mary Shelley's *Frankenstein* is a tale of technological innovation that went wrong, while the HAL computer in the film *2001: A Space Odyssey* was an early example of the idea that computers might supplant their human masters.

These worries continue into the modern era. The same technology that makes it easier for us to communicate with each other makes it easier for companies (and the government) to keep track of us. A study of smartphone apps in 2017 found that 88% of them could transmit data from users back to the Google group and 43% to Facebook.[29] Companies know not just what we searched for online but what we bought and where we are located. The power of the big social media groups means that they have an enormous influence. Twitter trolls and bots can bombard sites with false stories or allegations about political candidates, or about public health campaigns like vaccination. The same is true of stories spread via Facebook news feeds.

And the state can do even more than the corporate sector. China is developing a social credit system that will rank all its citizens by 2020. Actions that will cut the credit score include bad driving, smoking in the wrong place, buying too many video games, and, of course, expressing critical opinions about the government. Too low a score will restrict the jobs you can get, the hotels you can stay at, the schools your kids can attend, and your ability to take a train or a plane.[30] Chinese people already find their access to foreign websites blocked by the "great firewall", as it has been dubbed. Occasionally, this has ridiculous results, as when images of Winnie-the-Pooh were blocked because of an alleged resemblance to Xi Jinping, the Chinese leader.[31]

The instantaneous nature of social media can be a trap for the unwary. In 2013, Justine Sacco, a PR executive, who was boarding a flight to South Africa, tweeted what was meant to be an ironic comment about the impact of AIDS on different racial groups. She had just 170 followers and got no immediate reply. She thought no more about it until she landed, when an old acquaintance messaged her to say "I'm so sorry to see what's happening." For a while, she was the number 1 trending topic on Twitter, with many asking "Has Justine landed yet?" She was condemned for her racism and fired from her job.[32] Young adults who post pictures of their activities on Facebook can be alarmed to find that potential employers will check their online profile. Pictures of drug use or excessive alcohol consumption, and posts of a sexual nature, will dissuade many companies from hiring them.[33]

More and more devices in our homes may be connected to the internet so that we can turn them on and off while we are out. But who controls the data, and what happens if the information is hacked? Users of technology services are handing over vital data to the companies concerned. For example, a robot vacuum cleaner called iRobot not only cleans the room but creates a map of your house's interior.[34] Dealing with others over the internet also means that you cannot be sure that someone is who they claim to be, and nor can you be sure that others are not pretending to be you. The annual cost to American consumers of identity theft may exceed $16bn.[35]

Another worry is that scientific discoveries will harm the planet or have unwanted moral consequences. That this debate should persist is hardly surprising. Some innovations have been dogged by repeated setbacks. Nuclear power has seen accidents at Three Mile Island in the US, Chernobyl in Ukraine, and Fukushima in Japan. The number of deaths that resulted from these disasters is far lower than those in coal-mining accidents over the centuries, or from illnesses caused by atmospheric pollution caused by coal burning. But the risk of a catastrophic nuclear accident still weighs on the minds of voters and politicians: few want to see a nuclear power station built next door. And concerns have shifted to the way that bioengineering may alter plants and animals and inadvertently destroy the ecosystem on which we depend.

What about the concern that technology will destroy jobs? In the 1960s, President John F. Kennedy declared that the major domestic challenge was to "maintain full employment at a time when automation … is replacing men". It is worth remembering that many traditional jobs have disappeared altogether, but overall employment has continued to rise. The 1841 British census, for example, records more than 97,000 blacksmiths, 212,000 boot and shoe makers, 5,000 chimney sweeps, 18,000 coopers (barrel-makers), and over 1.1 million domestic servants.[36] Such jobs are scarce now.

Technology can eliminate mundane jobs (like those in the typing pool), allowing people to do more interesting stuff. The job of switchboard operator, once a key part of every office, has virtually disappeared. A study by the Federal Reserve Bank of St Louis found that the number of routine clerical and manual jobs in America had stagnated since the 1980s, while non-routine jobs had increased significantly.[37] The introduction of automated teller machines (ATMs) seemed to threaten the jobs of bank staff. From the mid-1990s, the average number of staff in a city branch did indeed fall from 21 to 13. But the ATM also made it cheaper for banks to operate branches, so they opened more sites. There are actually more people employed in American bank branches today than there were in 1980. Staff now interact with customers about their finances, rather than just cash their cheques.[38]

And technology can often do a better job than humans. Computers do not get tired or distracted. Programmes that analyse cancer scans can have lower error rates than do experienced doctors. The tedious task of searching mountains of legal documents, traditionally assigned to trainee lawyers, can be automated, with fewer mistakes resulting.

In the coming decades, many people will find jobs that require them to interact with computers. A study of the American economy between 1982 and 2012 found that employment grew faster than average in tasks, like graphic design, that made more use of computers.[39] And, as the population ages, jobs will be created in caring areas that cannot be automated at all. A study by Deloitte, a consultancy, found that the number of British nursing assistants increased by 909% between 1992 and 2014, while the number of teaching assistants had grown by 580%, and care workers by 168%.[40]

Some of these jobs are not very well paid, however. That links to another worry, that some of the new technology companies are bypassing traditional employment laws to create new and insecure forms of employment. This so-called "gig economy" involves workers having uncertain hours, and no paid holidays, sick pay or pensions rights. Instead, the worker (such as an Uber driver) will be hired at the whim of the customer, or on an irregular basis at a services company (on a zero-hours contract at a warehouse, for example). Some workers may like the freedom that a gig job brings, but surveys suggest that most would prefer full-time employment.[41]

Still, there are many people who do want to work part-time, and there are many people who are looking for services, whether it is an odd job or a car ride. In the past, it has been difficult for the two groups to find each other. The internet makes the process quick and cheap.

However, the anonymity of the internet creates a potential problem: how can the client trust the supplier to perform the service to a requisite standard, and how can the supplier trust the client to pay? Platforms such as Uber and TaskRabbit can perform this service too, acting as trusted middlemen for payment. They can also help customers and suppliers to choose each other, via the system of ratings. A bad supplier, or a bad customer, will eventually be shunned by the network.

## Pandora's Xbox

New technologies have often had the ability to cause as much harm as good. When people learned to forge metals, they made weapons as well as tools. The cotton gin gave slavery a longer lease of life in the US. Cars offered drivers freedom of movement, but at the cost of millions killed and injured. And radio broadcast Roosevelt's fireside chats, but also Hitler's speeches.

Even though it is nearly 30 years since the internet started to be developed, we are probably still at the early stages of understanding its influence on the economy. For all the worries about technological change, we need it, if ageing Western populations are to be cared for, and if young people in developing economies are to find jobs and enjoy a higher standard of living. Technology will be vital if we are to tackle issues like global warming. Innovation will be needed to capture energy from renewable sources like the sun, and to reduce the impact of traditional fossil fuels through approaches like carbon capture. As this book was being written, news was breaking of spinal implants that could help paralysed people walk again.

The time to worry will be when we stop making technological advances. Without them, we cannot hope to improve our standard of living or tackle global issues such as climate change. Indeed, technological change may be needed to pull the developed world economies out of the doldrums in which they became marooned in 2007.

# THE CRISIS AND AFTER:
## 2007 TO TODAY

Economists called the period from 1982 to 2007 "the great moderation", a long era of steady growth and low inflation. Gordon Brown, Britain's longest-serving finance minister, talked of "no more boom and bust". But the boom came to an end, in spectacular fashion, with the financial crisis of 2007 and its aftermath.

The depth of the crisis was worse than anything seen since the 1930s. It caught those in authority by surprise. In March 2007, just as the problems in the housing market were emerging, Ben Bernanke, the chairman of the Fed, said that the impact on the economy "seems likely to be contained". In May 2008, Mervyn King, governor of the Bank of England, said, "It's quite possible that at some point we may get an odd quarter or two of negative growth. But recession is not the central projection at all."[1] As it turned out, the recession had already started by that stage. Within four months, it seemed as if the entire financial system might collapse.

In some ways, the economic setback was like so many financial crises before it. Banks lent money to people so that they could buy property. The more money they lent, the more prices went up, because buyers could afford to pay higher prices. Rising property prices, in turn, meant that banks felt more confident about lending against the security of property. Over time, the relationship between house prices and buyers' incomes became ever more extended. That required lenders to lower their credit standards in order to keep making loans.

Lenders had a strong motivation to follow this path. In the old days, a bank, or other savings institution, lent money against a property and held the loan until it was repaid. That put them at risk if the borrower defaulted. But a step change in the market occurred in 1968 when the American government set up the Government National Mortgage Association (GNMA or Ginnie Mae). Like its sister organisation, the Federal National Mortgage Association (Fannie Mae), the corporation was set up to make it easier for homeowners to get loans, by guaranteeing those that met a certain standard.

In 1970, Ginnie Mae issued its first mortgage-backed security (MBS).[2] This was a $70m bond whose payments were linked to home mortgages; provided that homeowners serviced their debts, the interest on the MBS would still be paid. This attracted plenty of investors as it offered higher returns than government bonds, with plenty of security (hence the term, securitised loans).

The step that proved fatal in the long run was to create a more complex group of bonds, with fancy acronyms, that divided the money that flowed in from the mortgages into various tranches. The safest tranches got paid first and received a lower yield than the riskiest tranches which got paid last.[3]

For a long time, this was a relatively small market. In 1996, MBS issuance was less than $500m. But as house price rises accelerated, so did securitised lending. In 2003, issuance was nearly $3.2trn. An increasingly high proportion of these bonds were issued, not by Fannie Mae or Ginnie Mae, but by private lenders.[4]

What made this system dangerous was the increasingly risky nature of mortgage lending. There had been a deliberate attempt by the US authorities to expand home ownership in the 1990s and 2000s. The aim was to attract poorer people and citizens from ethnic minorities who had been excluded by the so-called "red lining" policies of mainstream lenders.[5] The proportion of the population owning homes rose from 63.8% in 1994 to 69.2% in 2004.[6]

The riskiest borrowers were known as "subprime"; these were people with low or irregular incomes. Some were dubbed NINJA borrowers, as they had no income, no job nor assets. But the people who made the loans were not too bothered. They would earn fees based on how many loans they originated and since the loans were quickly sold to others, the originators did not need to worry about whether they would be repaid. As for the homebuyers, taking out such a loan was the only way of getting on the property ladder; they did not worry about repayment since they assumed that they could always sell the house at a higher price.

Bundling together these loans seemed like a form of alchemy. The individual loans might be risky but issuers assured investors that it was unlikely lots of homeowners would default at once. Another financial instrument that emerged was designed to insure investors against the risk of a bond defaulting; in return for a premium, the investors would effectively be repaid the face value of the bond. These contracts were known as credit default swaps (CDS) and were themselves bundled together and sold to investors.

In other words, an entire pyramid of instruments was created on the willingness and ability of borrowers to repay mortgages. The total value of credit derivatives (as the instruments were called) went from $5trn in 2004 to $20trn in 2006.[7]

In 2005 and 2006 it was possible to believe that this was not a serious problem. By taking mortgage loans off the balance sheets of the banks, risk had been redistributed around the system to those who were more willing and able to bear it. In November 2005, Ben Bernanke, then a governor of the Federal Reserve, said that "With respect to their safety, derivatives, for the most part, are traded among very sophisticated financial institutions and individuals who have considerable incentive to understand them and to use them properly."[8]

But the real problem was that the banks were exposed to the subprime market after all. First, some of the securitised loans had not been easy to sell and remained on banks' balance sheets. Second, the banks had lent money to the people who bought the fancy securities. They were thus at risk if the market collapsed, and the borrowers failed to repay. Third, and most importantly, banks' balance sheets were much less secure than the regulators thought.

In past chapters, we have seen that banks are always at risk from a loss of depositor confidence. To offset this risk, banks are required to raise capital in the form of equity that can absorb any short-term losses. Under a global agreement known as Basel (after the Swiss city),[9] the amount of capital that banks were required to hold before 2007 was based on the riskiness of their assets. (A deposit is a liability of a bank, and the loans it makes are its assets.) In the crisis, however, the capital that banks had accumulated was shown to be insufficient. Five days before it went bust, Lehman Brothers, an investment bank, had an official capital ratio that was almost three times the regulatory minimum.[10]

There was a rotten cherry on the top of this particular cake. In the 1930s, it had been retail depositors who had panicked and started to demand their money back, triggering a liquidity crisis. But the two big US banks that collapsed in 2008 – Bear Stearns and Lehman Brothers – were not retail banks at all. They borrowed in the wholesale markets, where other banks were among their biggest lenders. Once a bank was deemed to be in trouble, no other bank was keen to lend to it for fear of suffering the kind of losses that might destroy its own balance sheet. The result was that the infection spread very quickly.

### Every bank for itself

The crisis began in early 2007, when subprime mortgage lenders started to default as homeowners failed to repay. In April, New Century, the largest subprime lender, filed for bankruptcy. In June, Bear Stearns had to halt redemptions in two of the funds it managed; both invested in subprime securities. In August, BNP Paribas, a French bank, suspended trading in three similar funds. By this stage, the bad news was sufficiently worrying to prompt central banks to lend money to banks that were suffering from liquidity problems. The Fed also cut interest rates by half a percentage point. September 2007 saw a run on Northern Rock, a British bank that had been one of the most aggressive lenders in the UK housing market and also depended on the wholesale markets for finance.

If that was a bad year, 2008 was much worse. In March, Bear Stearns needed to be rescued by J. P. Morgan (shades of 1907). The deal needed back-up financing by the Federal Reserve, which agreed to be responsible for up to $30bn of losses. That was a very controversial move with the public.

In early September, the government was forced to nationalise Fannie Mae and Freddie Mac, two of the bodies that guaranteed mortgage loans. Just a week later, Lehman Brothers teetered on the brink. Hank Paulson, the US Treasury secretary, was reluctant to engineer a public rescue for fear of the political row that would result. Rival banks, like Barclays, would not buy Lehman without a guarantee from the government that it would cover the bank's losses. So over the weekend of September 14th–15th, it was decided to let Lehman fold. The result was panic. Any investor who owned bank shares, or bank debt, feared that they would lose their money. Banks rushed to conserve their own cash.

The credit markets, the plumbing of the financial system, were blocked. The official short-term interest rate is the one set by the central bank (the federal funds rate in the US, for example). Normally, the rate at which banks borrow is a fraction of a percentage point above that official rate. But at the end of September 2008, American banks were paying three times the official rate to borrow overnight.[11]

Few banks seemed safe in the circumstances. Merrill Lynch was acquired by the Bank of America; when the deal showed signs of faltering, Hank Paulson pushed hard for its completion.[12] The authorities were forced to rescue AIG, a giant insurance company, which had guaranteed mortgage-backed securities. The fear was that a collapse of AIG would put more pressure on the banks, which were relying on the company to insure their assets. The AIG deal, which involved a loan of $85bn, led investors to be confused about which institutions qualified for rescue and which didn't. So they became even more nervous about lending to vulnerable banks, worsening the crisis. Congress rejected the first draft of a bailout package for the banks, causing further panic.

Alistair Darling, Britain's chancellor, was told that Royal Bank of Scotland was two to three hours from closing, at which point cash machines would stop working.[13] Lloyds was encouraged by the then prime minister, Gordon Brown, to take over the struggling Halifax Bank of Scotland.

In the end, politicians dared not risk a repeat of the 1930s, when a banking collapse led to the Great Depression. Governments and central banks introduced massive support packages for the banking system (the US Congress was persuaded to change its mind). Money was lent to the banks at cheap rates; governments bought shares to bolster bank capital; and interest rates were cut to record low levels.

## The Queen's question

So why didn't anyone see the crisis coming (as Queen Elizabeth II memorably asked when opening a new building at the London School of Economics)?[14] There were several causes. Regulators had been lulled into a false sense of security about the strength of the banking sector in the developed world. The introduction of deposit insurance, in the wake of the Great Depression, seemed to have solved the problem of banking runs.

But a moral hazard had been created, in which there was every incentive for bankers to take risk. In the late 19th century, banks in Britain had equity capital equivalent to 15–25% of their assets. By the 1980s, this cushion was just 5%.[15]

The long period of low interest rates and rising asset prices meant that bankers who were aggressive in their lending practices had been successful. Those bank executives were rewarded with share options, which soared in value. In turn, the performance of the share price was tied to the annual (or quarterly) change in profits. The result was a focus on short-term gain rather than long-term risks. The banks' top executives became very rich. Dick Fuld of Lehman Brothers was paid half a billion dollars between 1993 and 2007.

The credit boom, by driving up asset prices, had made ordinary people feel richer. It had also boosted government tax revenues. Politicians were reluctant to kill the golden goose of finance with regulation. There was a temptation to think that bankers were wise, because they had made so much money. Many were recruited into politics. (This brings to mind the anecdote of the financier who asked an academic, "If you're so smart, why aren't you rich?", to which the professor replied, "If you're so rich, why aren't you smart?")

The mood quickly turned in 2008 and the reputation of the financial sector may take a long time to recover. The bailout was just one issue. There were scandals, such as the attempts by traders to manipulate a benchmark interest rate called Libor, which affected some $350trn of financial contracts.[16] Banks were also penalised for mis-selling mortgage-backed bonds, money laundering, mis-selling of payment protection insurance, and, at Wells Fargo, for creating 2 million bogus accounts, without the permission of customers, in order to meet sales targets.[17] In the decade after the crisis, global banks paid $321bn in fines to national regulators, according to the Boston Consulting Group, with $204bn of those penalties imposed in North America.[18]

As well as imposing fines, regulators tried other ways of reforming the finance sector. In America, Congress passed the Dodd–Frank Act, which ran to a mammoth 848 pages; by contrast, the Glass–Steagall Act, passed during the Great Depression, was just 37 pages long.[19] By creating such complex legislation, the regulators may only have created more loopholes for banks to exploit, and pushed up the costs of the system by requiring banks to hire a great many more lawyers and compliance people.

A more effective change was to force banks to hold more capital, in the hope that such a cushion would reduce the extent of the next financial crisis. There is always a trade-off. The world needs banks that can lend to business and consumers and drive economic growth; too much regulation may restrict this process. But there always seems to come a point when banks lend too much and unwisely, and regulators must be alert to this possibility.

Economists were criticised in the wake of the crisis for paying too little attention to the role of the finance sector, and to the level of debt, in the economy. They regarded the banks as just a conduit between savers and borrowers. The important things to study, economists thought, were the factors that drove the overall levels of savings and investment, not the mechanics of the process. Few paid attention to the impact of rising consumer debt levels since the overall rate of inflation remained low. This proved to be a spectacular misjudgement.

## Depression avoided

In the early months of the crisis, economic data were deteriorating as fast as they did in the Great Depression of the 1930s. At the lowest point, industrial production had dropped 13% from its peak and the volume of world trade had fallen 20%.[20] But global governments and central banks stepped in with massive support programmes. In

November 2008, China unveiled a $586bn stimulus package for its own economy, the largest in its history.[21] The US Congress passed the American Recovery and Reinvestment Act in February 2009, one of the first achievements of Barack Obama's presidency, a combination of tax cuts and spending increases worth $787bn. Collectively, the leaders of the G20 nations agreed at a summit in London to pump $1.1trn into the global economy, by extending the ability of the IMF and World Bank to make loans.

In addition, central banks kept cutting rates to stimulate borrowing. By the end of 2008, the Federal Reserve's main rate was 0.25%; just 15 months previously it had been 5.25%. Quantitative easing (QE) also began that year. This involved central banks creating money and using it to buy government bonds. The aim was twofold. First, it prevented the kind of shrinkage in the money supply that occurred in the 1930s. When the central banks bought bonds, the sellers ended up with more money in their accounts. The second aim was to reduce the long-term bond yield as well as the short-term borrowing rate. This cut the cost of borrowing for companies and homebuyers and relieved the financial pressure on the economy.

These drastic measures were designed to deal with practical issues. One problem was dubbed the "zero level bound" – what to do when interest rates fell to zero. It has proved possible to impose negative rates in some parts of the system; for example, on commercial banks which are required to hold reserves at the central bank. But charging ordinary bank depositors a negative rate seems a step too far. The general public would be outraged if their deposits started falling in value. Many would withdraw their cash and keep it under the mattress, creating another run on the banks.

All this did have an effect. The stock market bottomed out in the spring of 2009 and started a long bull run. The decline in American output, from peak to trough, was 4.8%, smaller than the median decline in previous American recessions.[22] Nevertheless, the global recovery was painfully slow. Eight years after the crisis, only five out of 11 countries that had suffered a banking sector collapse had seen a full recovery in per capita GDP.[23]

These rescue measures were controversial. In the US, the "tea party" movement arose as a reaction to the bank bailout; it helped to fuel Republican victories in Congress in 2010 and aided the rise of Donald Trump. Some felt that QE was the equivalent of printing money to fund government spending; the same measure that led to hyperinflation in Germany. Others argued that QE, by pushing up the price of financial assets, boosted the wealth of the rich and thus made inequality worse.

### The euro zone divided

To add to the world's problems, a European crisis followed in short order. Many European banks were exposed to the US housing market and some of the most aggressive banks, like Deutsche and UBS, had balance sheets that were more than twice as risky as their US competitors. In 2007, the three largest banks in the world were all European.[24] When the crisis hit, European central banks and governments rushed to bail out their domestic banking sectors with cheap loans, share purchases, and the like. The effect was to take on to the national balance sheet debts that had previously been borne by the private sector. Between 2007 and 2013, the ratio of government debt to GDP in the euro zone rose from 66% to 93%.[25]

In some cases, the burden was too great. Ireland was dubbed the "Celtic Tiger" in the 1990s, and enjoyed a property boom, financed by its domestic banks, in the 2000s. When the banks collapsed in 2008 and 2009, the bill was two-fifths of the country's GDP. A recession then cost Ireland more than 11% of its output. As tax revenues slumped, government debt soared, reaching a peak of 120% of GDP. A bailout by the EU and the IMF was required in 2011.[26]

Things were even worse in Greece. The country adopted the euro in 2001, even though there were widespread doubts about its suitability (its debt-to-GDP ratio in 2000 was 104%).[27] Greece massaged its deficit numbers in order to meet the membership criteria. Like Italy, Spain and Portugal, Greece benefited from lower borrowing costs as interest rates in the euro zone converged. But things went wrong in the aftermath of the 2007 crisis. In 2009, George Papandreou, the Greek prime minister, announced that the year's budget deficit would not be 3.7% of GDP, as forecast, but 12.5%. At the same time, he revealed that the deficit for 2008 had been 7.7%, instead of the previously announced 5%.[28]

The country's credit rating was quickly downgraded and the government passed a series of austerity measures to try to bring the deficit under control. But that was not enough to reassure investors, and in April, the Greek government was paying 10 percentage points more to borrow money than was its German counterpart. Greece had to turn to the IMF and its EU partners for a bailout, which was only granted in return for the government imposing more austerity. That led to a round of strikes and violent protests, including the firebombing of a bank in which three people died.

The Greek people were caught in a trap. International creditors insisted on economic reform, but the austerity packages sent the economy into a further tailspin. Economic output declined by almost a quarter.[29] It was clear that Greece would have to default on some of its debt, but the prospect of default alarmed investors and sent bond yields even higher; the ten-year issue yielded 44% in the spring of 2012.

For a time, it seemed possible that Greece would have to quit the euro zone and readopt the drachma. But this was not a very appealing prospect. Switching to the drachma would have involved a substantial devaluation; 30% or more. So Greek bank depositors would have seen their savings decline sharply in value. Many would have tried to switch their money to foreign banks; capital controls would thus have been needed to prevent a run on the Greek banking system. Meanwhile the debt that Greece owed internationally would still be denominated in euros, and thus would be even more expensive to repay after a devaluation. Default on its debts would be inevitable.

In the immediate aftermath of default, it would be very expensive for the Greek government to borrow. So either the government would have to impose austerity anyway, or it would be forced into printing money to finance itself, pushing up inflation. Since devaluation would push up import prices, inflation would already be rising. It is hardly surprising, given all these disadvantages, that Greek governments of many different political persuasions kept opting for bailouts from the EU, despite the onerous conditions. By 2016, the country was enduring its thirteenth austerity package and its government debt to GDP ratio was still 180%. The euro zone was dubbed an economic "Hotel California"; countries could check out any time they wanted, but they could never leave.

## Whatever it takes

A complete collapse of the euro zone was averted with the help of the European Central Bank. In July 2012, Mario Draghi, the president of the ECB, pledged to do "whatever it takes" to save the euro. He cut interest rates to zero and below, and he unleashed a bond-buying programme that drove down the cost of borrowing for euro-zone governments. Such was his success that, by 2016, both Ireland and Spain were able to borrow for ten years at less than 1%.

Nevertheless, the crisis had some ugly moments, and created the sense of a continent in crisis. In turn, that played a part in the UK's vote to leave the EU in June 2016's referendum. In other countries, it contributed to the rise of populist anti-EU (and anti-immigrant) parties. The saga was seen as pitting "northern" creditor nations, such as Germany and the Netherlands, against "southern" debtors in (largely) Mediterranean states. The debtors got their own unwelcome acronym as "PIIGS", covering Portugal, Ireland, Italy, Greece and Spain.[30] The northern nations felt that the southerners had failed to show sufficient discipline and were "free riding" off the hard work of Germany and the rest. At the start of the crisis, the Greek retirement age was 61, while Germany had just announced plans to increase the retirement age to 67.[31] Greece was also notorious for its black, or unofficial, economy, which enabled citizens to avoid paying taxes.

For the southerners (and many economists), the problem was that Germany had pursued too restrictive a policy, aiming to run both trade and budget surpluses. In effect, Germany was saving too much and spending too little, thereby exporting deflation to the rest of the euro zone. (To compete with Germany, other countries had to reduce their wage bills.)[32] By definition, all countries cannot run a trade surplus; Germany was forcing the other countries into deficit and then blaming them for the result.

The crisis also confirmed the doubts of those who thought that the creation of the single currency had been mishandled. Too many countries had been allowed to join. Although Europeans had been annoyed by the repeated currency crises of the 1970s, 1980s and 1990s, those episodes had allowed countries to adjust their economic policies by the simple expedient of devaluation. When Greek or Italian exports became uncompetitive with those of Germany, the countries could devalue and start again. Within a single currency zone, that option was gone.

Furthermore, while the Europeans had eliminated currency risk, they could not get rid of risk altogether. Investors simply transferred their worries to the bond markets. Higher bond yields, by raising the cost of borrowing throughout the economy, had a more damaging effect than a small devaluation would have done.

More broadly, the EU created a currency zone without a common fiscal authority or regional deposit insurance. In a country with its own currency, like the UK or the US, the national government can transfer funds from strong regions to weak ones. That happens to an extent in the EU, but on nothing like a sufficient scale to cope with a recession. Banks were backed by their national governments, rather than by Brussels. This was understandable for political reasons; the Germans and Dutch were wary about underwriting the rest of Europe. But it made the system more fragile in the aftermath of 2008.

Another criticism is that the EU, like Western governments in general, became too obsessed with austerity. Critics on the left argue that politicians were frightened by the big budget deficits that appeared in 2009. The average budget deficit of 11 leading economies in 2007 was 0.3%; two years later it was 5.4%.[33] Both Britain and America had deficits of more than 10% of GDP. At the time, politicians worried that such huge deficits risked alienating bond investors, driving up borrowing costs, and thereby creating a Greek-style crisis.

But the critics argued that these fears were nonsensical. A country that issued debt in its own currency and had a compliant central bank (which could buy bonds through QE) need not fear the markets; indeed, bond yields were at historic lows despite the big deficits. Instead, the critics said, austerity was driven by the ideological desire, among conservative politicians on both sides of the Atlantic, for a smaller government. Austerity made matters worse, not better. The best way to close the deficit would be to let the economy grow more rapidly so that tax revenues could rise. This argument gained an unlikely ally in 2016 in the form of the IMF, which warned that "the costs of the tax increases or expenditure cuts required to bring down the debt may be much larger than the reduced crisis risk engendered by the lower debt". It added that "episodes of fiscal consolidation have been followed, on average, by drops rather than by expansions in output. On average, a consolidation of 1% of GDP increases the long-term unemployment rate by 0.6 percentage points."[34]

However, it is worth noting what economists mean when they talk of "austerity". They are talking about the trend in the deficit, rather than its absolute level. In other words, the UK government was still being "austere" when it borrowed 7.5% of GDP in 2011, even though that was one of the bigger deficits in its history. That is because the government had raised taxes and cut spending in order to bring the deficit down from 10.1% in 2009, thereby taking money out of people's pockets. Even after a prolonged period of austerity, 22 countries (out of 32) in the OECD were still spending more than 40% of GDP in 2015.[35]

There was little sign of a decline in social spending (unemployment benefits, health, pensions) as a proportion of GDP in the developed nations. As Western populations age, it seems likely that this ratio will continue to rise. In 1960, West Germany was unique in spending more than 15% of GDP on social benefits; now most nations spend much more. French social spending is more than 30% of GDP. To the extent that conservatives have attempted to shrink the government since the days of Margaret Thatcher and Ronald Reagan, they have often been running to stand still. A study by the Institute for Fiscal Studies in Britain found that, after years of austerity, public spending in 2017–18 was set to be around the same proportion of UK GDP as it had been in 2007–08.[36]

## The sins of wages

The stagnation of real wages was another source of voter discontent. Between the early 1970s and 2017, the wages of the median American worker grew at just 0.2% a year, while labour's share of GDP fell from nearly 65% to below 57% (as labour lost, owners of capital gained).[37] In Britain, by late 2016, workers were set for a decade without any real wage growth, a phenomenon not seen since the Second World War.[38] The essence of democracy is a deal in which workers give their votes to politicians in return for the promise of prosperity; politicians were perceived to be reneging on their side of the bargain. Populist politicians made gains across Europe, from Marine Le Pen in France to Matteo Salvini in Italy and Viktor Orbán in Hungary.

There have been plenty of attempts to explain the sluggish growth of real wages. On the political right, many have blamed immigration; they argue that an influx of unskilled workers has driven down wages by increasing the supply of labour. However, immigrants are not just workers, they are also consumers; as well as increasing the supply of labour, they increase the demand for goods. This "lump of labour" fallacy is hard to kill (see Chapter 9).

As noted earlier in the book, the real culprit could be found elsewhere. A study by the IMF found that the reason for around half the decline in labour's share of GDP was the impact of technology, as employers were able to automate low-skilled jobs. Another quarter of the shift was down to globalisation; companies in the developed world were shifting jobs to low-wage countries in the rest of the world.[39]

The sluggish overall level of growth that followed the financial crisis led some economists to rethink their previous models. Larry Summers, who was Treasury secretary under Bill Clinton and director of the National Economic Council under Barack Obama, argued that longer-term forces were at work. He revived a phrase first used by Alvin Hansen in 1938: secular stagnation.[40] Mr Summers claimed that the shock caused by the financial crisis seemed to have caused a permanent shift in the trend growth rate of output. The fear was that no level of interest rates would "permit the balance of savings and investment at full employment".

This shift was driven by a number of factors. As the population aged, economic growth slowed, and there was thus less need for businesses to invest in new plant and equipment. Furthermore, a larger proportion of capital investment was devoted to technological equipment, which needed regular updating and was declining steadily in price. The combination reduced the demand for investment. Meanwhile, rising inequality was transferring money from people who spend almost all of their income (the poor) to those who save a lot more of it (the rich). That shift was pushing up the level of savings.

At the same time, investing institutions like pension funds were being pressed, for regulatory reasons, to take a cautious approach.

This increased the demand for safe assets such as government bonds. All told, the combination of a lower propensity to invest and a higher propensity to save led to very low interest rates. Real (after inflation) interest rates were 3% or more at the global level through the 1990s and early 2000s but had dropped to less than 1% after 2010.[41]

Another issue is the impact of demographic change on economic growth. In 1950, a quarter of the Japanese population was aged over 40, and 5% was aged over 65; by 2010, more than half the population was aged over 40 and nearly a quarter was more than 65 years old. Between 2000 and 2018 the Japanese population of working people fell by 13%. It is very hard to grow an economy with fewer workers. A Federal Reserve paper estimated that, between 2011 and 2015, Japanese GDP growth was dragged down by 2 percentage points by this demographic decline.[42] Overall, Japan's annual growth rate averaged just 1.3% between 1988 and 2018, a far cry from the post-war miracle. Japan is still a prosperous and long-lived society, but its era of high growth looks gone for good.

Across the OECD as a whole, demography started to be a drag on growth after 2010 and will continue to be so until 2040.

## Workers' rights

The gig economy (see Chapter 17) can be viewed as a way of enhancing the productivity of the entire economy – by bringing unused resources (in this case, labour) into play. Similarly, the growth of flat- and house-sharing services, such as Airbnb, allows property to be used for a greater percentage of the time; it is a more efficient use of resources.

But the gig economy has raised questions about the issue of workers' rights. Over the course of the late 19th century and the 20th century, workers demanded, and were granted, more rights: paid holiday, sick leave, maternity leave, pensions and healthcare. These tended to be associated with full-time employment, rather than part-time or casual work. From the employer's point of view, they add significantly to the cost of hiring workers. The fear is that the gig economy represents a form of "regulatory arbitrage" in which companies replace full-time employees with casual or contract labour at less cost, and with fewer rights.

These lines can be difficult to draw. If a worker performs a service almost exclusively for a single company, and the company imposes sufficient conditions on the way in which the job is performed, then it may be proved that the worker is an employee, not a contractor.[43] Furthermore, such an employee may be entirely at the mercy of the platform provider. Comparisons have been drawn with the old system for employing dockers, who gathered at the port every day and were picked out by the foreman for work.

On the other hand, many people choose to operate as freelancers and independent contractors, and surveys show that they are happier than traditional employees.[44] The idea that everyone would have a full-time job in a factory or in an office, and would stay with a single employer for a large chunk of their career, developed in the 19th and 20th centuries. It was unusual before 1820 and may become unusual again.

But if employers fail to provide benefits, or a regular income, the state may have to step in to fill the gap. One suggestion is a "universal basic income", with the state providing an income to all citizens; this could, in part, replace the benefit system. The big question is how to create an income that is high enough to provide an acceptable standard of living without costing so much that the resulting tax burden would be crippling.[45]

The technology sector has also threatened a wide range of industries. Take music, for example. Listening to music used to involve the purchase of vinyl records, cassettes or compact discs; you could listen to the radio for free, but then the tunes were chosen by someone else. But the advent of streaming systems such as Spotify offered thousands of tracks, selected by the user, for a small monthly fee; indeed, I am listening to a playlist as I type this sentence. This was great news for the consumer but less great for the artists, who now need to depend more on the proceeds from touring. Something similar has occurred in newspapers. The availability of free information online has reduced the number of paid subscribers, while services like Craigslist have destroyed the market for classified advertising (jobs, cars for sale, etc.) on which so many papers relied.

These technology services have an enormous advantage over traditional suppliers. Once the network has been created or the software written, the costs of creating an additional unit, or adding a new customer, are close to zero. So a successful product can undercut its rivals. By the same token, however, logic suggests that if the cost of a product falls to zero in a competitive market, the price will fall towards zero too. Might this undermine the profitability of the corporate sector?

Not so far. Tech companies were piling on the profits in the second decade of the 21st century. One reason for this was that some seem to be natural monopolies; as already noted, people are on Facebook because their friends are on the site. A rival service would face an enormous task to catch up. Google, meanwhile, has become synonymous with "internet search" and thus can make money by selling advertised links. And Amazon's sheer scale means that it can undercut rival retailers, on price and on delivery.

However, the monopoly power that these companies have attained has caused a "techlash". People have started to worry about the Faustian bargain involved in giving personal information to corporate giants; as the saying goes, if you are being given a free service, that is because you are the product. Inevitably, the internet has been used to promote offensive views and hateful threats, and the tech companies have been accused of doing too little to prevent this. They have also been criticised for the way they have organised their tax affairs. Many have sited key parts of their organisations in low-tax regimes and they appear to make very little profit (and thus pay very little tax) in the bigger European states. The EU ruled that Apple owed Ireland €13bn in back taxes in 2016.[46] The notion that multinational companies were able to engineer their finances so as to reduce their tax bills was another factor in the rise of populism; a sense that there was one rule for the economic elite and another for the rest of us.

## Encouraging developments

Another change that continued in the wake of the debt crisis was the advance of the developing world, or emerging markets. In 1991 developed economies contributed more than 63% of global GDP. But with China growing fast, the rich world's share was shrinking; by 2000, it was down to 57%, and in 2008, the emerging markets moved ahead for the first time. As of 2018, the developed world's share was down to 40.6%, according to the IMF.[47]

Chinese growth slowed a bit from the double-digit percentage gains made in the early 2000s, but the government's target of 6–6.5% (as of 2019) was still enough to double the size of the economy in a little over a decade. The country's financial system has been liberalised a little, with the central bank allowing the yuan to be used in financial markets. But there has been an enormous build-up of debt, which reached 282% of GDP (excluding the finance sector) at the end of 2017 compared with just 158% at the end of 2008.[48] Economists tend to be divided between two camps. Some think that this debt has fuelled speculation in property and excess capacity in industry, and thus will inevitably lead to a crash. Others think that the government can handle the problem, thanks to its $3.1trn of foreign exchange reserves, as of June 2019.[49]

There has also been continued strength in the world's second-most populous nation, India, where the economy quadrupled in size between 1998 and 2018. The economy has managed a 7% annual growth rate despite a whole host of structural problems, including bureaucracy that makes it difficult for private businesses to expand. There is a lot of wasted Indian potential. As of 2018, a third of 15- to 29-year-olds were not in school, training or jobs; when 100,000 railway jobs were advertised, 20 million people applied.[50]

Of course, the term "developing economies" covers a wide range of countries. In 2014, there was much talk of the "fragile five"; economies dogged by high inflation and big current account deficits. The five in question were Brazil, Indonesia, India, South Africa and Turkey; some added Russia to the list to make a "suspect six".[51]

Emerging markets actually weathered the financial crisis in the developed world rather better than they might have done 20 years previously. Thanks to globalisation, many had become embedded in the supply chains of multinationals, which had established factories to make components or assemble parts made elsewhere. After building those factories, multinationals were unlikely to pull out again. But those countries that were dependent on commodities, like Russia, were vulnerable to the fall in the price of raw materials that followed the recession.

Perhaps the most prominent example of a failed economy was Venezuela. By 2017, 2.7 million of the country's 34 million people had left the country, many of them taking refuge in neighbouring Colombia. They were fleeing an economy in chaos, with inflation set to reach 10,000,000% in 2019, while output dropped by 18% in 2018.[52] In a poll, 93% of Venezuelans said that they could not afford the food they needed, while three-quarters had lost weight over the previous year. Income per head was back at the levels reached in the 1950s.[53]

All this in a country that claims bigger oil reserves than Saudi Arabia. The crisis is the result of the rule of Hugo Chávez, an ex-army major who first tried to seize power in a coup before being elected president, and his successor, Nicolás Maduro. Chávez governed in the name of revolutionary socialism, and spent heavily on social programmes, subsidies on food and energy, and aid for foreign allies. For a while, this programme was made affordable by a high oil price, bringing him popularity at home and support from left-wing politicians abroad. But Mr Chávez nationalised the oil company, ran it poorly and drove away private businesses; worse still, he harassed opponents, and closed down newspapers and radio stations that displeased him. His hapless successor Maduro simply printed money to finance the government's spending, leading to hyperinflation and empty supermarket shelves.[54] If anyone needed a post-Soviet illustration of the failings of socialist economics, Venezuela was it.

### Return of the nativist

In 2016, the world turned in a more nationalist direction. First, Britain voted to leave the EU in a referendum. Second, Donald Trump became US president on a protectionist ticket (despite losing the popular vote by nearly 3 million). At the time of writing, it is too early to say how disruptive the Brexit vote will be to European trade. But Mr Trump followed through by imposing tariffs on certain products (steel and aluminium) and against certain nations, most notably China.

It is hard to know how the trade war with China will pan out. In his negotiations with Mexico and Canada, Donald Trump seemed to follow a strategy of making big threats and settling for small concessions. The same thing may happen with China. More worrying was the ideology that underpinned his approach. First, he seemed to regard a trade deficit as both a loss for the US and a sign that the other side was cheating. This was a revival of mercantilism, a philosophy that Adam Smith debunked in 1776. In real life, trade deficits reflect an imbalance between domestic savings and investment. If the latter exceeds the former, then the economy must attract capital from abroad and this can only be done by running a current account deficit. Looked at another way, Americans save too little and spend too much on imports; neither factor has anything to do with foreign nations.

The second problem is that Mr Trump is under the mistaken impression that foreign companies pay the tariffs. In fact, those who import the goods do so. Businesses that import such goods will have to bear the extra cost in the form of lower profits (which means smaller dividends for investors), or they may have to recoup the cost in the form of lower wages for employees, or higher prices for consumers. In many cases, the imports may simply be components for products that are due to be exported; so the tariffs make the US company less competitive. Of course, it is possible that companies will switch to domestic suppliers. But those suppliers are bound to have higher costs. If they did not, companies would not be importing the product in the first place.

The net effect is to make the economy less efficient. The Trump tariffs are nothing like as bad as those that prevailed before the Second World War. But a survey by the Tax Foundation, a US think tank, calculated that if all the threatened tariffs were enacted, US GDP would be around 0.6% lower while wages would be reduced by 0.4% and employment would fall by around 460,000.[55]

In the last 300 years, the world has enjoyed long periods of growth, punctuated by occasional crises. The next crisis could well arise from an interruption to those trade patterns that carry boats to Singapore and Felixstowe.

# EPILOGUE

The story of the global economy has involved constant change. Consider the humble book. Printing technology was developed more than five hundred years ago and for a long time publishing was largely unchanged. But the industry grew hugely. First, there was a vast expansion of public libraries in the 19th century, which brought books to a much wider audience. Then books became even more widely disseminated with the development of the cheap paperback in the 20th century. In the 21st century, the rise of Amazon meant that book buyers could purchase a much wider range of publications than any individual shop could stock, and could have those volumes delivered to their homes. And electronic readers have changed the format in which books are read.

Change and trade are like conjoined twins. Economic history is all about connections. The more people with whom we can connect, the more likely it is that those connections will be useful. Either we will find someone whose expertise is helpful, or we will find someone who can offer a good or service that we desire but cannot provide for ourselves.

This book has tried to avoid equations, but think about a simple piece of maths. If you have three people, there are three ways in which they can connect: A can trade with B, or with C, and B can trade with C. With four people, there are six connections, and with five people there are ten. The formula is $n$ (for the number of people) multiplied by $n$ minus one and then divide the result by two. So as more and more people populated the world, the number of potential connections (or trades) rose dramatically.

Many of the elements of the modern economy such as long-distance trade and even financial instruments have existed for thousands of years. What has happened over the millennia is that more and more people have been drawn into the economic net and more connections have been made. As they have, the world has become richer, and people have grown taller and lived longer.

Hunter-gatherers largely lived off their own resources. Farmers specialised, and needed to trade for the things they did not produce. Agricultural societies created elites who sought luxury goods like silk or jewels from far-away places. And the great empires created "single markets" within their borders where merchants could trade.

Islamic and then Italian merchants established partnership structures that made long-distance trade easier. European traders muscled their way into Asia and then the Americas. The invention of the railways and the steamship reduced transport costs so that basic commodities like grain and (refrigerated) meat could be sold around the world. The telegraph, telephone and the internet increased the speed, and reduced the cost, of communication and information gathering. The global population is around 7.5 billion, so the number of potential connections is 28,000,000,000,000,000,000, or 28 quintillion.

Trade is good. A study of high-growth countries in the post-war period found that those that achieved per capita annual income growth of 3% or more saw similar growth in their trade. In contrast, countries that experience negligible or negative growth had a dismal trade performance.[1] Of course, correlation is not causality. But the contrasting growth records of, say, South Korea and China in the three post-war decades suggests that the former's export focus explains a lot of its success.

The modern economy is a place of dizzying complexity, and vast interconnections. Politicians who think they can disrupt the entire system and start again are taking a big risk. Unilever, the Anglo-Dutch consumer products company, operates in 190 countries and reckons that 2.5 billion people use its products every day, whether they are drinking a cup of PG Tips tea, cleaning their face with Dove soap, or disinfecting the toilet with Domestos.[2] Many more people must be involved in producing and distributing those products, not just those who work in Unilever factories, but those who produced the raw materials the company uses, drive the trucks and operate the ships that take those goods round the world, and manage the shops where they are sold. If it takes a village to raise a child, it takes the world to stock your house with goods.

This feat of coordination is beyond that of any individual. In the aftermath of the Soviet Union's break-up, the economist Paul Seabright was contacted by a Russian official who was keen to learn about the workings of the markets. "Tell me, for example," he asked "Who is in charge of the supply of bread to the population of London?"[3]

To anyone brought up in a Western economy, the question is laughable. Bread appears in the shops and we don't have to think about it. The big supermarkets know roughly how much their customers will buy every day and they order that amount from the big bakeries; smaller specialist shops make the same calculation. The result is that no one queues for bread, even if they complain about the price.

Richard Baldwin, an economist, has described economic development as a process of "unbundling".[4] First, we consumed the things that we ourselves produced. Then, we consumed some things produced by others in our local town or village. Later, thanks to the steamship, we consumed things that had been produced a long distance away. In the modern economy, every element of the system is "unbundled"; different people design the goods, produce the components, assemble them, market them, transport them, sell them and then consume them.

The system does involve greed and waste, and, in some regions and sectors, exploitation. Many worry about the dangers of environmental degradation. To give just one example, the cod was once so abundant off the coast of Canada that it enticed Viking and Basque sailors to risk their lives on a transatlantic journey. Dried cod is almost 80% protein, and by the middle of the 16th century, 60% of all fish eaten in Europe was cod. But industrialisation processes were applied to deep-sea fishing, with factory ships dragging the ocean floor. By the 1990s, Canada had to place a moratorium on cod fishing.[5]

Over the next few decades, humanity's impact on the climate may turn out to have significant economic costs. Unless action is taken to reduce carbon emissions, the global temperature may increase by more than two degrees centigrade and even as much as four to five degrees. The effect will be uneven. While countries like Canada may benefit from higher temperatures in the form of better crop yields, the same will not be true in the developing world. Warmer climates may mean an increase in pest infestation along with weather extremes such as floods, droughts and storms that damage crops. Storms and floods will also hit cities in the form of property damage, an effect that will be exacerbated as sea levels rise.

Climate change is a classic "collective action" problem, in which consumers, businesses and governments are reluctant to curtail their own energy consumption unless others do the same. The private sector will be able to help by developing new technologies that can produce renewable energy more cheaply, or by making homes and existing devices more energy-efficient. But some international action, in the form of a carbon tax that operates across borders, is probably needed to tackle the problem properly.

However, those who think that government planning will automatically reduce environmental exploitation should re-examine their assumptions. China, for instance, has a much more interventionist state than Europe and North America but its air pollution record is terrible. Another example of environmental destruction concerned the Aral Sea, once the fourth-largest lake in the world. A Soviet Union irrigation system diverted water from the lake, splitting it first into two before the eastern side dried up. It is now a fraction of its former size. Just because a government is in charge of planning doesn't mean that the environment will be protected.

This is not to say that governments are not important, as this book has emphasised. They are needed for a lot more than just policing and defence. The private sector needs governments to educate its workers, keep them healthy (in most countries), and to build the roads and infra-structure that bring its goods and services to market. A state also provides the legal system through which the business sector enforces contracts. Historically, the state provided the impetus and funding for some of the most important technologies in modern life, from the internet to satellite navigation systems to the development of life-saving drugs.

This book has avoided the use of the word neoliberalism, since it seems to be used as a term for the retreat of the state and its replacement by the private sector. But look across the OECD, a club of developed nations, and you find only two countries out of 35 where public spending was less than 30% of GDP in 2015 – Chile and Ireland. Another 31 countries had spending between 30% and 55% of GDP, and two (Finland and France) were above 55%.[6] If there has been a retreat, it has been very marginal. Public pressure to spend money on services, such as health, education and pensions, is very strong and difficult to resist.

The western economic model now faces a big challenge. In China the state operates a model of authoritarian capitalism where markets are allowed, but only under heavy government supervision. Rather than turning more democratic as it became more prosperous, the Chinese government has become even less tolerant of dissent. Nevertheless, its model may appeal to other developing nations, especially given the west's recent problems. Furthermore, China is a threat whether it succeeds or fails. China has kept growing at a rapid rate, but the weaknesses in its financial system may eventually cause a crash. And China is large enough that a crisis in its economy will inevitably cause problems for the rest of the world. There is very little that other countries can do to manage this risk.

Many improvements in our living standards arise from developments that could only happen as a result of economic change. As recently as 1940, 20% of American homes lacked electric light and 30% were without running water.[7] Better sanitation means better health. In 1870, 25% of American children died before their fifth birthday; now that number is down to 1%. The proportion of people living past their 65th birthday has risen from 34% to 77%.[8]

Globally, there has been just as dramatic a change. Life expectancy in 1820 was 36 in the developed world and 24 elsewhere; by 2000, the respective figures were 79 and 64. Over that same period, global population rose sixfold and income per capita ninefold (see

**A stronger economy supports a bigger population**
World population, bn

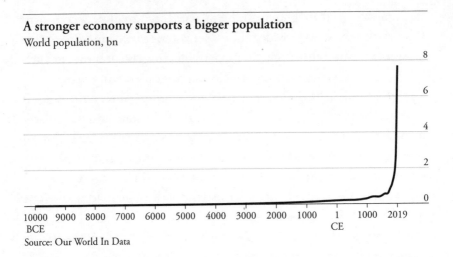

Source: Our World In Data

chart).[9] Occasionally, there are terrible famines, as in Ethiopia in the 1980s or in Yemen at the time of writing. But they are much rarer and more isolated than they used to be. Malthus has been conquered.

The most exciting news of the last 30 years has been that the developing world has been catching up. In 1980, average annual incomes in the developing world were $1,500, about where American incomes were (adjusting for inflation) in 1830. By 2015, the developing world average was $11,000, where the US was in the 1940s, meaning that they have caught up more than a century within 35 years.[10] The biggest advances were in China. In 1970, US per capita income was 20 times that of China; by 2010, the ratio was only 4.[11]

Of course, there are still too many people dying too early, and too many living in extreme poverty, or close to it. But things have in general been getting better. In the book he wrote with his son and daughter-in-law, the late Hans Rosling described 13 questions he often asked at global conferences.[12] Most people were too pessimistic in their answers, not realising, for example, that 60% of girls in low-income countries now finish primary school, 80% of children have been vaccinated, and 80% of people have access to electricity. Most remarkably, despite all the disasters you see on the news and the sevenfold rise in the global population, the absolute number of people who die in natural disasters every year has halved over the last century.

Economic growth also tends to make a society more liberal and tolerant. In 1993, in the aftermath of a recession, 64% of Americans said that immigrants hurt the economy. By 1999, at the height of a boom, only 40% felt the same. Trading encourages open minds, as it requires us to deal with people from other cultures and with other aspirations. By itself, this openness boosts economic growth because societies benefit from talented newcomers, as the British did with Flemish weavers or Ugandan Asians in the 1970s. Benjamin Friedman argues that "When economic growth gives way to stagnation, people's attitudes towards openness and mobility in their society harden accordingly."[13]

None of this can be taken for granted. As this book was being written, some politicians were preaching that ties with foreign nations should be reduced, that immigration should be kept to a minimum, and that other countries were out to cheat domestic workers out of their jobs. These policies only have appeal because the 2008 crisis seemed to suggest that there was something terribly wrong with the way the economy was operating; that it had been rigged in favour of the wealthy and those who work in the finance sector.

If this attitude persists, we will be in for a repeat of the 1914–45 period. As the economist Deirdre McCloskey has written, the danger of a corrupt society is that citizens start to feel that commerce is a zero-sum game and that the only way to get ahead is via theft or corruption.[14] China and India have made such rapid gains in the last 30 years because their citizens have been allowed to benefit from their own effort and ingenuity and have become part of a global trading market. It would be a terrible irony if Europeans and Americans, whose economic progress after 1820 astounded the world, were to forget the lesson.

But let us end on a more optimistic note. As this book was being finalised, the author attended an "Entrepreneur First" event in the King's Cross area of London. The idea of the programme was to bring bright young people together so that they could make connections and then form start-up businesses. At this event, previous attendees were making their pitch to investors. Two things were striking. The first was that the presenters came from all over the world, from Cameroon, China, Mexico and Switzerland, and many had postgraduate qualifications from top universities. The second was that many of the pitches were concerned with important social problems, like diagnosing sepsis quickly, spotting water leaks, monitoring arthritis, or reducing the carbon emissions involved in making concrete. The best pitches attracted whoops and cheers from the audience.

Here, assembled in one room, was an example of what economics can achieve. The public sector had educated these people to a high level and now they were turning to the private sector to fund ideas that would eventually bring gains for society as a whole. Three hundred years ago, these people would not have been educated to the same level, and would never have been able to meet like-minded people or attract the money needed to put their ideas into practice. But today they have the chance to make things better.

# APPENDIX

## The numbers game

The Great Depression was the biggest event in global economic history. When it struck, knowledge of the economy was very limited. The concept of gross domestic product (GDP) was not defined, let alone measured, until 1934 when it was defined as "national income". The task of establishing a measure of national income fell to a brilliant economist named Simon Kuznets, after a US Senate committee asked him to do so. With the help of staff from the Commerce Department and the National Bureau of Economic Research, Kuznets managed to set the blueprint for national accounts in 1934 within 12 months of being handed the assignment.[1] A fuller report followed in 1937.

The job was immense, both conceptually and logistically. The aim of GDP is to measure the final monetary value of all goods and services produced in a given year (or quarter). This requires a comprehensive survey of businesses, large and small, and it also needs to avoid double-counting. Take your morning cornflakes, for example. A farmer will have grown the corn, a mill will have processed it, someone will have made the cardboard box and the plastic sleeve, a truck will have charged money to drive the product to the store, a supermarket will have sold it, and so on. But GDP must measure only the final output. To the extent that it reflects the other parts of the process, it must merely include the "value added" at that stage.

There are three ways of measuring the figure. We can calculate the value of total output (the stuff we make), of total expenditure (retail sales, purchases of equipment by companies, etc.) and of total income (wages, profits, etc.).[2] In theory, these three measures should agree; in practice, there are some inevitable discrepancies.

Calculating the figure you hear quoted for growth on the national news – a 0.4% gain on the quarter, say – requires more adjustment. If the amount we produce rises in value just because of inflation, then we are no better off. So the figure must be recalculated to reflect changes in price; this is known as the GDP deflator. The eventual figure is the change in real (after inflation) GDP.

The earliest estimates for GDP come just a few weeks after the end of the quarter. So it is not surprising that the numbers have to be revised. Sometimes this means that a recession (defined as two quarters of declining output) has been declared inaccurately. The subsequent statistical adjustments get much less publicity than the initial bad news. This happened in Britain in 2012.[3] A study by the OECD of the period 1994 to 2013 found that, on average, annual GDP growth across 18 countries had been revised 0.2% higher after three years.[4]

As a measure, GDP, and its close relative gross national product (GNP),[5] has had many critics. In a speech, Senator Bobby Kennedy pointed out that the calculation included the value of guns and napalm and jails, but that

> the gross national product does not allow for the health of our children, the quality of their education or the joy of their play. It does not include the beauty of our poetry or the strength of our marriages, the intelligence of our public debate or the integrity of our public officials. It measures neither our wit nor our courage, neither our wisdom nor our learning, neither our compassion nor our devotion to our country, it measures everything in short, except that which makes life worthwhile.[6]

David Pilling, a *Financial Times* journalist (and former colleague), has written that GDP has five main flaws. It is much better at measuring physical goods than services; if fails to pick up gains to consumer welfare such as the ability to buy things cheaply online (indeed, such transactions could lower GDP); it has nothing to say about the distribution of income or wealth; it treats bigger as better, even though that might not be the case (a bigger finance sector was a problem in 2008); and it measures cash transactions, such as drug buying and prostitution, but not the labour of those who care for a relative or clean their house.[7]

Imperfect though it may be, calculating GDP at least gives elected politicians and central banks a rough idea of how the economy is performing, which allows them to set policy accordingly. Before the First World War, politicians were inclined to argue that the health of the economy was beyond their control, while central bankers were focused solely on maintaining the value of their currency or controlling domestic inflation (usually the same thing). The Depression created the demand for politicians to manage the economic cycle, and without some measure like GDP that would have been much more difficult.

## Inflation

Measuring other aspects of the economy is also hard. Inflation sounds easy; it is merely a matter of calculating the rise in prices. But which prices? The traditional answer has been to create a "representative basket" of goods after surveying consumers. But we differ enormously in our consumption patterns. The poor will spend more of their income, proportionately, on basics like food, rent and heating. It will be of little comfort to struggling families to learn that personal computers have fallen in price. So it is hard to find one measure that reflects changes in the standard of living of all consumers.

There are other problems with price indices. Consumption patterns are not fixed: if beef is expensive, people will switch to chicken. One of the biggest expenditures for many households is their mortgage payment, but when a central bank tries to tackle inflation, it tends to push up interest rates, increasing mortgage costs. Paradoxically, that means the bank's attempts to control inflation may push it higher in the short term. So central banks often target a measure that ignores mortgage costs.

Central banks may also exclude commodities like oil and food from their target measure; changes in such prices may be down to tension in the Middle East or a bad harvest rather than economic fundamentals. Another problem may be a one-off fall in the exchange rate, driving up import prices. This happened in Britain after the Brexit referendum of June 2016, when the Bank of England chose to focus on domestically generated inflation instead, rather than push up interest rates when confidence was shaky.

When all these adjustments are made, a central bank may well be targeting a "core" measure of inflation, which doesn't reflect the actual change in the standard of living of a typical consumer.

Another tricky issue is adjusting prices for changes in the quality of products; in other words, when we get a lot more features for the same price. This book's introduction recounted the changes in the quality of light from fires to candles to LED bulbs. A smartphone has more computing capacity than NASA did when it sent Apollo 11 to the moon.[8] A modern TV is lighter, less prone to failure, and carries many more channels than did its counterpart in the 1970s. Economists try to make adjustments for these "hedonic" improvements but may not get it right.

All these objections also apply to the GDP deflator. So as well as overestimating or underestimating inflation, economists may be overstating or understating real GDP growth.

## Unemployment

Another much-cited measure of economic performance is unemployment. Again, this was hard to measure until the existence of the modern state and the introduction of unemployment insurance. Precision here is difficult. Clearly, schoolchildren should not be included; the same goes for the very elderly and infirm, or parents looking after small children. But it is hard to draw an exact line. People go on working after the official retirement age; university students work in their holidays; and parents and those caring for the elderly may want to work part-time, or even full-time if alternative care arrangements are available.

A common measure of the unemployment rate is the "number of people out of work and claiming benefits". But that is quite a narrow definition. Governments like to control public spending and thus restrict the right to unemployment benefit; they do not want people to choose state handouts as an easy alternative to employment. So they may disallow claimants who refuse jobs because of the inconvenience, the unsociable hours, the commuting distance, or the mismatch with their qualifications, and so on.

The broadest measure of employment is the labour force participation rate: the proportion of people who are of working age and in employment. From this we can deduce how many people are not participating. As of June 2019, the official US unemployment rate was 3.8%, but 37% of the population was not taking part in the labour market.[9]

The existence of part-time jobs only adds to the complexity. Some people may be happy to work 15 hours a week because it suits their lifestyle; they need to pick up kids from school, for example. Others may only have a part-time job because they cannot find full-time employment. So there may well be "underemployment" as well as unemployment.

A whole host of other data are published every month, all with their own problems of measurement and definition. Surveys of businesses and consumers ask respondents whether they are "confident", or whether sales or new orders are "better than normal", "worse than expected" and so on. The results are inevitably subjective and prone to over-analysis. A fall in an index from 52 to 51 may look like a worrying decline but may prove to be a random event.

## A tricky task

Governments and central banks must attempt to set economic policy in the light of this data – a task that has been compared to driving while looking solely at a blurry rear-view mirror. Worse still, the impact of monetary and fiscal measures such as changing tax or interest rates may take a year or two to have an impact. By the time they take effect, economic conditions will probably have changed substantially.

The difficulties facing policymakers are made even worse because the relationship between economic variables can change. Take the Phillips curve, named after a study by William Phillips, an economist from New Zealand, of the relationship between unemployment and inflation in Britain between 1861 and 1957.[10] Phillips found that, as unemployment fell, inflation tended to rise. The logical explanation was that, as workers became harder to find, employers had to offer higher wages, requiring businesses to charge higher prices. In the 1960s, governments debated how much inflation they could tolerate in order to reduce unemployment.

Then, in the 1970s, stagflation emerged: the simultaneous appearance of high inflation and unemployment. Milton Friedman and Edmund Phelps argued that there could not be a long-run trade-off between higher inflation and lower unemployment, and that there was a "natural" rate of unemployment; trying to force the rate below that level would only lead to higher prices.[11]

But the late 1990s and early 2000s showed another change. There appeared to be no relationship between inflation and unemployment at all. In America, unemployment fell from 10% to just over 4% while inflation stayed in a 1–2% range.[12] Again, this made the life of central banks very difficult. A tighter labour market should, in theory, lead to higher wages and thus inflation, and it required the banks to take action to pre-empt this possibility. But if the theory were wrong, then policy would be tightened for no reason.

## The endless search for perfection

Economists' failure to forecast big events like recessions has made them the butt of jokes. For example, how can you tell that economists have a sense of humour? Because they put decimal points in their forecasts. The statistical agencies are always trying to refine their data in order to improve its accuracy. And economists are forever testing the past relationships between variables to see which policies might work.

The advent of the internet means that it is possible to gather much more information than previously about economic activity (for example, the number of cars parked at out-of-town shopping centres). In addition, economists also have more computing power with which to crunch the data. But we will never reach the stage where it is possible to accurately forecast the economic outlook. That is because economics is a social science and not a physical one.

When a chemist forecasts the result of two substances reacting, the substances are unaware of the forecast's existence. But if people knew, for certain, that there would be a recession next year, they would become more cautious immediately. Consumers would cut back on spending; businesses would postpone investment and new orders. The recession would be brought forward, rendering the forecast inaccurate. Economists need to be allowed a little slack, at least when it comes to forecasting.

# NOTES

**Introduction**

1. Christopher Minasians, "Where are Apple products made?", *Macworld*, September 18th 2017
2. https://www.zmescience.com/research/how-scientists-tught-monkeys-the-concept-of-money-not-long-after-the-first-prostitute-monkey-appeared/
3. Source: World Bank https://data.worldbank.org/indicator/NE.TRD.GNFS.ZS
4. Ecclesiastes 11:1, New Living Translation
5. Thomas Hobbes, *Leviathan*
6. "Worst tech predictions of all time", *The Daily Telegraph*, June 29th 2017, https://www.telegraph.co.uk/technology/0/worst-tech-predictions-of-all-time/thomas-watson-ibm-president-in-1943/
7. Vaclav Smil, *Energy and Civilization: A History*
8. https://www.tudorsociety.com/childbirth-in-medieval-and-tudor-times-by-sarah-bryson
9. Steven Pinker, *Enlightenment Now: The Case for Reason, Science, Humanism and Progress*
10. Hans Rosling, Ola Rosling and Anna Rosling Rönnlund, *Factfulness: Ten Reasons We're Wrong About the World – And Why Things Are Better Than You Think*

11. Ibid.; the figures comes from a World Bank study by Martin Ravallion and Shaohua Chen

12. Joe Hasell and Max Roser, "Famines", Our World in Data, https://ourworldindata.org/famines

13. Steven Radelet, *The Great Surge: The Ascent of the Developing World*

14. Jared Diamond, *Collapse: How Societies Choose to Fail or Survive*

15. Karen Bennett, "Disappearance of the Aral Sea", World Resources Institute, May 23rd 2008, http://www.wri.org/blog/2008/05/disappearance-aral-sea

16. The book is a biography of Cyrus the Great, a Persian emperor, and can be found at https://www.gutenberg.org/ebooks/2085

17. Deirdre N. McCloskey, "The great enrichment was built on ideas, not capital", Foundation for Economic Education, November 22nd 2017, https://fee.org/articles/the-great-enrichment-was-built-on-ideas-not-capital/

18. Angus Maddison, *Contours of the World Economy, 1–2030 AD*

19. William Easterly, *The Elusive Quest for Growth: Economists' Adventures and Misadventures in the Tropics*

20. Max Roser, "Light", Our World in Data, https://ourworldindata.org/light

21. Rachel Swaby, "One Man's Nearly Impossible Quest to Make a Toaster From Scratch", April 21st 2011, https://gizmodo.com/5794368/why-its-harder-than-you-think-to-make-a-simple-toaster

## Chapter 1 – The ancient economy

1. Grahame Clark, "Traffic in stone axes and adze blades", *The Economic History Review*, vol. 18 no. 1, 1965

2. Andrew Sherratt, "The Obsidian Trade in the Near East 14,000 to 6500BCE", *ArchAtlas*

3. Erin Wayman, "The Earliest Example of Hominid fire", April 4th 2012, www.smithsonianmag.com

4. John Lanchester, "How Civilization Started: Was it even a good idea?" *The New Yorker*, September 18th 2017

5. Chris Stringer and Julia Galway-Witham, "When did modern humans leave Africa?", *Science*, Jan 26th 2018

6. Nayan Chanda, *Bound Together: How Traders, Preachers, Adventurers and Warriors Shaped Globalization*

7. Richard Mabey, *The Cabaret of Plants: Botany and the Imagination*

8. The term just means "old stone". In layman's terms, it means Old Stone Age.

9. Mabey, *The Cabaret of Plants*, op. cit.

10. Lanchester, "How Civilisation Started", op. cit.

11. Yuval Noah Harari, *Sapiens: A Brief History of Humankind*

12. Tom Standage, *An Edible History of Humanity*

13. James C. Scott, *Against the Grain: A Deep History of the Earliest States*

14. Smil, *Energy and Civilization*, op. cit.

15. Megan Sweeney and Susan McCouch, "The complex history of the domestication of rice", *Annals of Botany*, vol. 100, no. 5, October 2007. Rice can be dated to around 10,000 years ago.

16. "Extinction: Dead as the moa", *The Economist*, September 14th 2013

17. Barry Cunliffe, *By Steppe, Desert, & Ocean: The Birth of Eurasia*

18. Scott, *Against the Grain*, op. cit.

19. Michael Wood, *The Story of India*

20. Steven Pinker, *The Better Angels of Our Nature: A History of Violence and Humanity*. The death rates are of course measured as a proportion of the existing population, not in absolute terms. They include, for modern states, both world wars and genocides.

21. Walter Scheidel, *The Great Leveler: Violence and the History of Inequality from the Stone Age to the Twenty-First Century*

22. Standage, *An Edible History of Humanity*, op. cit.

23. In his play *The Doctor's Dilemma*

24. Paul Kriwaczek, *Babylon: Mesopotamia and the Birth of Civilization*

25. Christopher Edens, "Dynamics of trade in the ancient Mesopotamian world system", *American Anthropologist*, vol. 94, no. 1, March 1992

26. Harari, *Sapiens*, op. cit.

27. Felix Martin, *Money: The Unauthorised Biography*

28. Kriwaczek, *Babylon*, op. cit.

29. Michael Jursa, "Babylonia in the first millennium BCE", in Larry Neal and Jeffrey G. Williamson, eds, *The Cambridge History of Capitalism, Volume 1*

30. Cunliffe, *By Steppe, Desert, & Ocean*, op. cit.

31. Peter Damerow, "Sumerian Beer: The Origins of Brewing Technology in Ancient Mesopotamia", Cuneiform Digital Library, 2012

32. The Avalon Project, Yale Law School, https://avalon.law.yale.edu/ancient/hamframe.asp

33. Steve Kummer and Christian Pauletto, "The History of Derivatives: A Few Milestones", EFTA Seminar on Regulation of Derivatives Markets, May 3rd 2012, Zurich. A derivative is a contract whose value derives from the price of another asset.

34. John P. Powelson, *The Story of Land: A World History of Land Tenure and Agrarian Reform*

35. Jursa, *The Cambridge History of Capitalism, Volume 1*, op. cit.

36. Standage, *Edible Humanity*, op. cit.

37. John Micklethwait and Adrian Wooldridge, *The Company: A Short History of a Revolutionary Idea*

38. Powelson, *The Story of Land*, op. cit.

39. Kostas Vlassopoulos, "Greek Slavery: From Domination To Property And Back Again", *Journal of Hellenic Studies*, vol. 131, 2011

40. Powelson, *The Story of Land*, op. cit.

41. Standage, op. cit.

42. Kassia St Clair, *The Golden Thread: How Fabric Changed History*

43. The first authenticated use of the wheel was in the Black Sea area around 3400BCE; see Jared Diamond, *Guns, Germs and Steel*

44. James D. Mauseth, *Plants & People*

45. John Keay, *India: A History*

46. Wood, *The Story of India*, op. cit.

47. Diamond, *Guns, Germs and Steel*, op. cit.

48. Jan Bakker, Stephan Maurer, Jörn-Steffen Pischke and Ferdinand Rauch, "Trade and growth in the Iron Age", August 23rd 2018, https://voxeu.org/article/trade-and-growth-iron-age

49. Alain Bresson, "Capitalism and the ancient Greek economy", *The Cambridge History of Capitalism, Volume 1*, op. cit.

50. Martin, *Money*, op. cit.

51. Ibid.

52. "The History of Derivatives", op. cit.

53. Stephen Hodkinson, "Female property ownership and status in Classical and Hellenistic Sparta", University of Manchester; paper given at a Women and Property conference at the Center for Hellenic Studies, Harvard University, 2003

54. Peter Frankopan, *The Silk Roads: A New History of the World*

55. An earlier version was built by Pharaoh Necho II. It followed a different route from the modern canal.

56. https://ciks.cbt.nist.gov/~garbocz/appendix1/node4.html

57. Smil, *Energy and Civilization*, op. cit.

58. Ibid.

59. Mancur Olson, *Power and Prosperity: Outgrowing Communist and Capitalist Dictatorships*

60. Willem M. Jongman, "Re-constructing the Roman economy", *The Cambridge History of Capitalism, Volume 1*, op. cit.

61. M.I. Finley, *The Ancient Economy*, second edition

62. Maddison, *Contours of the World Economy*, op. cit.

63. Ibid.

64. Colin Mayer, *Prosperity: Better Business Makes the Greater Good*

65. Micklethwait and Wooldridge, *The Company*, op. cit.

66. Rossella Lorenzi, "Roman 'factory town' for oil lamps found", http://www.nbcnews.com/id/28072109/ns/technology_and_science-science/t/roman-factory-town-oil-lamps-found/#.XHQFDaL7TIU

67. Pliny the Elder, *Natural History, Book XII*

68. Chanda, *Bound Together*, op. cit.

69. Lincoln Paine, *The Sea and Civilization: A Maritime History of the World*

70. The Erythraean Sea was the term used for a combination of the Red Sea, Arabian Sea and the northwest Indian Ocean.

71. Cunliffe, *By Steppe, Desert, & Ocean*, op. cit.

72. Around 2m square miles

73. Tamar Haspel, "In defense of corn, the world's most important food crop", *Washington Post*, July 12th 2015

74. David Landes, *The Wealth and Poverty of Nations*

75. Powelson, *The Story of Land*, op. cit.

76. John Keay, *China: A History*

77. E. G. Pulleyblank, "The Origins and Nature of Chattel Slavery in China", *Journal of the Economic and Social History of the Orient*, vol. 1, no. 2

78. Scheidel, *The Great Leveler*, op. cit.

79. Christopher Ford, *The Mind of Empire: China's History and Modern Foreign Relations*

80. Valerie Hansen, *The Silk Road: A New History*

81. All this is revealed in a fascinating paper in the *Journal of Roman Archaeology*, vol. 18, 2005: François de Callataÿ, "The Graeco-Roman economy in the super long-run: lead, copper and shipwrecks".

82. Maddison, *Contours of the World Economy*, op. cit.

83. Finley, *The Ancient Economy*, op. cit.

84. Cunliffe, *By Steppe, Desert, & Ocean*, op. cit.

85. Scott, *Against the Grain*, op. cit.
86. Ian Morris, *War: What Is it Good For? The Role of Conflict in Civilisation, from Primates to Robots*
87. Maddison, *Contours of the World Economy*, op. cit.

## Chapter 2 – Agriculture

1. "Arctic farms defy icy conditions with hydroponics", *Seattle Times*, November 3rd 2016, https://www.seattletimes.com/business/arctic-farming-town-turns-to-hydroponics-for-fresh-greens/
2. Source: https://data.worldbank.org/indicator/NV.AGR.TOTL.ZS
3. Joe Hasell and Max Roser, "Famines", Our World in Data, https://ourworldindata.org/famines. The figures for the years 2010–2016 were even lower at 0.5 per 100,000.
4. Giovanni Federico, *Feeding the World: An Economic History of Agriculture, 1800–2000*
5. Source: World Bank https://data.worldbank.org/indicator/SL.AGR.EMPL.ZS
6. A hectare is 2.47 acres.
7. Federico, *Feeding the World*, op. cit.
8. 2012 Census of Agriculture, https://www.agcensus.usda.gov/Publications/2012/Online_Resources/Highlights/Farms_and_Farmland/Highlights_Farms_and_Farmland.pdf
9. Shimelles Tenaw, K.M. Zahidul Islam and Tuulikki Parviainen, "Effects of land tenure and property rights on agricultural productivity in Ethiopia, Namibia and Bangladesh", University of Helsinki, 2009
10. See Frank Dikötter, *Mao's Great Famine: The History of China's Most Devastating Catastrophe 1958–1962;* or Anne Applebaum, *Red Famine: Stalin's War on Ukraine*
11. Radelet, *The Great Surge*, op. cit.
12. Paul McMahon, *Feeding Frenzy: The New Politics of Food*
13. Standage, *An Edible History of Humanity*, op. cit.
14. Mabey, *The Cabaret of Plants*, op. cit.
15. Chanda, *Bound Together*, op. cit.
16. Melinda Zeder, Smithsonian Institution, "The domestication of animals", *Journal of Anthropological Research*, vol. 68, no. 2, 2012
17. Lyudmila Trut, Irina Oskina and Anastasiya Kharlamova, "Animal evolution during domestication: the domesticated fox as a model",

Institute of Cytology and Genetics, Siberian Branch of Russian Academy of Sciences, Novosibirsk, Russia

18. Ed Yong, "A new origin story for dogs", https://www.theatlantic.com/science/archive/2016/06/the-origin-of-dogs/484976/

19. Diamond, *Guns, Germs and Steel*, op. cit.

20. Discovery is in inverted commas because, of course, the land was already inhabited. Indeed, the Vikings had reached Newfoundland a few centuries beforehand. But their travels were unknown in the rest of medieval Europe.

21. Standage, *An Edible History of Humanity*, op. cit.

22. Brendan O'Farrell and Lars Fehren-Schmitz, "Native Americans experienced a strong population bottleneck coincident with European contact", Proceedings of the National Academy of Sciences, December 20th 2011

23. The Maddison Project, https://www.rug.nl/ggdc/historicaldevelopment/maddison/releases/maddison-project-database-2018

24. Andrew M. Watson, "The Arab agricultural revolution and its diffusion 700–1100", *The Journal of Economic History*, vol. 34, no. 1, March 1974

25. Chanda, *Bound Together*, op. cit.

26. Ibid.

27. McMahon, *Feeding Frenzy*, op. cit.

28. Powelson, *The Story of Land*, op. cit.

29. Easterly, *The Elusive Quest for Growth*, op. cit.

30. The Chinese had already developed a breast-collar harness, which was far superior to European versions but did not arrive in Europe until the eighth century CE.

31. Jerome Blum, "The rise of serfdom in Eastern Europe", *The American Historical Review*, vol. 62, no. 4, July 1957

32. The folk rock group led by Ian Anderson was named after him.

33. See Professor Mark Overton, "Agricultural revolution in England 1500–1850" http://www.bbc.co.uk/history/british/empire_seapower/agricultural_revolution_01.shtml

34. Ibid.

35. Michael Turner, "Agricultural productivity in England in the eighteenth century: evidence from crop yields", *The Economic History Review*, vol. 35, no. 4, November 1982

36. Carlo M. Cipolla, *Before the Industrial Revolution: European Society and Economy 1000–1700*, third edition

37. Standage, *Edible History*, op. cit.

38. The National Museum of American History, "The Guano Trade", http://americanhistory.si.edu/norie-atlas/guano-trade

39. Bretislav Friedrich and Dieter Hoffmann, "Clara Haber, nee Immerwahr (1870–1915): Life, Work and Legacy", March 2016, https://www.ncbi.nlm.nih.gov/pmc/articles/PMC4825402/

40. Vaclav Smil, "Nitrogen cycle and world food production", *World Agriculture*, 2011. A megatonne is equal to 1m metric tonnes or 1 billion kilogrammes.

41. Tim Harford, *Fifty Things That Made the Modern Economy*

42. There are several types of rust, including *Puccinia triticina* (black rust) and *Puccinia recondita* (brown rust).

43. Noel Vietmeyer, *Our Daily Bread: the Essential Norman Borlaug*

44. 50 Years of IR8: A Tribute to the Miracle Rice that Helped India Fight One Of Its Worst Famines by Sanchari Pal, The Better India

45. Vietmeyer, *Our Daily Bread*, op. cit.

46. McMahon, *Feeding Frenzy*, op. cit.

47. Radelet, *The Great Surge*, op. cit.

48. Douglas Gollin, Casper Worm Hansen and Asger Wingender, "Two blades of grass: the impact of the green revolution", Centre for Economic Policy Research, November 2016

49. https://www.epa.gov/nutrientpollution/effects-dead-zones-and-harmful-algal-blooms

50. Geoffrey Carr, "The future of agriculture", Technology Quarterly, *The Economist*, June 9th 2016

51. Source: https://www.statista.com/statistics/263962/number-of-chickens-worldwide-since-1990/

52. David Edgerton, *The Shock of the Old: Technology and Global History Since 1900*

53. Source: https://www.ciwf.org.uk/farm-animals/chickens/meat-chickens/

54. Source: http://www.fao.org/newsroom/common/ecg/1000505/en/stocks.pdf

55. "Getting serious about overfishing", *The Economist*, May 27th 2017

56. "A bigger rice bowl", *The Economist*, May 10th 2014

57. Elizabeth Weise, "Academies of Science finds GMOs not harmful to human health", *USA Today*, May 17th 2016

58. "Field research", *The Economist*, November 12th 2014

59. Adam Aton, "For Crop Harvests, Every Degree of Warming Counts", *Scientific American*, August 16th 2017

## Chapter 3 – The Asian market: 200–1000CE

1. John Keay, *China: A History*

2. Dr Tim Newfield, Princeton University, "The global cooling event of the sixth century. Mystery no longer?" https://www. historicalclimatology.com/blog/something-cooled-the-world-in-the-sixth-century-what-was-it

3. Rhys Blakeley, "Worst year in history puts our problems in the shade", *The Times*, November 20th 2018

4. Frankopan, *The Silk Roads*, op. cit.

5. John Keay, *India: A History*

6. Hansen, *The Silk Road*, op. cit.

7. Chanda, *Bound Together*, op. cit.

8. Étienne de la Vaissière, "Sogdians in China: A Short History and Some New Discoveries", The Silkroad Foundation Newsletter

9. Hansen, *The Silk Road*, op. cit.

10. Ibid.

11. St Clair, *The Golden Thread*, op. cit.

12. Etienne de las Vaissière, "Trans-Asian trade, or the Silk Road deconstructed", *The Cambridge History of Capitalism, Volume 1*, op. cit.

13. Tom Phillips, "The $900bn question: what is the Belt and Road initiative?" *The Guardian*, May 12th 2017

14. Source: https://en.unesco.org/silkroad/silk-road-themes/underwater-heritage/belitung-shipwreck. Oddly, this boat seems to have strayed from the traditional route.

15. David Abulafia, professor of Mediterranean history, Cambridge University, speaking at the Silk Road seminar at the Legatum Institute, October 25th 2016

16. Janet L. Abu-Lughod, *Before European Hegemony: The World System AD 1250–1350*

17. Hansen, *The Silk Road*, op. cit.

18. Ibid.

19. Albert Hourani, *A History of the Arab Peoples*

20. Abu-Lughod, *Before European Hegemony*, op. cit.

21. Hourani, *A History of the Arab Peoples,* op. cit.

22. Source: http://www.muslimheritage.com/article/umayyad-coins-661–750ce

23. Cunliffe, *By Steppe, Desert, & Ocean,* op. cit.

24. Paul Vallely, "How Islamic inventors changed the world", *The Independent,* March 11th 2006

25. Hourani, *A History of the Arab Peoples,* op. cit.

26. Frankopan, *The Silk Roads,* op. cit.

27. Keay, *China: A History,* op. cit.

28. Greg Clark, *Global Cities: A Short History*

29. Steven A. Epstein, *An Economic and Social History of Later Medieval Europe, 1000–1500*

30. Ibid.

31. Branko Milanovic, *Global Inequality: A New Approach for the Age of Globalization*

32. It is striking how these areas in the middle kingdom were still the subject of territorial dispute in the 20th century.

33. Maddison, *Contours of the World Economy,* op. cit.

## Chapter 4 – Europe revives: 1000–1500

1. Smil, *Energy and Civilization,* op. cit.

2. Robert Bartlett, *The Making of Europe: Conquest, Colonization and Cultural Change 950–1350*

3. Ibid.

4. From the hymn "All Things Bright and Beautiful" written by Cecil Frances Alexander

5. Epstein, *An Economic and Social History of Later Medieval Europe,* op. cit.

6. Abu-Lughod, *Before European Hegemony,* op. cit.

7. Fernand Braudel, *Civilization & Capitalism, 15th–18th Century, Volume 1: The Structures of Everyday Life*

8. Robert S. Lopez, *The Commercial Revolution of the Middle Ages, 950–1350*

9. Abu-Lughod, *Before European Hegemony,* op. cit.

10. Ibid.

11. Epstein, *An Economic and Social History of Later Medieval Europe,* op. cit.

12. Ibid.

13. Abu-Lughod, *Before European Hegemony,* op. cit.

14. Lopez, *The Commercial Revolution of the Middle Ages, 950–1350,* op. cit.

15. The Florentine coin was the florin, a name that survived into the modern era as a two-shilling coin in the UK.

16. Norman Davies, *Europe: A History*

17. It is possible that the author's name, Coggan, stems from this root.

18. Fernand Braudel, *Civilization & Capitalism, 15th–18th Century, Volume 3: The Perspective of the World*

19. James Kynge, *China Shakes the World: The Rise of a Hungry Nation*

20. Michael Pye, *The Edge of the World: How the North Sea Made Us*

21. Abu-Lughod, *Before European Hegemony*, op. cit.

22. Braudel, *Civilization & Capitalism, 15th–18th Century, Volume 3*, op. cit.

23. Abu-Lughod, *Before European Hegemony*, op. cit.

24. John Keay, *China: A History*

25. Clark, *Global Cities*, op. cit.

26. John Darwin, *After Tamerlane: The Rise & Fall of Global Empires 1400–2000*

27. Braudel, *Civilization & Capitalism, 15th–18th Century, Volume 1*, op. cit.

28. Epstein, *An Economic and Social History of Later Medieval Europe,* op. cit.

29. Ibid.

30. Ibid.

31. Keay, *China: A History*, op. cit.

32. Abby Rogers, "The 10 Greatest Empires in the History of the World", https://www.businessinsider.com/the-10-greatest-empires-in-history-2011–9?IR=T#2-the-mongol-empire-was-the-largest-contiguous-empire-the-world-has-ever-seen-9

33. Frankopan, *The Silk Roads*, op. cit.

34. Michael Prawdin, *The Mongol Empire: Its Rise and Legacy*

35. Ole Benedictow, "The Black Death: The Greatest Catastrophe Ever", *History Today*, March 2005

36. "Distinct clones of *Yersinia pestis* caused the Black Death", Stephanie Haensch, et al., *PLOS Pathogens*, October 7th 2010

37. Victoria Gill, "Black Death 'spread by humans not rats'", BBC Science and Environment, 15th January 2018 https://www.bbc.co.uk/news/science-environment-42690577

38. British Library, "Chronicle of the Black Death", http://www.bl.uk/learning/timeline/item126557.html

39. Hanawalt, *The Ties That Bound*, op. cit.

40. Epstein, *An Economic and Social History of Later Medieval Europe*, op. cit.

41. Scheidel, *The Great Leveler*, op. cit.

42. Robert Bideleux and Ian Jeffries, *A History of Eastern Europe: Crisis and Change*

43. Karl Gunnar Persson, "Markets and coercion in medieval Europe", *The Cambridge History of Capitalism, Volume 1*, op. cit.

44. Landes, *The Wealth and Poverty of Nations*, op. cit.

45. Frankopan, *The Silk Roads*, op. cit.

46. Mark Kurlansky, *Cod: A Biography of the Fish That Changed the World*

47. Chanda, *Bound Together*, op. cit.

48. "Paper Money, a Chinese invention?" National Bank of Belgium https://www.nbbmuseum.be/en/2007/09/chinese-invention.htm

49. Ibid.

50. Wood, *The Story of India*, op. cit.

51. Ha-Joon Chang, *Economics: The User's Guide*

52. Angus Maddison, *Growth and Interaction in the World Economy: The Roots of Modernity*

53. Kenneth Pomeranz, *The Great Divergence: China, Europe, And the Making of the Modern World Economy*

## Chapter 5 – The quest for energy

1. Ali Sundermier, "Penn researchers working to mimic giant clams to enhance the production of biofuel", *Penn Today*, November 2nd 2017

2. The numbers come from Smil, *Energy and Civilization*. The original research was done by Roger Fouquet.

3. Richard Rhodes, *Energy: A Human History*

4. Charles A. S. Hall, Jessica G. Lambert and Steven B. Balogh, "EROI of different fuels and the implications for society", https://www.sciencedirect.com/science/article/pii/S0301421513003856

5. Ibid.

6. Rachel Nuwer, "Oil sands mining uses up almost as much energy as it produces", *Inside Climate News*, https://insideclimatenews.org/news/20130219/oil-sands-mining-tar-sands-alberta-canada-energy-return-on-investment-eroi-natural-gas-in-situ-dilbit-bitumen

7. E. A. Wrigley, *Energy and the English Industrial Revolution*

8. Ibid.

9. Rhodes, *Energy: A Human History*, op. cit.

10. Ibid.

11. Ibid.

12. Wrigley, *Energy and the English Industrial Revolution*, op. cit.

13. Alan Fernihough and Kevin Hjortshøj O'Rourke, "Coal and the European Industrial Revolution", https://www.economics.ox.ac.uk/materials/papers/13183/Coal%20-%200%27Rourke%20124.pdf

14. Wrigley, *Energy and the English Industrial Revolution*, op. cit.

15. David Wootton, *The Invention of Science: A New History of the Scientific Revolution*

16. Joel Mokyr, *The Enlightened Economy: An Economic History of Britain 1700–1850*

17. Landes, *The Wealth and Poverty of Nations,* op. cit.

18. Timothy Mitchell, *Carbon Democracy: Political Power in the Age of Oil*

19. Smil, *Energy and Civilization*, op. cit.

20. Rhodes, *Energy: A Human History*, op. cit.

21. Ibid.

22. Daniel Yergin, *The Prize: The Epic Quest for Oil, Money, and Power*

23. Alan Greenspan and Adrian Wooldridge, *Capitalism in America: A History*

24. T. K. Derry and Trevor I. Williams, *A Short History of Technology*

25. "History of the light bulb", https://www.bulbs.com/learning/history.aspx

26. Rhodes, *Energy: A Human History*, op. cit.

27. Ibid.

28. Greenspan and Wooldridge, *Capitalism in America*, op. cit.

29. Robert Caro, *The Years of Lyndon Johnson: The Path To Power*

30. The company survived long enough into the modern era for Margaret Thatcher's husband, Denis, to be a director.

31. Anthony Sampson, *The Seven Sisters: The Great Oil Companies and the World They Made.* Many of those companies have changed their names several times.

32. Rhodes, *Energy: A Human History*, op. cit.

33. Peter Mansfield, *A History of the Middle East*

34. E. Roger Owen, "One hundred years of Middle Eastern oil", https://www.brandeis.edu/crown/publications/meb/MEB24.pdf

35. Source: http://www.opec.org/opec_web/en/data_graphs/330.htm

36. Yergin, *The Prize*, op. cit.
37. Gregory Zuckerman, *The Frackers: The Outrageous Inside Story of the New Energy Revolution*
38. Source: https://www.eia.gov/dnav/ng/hist/n9050us2A.htm
39. Source: https://www.eia.gov/dnav/ng/hist/rngwhhdM.htm
40. Source: https://www.eia.gov/dnav/pet/hist/LeafHandler. ashx?n=pet&s=mcrfpus2&f=m
41. Adam Vaughan, "Fracking – the reality, the risks and what the future holds", *The Guardian*, February 26th 2018
42. Source: Key World Energy Statistics, International Energy Agency https://www.iea.org/publications/freepublications/publication/ KeyWorld2017.pdf
43. Source: https://data.worldbank.org/indicator/EG.ELC.ACCS.ZS
44. Catherine Wolfram, "The developing world is connecting to the power grid, but reliability lags", Energy Institute Blog, May 30th 2017 https://energyathaas.wordpress.com/2017/05/30/the-developing-world-is-connecting-to-the-power-grid-but-reliability-lags/
45. Vivian Sequera, Corina Pons, "Second major blackout leaves Venezuelans fearing power cuts will be the norm", Reuters, March 26th 2019
46. Source: Global Energy Statistical Yearbook 2017 https://yearbook. enerdata.net/electricity/world-electricity-production-statistics.html
47. "Clean energy's dirty secret", *The Economist*, February 25th 2017
48. Adam Vaughan, "UK renewable energy capacity surpasses fossil fuels for first time", *The Guardian*, November 6th 2018

## Chapter 6 – The great change: 1000–1500

1. C.A. Bayly, *The Birth of the Modern World 1780–1914*
2. N.F.R. Crafts and C.K. Harley, "Output growth and the British Industrial Revolution: a restatement of the Crafts-Harley view", *The Economic History Review*, vol. 45, no. 4, November 1992
3. Maddison, *Growth and Interaction in the World Economy*, op. cit.
4. Ibid.
5. Thomas Malthus, *An Essay on the Principle of Population*
6. Maddison, *Contours of the World Economy*, op. cit.
7. Jürgen Osterhammel, *The Transformation of the World: A Global History of the 19th Century*
8. Ibid.

9. Douglass C. North and Robert Paul Thomas, *The Rise of the Western World: A New Economic History*

10. Standage, *An Edible History of Humanity*, op. cit.

11. Fernand Braudel, *Civilization & Capitalism, 15th–18th Century, Volume 2: The Wheels of Commerce*

12. Charles C. Mann, *1493: Uncovering the New World Columbus Created*

13. Pomeranz, *The Great Divergence*, op. cit.

14. Eric Williams, *Capitalism & Slavery*

15. Shashi Tharoor, *Inglorious Empire: What the British Did to India*

16. Mann, *1493*, op. cit.

17. Edwin Williamson, *The Penguin History of Latin America*

18. See Niall Ferguson, *Civilization: The West and the Rest* for this argument.

19. Maddison, *Contours of the World Economy*, op. cit.

20. Wootton, *The Invention of Science: A New History of the Scientific Revolution*

21. Deirdre Nansen McCloskey, *Bourgeois Equality: How Ideas, Not Capital or Institutions, Enriched the World*

22. Joel Mokyr, *A Culture of Growth: The Origins of the Modern Economy*

23. See, for example, Douglass North, "Institutions", *The Journal of Economic Perspectives*, vol. 5, no. 1, Winter 1991

24. Ibid.

25. Braudel, *Civilization & Capitalism, 15th–18th Century, Volume 2*, op. cit.

26. North and Thomas, *The Rise of the Western World*, op. cit.

27. See Wrigley, *Energy and the English Industrial Revolution*, op. cit.

28. Roger Osborne, *Iron, Steam & Money: The Making of the Industrial Revolution*

29. See David Eltis and Stanley L. Engerman, "The importance of slavery and the slave trade to industrialising Britain", *The Journal of Economic History*, vol. 60, no. 1, March 2000

30. The Belgians did not exploit the Congo (as they did horribly) until the late 19th century.

31. Beckert, *Empire of Cotton*, op. cit.

32. Robert C. Allen, *The British Industrial Revolution in Global Perspective*

33. Jan de Vries, *The Industrious Revolution: Consumer Behavior and the Household Economy, 1650 to the Present*

34. Not everyone accepts the idea. See Gregory Clark and Ysbrand

van der Werf "Work in progress? The Industrious Revolution", *The Journal of Economic History*, vol. 58, no. 3, which finds little evidence of the phenomenon.

35. Áine Cain, "Here's why people loved Monday hundreds of years ago", https://www.businessinsider.com/why-people-hundreds-of-years-ago-loved-monday-2016-9?r=US&IR=T

36. Braudel, *Civilization & Capitalism, 15th–18th Century, Volume 2*, op. cit.

37. Mokyr, *A Culture of Growth* op. cit.

38. C. Knick Harley, "British and European industrialization", *The Cambridge History of Capitalism, Volume 1*, op. cit.

39. Allen, *The British Industrial Revolution in Global Perspective,* op. cit.

40. North and Thomas, *The Rise of the Western World,* op. cit.

41. Osborne, *Iron, Steam & Money*, op. cit.

42. Daron Acemoglu and James A. Robinson, *Why Nations Fail: The Origins of Power, Prosperity and Poverty*

43. Allen, *The British Industrial Revolution in Global Perspective,* op. cit.

44. Osborne, *Iron, Steam & Money*, op. cit.

45. Robert Skidelsky, *Money and Government: A Challenge to Mainstream Economics*

46. This inflow was a mixed blessing as it gave Spain little incentive to develop the rest of its economy.

47. Keith Wrightson, *Earthly Necessities: Economic Lives in Early Modern Britain, 1450–1750*

48. Judy Stephenson, "Real contracts and mistaken wages: the organisation of work and pay in London building trades, 1650–1800", LSE working papers, no. 231, January 2016

49. "The Industrial Revolution Could Shed Light on Modern Productivity", Free Exchange, *The Economist*, August 2nd 2018

50. Allen, *The British Industrial Revolution in Global Perspective,* op. cit.

51. Ibid.

52. Wrightson, *Earthly Necessities*, op. cit.

53. Cunliffe, *By Steppe, Desert, & Ocean,* op. cit.

54. The letter can be found at https://china.usc.edu/emperor-qianlong-letter-george-iii-1793

55. Bayly, *The Birth of the Modern World 1780–1914,* op. cit.

56. Pomeranz, *The Great Divergence*, op. cit.

57. Allen, *The British Industrial Revolution in Global Perspective*, op. cit.

58. Sevket Pamuk, "Institutional change and economic development in

the Middle East 700–1800", *The Cambridge History of Capitalism, Volume 1*, op. cit.

59. Bayly, *The Birth of the Modern World 1780–1914*, op. cit.
60. Wood, *The Story of India*, op. cit.
61. Keay, *India: A Short History*, op. cit. A big part of his fortune was a giant jewel called the Pitt diamond.
62. Tharoor, *Inglorious Empire*, op. cit.
63. Ibid.
64. Clark, *Global Cities*, op. cit.
65. Joel Mokyr, "The Industrial Revolution in the Low Countries in the first half of the nineteenth century: a comparative case study", *The Journal of Economic History*, vol. 34, no. 2, June 1974
66. "Population and the Thirty Years War", HistoryLearning. com, http://historylearning.com/the-thirty-years-war0/ social-economic-thirty-years/population-thirty-years-war/
67. Bhu Srinivasan, *Americana: A 400-Year History of American Capitalism*
68. Douglas Irwin, *Clashing Over Commerce: A History of US Trade Policy*
69. Ron Chernow, *Alexander Hamilton*
70. Gordon S. Wood, *Empire of Liberty: A History of the Early Republic, 1789–1815*
71. Named after Sir Thomas Gresham, an adviser to Elizabeth I.
72. John Locke, *Some Considerations of the Consequences of the Lowering of Interest and the Raising the Value of Money*, found at http:// la.utexas.edu/users/hcleaver/368/368LockeSomeConsiderationsAllta ble.pdf

## Chapter 7 – Manufacturing: worshipping our makers

1. Value added is an economic term used to describe the extra value created by a company when it turns inputs (parts or raw materials) into outputs. It is used to avoid double counting when compiling economic data.
2. "Changing global production landscape and Asia's flourishing supply chain", HKTDC Research, October 3rd 2017, http://economists-pick-research.hktdc.com/business-news/article/Research-Articles/ Changing-Global-Production-Landscape-and-Asia-s-Flourishing-Supply-Chain/rp/en/1/1X000000/1X0ABHUR.htm
3. Source: https://fred.stlouisfed.org/graph/?g=cAYh

4.  Federica Cocco, "Most US manufacturing jobs lost to technology, not trade", *Financial Times*, December 2nd 2016

5.  "Politicians cannot bring back old-fashioned factory jobs", *The Economist*, January 14th 2017

6.  See the evidence of employees as recounted in E.P. Thompson, "Time, work-discipline and industrial capitalism", *Past & Present*, vol. 38, no. 1, December 1967

7.  Sitala Peek, "Knocker uppers: Waking up the workers in industrial Britain", March 27th 2016, https://www.bbc.co.uk/news/uk-england-35840393. Alas there is no record of the urban legend, the knocker-upper's knocker-upper, the person employed to wake the knocker-upper.

8.  Osborne, *Iron, Steam & Money*, op. cit.

9.  Peter Razzell and Christine Spence, "Social capital and the history of mortality in Britain", *International Journal of Epidemiology*, vol. 34, no. 2, 2005

10. Beckert, *Empire of Cotton*, op. cit.

11. Osborne, *Iron, Steam & Money*, op. cit.

12. Ibid.

13. Beckert, *Empire of Cotton*, op. cit.

14. Andrew L. Russell, "Standardization in history: a review essay with an eye to the future", Johns Hopkins University, http://arussell.org/papers/futuregeneration-russell.pdf

15. Chanda, *Bound Together*, op. cit.

16. Joshua B. Freeman, *Behemoth: A History of the Factory and the Making of the Modern World*

17. Ibid.

18. Michael Pooler and Emily Feng, "Steel industry grapples with curse of oversupply", *Financial Times*, October 29th 2017

19. Source: https://www.ranker.com/list/life-in-steel-producing-pittsburgh/nicole-sivens

20. Quote taken from "The Steel Business", https://www.pbs.org/wgbh/americanexperience/features/carnegie-steel-business/

21. Peter Krass. *Carnegie*. Carnegie was also ruthless in dealing with strikers, as we shall see in Chapter 9. In later life, he became a noted philanthropist.

22. "Frederick Winslow Taylor, Guru", *The Economist*, February 6th 2009

23. Quoted in Emily Guendelsberger, *On the Clock: What Low-Wage Work Did to Me and How It Drives America Insane*

24. Richard Donkin, *Blood, Sweat & Tears: The Evolution of Work*

25. "Lean production", *The Economist*, October 19th, 2009

26. Oya Celasun and Bertrand Gruss, "The declining share of industrial jobs", May 25th 2018, https://voxeu.org/article/declining-share-manufacturing-jobs

27. Source: https://data.worldbank.org/indicator/sl.srv.empl.zs

28. "Lean production", *The Economist*, op. cit.

29. Ondrej Burkacky, Johannes Deichmann, Georg Doll, and Christian Knochenhauer, "Rethinking car software and electronics architecture", February 2018, https://www.mckinsey.com/industries/automotive-and-assembly/our-insights/rethinking-car-software-and-electronics-architecture

30. Smil, *Energy and Civilization*, op. cit.

31. "Industrial metamorphosis", *The Economist*, September 29th 2005

32. "An incurable disease", *The Economist*, September 29th 2012

33. Jonathan Aldred, *Licence to be Bad: How Economics Corrupted Us*

34. Finbarr Livesey, "Defining high-value manufacturing", 2006, https://www.ifm.eng.cam.ac.uk/uploads/Research/CIG/DefiningHVM.pdf

35. Steve Lohr, "Huge payoff for IBM after a shift", *The New York Times*, January 19th 2010

36. Ashling Withers, "Hitting peak stuff – is this the end of traditional consumerism?", *Marketing* magazine, July 11th 2018

37. Kellie Ell, "Video game industry is booming with continued revenue", https://www.cnbc.com/2018/07/18/video-game-industry-is-booming-with-continued-revenue.html

38. Source: Arthur Wang, Ting Wu and Tony Zhou, "Riding China's huge, high-flying car market", October 2017, https://www.mckinsey.com/industries/automotive-and-assembly/our-insights/riding-chinas-huge-high-flying-car-market

39. Source: https://www.marklines.com/en/statistics/flash_sales/salesfig_china_2017

40. Wang, Wu and Zhou, "Riding China's huge, high-flying car market", op. cit.

41. "Emerging market insights: The coming emerging market demand shock", Deloitte, September 2017

42. David Teather, "Nike lists abuses at Asian factories", *The Guardian*, April 14th 2005

43. Elizabeth Segran, "Escalating sweatshop protests keep Nike sweating", Fast Company, July 28th 2017

44. Jamie Fullerton, "Suicide at Chinese iPhone factory reignites concern over working conditions", *The Daily Telegraph*, January 7th 2018

45. Gary Burtless, "Workers' rights: Labor standards and global trade", Brookings Institute, September 1st 2001, https://www.brookings.edu/articles/workers-rights-labor-standards-and-global-trade/

46. "In pieces", *The Economist*, February 19th 2009

47. Source: https://www.mema.org/about-us

48. For a full explanation of this process, see Richard Baldwin, *The Great Convergence: Information Technology and the New Globalization.*

49. Chang, *Economics: The User's Guide*, op. cit.

50. Source: https://www.mema.org/sites/default/files/A_World_Without_NAFTA_0.pdf

51. Daron Acemoglu and Pascual Restrepo, "Robots and jobs: evidence from US labor markets", NBER working paper 23285

52. "The growth of industrial robots", Daily Chart, *The Economist*, March 27th 2017

53. Celasun and Gruss, "The declining share of industrial jobs", op. cit.

54. Ryan Avent, *The Wealth of Humans: Work and Its Absence in the Twenty-First Century*

## Chapter 8 – The first era of globalisation: 1820–1914

1. John Maynard Keynes, *The Economic Consequences of the Peace*

2. The Maddison Project, https://www.rug.nl/ggdc/historicaldevelopment/maddison/releases/maddison-project-database-2018

3. Gregory Clark, *A Farewell to Alms: A Brief Economic History of the World*

4. Source: http://www.ggdc.net/maddison/oriindex.htm

5. Max Roser, "Life expectancy", Our World in Data, https://ourworldindata.org/life-expectancy

6. Quoted in Nicholas Crafts and Anthony J. Venables, "Globalization in history: a geographical perspective", http://www.nber.org/chapters/c9592

7. Frank Trentmann, *Empire of Things: How We Became a World of Consumers from the Fifteenth Century to the Twenty-First*

8. Keay, *China: A Short History*, op. cit.

9. Source: https://www.battlefields.org/learn/articles/civil-war-facts

10. Jean-Yves Huwart and Loïc Verdier, *Economic Globalisation: Origins and Consequences*

11. Kevin O'Rourke and Jeffrey G. Williamson, "When did globalization begin?", NBER working paper 7632

12. Both statistics from William Bernstein, *A Splendid Exchange: How Trade Shaped the World*

13. Kevin O'Rourke and Jeffrey G. Williamson, "The spread of, and resistance to, global capitalism", in Larry Neal and Jeffrey G. Williamson, eds, *The Cambridge History of Capitalism, Volume 2*

14. Sidney Pollard, *Peaceful Conquest: The Industrialisation of Europe 1760–1970*

15. Kevin H. O'Rourke and Jeffrey G. Williamson, *Globalization and History: The Evolution of a Nineteenth-Century Atlantic Economy*

16. Pollard, *Peaceful Conquest,* op. cit.

17. Source: https://www.britannica.com/topic/colonialism/European-expansion-since-1763

18. Paul Bairoch, *Victoires et déboires II: Histoire économique et sociale du monde du XVI^e siècle à nos jours*

19. Gareth Austin, "Capitalism and the colonies", *The Cambridge History of Capitalism, Volume 2,* op. cit.

20. Lance E. Davis and Robert A. Huttenback, "The political economy of British imperialism: measures of benefits and support", *The Journal of Economic History*, vol. 42, no. 1, 1982

21. Avner Offer, "The British Empire 1870–1914: a waste of money?" *The Economic History Review*, vol. 46, no. 2, 1993

22. Austin, "Capitalism and the colonies", op. cit.

23. Vanessa Mock, "Belgium revisits the scene of its colonial shame", *The Independent*, June 30th 2010

24. Austin, "Capitalism and the colonies", op. cit.

25. John R. Oneal and Frances H. Oneal, "Hegemony, imperialism, and the profitability of foreign investments", *International Organization*, vol. 42, no. 2, 1988

26. Williamson, *The Penguin History of Latin America*, op. cit.

27. Ibid.

28. "The eighth default of Argentina: from independence to Elliott Management", ValueWalk, https://www.valuewalk.com/2014/10/argentina-defaults-history/

29. Harold James, "International capital movements and the global order", *The Cambridge History of Capitalism, Volume 2*, op. cit.

30. Tharoor, *Inglorious Empire*, op. cit.
31. Soutik Biswas, "How Churchill 'starved' India", http://www.bbc.co.uk/blogs/thereporters/soutikbiswas/2010/10/how_churchill_starved_india.html
32. Charles Read, "British economic policy and Ireland c. 1841–1845", unpublished University of Cambridge PhD thesis
33. Brian Inglis, *The Opium War*
34. Clark, *A Farewell to Alms*, op. cit.
35. Osterhammel, *The Transformation of the World*, op. cit.
36. Mansfield, *A History of the Middle East*, op. cit.
37. Ibid.
38. David Cannadine, *Victorious Century: The United Kingdom 1800–1906*
39. Robert C. Allen, *Global Economic History: A Very Short Introduction*
40. Alexander Watson, *Ring of Steel: Germany and Austria-Hungary at War 1914–1918*
41. Irwin, *Clashing Over Commerce*, op. cit.
42. Srinivasan, *Americana*, op. cit.
43. Irwin, *Clashing Over Commerce*, op. cit.
44. Jutta Bolt, Marcel Timmer and Jan Luiten van Zanden, "GDP per capita since 1820", in *How was Life? Global Well-Being Since 1820*, OECD, 2014
45. Irwin, *Clashing Over Commerce*, op. cit.
46. Greenspan and Wooldridge, *Capitalism in America*, op. cit.
47. Irwin, *Clashing Over Commerce*, op. cit.
48. Fritz Stern, *Gold and Iron: Bismarck, Bleichröder, and the Building of the German Empire*
49. Richard J. Evans, *The Pursuit of Power: Europe, 1815–1914*
50. Pollard, *Peaceful Conquest*, op. cit.
51. Osterhammel, *The Transformation of the World*, op. cit.
52. Stern, *Gold and Iron*, op. cit.
53. The Maddison Project, https://www.rug.nl/ggdc/historicaldevelopment/maddison/releases/maddison-project-database-2018
54. Pollard, *Peaceful Conquest*, op. cit.
55. "Textile crafts", Switzerland Tourism, https://www.myswitzerland.com/en-gb/textile-crafts.html
56. Pollard, *Peaceful Conquest*, op. cit.
57. Russia sold Alaska to the US in 1867 for $7.2m. The cold war might

have been a lot more tense had it kept hold of territory in North America.

58. Landes, *The Wealth and Poverty of Nations*, op. cit.

59. Evans, *The Pursuit of Power*, op. cit.

60. Pollard, *Peaceful Conquest*, op. cit.

61. Pomeranz, *The Great Divergence*, op. cit.

62. Clark, *A Farewell to Alms*, op. cit.

63. The Maddison Project, https://www.rug.nl/ ggdc/historicaldevelopment/maddison/releases/ maddison-project-database-2018

64. G.C. Allen, *A Short Economic History of Modern Japan 1867–1937*

65. Darwin, *After Tamerlane*, op. cit.

66. Kenichi Ohno, *The Economic Development of Japan: The Path Travelled by Japan as a Developing Country*

67. Lewis Freeman, "How the railroad is modernising Asia", https:// trove.nla.gov.au/newspaper/article/5385284

68. Osterhammel, *The Transformation of the World*, op. cit.

69. O'Rourke and Williamson, *Globalization and History*, op. cit.

70. Landes, *The Wealth and Poverty of Nations*, op. cit.

71. Kristine Bruland and David Mowery, "Technology and the spread of capitalism", *The Cambridge History of Capitalism, Volume 2*, op. cit.

72. Micklethwait and Wooldridge, *The Company*, op. cit.

73. "The beauty of bubbles", *The Economist*, December 18th 2008

74. "Coase's theory of the firm", *The Economist*, July 27th 2017

75. Tim Harford, *Fifty Things That Made the Modern Economy*

76. Yergin, *The Prize*, op. cit.

77. Matthew DiLallo, "Carnegie Steel Company: An early model of efficiency and innovation", https://www.fool.com/investing/ general/2015/06/12/carnegie-steel-company-an-early-model-of-efficienc.aspx

78. Source: http://www.company-histories.com/United-States-Steel-Corporation-Company-History.html

79. Micklethwait and Wooldridge, *The Company*, op. cit.

80. Greenspan and Wooldridge, *Capitalism in America*, op. cit.

81. Ibid.

82. Suzanne Raga, "Why are the majority of US companies incorporated in Delaware?", http://mentalfloss.com/article/76951/ why-are-so-many-us-companies-incorporated-delaware

83. Quoted in Edmund Morris, *Theodore Rex*

84. Ricardo Minesotor, "Teddy Roosevelt and trust busting", *Foreign Policy*, July 3rd 2018, https://foreignpolicyi.org/teddy-roosevelt-and-trust-busting/

85. Evans, *The Pursuit of Power*, op. cit.

86. Geoffrey Jones, *Multinationals and Global Capitalism: from the Nineteenth to the Twenty-first Century*

87. The index is calculated by dividing the prices of the components. This means that companies with a higher share price have a bigger weight in the average, even though the company's overall market value is not connected to the nominal price. Most indices use market value weights, so a $2bn company has double the weight of a $1bn business.

88. Osterhammel, *The Transformation of the World*, op. cit.

89. Paul Cornish, "The naval race between Britain and Germany before The First World War", January 5th 2018, https://www.iwm.org.uk/history/the-naval-race-between-britain-and-germany-before-the-first-world-war

90. Robert C. Allen, "Engels' pause: technical change, capital accumulation and inequality in the British industrial revolution", *Explorations in Economic History*, vol. 46, no. 4, October 2009

91. Ibid.

92. Cannadine, *Victorious Century*, op. cit.

93. Milanovic, *Global Inequality*, op. cit.

94. William A. Pelz, *A People's History of Modern Europe*

95. Evans, *The Pursuit of Power*, op. cit.

96. Simon Heffer, *The Age of Decadence: Britain 1880 to 1914*

97. Donkin, *Blood, Sweat & Tears*, op. cit.

98. Giovanni Federico, "Growth, specialization, and organization of world agriculture", *The Cambridge History of Capitalism, Volume 2*, op. cit.

99. Evans, *The Pursuit of Power*, op. cit.

100. Source: http://brighttolife.sciencemuseum.org.uk/broughttolife/people/ignazsemmelweis

101. Source: http://www.bbc.co.uk/history/historic_figures/snow_john.shtml

102. "Subterranean dreams", *The Economist*, July 16th 2013

103. Evans, *The Pursuit of Power*, op. cit.

104. Sun Go and Peter Lindert, "The curious dawn of American public schools", NBER working paper 1335

105. Evans, *The Pursuit of Power*, op. cit.
106. Daron Acemoglu and James A. Robinson, "Why did the West extend the franchise? Democracy, inequality and growth in historical perspective", http://web.mit.edu/daron/www/qje_kuz6.pdf
107. Trentmann, *Empire of Things*, op. cit.
108. Source: http://www.searsarchives.com/catalogs/history.htm
109. Ibid.
110. Source: http://www.conspicuousconsumption.org/
111. Source: http://www.woolworthsmuseum.co.uk/aboutwoolies.html
112. Tom Standage, *A History of the World in Six Glasses*
113. For a more technical explanation, see Christopher Freeman and Carlota Perez, "Structural crises of adjustment, business cycles and investment behaviour", http://www.carlotaperez.org/downloads/pubs/StructuralCrisesOfAdjustment.pdf

## Chapter 9 – Immigration

1.   The words were written by poet Emma Lazarus, and were added in 1903.
2.   That is the view of the Ancient History Encyclopaedia, https://www.ancient.eu/Huns/
3.   Peter Heather, "The Huns and the end of the Roman Empire in Western Europe", *The English Historical Review*, vol. 110, no. 435, 1995
4.   Morris, *War, What Is It Good For?*, op. cit.
5.   See Niall Ferguson, *Civilisation*, op. cit., for an exploration of this dichotomy.
6.   Cipolla, *Before the Industrial Revolution*, op. cit.
7.   Paul Harris, "They fled with nothing but built a new empire", *The Observer*, August 11th 2002
8.   Boyd Tonkin, "The Huguenots count among the most successful of Britain's immigrants", *The Independent*, June 18th 2015
9.   Chanda, *Bound Together*, op. cit.
10.  Paine, *The Sea and Civilization*, op. cit.
11.  Hugh Thomas, *The Slave Trade: The History of the Atlantic Slave Trade*
12.  "Living Africans Thrown Overboard", http://www.pbs.org/wgbh/aia/part1/1h280.html
13.  Robert M. Harveson, "History of sugarbeets", University of Nebraska–Lincoln, https://cropwatch.unl.edu/history-sugarbeets

14. J. H. Galloway, "The Mediterranean sugar industry", *Geographical Review*, vol. 67, no. 2, April 1977

15. Thomas, *The Slave Trade*, op. cit.

16. Jason W. Moore, "Madeira, sugar, and the conquest of nature in the 'first' sixteenth century, Part 1: from 'island of timber' to sugar revolution, 1420–1506", *Review* (*Fernand Braudel Center*), vol. 32, no. 4, 2009

17. Thomas, *The Slave Trade*, op. cit.

18. "Conditions in the sugar works", International Slavery Museum, Liverpool, http://www.liverpoolmuseums.org.uk/ism/slavery/archaeology/caribbean/plantations/caribbean35.aspx

19. Maddison, *Contours of the World Economy*, op. cit.

20. Hourani, *A History of the Arab Peoples*, op. cit.

21. Thomas, *The Slave Trade*, op. cit.

22. Mann, *1493*, op. cit.

23. Thomas, *The Slave Trade*, op. cit.

24. Ibid.

25. David Sheward, "The real story behind 'Amazing Grace'", Biography.com, August 11th 2015, https://www.biography.com/news/amazing-grace-story-john-newton

26. John Thornton, *Africa and Africans in the Making of the Atlantic World, 1400–1800*

27. Mann, *1493*, op. cit.

28. Thomas, *The Slave Trade*, op. cit.

29. Mann, *1493*, op. cit.

30. Nathan Nunn, "The long-term effects of Africa's slave trades", *The Quarterly Journal of Economics*, vol. 123, no. 1, February 2008

31. Timothy Hatton and Jeffrey Williamson, *Global Migration and the World Economy: Two Centuries of Policy and Performance*

32. Mann, *1493*, op. cit.

33. Hatton and Williamson, *Global Migration and the World Economy*, op. cit.

34. Chanda, *Bound Together*, op. cit.

35. Sherry-Ann Singh, "The experience of Indian indenture in Trinidad: living conditions on the estates", University of the West Indies, St Augustine, http://www.caribbean-atlas.com/en/themes/waves-of-colonization-and-control-in-the-caribbean/daily-lives-of-caribbean-people-under-colonialism/the-experience-of-indian-indenture-in-trinidad-living-conditions-on-the-estates.html

36.  Paine, *The Sea and Civilization*, op. cit.

37.  Evelyn Hu-Dehart, "Chinese coolie labor in Cuba in the nineteenth century: free labour or neo-slavery?", *Contributions in Black Studies*, vol. 12, 1994

38.  Hatton and Williamson, *Global Migration and the World Economy*, op. cit.

39.  Chanda, *Bound Together*, op. cit.

40.  Hatton and Williamson, *Global Migration and the World Economy*, op. cit.

41.  Huwart and Verdier, *Economic Globalisation*, op. cit.

42.  Hatton and Williamson, *Global Migration and the World Economy*, op. cit.

43.  Ibid.

44.  Ibid.

45.  Jeffrey Frieden, *Global Capitalism: Its Fall and Rise in the Twentieth Century*

46.  Lorraine Boissoneault, "How the 19th-century Know Nothing Party reshaped American politics", Smithsonian.com, January 26th 2017, https://www.smithsonianmag.com/history/immigrants-conspiracies-and-secret-society-launched-american-nativism-180961915/

47.  Chinese Exclusion Act (1882), "Immigration to the United States, 1789–1930", Harvard Library, http://ocp.hul.harvard.edu/immigration/exclusion.html

48.  Fred Dews, "What percentage of US population is foreign born?", Brookings Now, October 3rd 2013

49.  "Great Migration", History.com, March 4th 2010, https://www.history.com/topics/black-history/great-migration

50.  Pieter C. Emmer and Leo Lucassen, "Migration from the colonies to Western Europe since 1800", European History Online, http://ieg-ego.eu/en/threads/europe-on-the-road/economic-migration/pieter-c-emmer-leo-lucassen-migration-from-the-colonies-to-western-europe-since-1800

51.  Tom Gjelten, "The Immigration Act that inadvertently changed America", *The Atlantic*, October 2nd 2015

52.  Dews, "What percentage of US population is foreign born?", op. cit.

53.  Ibid.

54.  Audrey Singer, "Contemporary immigrant gateways in historical perspective", Brookings Institute, September 5th 2013

55.  Phillip Connor, "International migration: key findings from the US,

Europe and the world", Pew Research Center, December 15th 2016, http://www.pewresearch.org/fact-tank/2016/12/15/international-migration-key-findings-from-the-u-s-europe-and-the-world/

56. The International Migration Report 2017, UN Department of Economic and Social Affairs

57. Source: UNHCR. Another 6.6 million Syrians were displaced within their own country.

58. Tom Nuttall, "Looking for a home: special report on migration", *The Economist*, May 28th 2016

59. Claudia Goldin, "The political economy of immigration restriction in the United States, 1890 to 1921", in *The Regulated Economy: A Historical Approach to Political Economy*, Claudia Goldin and Gary D. Libecap, eds

60. Jonathan Portes, "How small is small? The impact of immigration on UK wages", National Institute of Economic and Social Research, January 17th 2016

61. Farhad Manjoo, "Why Silicon Valley wouldn't work without immigrants", *The New York Times*, February 8th 2017

62. "A world of free movement would be $78trn richer", *The Economist*, July 13th 2017

### Chapter 10 – World wars and depression: 1914–1945

1. Esteban Ortiz-Ospina, Diana Beltekian and Max Roser, "Trade and globalization", Our World in Data, https://ourworldindata.org/trade-and-globalization

2. Bernstein, *A Splendid Exchange*, op. cit.

3. Geoffrey Jones, "Firms and global capitalism", in *The Cambridge History of Capitalism, Volume 2*, op. cit.

4. See Christopher Clark, *The Sleepwalkers: How Europe Went to War in 1914*

5. Niall Ferguson, "Earning from history? Financial markets and the approach of world wars", Brookings Institute, https://www.brookings.edu/wp-content/uploads/2008/03/2008a_bpea_ferguson.pdf

6. Niall Ferguson, *The Pity of War: Explaining World War I*

7. Stern, *Gold and Iron*, op. cit.

8. Esteban Ortiz-Ospina and Max Roser, "Public spending", Our World in Data, https://ourworldindata.org/public-spending

9. Matthias Blum, Jari Eloranta and Pavel Osinsky, "Organization of

war economies", https://encyclopedia.1914–1918-online.net/article/organization_of_war_economies

10. Source: https://www.iwm.org.uk/history/rationing-and-food-shortages-during-the-first-world-war

11. Stephen Broadberry and Mark Harrison, *The Economics of the Great War: A Centennial Perspective*

12. Source: https://scottmanning.com/content/world-war-i-troop-statistics/

13. Eleanor Beardsley, "WWI munitions still live beneath Western Front", NPR, November 11th 2007, https://www.npr.org/templates/story/story.php?storyId=16131857&t=1540290769223

14. Jordan Golson, "How WWI's U-boats launched the age of unrestricted warfare", *Wired*, September 22nd 2014

15. Ferguson, *The Pity of War*, op. cit.

16. Ibid.

17. Blum, Eloranta and Osinsky, "Organization of war economies", op. cit.

18. Ellen Castelow, "World War One: women at war", Historic UK *History Magazine*, https://www.historic-uk.com/HistoryUK/HistoryofBritain/World-War-One-Women-at-War/

19. The voting age was equalised in 1928 at 21.

20. "The centenary of the 20th century's worst catastrophe", *The Economist*, September 29th 2018

21. As Sellar and Yeatman wrote in their classic *1066 and All That*, "America was thus clearly top nation and thus history came to a full stop".

22. Source: https://www.nber.org/cycles.html

23. "The searing Twenties", *The Economist*, November 8th 2014

24. A.J.P. Taylor, *English History 1914–1945*

25. Ibid.

26. See David Edgerton, *The Rise and Fall of the British Nation: A Twentieth-Century History*

27. Barry Eichengreen, "The British economy between the wars", https://eml.berkeley.edu/~eichengr/research/floudjohnsonchaptersep16–03.pdf

28. Richard J. Evans, *The Coming of the Third Reich*

29. Ibid.

30. Liaquat Ahamed, *Lords of Finance: The Bankers Who Broke the World*

31. Barry Eichengreen, *Golden Fetters: The Gold Standard and the Great Depression 1919–1939*

32. Barry Eichengreen, *Globalizing Capital: A History of the International Monetary System*

33. Philip Coggan, *Paper Promises: Money, Debt and the New World Order*

34. David M. Kennedy, *Freedom from Fear: The American People in Depression and War 1929–1945*

35. Source: https://inflationdata.com/articles/inflation-consumer-price-index-decade-commentary/inflation-cpi-consumer-price-index-1920–1929/

36. Ahamed, *Lords of Finance*, op. cit.

37. Source: https://fred.stlouisfed.org/series/M1109BUSM293NNBR

38. The figures come from Robert Shiller of Yale University and his website: www.irrationalexuberance.com

39. "Florida's land boom", https://fcit.usf.edu/florida/lessons/ld_boom/ld_boom1.htm

40. The city's name had been changed from St Petersburg during the war. It would be changed again to Leningrad before reverting to St Petersburg in the post-communist era.

41. Robert Service, *The Penguin History of Modern Russia: From Tsarism to the Twenty-First Century*

42. The Russians had not adopted the Gregorian calendar, so this took place in October by their reckoning.

43. Service, *The Penguin History of Modern Russia*, op. cit.

44. Source: http://www.orlandofiges.info/section10_RevolutionfromAbove/TheWaragainsttheKulaks.php

45. "Stalin's famine, a war on Ukraine", *The Economist*, September 30th 2017

46. Frieden, *Global Capitalism*, op. cit.

47. Service, *The Penguin History of Modern Russia*, op. cit.; 1930 was the exceptional year.

48. "What there is to learn from the Soviet economic model", *The Economist*, November 9th 2017

49. Anton Cheremukhin, Mikhail Golosov, Sergei Guriev, and Aleh Tsyvinski, "Was Stalin necessary for Russia's economic development?", October 10th 2013, https://voxeu.org/article/stalin-and-soviet-industrialisation

50. Ahamed, *Lords of Finance*, op. cit.

51. Peter H. Lindert, *Key Currencies and Gold, 1900–1913* (Princeton Studies in International Finance, no. 24)

52. John Maynard Keynes, *The Economic Consequences of Mr Churchill*

53. Eichengreen, *Golden Fetters*, op. cit.

54. Quoted in Robert Skidelsky, *John Maynard Keynes: The Economist as Saviour 1920–1937*

55. Evans, *The Coming of the Third Reich*, op. cit.

56. Ahamed, *Lords of Finance*, op. cit.

57. Source: https://fred.stlouisfed.org/series/INDPRO

58. Source: https://www.nber.org/cycles.html

59. Ahamed, *Lords of Finance*, op. cit.

60. Kimberly Amadeo, "Black Thursday 1929: what happened, and what caused it", The Balance, May 15th 2018

61. Because one thing occurred before another, it must have caused the latter event.

62. Kennedy, *Freedom from Fear*, op. cit.

63. Irwin, *Clashing Over Commerce*, op. cit.

64. Frieden, *Global Capitalism*, op. cit.

65. Michael Reid, *Forgotten Continent: The Battle for Latin America's Soul*

66. Ahamed, *Lords of Finance*, op. cit.

67. Evans, *The Coming of the Third Reich*, op. cit.

68. Eichengreen, *Golden Fetters*, op. cit.

69. Irwin, *Clashing Over Commerce*, op. cit.

70. David Wheelock, "The Great Depression: an overview", https://www.stlouisfed.org/~/media/files/pdfs/great-depression/the-great-depression-wheelock-overview.pdf

71. Milton Friedman and Anna Jacobson Schwartz, *A Monetary History of the United States, 1867–1960*

72. Rasheed Saleuddin, "Agricultural markets and the Great Depression: lessons from the past", May 7th 2014, https://www.cam.ac.uk/research/features/agricultural-markets-and-the-great-depression-lessons-from-the-past

73. Nicholas Crafts and Peter Fearon, "Lessons from the 1930s Great Depression", *Oxford Review of Economic Policy*, vol. 26, no. 3, October 2010

74. Robert Dallek, *Franklin D. Roosevelt: A Political Life*

75. Ibid.

76. William L. Silber, "Why did FDR's Bank Holiday succeed?" https://

www.newyorkfed.org/medialibrary/media/research/epr/
09v15n1/0907silb.pdf

77. Ibid.

78. Irwin, *Clashing Over Commerce,* op. cit.

79. Greenspan and Wooldridge, *Capitalism in America*, op. cit.

80. Quoted in Dallek, *Franklin D. Roosevelt,* op. cit.

81. Patricia Waiwood, "Recession of 1937–38", https://www.
federalreservehistory.org/essays/recession_of_1937_38

82. Eichengreen, *Golden Fetters*, op. cit.

83. Adam Tooze, *The Wages of Destruction: The Making and Breaking of
the Nazi Economy*

84. Ibid.

85. Ibid.

86. Ibid.

87. "Foreign trade in German economy", CQ Researcher
Online, https://library.cqpress.com/cqresearcher/document.
php?id=cqresrre1939030900

88. Frieden, *Global Capitalism,* op. cit.

89. Gregg Huff and Shinobu Majima, "Financing Japan's World War
II occupation of Southeast Asia", https://www.economics.ox.ac.uk/
materials/working_papers/2504/huffmajima109.pdf

90. Tooze, *The Wages of Destruction,* op. cit.

91. Filippo Occhino, Kim Oosterlinck and Eugene White, "How
occupied France financed its own exploitation in World War II",
NBER working paper 12137, https://www.nber.org/papers/w12137.pdf

92. Pollard, *Peaceful Conquest,* op. cit.

93. Iris Kesternich, Bettina Siflinger, James Smith and Joachim Winter,
"The effects of World War II on economic and health outcomes
across Europe", https://www.ncbi.nlm.nih.gov/pmc/articles/
PMC4025972/

94. Mark Harrison, "The economics of World War II: an overview",
in *The Economics of World War II: Six Great Powers in International
Comparison*, Mark Harrison, ed.

95. Ibid.

96. Christopher Tassava, "The American economy during World War
II", Economic History Association, https://eh.net/encyclopedia/
the-american-economy-during-world-war-ii/

97. Claudia Goldin, "The role of World War II in the rise of women's

work", NBER working paper 3203, https://www.nber.org/papers/w3203.pdf

98. Smil, *Energy and Civilisation*, op. cit.

99. Alan L. Olmstead and Paul W. Rhode, "The diffusion of the tractor in American agriculture 1910–1960", NBER working paper 7947, www.nber.org/papers/w7947

100. Robert Gordon, *The Rise and Fall of American Growth: The US Standard of Living Since the Civil War*

101. Barbara Krasner-Khait, "The impact of refrigeration", *History Magazine*, https://www.history-magazine.com/refrig.html

102. Frieden, *Global Capitalism*, op. cit.

103. St Clair, *The Golden Thread*, op. cit.

104. Michael Huberman, "Labor movements", *The Cambridge History of Capitalism, Volume 2*, op. cit.

105. Barry Eichengreen and Tim Hatton, "Interwar unemployment in international perspective", IRLE, http://www.irle.berkeley.edu/files/1998/Interwar-Unemployment-In-International-Perspective.pdf

106. Frieden, *Global Capitalism*, op. cit.

## Chapter 11 – Transport: the vital network

1. James T. Patterson, *Grand Expectations: The United States 1945–1974*

2. Hugh Morris, "How many planes are there in the world right now?", *The Daily Telegraph*, August 16th 2017

3. Source: https://afdc.energy.gov/data/10309

4. Sarah Gibbens, "Human arrival in Australia pushed back 18,000 years", *National Geographic*, July 20th 2017

5. Cunliffe, *By Steppe, Desert, & Ocean*, op. cit.

6. Simon Webb, *Commuters: The History of a British Way of Life*

7. Rhodes, *Energy: A Human History*, op. cit.

8. Christian Wolmar, *Blood, Iron and Gold: How the Railways Transformed the World*

9. Wrigley, *Energy and the English Industrial Revolution*, op. cit.

10. Tom Standage, *The Victorian Internet: The Remarkable Story of the Telegraph and the Nineteenth Century's Online Pioneers*

11. Wolmar, *Blood, Iron and Gold*, op. cit.

12. Evans, *The Pursuit of Power*, op. cit.

13. Edward Chancellor, "Bubbles: a Victorian lesson in mania", *Financial Times*, April 11th 2010

14. Richard White, *Railroaded: The Transcontinentals and the Making of Modern America*
15. Ibid.
16. Simon Bradley, *The Railways: Nation, Network and People*
17. Wolmar, *Blood, Iron and Gold*, op. cit.
18. Randy Alfred, "Nov 18, 1883: Railroad time goes coast to coast", *Wired*, November 18th 2010
19. Webb, *Commuters*, op. cit.
20. Rhodes, *Energy: A Human History*, op. cit.
21. Ibid.
22. Mokyr, *The Enlightened Economy*, op. cit.
23. John Steele Gordon, *The Business of America*
24. Steven Parissien, *The Life of the Automobile: A New History of the Motor Car*
25. Ibid.
26. John Steele Gordon, *The Business of America*, op. cit.
27. Srinivasan, *Americana*, op. cit.
28. Avent, *The Wealth of Humans*, op. cit.
29. Parissien, *The Life of the Automobile*, op. cit.
30. Ibid.
31. His famous quote was that the customer could have "any color so long as it is black".
32. Parissien, *The Life of the Automobile*, op. cit.
33. Kat Eschner, "A short picture history of gas stations", Smithsonian. com, December 1st 2017, https://www.smithsonianmag.com/ smart-news/short-picture-history-gas-stations-180967337/
34. David Halberstam, *The Fifties*
35. Brad Tuttle, "10 things you didn't know about the fast food drive-thru", MSM.com, November 25th 2014
36. Richard A. Feinberg and Jennifer Meoli, "A brief history of the mall", *Advances in Consumer Research*, vol. 18, no. 1, 1991
37. "First drive-in movie theater opens", History.com, November 13th 2009, https://www.history.com/this-day-in-history/ first-drive-in-movie-theater-opens
38. Patterson, *Grand Expectations*, op. cit.
39. David A. Pfeiffer, "Ike's interstates at 50", *Prologue Magazine*, vol. 38, no. 2, 2006, National Archives, https://www.archives.gov/ publications/prologue/2006/summer/interstates.html

40. Kirsten Korosec, "The 10 most congested cities in the world", *Fortune*, February 6th 2018

41. Adam Mann, "What's up with that: building bigger roads actually makes traffic worse", *Wired*, June 17th 2014

42. "The hidden cost of congestion", graphic detail, *The Economist*, February 28th 2018, https://www.economist.com/graphic-detail/2018/02/28/the-hidden-cost-of-congestion

43. Elena Holodny, "Traffic fatalities in the US have been mostly plummeting for decades", Business Insider, April 20th 2016

44. Source: https://www.statista.com/statistics/200002/international-car-sales-since-1990/

45. Source: www.trucking.org

46. Dom Phillips and Sam Cowie, "Brazilian president sends in army as truck protest paralyses country", *The Guardian*, May 25th 2018

47. Ross Logan, "Think your commute's bad?", *Daily Record*, November 21st 2015

48. Marc Levinson, *The Box: How the Shipping Container Made the World Smaller and the World Economy Bigger*

49. Daniel M. Bernhofen, Zouheir El-Shali and Richard Kneller, "Estimating the effects of the container revolution on world trade", CESIfo working paper series no. 4136, March 2013

50. Levinson, *The Box*, op. cit.

51. Bernhofen, El-Sahli and Kneller, "Estimating the effects of the container revolution", op. cit.

52. Source: https://library.duke.edu/digitalcollections/adaccess/guide/transportation/airlines/

53. Thomas Petzinger, *Hard Landing: The Epic Contest for Power and Profits That Plunged the Airlines into Chaos*

54. Source: https://www.bts.gov/newsroom/2017-traffic-data-us-airlines-and-foreign-airlines-us-flights

55. "The package holiday revolution", History extra, https://www.historyextra.com/period/victorian/the-package-holiday-revolution/

56. Buffett, in the annual letter to Berkshire Hathaway shareholders, 2007

57. "Plumb centre", *The Economist*, February 22nd 2014

58. Source: https://www.wttc.org/-/media/files/reports/economic-impact-research/2017-documents/global-economic-impact-and-issues-2017.pdf

## Chapter 12 – From the wonder years to the malaise: 1945–1979

1. Quoted in Armand van Dormael, *Bretton Woods: Birth of a Monetary System*

2. Frieden, *Global Capitalism,* op. cit.

3. Von Braun was the man behind the V1 and V2 rockets that fell on London. He subsequently became part of the US space programme. As Tom Lehrer sang, "Once the rockets are up, who cares where they come down?/That's not my department, says Wernher von Braun".

4. Stephen D. King, *Grave New World: The End of Globalisation, The Return of History*

5. David Pilling, *Bending Adversity: Japan and the Art of Survival*

6. Source: https://history.state.gov/milestones/1945–1952/japan-reconstruction

7. Pilling, *Bending Adversity*, op. cit.

8. Barry Eichengreen, *The European Economy Since 1945: Coordinated Capitalism and Beyond*

9. Keith Lowe, *Savage Continent: Europe In The Aftermath of World War II*

10. Ibid.

11. Tony Judt, *Postwar: A History of Europe Since 1945*

12. Eichengreen, *The European Economy Since 1945*, op. cit.

13. Ibid.

14. Davies, *Europe: A History*, op. cit.

15. Ibid.

16. The European Court of Human Rights is a separate body, not connected with the EU.

17. "A short introduction to 50 years of EFTA", http://www.efta.int/sites/default/files/publications/fact-sheets/General-EFTA-fact-sheets/efta-50-years.pdf

18. Eichengreen, *The European Economy Since 1945*, op. cit.

19. De Gaulle was suspicious of Britain's ties to the US; he had clashed with Roosevelt during the war and resented American power. He withdrew from NATO in 1966. His attitude was not appreciated in Britain, which sheltered him during the war, or in the US. Told that France wanted all American troops removed from France, Dean Rusk, the secretary of state, under instruction from President Johnson, asked whether this also included the 60,000 who were buried in French cemeteries thanks to the two world wars.

20. Nauro Campos and Fabrizio Coricelli, "Why did Britain join the

EU? A new insight from economic history", February 3rd 2015, https://voxeu.org/article/britain-s-eu-membership-new-insight-economic-history

21. Edgerton, *The Rise and Fall of the British Nation*, op. cit.
22. Horst Siebert, *The German Economy: Beyond the Social Market*
23. Geoffrey Owen, "Industrial policy in Europe since the Second World War: what has been learnt?", 2012, The European Centre for International Political Economy, http://eprints.lse.ac.uk/41902/1/Industrial_policy_in_Europe_since_the__Second_World_War_what_has_been_learnt%281sero%29.pdf
24. Roger Backhouse, Bradley Bateman, Tamotsu Nishizawa and Dieter Plehwe, eds, *Liberalism and the Welfare State: Economists and Arguments for the Welfare State*
25. Source: https://www.eastonbh.ac.nz/2002/08/new_zealands_postwar_economic_growth_performance_comparison_with_the_oecd/
26. Scheidel, *The Great Leveler*, op. cit.
27. Thomas Piketty, *Capital in the 21st Century*
28. Milanovic, *Global Inequality*, op. cit.
29. Scheidel, *The Great Leveler*, op. cit.
30. Source: https://taxfoundation.org/us-federal-individual-income-tax-rates-history-1913–2013-nominal-and-inflation-adjusted-brackets/
31. Claudia Goldin and Robert Margo, "The great compression: the wage structure in the United States at mid-century", NBER working paper 3817, https://www.nber.org/papers/w3817.pdf
32. Timothy Noah, "The United States of inequality", *Slate*, http://www.slate.com/articles/news_and_politics/the_great_divergence/features/2010/the_united_states_of_inequality/introducing_the_great_divergence.html?via=gdpr-consent
33. Patterson, *Grand Expectations*, op. cit.
34. Wooldridge and Greenspan, *Capitalism in America*, op. cit.
35. Ezra Vogel, "Guided free enterprise in Japan", *Harvard Business Review*, May 1978
36. Pilling, *Bending Adversity*, op. cit.
37. Ibid.
38. "W. Edwards Deming", *The Economist*, June 5th 2009
39. Greenspan and Wooldridge, *Capitalism in America*, op. cit.
40. Jonathan Fenby, *The Penguin History of Modern China: The Fall and Rise of a Great Power*

41. Maddison, *Growth and Interaction in the World Economy*, op. cit.
42. Fenby, *The Penguin History of Modern China*, op. cit.
43. Ibid.
44. Ibid.
45. Dikötter, *Mao's Great Famine*, op. cit.
46. Maddison, *Contours of the World Economy*, op. cit.
47. Service, *The Penguin History of Modern Russia*, op. cit.
48. Ibid.
49. Frieden, *Global Capitalism*, op. cit.
50. Eichengreen, *The European Economy since 1945*, op. cit.
51. As recounted in Acemoglu and Robinson, *Why Nations Fail*, op. cit.
52. Maddison, *Contours of the World Economy*, op. cit.
53. Kwan S. Kim, "The Korean miracle (1962–1980) revisited: myths and realities in strategy and development", https://kellogg.nd.edu/sites/default/files/old_files/documents/166_0.pdf
54. Acemoglu and Robinson, *Why Nations Fail*, op. cit.
55. Jinn-Yuh Hsu and Lu-Lin Cheng, "Revisiting economic development in post-war Taiwan: the dynamic process of geographical industrialization", *Regional Studies*, vol. 36, no. 8, 2002
56. Kelly Olds, " The economic history of Taiwan", Economic History Association, https://eh.net/encyclopedia/the-economic-history-of-taiwan/
57. Maddison, *Contours of the World Economy*, op. cit.
58. K. Srinivasan, "Population and development In India since independence: an overview", http://medind.nic.in/jah/t04/s1/jaht04s1p5g.pdf
59. Niranjan Rajadhyaksha, "The economics of Jawaharlal Nehru", Mint, https://www.livemint.com/Opinion/TMk7svMznR8sJHayMAXW1M/The-economics-of-Jawaharlal-Nehru.html
60. Robert Fogel, "The impact of the Asian miracle on the theory of economic growth", NBER working paper 14967, https://www.nber.org/papers/w14967.pdf
61. Jagdish Bhagwati, *In Defense of Globalization*
62. Reid, *Forgotten Continent*, op. cit.
63. Victor Bulmer-Thomas, *The Economic History of Latin America Since Independence*, second edition
64. Frieden, *Global Capitalism*, op. cit.
65. Bulmer-Thomas, *The Economic History of Latin America*, op. cit.

66. Ibid.

67. Reid, *Forgotten Continent*, op. cit.

68. "A century of decline", *The Economist*, February 17th 2014

69. Bulmer-Thomas, *The Economic History of Latin America*, op. cit.

70. "System in crisis (1959–1971): The dollar glut", https://www.imf.org/external/np/exr/center/mm/eng/mm_sc_03.htm

71. "System in crisis (1959–1971): The incredible shrinking gold supply", https://www.imf.org/external/np/exr/center/mm/eng/sc_sub_3.htm

72. "System in crisis (1959–1971): Searching for solutions", https://www.imf.org/external/np/exr/center/mm/eng/mm_sc_04.htm

73. The Watergate tapes, Nixon library, https://www.nixonlibrary.gov/sites/default/files/forresearchers/find/tapes/watergate/wspf/741–002.pdf

74. Eichengreen, *The European Economy since 1945*, op. cit.

75. Milton Friedman, "The case for flexible exchange rates", in *Essays in Positive Economics*

76. Quoted in Coggan, *Paper Promises*, op. cit.

77. Source: https://www.minneapolisfed.org/community/financial-and-economic-education/cpi-calculator-information/consumer-price-index-and-inflation-rates-1913

78. Source: https://fred.stlouisfed.org/series/CPIIUKA

79. Source: https://inflationdata.com/articles/historical-inflation-rates-japan-1971–2014/

80. Edward Nelson, "The great inflation of the Seventies: what really happened?", Federal Reserve Bank of St Louis, https://files.stlouisfed.org/files/htdocs/wp/2004/2004–001.pdf

81. "Reinventing the system (1972–1981): Opec takes center stage", https://www.imf.org/external/np/exr/center/mm/eng/mm_rs_02.htm

82. Kimberley Amadeo, "Stagflation and its causes", The Balance, https://www.thebalance.com/what-is-stagflation-3305964

83. Bethan Bell and Mario Cacciottoio, "Torrey Canyon oil spill: the day the sea turned black", BBC News, March 17th 2017, https://www.bbc.co.uk/news/uk-england-39223308

84. It had caught fire many times before but this incident caught public attention. See http://edition.cnn.com/2008/TECH/science/12/10/history.environmental.movement/index.html

85. Donella Meadows, Dennis L. Meadows, Jorgen Randers and William W. Behrens III, *The Limits to Growth*

86. "Examining Carter's 'Malaise Speech', 30 years later", NPR,

July 12th 2009, https://www.npr.org/templates/story/story.
php?storyId=106508243

## Chapter 13 – Central banks: money and technocrats

1.  This chapter is based on an *Economist* briefing, written by the author,
    "The history of central banks", April 27th 2017.
2.  L. Randall Wray, "The Neo-Chartalist approach to money", The
    Levy Economics Institute, July 1st 2000
3.  Chernow, *Alexander Hamilton*, op. cit.
4.  Roger Bootle, *The Death of Inflation: Surviving and Thriving in the
    Zero Era*
5.  P. Richardson, "A Letter to the shareholders in the Bank of Western
    India", 1842. The same Huskisson was to be the first-ever railway
    fatality.
6.  Charles P. Kindleberger, *A Financial History of Western Europe*
7.  Ahamed, *Lords of Finance*, op. cit.
8.  Federal Reserve, https://www.federalreserve.gov/BOARDDOCS/
    SPEECHES/2002/20021108/
9.  Sebastian Mallaby, *The Man Who Knew: The Life and Times of Alan
    Greenspan*
10. Ibid.
11. Dietrich Domanski, Michela Scatigna and Anna Zabai, "Wealth
    inequality and monetary policy", BIS, https://www.bis.org/publ/
    qtrpdf/r_qt1603f.htm
12. Brendan Greeley, "America has never worried about financing its
    priorities", *Financial Times*, January 16th 2019

## Chapter 14 – The second era of globalisation: the developed world, 1979–2007

1.  Many people use the word neoliberal for this trend, but its definition
    is fairly vague, and it has become a catch-all term of abuse.
2.  Jones, *Multinationals and Global Capitalism*, op. cit.
3.  Max Roser, "Life expectancy", Our World in Data, https://
    ourworldindata.org/life-expectancy
4.  Laurel Graefe, "Oil shock of 1978–79", https://www.
    federalreservehistory.org/essays/oil_shock_of_1978_79
5.  Ibid.
6.  Source: https://www.nber.org/cycles.html

7. J.-P. Fitoussi and E.S. Phelps, "Causes of the 1980s slump in Europe", https://core.ac.uk/download/pdf/6252244.pdf

8. Olivier Blanchard and Lawrence Summers, "Hysteresis and the European unemployment problem", https://www.nber.org/chapters/c4245.pdf

9. Blanchard and Summers mentioned this issue but thought that shortfalls in aggregate demand were just as likely an explanation.

10. Source: https://www.indexmundi.com/g/g.aspx?c=gm&v=74

11. Christian Odendahl, "Germany after the Hartz reforms", *Foreign Affairs*, September 11th 2017, https://www.foreignaffairs.com/articles/germany/2017–09–11/germany-after-hartz-reforms

12. https://www.ilo.org/wcmsp5/groups/public/---dgreports/---inst/documents/publication/wcms_557245.pdf

13. "Hayek, Popper and Schumpeter formulated a response to tyranny", *The Economist*, August 23rd 2018

14. Quoted in Robert Skidelsky, *Money and Government,* op. cit.

15. Ibid.

16. Friedman, "The counter-revolution in monetary theory", occasional paper for the Institute of Economic Affairs, 1970

17. Source: https://fred.stlouisfed.org/series/M2V

18. Tyler Fisher, "How past income tax rate cuts on the wealthy affected the economy", Politico, September 27th 2017, https://www.politico.com/interactives/2017/gop-tax-rate-cut-wealthy/

19. Coggan, *Paper Promises*, op. cit.

20. "Coming home to roost", *The Economist*, June 27th 2002

21. Ibid.

22. Source: http://law2.wlu.edu/deptimages/Powell%20Archives/PowellMemorandumPrinted.pdf

23. Source: https://www.opensecrets.org/overview/cost.php

24. Source: https://www.opensecrets.org/lobby/ and Lee Drutman, *The Business of America is Lobbying: How Corporations Became Politicized and Politics Became More Corporate*

25. Source:https://www.opensecrets.org/lobby/top.php?indexType=s&showYear=2018

26. Source: www.vox.com/2016/1/15/10775788/revolving-door-lobbying

27. Larry Bartels, *Unequal Democracy: The Political Economy of the New Gilded Age*

28. Milanovic, *Global Inequality,* op. cit.

29. John Barrymore, "How S&Ls work", https://money.howstuffworks. com/personal-finance/banking/savings-and-loans2.htm

30. General Electric, one of the oldest conglomerates, managed to survive, in part because it went on its own takeover spree.

31. Irwin, *Clashing Over Commerce,* op. cit.

32. Ibid.

33. The Clancy novel contained a prescient scene where an enraged Japanese pilot crashed his plane into Washington's Capitol. This was well before the 2001 attacks.

34. "Did the Plaza Accord cause Japan's lost decades?", IMF World Economic Outlook, April 2011

35. Robert L. Cutts, "Power from the ground up: Japan's land bubble", *Harvard Business Review*, May–June 1990

36. Coggan, *Paper Promises*, op. cit.

37. Thomas Philippon, "Has the US finance industry become less efficient? On the theory and measurement of financial intermediation", September 2014, http://pages.stern.nyu. edu/~tphilipp/papers/Finance_Efficiency.pdf

38. Barry Eichengreen and Charles Wyplosz, "The unstable EMS", https://www.Brookings.Edu/Wp-Content/Uploads/1993/01/1993a_ Bpea_Eichengreen_Wyplosz_Branson_Dornbusch.Pdf

39. Source: https://www.nber.org/cycles.html

40. The day was dubbed Black Wednesday although, in fact, it allowed Britain to slash interest rates and let the economy recover. Longer term, it soured British politics by making many on the right hostile to the EU in general.

41. Robert Shiller, *Irrational Exuberance*, third edition

42. Judith Yates, "Housing in Australia in the 2000s: on the agenda too late?", https://www.rba.gov.au/publications/confs/2011/yates.html

43. Tobias Buck, "Spain: boom to bust and back again", *Financial Times*, April 6th 2017

44. Ben S. Bernanke, "The global saving glut and the US current account deficit", the Sandridge Lecture, Virginia Association of Economists, Richmond, Virginia, March 10th 2005

## Chapter 15 – Government: an ever-present force

1. Some of the reporting for this chapter also featured in my article for *The Economist*, "A welcome upgrade to apprenticeships", July 12th 2018

2. John Yates, "At the cutting edge of a new era", *Yorkshire Post*, February 15th 2001

3. Source: https://ourworldindata.org/government-spending

4. Greenspan and Wooldridge, *Capitalism in America*, op. cit.

5. Quentin Peel, "Merkel warns on costs of welfare", *Financial Times*, December 16th 2012

6. Source: https://ourworldindata.org/literacy

7. Jens Andersson and Thor Berger, "Elites and the expansion of education in 19th-century Sweden", http://portal.research.lu.se/ws/files/13625993/LUP149.pdf

8. A few developing countries only require education to the ages of 11 or 12.

9. Evan Schofer and John W. Meyer, "The worldwide expansion of higher education in the twentieth century", *American Sociological Review*, vol. 70, no. 6, December 2005

10. Robert G. Valletta, "Recent flattening In the higher education wage premium: polarization, skill downgrading or both?", NBER working paper 22935

11. Max Roser, "Life expectancy", Our World in Data, https://ourworldindata.org/life-expectancy

12. Pinker, *Enlightenment Now*, op. cit.

13. Ibid.

14. Rosling, *Factfulness*, op. cit.

15. Source: https://gateway.euro.who.int/en/indicators/hfa_566–6711-total-health-expenditure-as-of-gdp/

16. Kimberly Amadeo, "The rising cost of health care per year and its causes", The Balance, July 26th 2018

17. Bradley Sawyer and Gary Claxton, "How do health expenditures vary across the population?", Kaiser Family Foundation, January 16th 2019

18. Lisa Rapaport, "US health spending twice other countries' with worse results", Reuters, March 13th 2018

19. Jeffrey Pfeffer, *Dying for a Paycheck: How Modern Management Harms Employee Health and Company Performance – And What We Can Do About It*

20. "Top five reasons to end US sugar subsidies", Americans for Tax Reform, November 15th 2015, https://www.atr.org/top-five-reasons-end-us-sugar-subsidies

21. "The entrepreneurial state", Schumpeter, *The Economist*, August 31st 2013
22. See Mariana Mazzucato, *The Entrepreneurial State: Debunking Public vs Private Sector Myths*
23. Jonathan Haskel and Stian Westlake, *Capitalism Without Capital: The Rise of the Intangible Economy*
24. Hernando de Soto, *The Mystery of Capital: Why Capitalism Triumphs in the West and Fails Everywhere Else*
25. Source: http://www.doingbusiness.org/rankings
26. Source: https://data.oecd.org/gga/general-government-spending.htm

## Chapter 16 – A truly global economy: the developing world, 1979–2007

1. Radelet, *The Great Surge*, op. cit.
2. Yuen Yuen Ang, *How China Escaped the Poverty Trap*
3. Fenby, *The Penguin History of Modern China*, op. cit.
4. Joe Studwell, *The China Dream: The Elusive Quest for the Greatest Untapped Market on Earth*
5. Ang, *How China Escaped the Poverty Trap*, op. cit.
6. Fenby, *The Penguin History of Modern China*, op. cit.
7. Ang, *How China Escaped the Poverty Trap*, op. cit.
8. "The story of China's economy as told through the world's biggest building", *The Economist*, February 23rd 2019
9. "Theme and variations", *The Economist*, January 21st 2012
10. "Chinese tycoons in trouble", *The Straits Times*, June 14th 2017
11. Studwell, *The China Dream*, op. cit.
12. "China's grip on electronics manufacturing will be hard to break", *The Economist*, October 11th 2018
13. Greenspan and Wooldridge, *Capitalism in America: A History*, op. cit.
14. Dennis Yang, Junsen Zhang and Shaojie Zhou, "Why are savings rates so high in China?", NBER working paper 16771, https://www.nber.org/papers/w16771.pdf
15. Niall McCarthy, "China used more concrete in 3 years than the US used in the entire 20th century", *Forbes*, December 5th 2014
16. Giovanni Federico and Antonio Tena-Junguito, "World trade 1800–2015", February 7th 2016, https://voxeu.org/article/world-trade-1800–2015
17. Irwin, *Clashing Over Commerce*, op. cit.

18. Paul Kuznets, "An East Asian model of economic development: Japan, Taiwan, and South Korea", *Economic Development and Cultural Change*, vol. 36, no. 3, April 1988

19. Pam Woodall, "Tigers adrift", *The Economist*, March 5th 1998

20. Ibid.

21. Philip Shenon, "The Suharto billions", *The New York Times*, Jan 16th 1998

22. Victor Mallet, *The Trouble with Tigers: The Rise and Fall of South-East Asia*

23. Alan Beattie, "Suharto and the crisis of Asian crony capitalism, January 1998", *Financial Times*, July 19th 2008

24. Paul Krugman, "The myth of Asia's miracle", *Foreign Affairs*, November/December 1994, https://www.foreignaffairs.com/articles/asia/1994–11–01/myth-asias-miracle

25. Mallet, *The Trouble with Tigers*, op. cit.

26. "One more push", *The Economist*, July 21st 2011

27. "The Bangalore paradox", *The Economist*, April 21st 2005

28. "India no longer home to the largest number of poor", *Times of India*, June 27th 2018

29. Andrei Shleifer, "Normal countries: the east 25 years after communism", *Foreign Affairs*, November/December 2014

30. Stanley Fischer, Ratna Sahay and Carlos A. Végh, "Stabilization and growth in transition economies: the early experience", *Journal of Economic Perspectives*, vol. 2, no. 10, Spring 1996

31. Jan Lopatka, "No more low cost: East Europe goes up in the world", Reuters, July 25th 2017

32. Shleifer, "Normal countries", op. cit.

33. Source: https://www.statista.com/statistics/262858/change-in-opec-crude-oil-prices-since-1960/

34. Jocelyn Sims and Jessie Romero, "Latin American debt crisis of the 1980s", https://www.federalreservehistory.org/essays/latin_american_debt_crisis

35. Ibid.

36. "Missed opportunities: the economic history of Latin America", October 5th 2017, https://www.imf.org/en/News/Articles/2017/10/05/NA100517-Missed-Opportunities-The-Economic-History-of-Latin-America

37. Reid, *Forgotten Continent*, op. cit.

38. Ibid.

39. "Why Argentine orthodoxy has worked no better than Turkish iconoclasm", *The Economist*, September 6th 2018

40. James McBride and Mohammed Aly Sergie, "NAFTA's economic impact", https://www.cfr.org/backgrounder/naftas-economic-impact

41. Milanovic, *Global Inequality*, op. cit. The Gini coefficient measures the concentration of income. The nearer the figure gets to 1, the more unequal the distribution.

42. Brian Keeley, "Income inequality: The gap between rich and poor", December 15th 2015, https://www.oecd-ilibrary.org/social-issues-migration-health/income-inequality_9789264246010-en

43. Source: https://fred.stlouisfed.org/series/SIPOVGINIUSA

44. Gordon, *The Rise and Fall of American Growth*, op. cit.

45. David Card and John DiNardo, "Skill-biased technological change and rising wage inequality: some problems and puzzles", 2002, http://davidcard.berkeley.edu/papers/skill-tech-change.pdf

46. "Chief executives win the pay lottery", *The Economist*, October 20th 2018

47. "Sex, brains and inequality", *The Economist*, February 8th 2014

48. Milanovic, *Global Inequality*, op. cit.

49. Ibid.

50. All stats in this paragraph come from Radelet, *The Great Surge*, op. cit.

51. Paul Collier, *The Bottom Billion: Why the Poorest Countries Are Failing and What Can Be Done About It*

52. Avent, *The Wealth of Humans*, op. cit.

53. Collier, *The Bottom Billion*, op. cit.

54. McMahon, *Feeding Frenzy*, op. cit.

55. Robert Guest, *The Shackled Continent: Africa's Past, Present and Future*

56. "Mobile phones are transforming Africa", *The Economist*, December 10th 2016

57. Oliver August, "A hopeful continent", *The Economist*, March 2nd 2013

## Chapter 17 – Technology and innovation

1. Paul Krugman, *Peddling Prosperity: Economic Sense and Nonsense in the Age of Diminished Expectations*

2. Robert M. Solow, "Technical change and the aggregate production

function", *The Review of Economics and Statistics*, vol. 39, no. 3, August 1957

3. Paul M. Romer, "Increasing returns and long-run growth", *Journal of Political Economy*, vol. 94, no. 5, October 1986

4. David Warsh, *Knowledge and the Wealth of Nations: A Story of Economic Discovery*

5. Alasdair Nairn, *Engines That Move Markets: Technology Investing from Railroads to the Internet and Beyond*

6. Ibid.

7. Robert Friedel, *A Culture of Improvement: Technology and The Western Millennium*

8. Gordon, *The Rise and Fall of American Growth*, op. cit.

9. Mary Bellis, "Who invented the microchip?", ThoughtCo., https://www.thoughtco.com/what-is-a-microchip-1991410

10. "The end of Moore's law", *The Economist*, April 19th 2015

11. Nairn, *Engines That Move Markets*, op. cit.

12. Ibid.

13. Elli Narewska, "The end of hot metal printing", *The Guardian*, March 3rd 2015

14. Greenspan and Wooldridge, *Capitalism in America: A History*, op. cit.

15. Adam Pothitos, "The history of the smartphone", Mobile Industry Review, October 31st 2016

16. Tuan Nguyen, "The history of smartphones", ThoughtCo., https://www.thoughtco.com/history-of-smartphones-4096585

17. Adam Gale, "Will Mark Zuckerberg's mobile-first strategy make Facebook bigger than Google?", *Management Today*, July 28th 2016

18. Robert J. Gordon, "The demise of US economic growth: restatement, rebuttal, and reflections", NBER working paper 19895

19. Gordon, *The Rise and Fall of American Growth*, op. cit.

20. Amie Gordon and Tom Rawstorne, "Traffic is slower than a horse drawn carriage", *Daily Mail*, October 16th 2016

21. Andrew McAfee and Erik Brynjolfsson, *Machine, Platform, Crowd: Harnessing Our Digital Future*

22. "DeepMind AI reduces Google data centre cooling bill by 40%", https://deepmind.com/blog/deepmind-ai-reduces-google-data-centre-cooling-bill-40/

23. Nathan Rosenberg, *Exploring the Black Box: Technology, Economics, and History*

24. Ami Sedghi, "Facebook: 10 years of social networking, in numbers", *The Guardian*, February 4th 2014

25. Source: https://www.statista.com/statistics/264810/ number-of-monthly-active-facebook-users-worldwide/

26. Source: https://www.statista.com/statistics/263401/ global-apple-iphone-sales-since-3rd-quarter-2007/

27. Cheryl Conner, "Wasting time at work: the epidemic continues", *Forbes*, July 31st 2015

28. Mokyr, *The Enlightened Economy*, op. cit.

29. Aliya Ram, Aleksandra Wisniewska, Joanna Kao, Andrew Rininsland and Caroline Nevitt, "How smartphone apps track users and share data", *Financial Times*, October 23rd 2018

30. Alexandra Ma, "China has started ranking citizens with a creepy 'social credit' system", Business Insider, October 29th 2018, http:// uk.businessinsider.com/china-social-credit-system-punishments-and-rewards-explained-2018–4/#1-banning-you-from-flying-or-getting-the-train-1

31. Emily Stewart, "Christopher Robin, denied Chinese release, is the latest victim in China's war on Winnie the Pooh", August 4th 2018, https://www.vox.com/2018/8/4/17651630/ christopher-robin-banned-in-china-pooh

32. Jon Ronson, *So You've Been Publicly Shamed*

33. "The top three things that employers want to see in your social media profile", https://careers.workopolis.com/advice/ the-three-things-that-employers-want-to-find-out-about-you-online/

34. "How digital devices challenge the nature of ownership", *The Economist*, September 30th 2017

35. "America should borrow from Europe's data-privacy law", *The Economist*, April 5th 2018

36. Source: http://www.visionofbritain.org.uk/census/table/ GB1841oCC_M[1]

37. Maximiliano Dvorkin, "Jobs involving routine tasks aren't growing", https://www.stlouisfed.org/on-the-economy/2016/january/ jobs-involving-routine-tasks-arent-growing

38. James Pethokoukis, "What the story of ATMs and bank tellers reveals about the 'rise of the robots' and jobs", American Enterprise Institute, June 6th 2016, http://www.aei.org/publication/ what-atms-bank-tellers-rise-robots-and-jobs/

39. "Automation and anxiety", *The Economist*, June 23rd 2016

40. Ian Stewart, Debapratim De and Alex Cole, "Technology and people: The great job-creating machine", Deloitte, 2015, https://www2.deloitte.com/content/dam/Deloitte/uk/Documents/finance/deloitte-uk-technology-and-people.pdf

41. "The insecurity of freelance work", *The Economist*, June 14th 2018

## Chapter 18 – The crisis and after: 2007 to today

1. Chris Giles, "The vision thing", *Financial Times*, November 25th 2008

2. John J. McConnell and Stephen A. Buser, "The origins and evolution of the market for mortgage-backed securities", *Annual Review of Financial Economics*, vol. 3, 2011

3. Of course, we are talking about "initial yield" here. The investors owning the least secure tranche might not get paid at all. Their higher theoretical return compensated for this risk.

4. McConnell and Buser, The origins and evolution of the market for mortgage-backed securities", op. cit.

5. Adam Tooze, *Crashed: How a Decade of Financial Crises Changed the World*

6. Source: https://fred.stlouisfed.org/series/RHORUSQ156N

7. "At the risky end of finance", *The Economist*, April 19th 2007; written by the author

8. Michael Snyder, "30 Bernanke quotes that are so absurd you won't know whether to laugh or cry", Business Insider, December 8th 2010

9. The first Basel Accord was produced in 1988 and an updated version (Basel 2) came out in 2004.

10. "Base camp Basel", *The Economist*, January 21st 2010

11. "Blocked pipes", *The Economist*, October 2nd 2008

12. David Fiderer, "Hank Paulson, the unnamed 'decider' in the Merrill Lynch saga", *HuffPost*, December 6th 2017

13. "Alistair Darling: from here to uncertainty", *Financial Times*, August 31st 2017

14. Andrew Pierce, "The Queen asks why no one saw the credit crunch coming", *The Daily Telegraph*, November 5th 2008. This was not quite fair. Some, like Bill White at the Bank for International Settlements, had been warning for years of the dangers of excessive credit growth.

15. Piergiorgio Alessandri and Andrew Haldane, "Banking on the state", Bank of England, November 2009

16. "A crucial interest-rate benchmark faces a murky future", *The Economist*, August 3rd 2017

17. "Stumpfed", *The Economist*, October 13th 2016

18. Vishaka George, "Banks paid $321 billion in fines since financial crisis: BCG", Reuters, March 2nd 2017

19. "Too big not to fail", *The Economist*, February 18th 2012

20. Barry Eichengreen and Kevin O'Rourke, "What do the new data tell us?", March 7th 2010, https://voxeu.org/article/tale-two-depressions-what-do-new-data-tell-us-february-2010-update

21. "China seeks stimulation", *The Economist*, November 10th 2008

22. Carmen Reinhart, "Eight years later: post-crisis recovery and deleveraging", The Clearing House, https://www.theclearinghouse.org/banking-perspectives/2017/2017-q1-banking-perspectives/articles/post-crisis-recovery-and-deleveraging

23. Ibid.

24. Tooze, *Crashed*, op. cit. The three were Royal Bank of Scotland, UBS and Deutsche.

25. "Back to reality", *The Economist*, October 23rd 2014

26. "Celtic phoenix", *The Economist*, November 19th 2015

27. Tooze, *Crashed*, op. cit.

28. Tony Barber, "Greece condemned for falsifying data", *Financial Times*, January 12th 2010

29. Reinhart, "Eight years later: post-crisis recovery and deleveraging", op. cit.

30. An aggrieved *Economist* reader pointed out that the UK nations could be recast as "SWINE", Scotland, Wales, Ireland (Northern) and England.

31. Charlemagne, "What Makes Germans So Very Cross About Greece?", *The Economist*, February 23rd 2010

32. See, for example, Martin Wolf, "Germany is a weight on the world", *Financial Times*, November 5th 2013.

33. The economies were Australia, Canada, China, France, Germany, Italy, Japan, South Korea, Mexico, the UK and the US. Source: https://data.oecd.org/gga/general-government-deficit.htm

34. Larry Elliott, "Austerity policies do more harm than good, IMF study concludes", *The Guardian*, May 27th 2016

35. Source: https://data.oecd.org/gga/general-government-spending.htm

36. Joe Watts, "Years of austerity 'have left UK with same level of public

spending as it had 10 years ago' says IFS", *The Independent*, October 30th 2017

37. Jay Shambaugh and Ryan Nunn, "Why wages aren't growing in America", *Harvard Business Review*, October 24th 2017

38. Nathalie Thomas, "UK facing 'dreadful' prospect of 10+ years without real wage growth – IFS" *Financial Times*, November 24th 2016

39. Mai Chi Dao, Mitali Das, Zsoka Koczan and Weicheng Lian, "Drivers of declining share of labor income", April 12th 2017, https://blogs.imf.org/2017/04/12/drivers-of-declining-labor-share-of-income/

40. Lawrence H. Summers, "Reflections on the new 'Secular Stagnation hypothesis'", October 30th 2014, https://voxeu.org/article/larry-summers-secular-stagnation

41. Ibid.

42. Jinill Kim, "The effects of demographic change on GDP growth in OECD economies", September 28th 2016, www.federalreserve.gov

43. This was the issue at the heart of the Uber case, working its way through the British courts at the time of writing. See Rob Davies, "Uber to take appeal over ruling on drivers' status to UK supreme court", *The Guardian*, November 24th 2017

44. McKinsey, "Independent work: choice, necessity, and the gig economy", October 2016

45. For a debate on the issue, see https://www.johnkay.com/2017/10/09/paying-everyone-basic-income-not-realistic-fairer-way-tackle-poverty/

46. Bizarrely, Ireland, which prides itself on attracting multinationals through its low tax regime, did not want to collect the money. The EU had to threaten to take Ireland to court in order to make them do so. See Rochelle Toplensky, Arthur Beesley and Adam Samson, "EU takes Ireland to court over Apple taxes", *Financial Times*, October 4th 2017.

47. The figures are based on purchasing power parity, a calculation that adjusts exchange rates on the basis of tradable goods prices. Source: http://www.imf.org/external/datamapper/PPPSH@WEO/OEMDC/ADVEC/WEOWORLD

48. Dan McCrum, "Over in China, a debt boom mapped", FT Alphaville, March 5th 2018

49. "China June forex reserves rise more than expected amid trade truce", Reuters, July 8th 2019

50. "India's economy is back on track. Can it pick up speed?", *The Economist*, March 28th 2018

51. "The dodgiest duo in the suspect six", *The Economist*, November 7th 2014

52. "IMF sees Venezuela inflation at 10 million per cent in 2019", *The Economic Times of India*, October 9th 2018

53. "How to deal with Venezuela", *The Economist*, July 29th 2017

54. John Otis, "'We loot or we die of hunger': food shortages fuel unrest in Venezuela", *The Guardian*, January 21st 2018

55. Erica York, Kyle Pomerleau and Robert Bellafiore, "Tracking the economic impact of US tariffs and retaliatory actions", https://taxfoundation.org/tracker-economic-impact-tariffs/

## Epilogue

1. Jagdish Bhagwati, *In Defense of Globalization*, op. cit.

2. Unilever Annual Report and Accounts, 2017, https://www.unilever.com/Images/unilever-annual-report-and-accounts-2017_tcm244–516456_en.pdf

3. Paul Seabright, *The Company of Strangers: A Natural History of Economic Life*

4. Richard Baldwin, "A long view of globalisation in short", December 5th 2018, https://voxeu.org/content/long-view-globalisation-short-new-globalisation-part-5–5

5. Kurlansky, *Cod*, op. cit.

6. Source https://data.oecd.org/gga/general-government-spending.htm

7. Gordon, *The Rise and Fall of American Growth*, op. cit.

8. Ibid.

9. Maddison, *Growth and Interaction in the World Economy*, op. cit.

10. Avent, *The Wealth of Humans*, op. cit.

11. Milanovic, *Global Inequality*, op. cit.

12. Rosling, *Factfulness*, op. cit.

13. Benjamin Friedman, *The Moral Consequences of Economic Growth*

14. McCloskey, *Bourgeois Equality*, op. cit.

## Appendix

1. Dirk Philipsen, *The Little Big Number: How GDP Came to Rule the World and What to Do about It*

2. See Tim Callen, "Gross Domestic Product: an economy's all", http://www.imf.org/external/pubs/ft/fandd/basics/gdp.htm

3.  "UK double-dip recession revised away", BBC News, June 27th 2013

4.  Jorrit Zwijnenburg, "Revisions of quarterly GDP in selected OECD countries", July 2015, http://www.oecd.org/sdd/na/Revisions-quarterly-GDP-selected-OECD-countries-OECDSB22.pdf

5.  GNP includes income earned abroad, and not generated within the country. Goods made for export are part of GDP; profits earned in an overseas factory are in GNP.

6.  Speech given by Bobby Kennedy at an election rally in Kansas on March 18th 1968. He was assassinated in June that year.

7.  This summary is taken from an article for the World Economic Forum, https://www.weforum.org/agenda/2018/01/gdp-frog-matchbox-david-pilling-growth-delusion/. David Pilling's book is *The Growth Delusion: The Wealth and Well-Being of Nations*.

8.  Tibi Puiu, "Your smartphone is millions of times more powerful than all of NASA's combined computing in 1969", ZME Science, September 10th 2017

9.  Source: the St Louis Federal Reserve, https://fred.stlouisfed.org/series/CIVPART. It has an excellent and accessible database on the economy.

10. For an excellent explanation, see Kevin D. Hoover, "Phillips Curve", http://www.econlib.org/library/Enc/PhillipsCurve.html

11. This is now dubbed the non-accelerating rate of inflation or NAIRU.

12. "The Phillips curve may be broken for good", *The Economist*, November 1st 2017

# BIBLIOGRAPHY

What follows is a list of the books and academic papers consulted. Newspaper, magazine and blog articles appear in the Notes (pages 371–423), along with data sources.

Abu-Lughod, Janet L. *Before European Hegemony: The World System AD 1250–1350*, Oxford University Press, 1989

Acemoglu, Daron, and Restrepo, Pascual "Robots and jobs: evidence from US labor markets", NBER working paper 23285, 2017

Acemoglu, Daron, and Robinson, James A. *Why Nations Fail: The Origins of Power, Prosperity, and Poverty*, Penguin Random House, 2012

—— "Why did the West extend the franchise? Democracy, inequality and growth in historical perspective", http://web.mit.edu/daron/www/qje_kuz6.pdf, 2000

Ahamed, Liaquat *Lords of Finance: 1929, The Great Depression, and the Bankers who Broke the World,* Windmill Books, 2010

Aldred, Jonathan *Licence to be Bad: How Economics Corrupted Us*, Allen Lane, 2019

Allen, G.C. *A Short Economic History of Modern Japan 1867–1937*, Palgrave Macmillan, 1981

Allen, Robert C. *The British Industrial Revolution in Global Perspective*, Cambridge University Press, 2009

—— *Global Economic History: A Very Short Introduction*, Oxford University Press, 2011

—— "Engels' pause: technical change, capital accumulation and inequality in the British industrial revolution", *Explorations in Economic History*, vol. 46, no. 4, October 2009

Andersson, Jens, and Berger, Thor "Elites and the expansion of education in 19th-century Sweden", http://portal.research.lu.se/ws/files/13625993/LUP149.pdf, 2016

Ang, Yuen Yuen *How China Escaped the Poverty Trap*, Cornell University Press, 2016

Angell, Sir Norman *The Great Illusion*, Cosimo Classics, 2007

Applebaum, Anne *Red Famine: Stalin's War on Ukraine*, Penguin Random House, 2017

Avent, Ryan *The Wealth of Humans: Work and Its Absence in the Twenty-First Century*, Penguin, 2017

Backhouse, Roger *The Penguin History of Economics*, Penguin, 2002

—— and Bateman, Bradley, Nishizawa, Tamotsu, and Plehwe, Dieter, eds, *Liberalism and the Welfare State: Economists and Arguments for the Welfare State*, Oxford University Press, 2017

Bagehot, Walter *Lombard Street: A Description of the Money Market*, Dodo Press, 2006 (originally published in 1873)

Bairoch, Paul *Victoires et déboires II: Histoire économique et sociale du monde du XVIᵉ siècle à nos jours*, Folio, 1997

Bakker, Jan, Maurer, Stephan, Pischke, Jörn-Steffen, and Rauch, Ferdinand "Trade and growth in the Iron Age", August 23rd 2018, https://voxeu.org/article/trade-and-growth-iron-age

Baldwin, Richard *The Great Convergence: Information Technology and the New Globalization*, Harvard University Press, 2016

Bartels, Larry *Unequal Democracy: The Political Economy of the New Gilded Age*, Princeton University Press, 2016

Bartlett, Robert *The Making of Europe: Conquest, Colonization and Cultural Change 950–1350*, Penguin, 1994

Bayly, C.A. *The Birth of the Modern World 1780–1914*, Wiley-Blackwell, 2004

Beckert, Sven *Empire of Cotton: A New History of Global Capitalism*, Penguin, 2014

Bennett, Karen "Disappearance of the Aral Sea", World Resources Institute, May 23rd 2008, http://www.wri.org/blog/2008/05/disappearance-aral-sea

Bernstein, William *A Splendid Exchange: How Trade Shaped the World*, Atlantic Books, 2009

Bhagwati, Jagdish, *In Defense of Globalization*, Oxford University Press, 2004

Bideleux, Robert, and Jeffries, Ian *A History of Eastern Europe: Crisis and Change*, Routledge, 2007

Blanchard, Olivier, and Summers, Lawrence "Hysteresis and the European unemployment problem", https://www.nber.org/chapters/c4245.pdf, 1986

Blum, Jerome "The rise of serfdom in Eastern Europe", *The American Historical Review*, vol. 62, no. 4, July 1957

Blundell-Wignall, Adrian "The private equity boom: causes and policy issues", https://www.oecd.org/finance/financial-markets/40973739.pdf, 2007

Bootle, Roger *The Death of Inflation: Surviving and Thriving in the Zero Era*, Nicholas Brealey Publishing, 1996

Bourguignon, François, and Morrisson, Christian "Inequality among world citizens 1820–1992", *American Economic Review*, vol. 92, no. 4, February 2002

Bradley, Simon *The Railways: Nation, Network and People*, Profile Books, 2016

Braudel, Fernand *Civilization & Capitalism, 15th–18th Century, Volume 1: The Structures of Everyday Life*, Fontana, 1985
—— *Volume 2: The Wheels of Commerce*, Fontana, 1992
—— *Volume 3: The Perspective of the World*, Fontana, 1992

Broadberry, Stephen, and Harrison, Mark *The Economics of the Great War: A Centennial Perspective*, Vox e-book, November 2018

Bulmer-Thomas, Victor *The Economic History of Latin America Since Independence*, second edition, Cambridge University Press, 2003

Burkacky, Ondrej, Deichmann, Johannes, Doll, Georg, and Knochenhauer, Christian "Rethinking car software and electronics architecture", February 2018, https://www.mckinsey.com/industries/automotive-and-assembly/our-insights/rethinking-car-software-and-electronics-architecture

Burroughs, Bryan, and Helyar, John *Barbarians at the Gate*, Arrow, 2010

Cannadine, David *Victorious Century: The United Kingdom 1800–1906*, Penguin, 2018

Card, David, and DiNardo, John "Skill-biased technological change and rising wage inequality: some problems and puzzles", http://davidcard.berkeley.edu/papers/skill-tech-change.pdf, 2002

Caro, Robert A. *The Years of Lyndon Johnson: The Path to Power*, Vintage, 1983

Chanda, Nayan *Bound Together: How Traders, Preachers, Adventurers, and Warriors Shaped Globalization*, Yale University Press, 2008

Chang, Ha-Joon *Economics: The User's Guide*, Pelican, 2014

Chernow, Ron *Alexander Hamilton*, Head of Zeus, 2017

Cipolla, Carlo M. *Before the Industrial Revolution: European Society and Economy, 1000–1700*, third edition, Routledge, 1993

Clark, Christopher *The Sleepwalkers: How Europe Went to War in 1914*, Penguin, 2013

Clark, Grahame "Traffic in stone axes and adze blades", *The Economic History Review*, 1965

Clark, Greg *Global Cities: A Short History*, The Brookings Institution, 2016

Clark, Gregory *A Farewell to Alms: A Brief Economic History of the World*, Princeton University Press, 2007

Clark, Gregory, and Van der Werf, Ysbrand "Work in progress? The Industrious Revolution", *The Journal of Economic History*, vol. 58, no. 3, September 1998

Coggan, Philip *Paper Promises: Money, Debt and the New World Order*, Allen Lane, 2011

Collier, Paul *The Bottom Billion: Why the Poorest Countries Are Failing and What Can Be Done About It*, Oxford University Press, 2007

Crafts, N.F.R., and Harley, C.K. "Output Growth and the British Industrial Revolution: A Restatement of the Crafts-Harley View", *The Economic History Review*, vol. 45, no. 4, November 1992

Crafts, Nicholas and Venables, Anthony J. "Globalization in History: A Geographical Perspective", http://www.nber.org/chapters/c9592, 2003

Cunliffe, Barry *By Steppe, Desert, & Ocean: The Birth of Eurasia*, Oxford University Press, 2015

Dallek, Robert *Franklin D. Roosevelt: A Political Life*, Allen Lane, 2017

Darwin, John *After Tamerlane: The Rise & Fall of Global Empires 1400–2000*, Penguin, 2008

Davies, Aled "The evolution of British monetarism: 1968–1979", October 2012, http://www.nuff.ox.ac.uk/Economics/History/Paper104/davies104.pdf

Davies, Norman *Europe: A History*, Oxford University Press, 1996

Davis, Lance E., and Huttenback, Robert E. "The political economy of

British imperialism: measures of benefits and support", *The Journal of Economic History*, vol. 42, no. 1, 1982

De Callataÿ, François "The Graeco-Roman economy in the super long-run: lead, copper and shipwrecks", *Journal of Roman Archaeology*, vol. 18, 2005

Derry, T.K., and Williams, Trevor I. *A Short History of Technology*, Dover Publications, 1993

De Vries, Jan *The Industrious Revolution: Consumer Behavior and the Household Economy, 1650 to the Present*, Cambridge University Press, 2008

Diamond, Jared *Collapse: How Societies Choose to Fail or Survive*, Allen Lane, 2005

—— *Guns, Germs and Steel*, Vintage, 1998

Dikötter, Frank *Mao's Great Famine: The History of China's Most Devastating Catastrophe 1958–1962*, Bloomsbury, 2017

Domanski, Dietrich, Scatigna, Michela, and Zabai, Anna "Wealth inequality and monetary policy", BIS, March 2016, https://www.bis.org/publ/qtrpdf/r_qt1603f.htm

Donkin, Richard *Blood, Sweat & Tears: The Evolution of Work*, Texere Publishing, 2001

Dormael, Armand van *Bretton Woods: Birth of a Monetary System*, Palgrave, 1978

Drutman, Lee *The Business of America is Lobbying: How Corporations Became Politicized and Politics Became More Corporate*, Oxford University Press, 2015

Easterly, William *The Elusive Quest for Growth: Economists' Adventures and Misadventures in the Tropics*, MIT Press

Edens, Christopher "Dynamics of trade in the ancient Mesopotamian world system", *American Anthropologist*, vol. 94, no. 1, 1992

Edgerton, David *The Rise and Fall of the British Nation: A Twentieth-Century History*, Penguin, 2018

—— *The Shock of the Old: Technology and Global History since 1900*, Profile Books, 2019

Eichengreen, Barry *The European Economy since 1945: Coordinated Capitalism and Beyond*, Princeton University Press, 2008

—— *Globalizing Capital: A History of the International Monetary System*, Princeton University Press, 2008

—— *Golden Fetters: The Gold Standard and the Great Depression 1919–1939*, Oxford University Press, 1995

—— "The British economy between the wars", April 2002, https://eml. berkeley.edu/~eichengr/research/floudjohnsonchaptersep16–03.pdf

Eichengreen, Barry, and Hatton, Tim "Interwar unemployment in international perspective", IRLE, http://www.irle.berkeley.edu/ files/1998/Interwar-Unemployment-In-International-Perspective.pdf

Eichengreen, Barry, and Mitchener, Kris "The Great Depression as a credit boom gone wrong", BIS working papers, no. 137, https://www. bis.org/publ/work137.pdf, 2004

Eichengreen, Barry, and Wypolsz, Charles "The unstable EMS", https:// www.brookings.edu/wp-content/uploads/1993/01/1993a_bpea_ eichengreen_wyplosz_branson_dornbusch.pdf

Eltis, David, and Engerman, Stanley L. "The importance of slavery and the slave trade to industrialising Britain", *Journal of Economic History*, vol. 60, no. 1, March 2000

Epstein, Steven A. *An Economic and Social History of Later Medieval Europe, 1000–1500,* Cambridge University Press, 2009

Erixon, Fredrik, and Marel, Erik van der "What is driving the rise in health care expenditures? An inquiry into the nature and causes of the cost disease", ECIPE working paper, no. 5, 2011

Evans, Richard J. *The Coming of the Third Reich*, Allen Lane, 2003

—— *The Pursuit of Power: Europe 1815–1914*, Allen Lane, 2016

—— *The Third Reich in Power*, Allen Lane, 2005

Federico, Giovanni *Feeding the World: An Economic History of Agriculture 1800–2000*, Princeton University Press, 2005

Feinberg, Richard A., and Meoli, Jennifer "A brief history of the mall", *Advances in Consumer Research*, vol. 18, no. 1, 1991

Fenby, Jonathan *The Penguin History of Modern China: The Fall and Rise of a Great Power*, Penguin, 2019

Ferguson, Niall *Civilization: The West and the Rest*, Allen Lane, 2011

—— *The Pity of War: Explaining World War I*, Allen Lane, 1998

Fernihough, Alan, and O'Rourke, Kevin Hjortshøj "Coal and the European Industrial Revolution", https://www.economics.ox.ac.uk/ materials/papers/13183/Coal%20-%200%27Rourke%20124.pdf, 2014

Findlay, Ronald, and O'Rourke, Kevin H. *Power and Plenty: Trade, War, and the World Economy in the Second Millennium*, Princeton University Press, 2009

Finley, M. I. *The Ancient Economy:* second edition, University of California Press, 1999

Fischer, Stanley, Sahay, Ratna, and Végh, Carlos A. "Stabilization and growth in transition economies: the early experience", *Journal of Economic Perspectives*, vol. 2, no. 10, Spring 1996

Fitoussi, J.-P., and Phelps, E.S. "Causes of the 1980s slump in Europe", https://core.ac.uk/download/pdf/6252244.pdf, 1986

Fogel, Robert "The impact of the Asian miracle on the theory of economic growth", NBER working paper 14967, https://www.nber.org/papers/w14967.pdf, 2009

Ford, Christopher *The Mind of Empire: China's History and Modern Foreign Relations*, University Press of Kentucky, 2010

Frankopan, Peter *The Silk Roads: A New History of the World*, Bloomsbury, 2015

Freeman, Christopher, and Perez, Carlota "Structural crises of adjustment, business cycles and investment behaviour", http://www.carlotaperez.org/downloads/pubs/StructuralCrisesOfAdjustment.pdf

Freeman, Joshua B. *Behemoth: A History of the Factory and the Making of the Modern World*, W.W. Norton, 2018

Friedel, Robert *A Culture of Improvement: Technology and the Western Millennium*, MIT Press, 2010

Frieden, Jeffrey *Global Capitalism: Its Fall and Rise in the Twentieth Century*, W.W. Norton, 2006

Friedman, Benjamin *The Moral Consequences of Economic Growth*, Knopf, 2005

Friedman, Milton *Essays in Positive Economics,* University of Chicago Press, 1966

Friedman, Milton, and Schwartz, Anna Jacobson (National Bureau of Economic Research), *A Monetary History of the United States, 1867–1960*, Princeton University Press, 1963

Galloway, J.H. "The Mediterranean sugar industry", *Geographical Review*, vol. 67, no. 2, April 1977

Go, Sun, and Lindert, Peter "The curious dawn of American public schools", NBER working paper 1335, 2007

Goldin, Claudia "The political economy of immigration restriction in the United States 1890 to 1921", in *The Regulated Economy: A Historical Approach to Political Economy*, Claudia Goldin and Gary D. Libecap, eds, University of Chicago Press, 1994

—— "The role of World War II in the rise of women's work", NBER working paper 3203, https://www.nber.org/papers/w3203.pdf, 1991

Goldin, Claudia, and Margo, Robert "The great compression: the wage structure in the United States at mid-century", NBER working paper 3817, https://www.nber.org/papers/w3817.pdf, 1991

Gollin, Douglas, Hansen, Casper Worm, and Wingender, Asger "Two blades of grass: the impact of the green revolution", Centre for Economic Policy Research, November 2016

Gordon, John Steele *The Business of America*, Walker Books, 2001

Gordon, Robert *The Rise and Fall of American Growth: The US Standard of Living since the Civil War,* Princeton University Press, 2016

—— "The demise of US economic growth: restatement, rebuttal, and reflections", NBER working paper 19895, 2014

Greenspan, Alan, and Wooldridge, Adrian *Capitalism in America: A History*, Allen Lane, 2018

Guendelsberger, Emily *On the Clock: What Low-Wage Work Did to Me and How It Drives America Insane*, Little, Brown and Company, 2019

Guest, Robert *The Shackled Continent: Africa's Past, Present and Future*, Pan Macmillan, 2004

Haensch, Stephanie, et al. "Distinct clones of *Yersinia pestis* caused the Black Death", *PLOS Pathogens*, October 7, 2010

Halberstam, David *The Fifties*, Fawcett Columbine, 1993

Hanawalt, Barbara *The Ties That Bound: Peasant Families in Medieval England*, Oxford University Press, 1986

Hansen, Valerie *The Silk Road: A New History*, Oxford University Press, 2012

Harari, Yuval Noah *Sapiens: A Brief History of Humankind*, Vintage, 2015

Harford, Tim *Fifty Things That Made the Modern Economy*, Abacus, 2017

Harrison, Mark "The Economics of World War II: An Overview", in Mark Harrison, ed., *The Economics of World War II: Six Great Powers in International Comparison*, Cambridge University Press, 1998

Haskel, Jonathan, and Westlake, Stian *Capitalism Without Capital: The Rise of the Intangible Economy,* Princeton University Press, 2017

Hatton, Timothy, and Williamson, Jeffrey *Global Migration and the World Economy: Two Centuries of Policy and Performance*, MIT Press, 2008

Heather, Peter "The Huns and the end of the Roman Empire in Western Europe", *The English Historical Review*, vol. 110, no. 435, 1995

Heffer, Simon *The Age of Decadence: Britain 1880 to 1914*, Random House, 2017

Hellebrandt, Tomáš and Mauro, Paolo, "The future of worldwide income distribution", working paper 15–7, Peterson Institute for International Economics, April 2015

Hobbes, Thomas *Leviathan*, Penguin Classics, 2016 (originally published in 1651)

Hodkinson, Stephen "Female property ownership and status in Classical and Hellenistic Sparta", University of Manchester, 2003

Hourani, Albert *A History of the Arab Peoples*, Faber & Faber, 2013

Hsu, Jinn-Yuh, and Cheng, Lu-Lin "Revisiting economic development in post-war Taiwan: the dynamic process of geographical industrialization", *Regional Studies*, vol. 36, no. 8, 2002

Hu-Dehart, Evelyn "Chinese coolie labor in Cuba in the nineteenth century: free labour or neo-slavery?", *Contributions in Black Studies*, vol. 12, 1994

Huff, Gregg, and Majima, Shinobu "Financing Japan's World War II occupation of Southeast Asia", https://www.economics.ox.ac.uk/materials/working_papers/2504/huffmajima109.pdf, 2013

Huwart, Jean-Yves, and Verdier, Loïc *Economic Globalisation: Origins and Consequences*, OECD Insights, OECD Publishing, 2013

Inglis, Brian *The Opium War*, Endeavour Ink, 2017

Irwin, Douglas *Clashing over Commerce: A History of US Trade Policy*, University of Chicago Press, 2017

Johnson, Simon, and Kwak, James *13 Bankers: The Wall Street Takeover and the Next Financial Meltdown*, Pantheon Books, 2010

Jones, Geoffrey *Multinationals and Global Capitalism: from the Nineteenth to the Twenty-first Century*, Oxford University Press, 2005

Judt, Tony *Postwar: A History of Europe Since 1945*, Vintage, 2010

Keay, John *India: A History*, HarperPress, 2010

—— *China, A History*, HarperCollins, 2009

Kennedy, David M. *Freedom from Fear: The American People in Depression and War 1929–1945*, Oxford University Press, 1999

Kesternich, Iris, Siflinger, Bettina, Smith, James, and Winter, Joachim "The effects of World War II on economic and health outcomes across Europe", https://www.ncbi.nlm.nih.gov/pmc/articles/PMC4025972/, 2014

Keynes, John Maynard *The Economic Consequences of Mr Churchill*, Royal Economic Society, 1925

—— *The Economic Consequences of the Peace*, Freeland Press, 2017 (originally published in 1919)

Kim, Kwan S. "The Korean miracle (1962–1980) revisited: myths and realities in strategy and development", https://kellogg.nd.edu/sites/default/files/old_files/documents/166_0.pdf, 1991

Kindleberger, Charles P. *A Financial History of Western Europe*, Routledge, 2007

King, Stephen D. *Grave New World: The End of Globalisation, The Return of History*, Yale University Press, 2017

Krass, Peter *Carnegie*, John Wiley & Sons, 2002

Kriwaczek, Paul *Babylon: Mesopotamia and the Birth of Civilization*, Atlantic, 2012

Krugman, Paul *Peddling Prosperity: Economic Sense and Nonsense in the Age of Diminished Expectations*, Norton, 1995

Kurlansky, Mark *Cod: A Biography of the Fish That Changed the World*, Vintage, 1999

Kynge, James *China Shakes the World: The Rise of a Hungry Nation*, W&N, 2006

Landes, David *The Wealth and Poverty of Nations*, Abacus, 1999

Levinson, Marc *The Box: How the Shipping Container Made the World Smaller and the World Economy Bigger*, Princeton University Press, 2016

Lindert, Peter H. *Key Currencies and Gold, 1900–1913*, Princeton Studies in International Finance, no. 24, 1969

Lopez, Robert S. *The Commercial Revolution of the Middle Ages 950–1350*, Cambridge University Press, 1976

Lowe, Keith *Savage Continent: Europe in the Aftermath of World War II*, Penguin, 2013

Lyons, Dan *Lab Rats: Why Modern Work Makes People Miserable*, Atlantic Books, 2019

Mabey, Richard *The Cabaret of Plants: Botany and the Imagination*, Profile Books, 2015

Maddison, Angus *Contours of the World Economy, 1–2030 AD*, Oxford University Press, 2007

—— *Growth and Interaction in the World Economy: The Roots of Modernity*, AEI Press, 2004

Mallaby, Sebastian *The Man Who Knew: The Life and Times of Alan Greenspan*, Bloomsbury, 2016

Mallet, Victor *The Trouble with Tigers: The Rise and Fall of South-East Asia*, HarperCollins Business, 1999

Malthus, Thomas, *An Essay on the Principle of Population*, Oxford World Classics, 2008 (originally published in 1798)

Mann, Charles C. *1493: Uncovering the New World Columbus Created*, Knopf, 2011

Mansfield, Peter *A History of the Middle East*, fourth edition, Penguin, 2013

Martin, Felix *Money: The Unauthorised Biography*, Vintage, 2014

Mauseth, James D. *Plants & People,* Jones & Bartlett, 2012

Mayer, Colin *Prosperity: Better Business Makes the Greater Good*, Oxford University Press, 2018

Mazzucato, Marianna *The Entrepreneurial State: Debunking Public vs Private Sector Myths*, Perseus Books, 2015

McAfee, Andrew and Brynjolfsson, Erik *Machine, Platform, Crowd: Harnessing Our Digital Future*, W.W. Norton, 2017

—— *Race Against the Machine*, Digital Frontier Press, 2012

—— *The Second Machine Age*, W.W. Norton, 2016

McCloskey, Deirdre Nansen *Bourgeois Equality: How Ideas, Not Capital or Institutions, Enriched the World*, University of Chicago Press, 2016

—— "The great enrichment was built on ideas, not capital", Foundation for Economic Education, https://fee.org

McConnell, John J. and Buser, Stephen A. "The origins and evolution of the market for mortgage-backed securities", *Annual Review of Financial Economics*, vol. 3, 2011

McMahon, Paul *Feeding Frenzy: The New Politics of Food*, Profile Books, 2013

Micklethwait, John and Wooldridge, Adrian *The Company: A Short History of a Revolutionary Idea*, Modern Library, 2003

Milanovic, Branko *Global Inequality: A New Approach for the Age of Globalization*, Belknap Press, 2018

Mitchell, Timothy *Carbon Democracy: Political Power in the Age of Oil*, Verso, 2013

Mitchener, Kris and Weidenmier, Marc "The Barings crisis and the great Latin American meltdown of the 1890s", August 2006, http://www.helsinki.fi/iehc2006/papers1/Mitchener.pdf

Mokyr, Joel *The Culture of Growth: The Origins of the Modern Economy*, Princeton University Press, 2017

—— *The Enlightened Economy: An Economic History of Britain 1700–1850*, Yale University Press, 2010

—— "The Industrial Revolution in the Low Countries in the first half of the nineteenth century: a comparative case study", *The Journal of Economic History*, vol. 34, no. 2, June 1974

Moore, Jason W. "Madeira, sugar and the conquest of nature in the 'first' sixteenth century: Part 1: from 'island of timber' to sugar revolution, 1420–1506", *Review (Fernand Braudel Center)*, vol. 32, no. 4, 2009

Morris, Edmund *Theodore Rex*, HarperCollins, 2002

Morris, Ian *War: What Is it Good For? The Role of Conflict in Civilisation, from Primates to Robots*, Profile Books, 2015

Nader, Ralph *Unsafe at Any Speed: The Designed-In Dangers of the American Automobile*, Pocket, 1965

Nagarajan, K.V. "The Code of Hammurabi: an economic interpretation", *International Journal of Business and Social Science*, May 2011

Nairn, Alasdair *Engines That Move Markets: Technology Investing from Railroads to the Internet and Beyond*, John Wiley & Sons, 2002

Neal, Larry, and Williamson, Jeffrey G. *The Cambridge History of Capitalism, Volume I. The Rise of Capitalism: From Ancient Origins to 1848*, Cambridge University Press, 2014

—— *Volume II. The Spread of Capitalism: From 1848 to the Present*, Cambridge University Press, 2014

North, Douglass C. "Institutions", *The Journal of Economic Perspectives*, vol. 5, no. 1, Winter 1991

North, Douglass C., and Thomas, Robert Paul *The Rise of the Western World: A New Economic History*, Cambridge University Press, 1973

Nunn, Nathan "The long-term effects of Africa's slave trades", *The Quarterly Journal of Economics*, vol. 123, no. 1, February 2008

Occhino, Filippo, Oosterlinck, Kim, and White, Eugene "How occupied France financed its own exploitation in World War II", NBER working paper 12137, https://www.nber.org/papers/w12137.pdf, 2006

Ohno, Kenichi *The Economic Development of Japan: The Path Travelled by Japan as a Developing Country*, http://www.grips.ac.jp/forum/pdf06/EDJ.pdf, 2006

Olson, Mancur *Power and Prosperity: Outgrowing Communist and Capitalist Dictatorships*, Basic Books, 2000

Oneal, John R., and Frances H. "Hegemony, imperialism, and the profitability of foreign investments", *International Organization*, vol. 42, no. 2, 1988

O'Rourke, Kevin H., and Williamson, Jeffrey G. *Globalization and History: The Evolution of a Nineteenth-Century Atlantic Economy*, MIT Press, 1999

—— "When did globalization begin?", NBER working paper 7632, April 2000

Osborne, Roger *Iron, Steam & Money: The Making of the Industrial Revolution*, Pimlico, 2014

Osterhammel, Jürgen *The Transformation of the World: A Global History of the 19th Century*, Princeton University Press, 2014

Owen, Geoffrey "Industrial policy in Europe since the Second World War: what has been learnt?", 2012, The European Centre for International Political Economy, http://eprints.lse.ac.uk/41902/1/Industrial_policy_in_Europe_since_the__Second_World_War_what_has_been_learnt%281sero%29.pdf

Owen, E. Roger "One hundred years of Middle Eastern oil", January 2008, https://www.brandeis.edu/crown/publications/meb/MEB24.pdf

Paine, Lincoln *The Sea and Civilization: A Maritime History of the World*, Knopf, 2013

Parissien, Steven *The Life of the Automobile: A New History of the Motor Car*, Atlantic Books, 2013

Patterson, James T. *Grand Expectations: The United States 1945–1974*, Oxford University Press, 1996

Pelz, William A. *A People's History of Modern Europe*, Pluto Press, 2016

Pethokoukis, James "What the story of ATMs and bank tellers reveals about the 'rise of the robots' and jobs", American Enterprise Institute, June 6th 2016, http://www.aei.org/publication/what-atms-bank-tellers-rise-robots-and-jobs

Petzinger, Thomas *Hard Landing: The Epic Contest for Power and Profits That Plunged the Airlines into Chaos*, Random House, 1995

Pfeffer, Jeffrey *Dying for a Paycheck: How Modern Management Harms Employee Health and Company Performance – And What We Can Do About It*, HarperBusiness, 2018

Philippon, Thomas "Has the US finance industry become less efficient? On the theory and measurement of financial intermediation", September 2014, http://pages.stern.nyu.edu/~tphilipp/papers/Finance_Efficiency.pdf

Philipsen, Dirk *The Little Big Number: How GDP Came to Rule the World and What to Do about It*, Princeton University Press, 2015

Piketty, Thomas *Capital in the 21st Century*, Harvard University Press, 2014

Pilling, David *Bending Adversity: Japan and the Art of Survival*, Penguin, 2014

—— *The Growth Delusion: The Wealth and Well-Being of Nations*, Bloomsbury, 2018

Pinker, Steven *The Better Angels of Our Nature: A History of Violence and Humanity*, Penguin, 2011

—— *Enlightenment Now: The Case for Reason, Science, Humanism and Progress*, Viking, 2018

Pollard, Sidney *Peaceful Conquest: The Industrialization of Europe, 1760– 1970*, Oxford University Press, 1981

Pomeranz, Kenneth *The Great Divergence: China, Europe, and the Making of the Modern World*, Princeton University Press, 2000

Portes, Jonathan "How small is small? The impact of immigration on UK wages", National Institute of Economic and Social Research, January 17th 2016

Powelson, John P. *The Story of Land: A World History of Land Tenure and Agrarian Reform*, Lincoln Institute of Land Policy, 1988

Prawdin, Michael *The Mongol Empire: Its Rise and Legacy*, George Allen & Unwin, 1967

Pye, Michael *The Edge of the World: How the North Sea Made Us*, Pegasus Books, 2016

Radelet, Steven: *The Great Surge: The Ascent of the Developing World*, Simon & Schuster, 2016

Razzell, Peter, and Spence, Christine "Social capital and the history of mortality in Britain", *International Journal of Epidemiology*, vol. 34, no. 2, 2005

Read, Charles "British economic policy and Ireland c. 1841–1845", unpublished University of Cambridge PhD thesis, 2017

Reid, Michael *Forgotten Continent: The Battle for Latin America's Soul*, Yale University Press, 2007

Rhodes, Richard *Energy: A Human History*, Simon & Schuster, 2018

Romer, Paul "Increasing returns and long-term growth", *Journal of Political Economy*, vol. 94, no. 5, 1986

Ronson, Jon *So You've Been Publicly Shamed*, Picador, 2015

Rosenberg, Nathan *Exploring the Black Box: Technology, Economics, and History*, Cambridge University Press, 1994

Rosling, Hans, Rosling, Ola, and Rosling Rönnlund, Anna *Factfulness: Ten Reasons We're Wrong About the World – And Why Things Are Better Than You Think*, Sceptre, 2018

Russell, Andrew L. "Standardization in history: a review essay with an eye

to the future", Johns Hopkins University, http://arussell.org/papers/
futuregeneration-russell.pdf

Sampson, Anthony *The Seven Sisters: The Great Oil Companies and the
World They Made*, Hodder & Stoughton, 1975

Scheidel, Walter *The Great Leveler: Violence and the History of Inequality
from the Stone Age to the Twenty-First Century*, Princeton University
Press, 2017

Schofer, Evan, and Meyer, John W. "The worldwide expansion of higher
education in the twentieth century", *American Sociological Review*,
vol. 70, no. 6, December 2005

Scott, James C. *Against the Grain: A Deep History of the Earliest States*, Yale
University Press, 2017

Seabright, Paul *The Company of Strangers: A Natural History of Economic
Life*, Princeton University Press, 2010

Service, Robert *The Penguin History of Modern Russia: From Tsarism to the
Twenty-First Century*, Penguin, 2015

Shiller, Robert *Irrational Exuberance*, third edition, Princeton University
Press, 2015

Siebert, Horst *The German Economy: Beyond the Social Market*, Princeton
University Press, 2014

Skidelsky, Robert *John Maynard Keynes: The Economist As Saviour 1920–
1937*, Papermac, 1994

—— *Money and Government: A Challenge to Mainstream Economics*, Allen
Lane, 2018

Smil, Vaclav *Energy and Civilization: A History*, MIT Press, 2017

—— "Nitrogen cycle and world food production", *World Agriculture,* 2011

Smith, Adam *The Theory of Moral Sentiments*, Penguin Classics, 2010
(originally published in 1759)

—— *The Wealth of Nations*, Wordsworth Editions, 2012 (originally
published in 1776)

Solow, Robert M. "Technical change and the aggregate production
function", *The Review of Economics and Statistics*, vol. 39, no. 3,
August 1957

Soto, Hernando de *The Mystery of Capital: Why Capitalism Triumphs in the
West and Fails Everywhere Else*, Black Swan, 2001

Srinivasan, Bhu *Americana: A 400-Year History of American Capitalism*,
Penguin, 2017

Srinivasan, K. "Population and development in India since independence:
an overview", http://medind.nic.in/jah/t04/s1/jaht04s1p5g.pdf, 2004

Standage, Tom *An Edible History of Humanity*, Atlantic Books, 2010

—— *A History of the World in Six Glasses*, Walker & Company, 2006

—— *The Victorian Internet: The Remarkable Story of the Telegraph and the Nineteenth Century's Online Pioneers*, Weidenfeld & Nicolson, 1998

St Clair, Kassia *The Golden Thread: How Fabric Changed History*, John Murray, 2018

Stephenson, Judy "Real contracts and mistaken wages: the organisation of work and pay in London building trades, 1650–1800", LSE working papers, no. 231, January 2016

Stern, Fritz *Gold and Iron: Bismarck, Bleichröder, and the Building of the German Empire*, Random House, 1979

Studwell, Joe *The China Dream: The Elusive Quest for the Greatest Untapped Market on Earth*, Profile Books, 2002

Sweeney, Megan, and McCouch, Susan "The complex history of the domestication of rice", *Annals of Botany*, vol. 100, no. 5, October 2007

Tanzi, Vito *Government versus Markets: The Changing Economic Role of the State*, Cambridge University Press, 2011

Taylor A.J.P. *English History 1914–1945*, Pelican, 1970 (originally published in 1965)

Tenaw, Shimelles, Islam, K.M. Zahudul, and Parviainen, Tuulikki "Effects of land tenure and property rights on agricultural productivity in Ethiopia, Namibia and Bangladesh", University of Helsinki, 2009

Tharoor, Shashi *Inglorious Empire: What the British Did to India*, C. Hurst & Co., 2017

Thomas, Hugh *The Slave Trade: The History of the Atlantic Slave Trade, 1440–1870*, Phoenix, 2006

Thompson, E.P. "Time, work-discipline and industrial capitalism", *Past & Present*, vol. 38, no. 1, December 1967

Thornton, John *Africa and Africans in the Making of the Atlantic World, 1400–1800*, Cambridge University Press, 1998

Timmins, Nicholas *The Five Giants: A Biography of the Welfare State*, new edition, HarperCollins, 2001

Tooze, Adam *Crashed: How A Decade of Financial Crises Changed the World*, Allen Lane, 2018

—— *The Wages of Destruction: The Making and Breaking of the Nazi Economy*, Penguin, 2006

Trentmann, Frank *Empire of Things: How We Became a World of Consumers from the Fifteenth Century to the Twenty-First*, Allen Lane, 2016

Trut, Lyudmila, Oskina, Irina, and Kharlamova, Anastasiya "Animal
    evolution during domestication: the domesticated fox as a model",
    Institute of Cytology and Genetics, Siberian Branch of Russian
    Academy of Sciences, Novosibirsk, Russia, 2009

Turner, Michael "Agricultural productivity in England in the eighteenth
    century: evidence from crop yields", *The Economic History Review*,
    vol. 35, no. 4, November 1982

Valletta, Robert G. "Recent flattening in the higher education wage
    premium: polarization, skill downgrading or both?", NBER working
    paper 22935, 2016

Vietmeyer, Noel *Our Daily Bread: the Essential Norman Borlaug*, Bracing
    Books, 2011

Wang, Arthur, Wu, Ting, and Zhou, Tony "Riding China's huge,
    high-flying car market", October 2017, https://www.mckinsey.
    com/industries/automotive-and-assembly/our-insights/
    riding-chinas-huge-high-flying-car-market

Warsh, David *Knowledge and the Wealth of Nations: A Story of Economic
    Discovery*, W.W. Norton, 2006

Watson, Alexander *Ring of Steel: Germany and Austria-Hungary At War
    1914–1918*, Penguin, 2015

Watson, Andrew M. "The Arab agricultural revolution and its diffusion
    700–1100", *The Journal of Economic History*, vol. 34, no. 1, March
    1974

Webb, Simon *Commuters: The History of a British Way of Life*, Pen &
    Sword History, 2016

White, Richard *Railroaded: The Transcontinentals and the Making of
    Modern America*, W.W. Norton & Company, 2013

Williams, Eric *Capitalism & Slavery*, University of North Carolina Press,
    1994

Williamson, Edwin *The Penguin History of Latin America*, Penguin, 2009

Wolmar, Christian *Blood, Iron and Gold: How the Railways Transformed
    the World*, Atlantic Books, 2009

Wood, Gordon S. *Empire of Liberty: A History of the Early Republic, 1789–
    1815*, Oxford University Press, 2009

Wood, Michael *The Story of India*, BBC Books, 2008

Wootton, David *The Invention of Science: A New History of the Scientific
    Revolution*, Penguin, 2016

Wray, L. Randall "The Neo-Chartalist approach to money", The Levy

Economics Institute, July 1st 2000, https://papers.ssrn.com/s013/papers.cfm?abstract_id=1010334

Wrightson, Keith *Earthly Necessities: Economic Lives in Early Modern Britain 1450–1750*, Penguin, 2002

Wrigley, E.A. *Energy and the English Industrial Revolution*, Cambridge University Press, 2010

Yang, Dennis, Zhang, Junsen, and Zhou, Shaojie "Why are savings rates so high in China?" NBER working paper 16771, https://www.nber.org/papers/w16771.pdf, 2011

Yergin, Daniel *The Prize: The Epic Quest for Oil, Money, and Power*, Simon & Schuster, 2009

Zeder, Melinda, Smithsonian Institution "The domestication of animals", *Journal of Anthropological Research*, vol. 68, no. 2, 2012

Zuckerman, Gregory *The Frackers: The Outrageous Inside Story of the New Energy Revolution*, Portfolio, 2013

# INDEX

Credit: Nephi Niven

**Philip Coggan** writes the Bartleby column for *The Economist* and is the former writer of the Buttonwood column. Previously, he worked for the *Financial Times* for twenty years. In 2009, he was voted senior financial journalist of the year in the Wincott awards and best communicator in the Business Journalist of the Year Awards. Among his books are *The Money Machine, The Economist Guide to Hedge Funds* and *Paper Promises*.

PublicAffairs is a publishing house founded in 1997. It is a tribute to the standards, values, and flair of three persons who have served as mentors to countless reporters, writers, editors, and book people of all kinds, including me.

I. F. STONE, proprietor of *I. F. Stone's Weekly*, combined a commitment to the First Amendment with entrepreneurial zeal and reporting skill and became one of the great independent journalists in American history. At the age of eighty, Izzy published *The Trial of Socrates*, which was a national bestseller. He wrote the book after he taught himself ancient Greek.

BENJAMIN C. BRADLEE was for nearly thirty years the charismatic editorial leader of *The Washington Post*. It was Ben who gave the *Post* the range and courage to pursue such historic issues as Watergate. He supported his reporters with a tenacity that made them fearless and it is no accident that so many became authors of influential, best-selling books.

ROBERT L. BERNSTEIN, the chief executive of Random House for more than a quarter century, guided one of the nation's premier publishing houses. Bob was personally responsible for many books of political dissent and argument that challenged tyranny around the globe. He is also the founder and longtime chair of Human Rights Watch, one of the most respected human rights organizations in the world.

·     ·     ·

For fifty years, the banner of Public Affairs Press was carried by its owner Morris B. Schnapper, who published Gandhi, Nasser, Toynbee, Truman, and about 1,500 other authors. In 1983, Schnapper was described by *The Washington Post* as "a redoubtable gadfly." His legacy will endure in the books to come.

Peter Osnos, *Founder*